italiana

ITALIANA
Narratori Giunti

Simonetta Agnello Hornby

Il pranzo di Mosè

Con le ricette di Chiara Agnello

Il pranzo di Mosè
di Simonetta Agnello Hornby
«Italiana» Giunti

http://narrativa.giunti.it

© 2014 Giunti Editore S.p.A.
Via Bolognese 165 – 50139 Firenze – Italia
Piazza Virgilio 4 – 20123 Milano – Italia

Immagini:
per le fotografie alle pp. 27, 32, 39, 55, 60, 90, 101, 109 si ringrazia la famiglia Agnello,
per la fotografia a p. 81 © Fausto Giaccone,
per le fotografie alle pp. 193 (in basso), 198-199, 208 si ringrazia Aurora Di Girolamo,
per le fotografie alle pp. 202-203, 205 (in alto), 206-207 © Roberto Collovà,
per tutte le altre fotografie © 2014 Discovery Communications, LLC, Real Time and related
logos are trademarks of Discovery Communications, LLC used under license. All rights
reserved.

Prima edizione: novembre 2014

Ristampa						Anno				
5	4	3	2	1	0	2018	2017	2016	2015	2014

A Cristiana e Riccardo

Ringraziamenti

Un triplice ringraziamento è dovuto a mia sorella Chiara, schiva di natura e che non ama di essere truccata, per avere accettato la sfida di partecipare a *Il pranzo di Mosè*, per avere avuto fiducia in me e in quello che le proponevo, e per essere stata generosa con le sue ricette.

Mio figlio Giorgio ha aiutato Chiara e me nella scelta dei menù, e lo ringrazio per i suggerimenti offerti durante la stesura del testo, per i commenti sulla bozza finale e per la scelta delle fotografie. Le sue ricerche storiche sono state di grande aiuto. A lui devo inoltre la levità e il buon umore che hanno accompagnato questo libro dall'inizio alla fine, e che spero siano riflessi nel testo.

Ringrazio Vincenzo Vella per le sue storie e per l'affetto che ci lega. Ringrazio Totu Vella, a cui dobbiamo le squisite quagliata, tuma e ricotta; Concetta, sua moglie, che ci ha insegnato a preparare i biscotti ricci, e i loro figli. Luigi si prende cura di Mosè come faceva un tempo suo zio Vincenzo, e Linda, abile assistente in cucina, è sempre pronta al sorriso.

Ringrazio Roberto Collovà, Aurora Di Girolamo e Fausto Giaccone per le loro fotografie.

Ringrazio Giuseppe Barbera al cui libro *Tuttifrutti* ho attinto per descrivere alcuni degli ingredienti da me preferiti, e ringrazio Massimo Montanari ai cui testi sono indebitata per le informazioni storiche e culinarie. Ovviamente sono la sola responsabile di qualsiasi errore o inaccuratezza su quanto riportato dalle loro opere.

Ringrazio Chiara Mancini per le traduzioni dall'inglese in italiano, per aver scritto e corretto quanto da me dettato, e per il supporto offerto nei momenti di bisogno.

Ringrazio Beatrice Fini, direttore editoriale di Giunti, per il costante supporto e Silvia Valmori, che ha seguito con attenzione e maestria questo libro.

Un ringraziamento particolare a Valentina Alferj, validissima amica, che mi è stata vicina nella genesi del testo e mi ha aiutata generosamente nei momenti di incertezza.

Indice

Il pranzo di Mosè

PARTE PRIMA

1

Un medico di Favara

Ho trascorso tutte le estati, dall'età di tre anni, nella casa di Mosè, la nostra campagna a pochi chilometri da Agrigento. Ma il mio ricordo più bello di Mosè, non è a Mosè. È legato ai tempi in cui avevo non più di cinque anni e abitavamo ad Agrigento. Talvolta, nel primo pomeriggio, Papà apriva la porta della stanza dove io e mia sorella Chiara, piccina, trascorrevamo le giornate con Giuliana, la nostra bambinaia, e annunciava dalla soglia: "Vado a Mosè. Mi porto Simonetta".

Erano gite meravigliose.

Papà stava poco in casa, e ancor meno con noi figlie. Era presidente dell'Ente del Turismo di Agrigento e voleva migliorare e valorizzare la Valle dei Templi. In più badava alle proprie campagne e andava dall'una all'altra sulla sua bella Lancia coupé color amaranto, che guidava con maestria. Sprofondata nel sedile accanto a lui, mi guardavo intorno soddisfatta e godevo del panorama della Valle. Uomo di poche parole, quando era al volante mio padre diventava quasi loquace: si lasciava andare a un commentario che in realtà era un soliloquio. "Questa strada unisce Agrigento alla statale 115; secondo me segue il tracciato di quella dei greci, perché raggiunge la costa passando attraverso Porta Aurea." Guidava cauto tra le alte facciate lisce e gialle che formavano le pareti del passaggio a gomito, un tempo porta tra le mura greche, e spiegava che gli archeologi l'avevano chiamata la Quarta porta della enorme cinta di Akragas: era stata scavata nel costone di tufo; la grande muraglia aveva protetto la città dagli invasori d'oltremare. "Ma non riuscì a fermare i Cartaginesi: quelli misero Akragas a ferro e fuoco e ne incendiarono i templi".

Imboccato il rettilineo sotto il costone della zona sacra, Papà rallentava; orgoglioso della nostra terra, ripeteva i nomi dei templi sul crinale indicandoli con ampi gesti, le mani sollevate dal volante. "Le colonne del tempio di Ercole sono le più antiche: sembrano davvero dei tronchi d'albero." Poi, tutto a un tratto rabbioso, esclamava: "Queste colonne furono sollevate da un inglese, e a spese sue! Quando avremmo dovuto farlo noi siciliani!". Eravamo sotto il tempio della Concordia, giallo come la pietra su cui poggiava, con il colonnato e il naos intatti. Pensieroso, borbottava tra sé e sé: "Questo s'è salvato dallo scempio soltanto perché era stato trasformato in chiesa".

Guardava la singola fila di colonne semidiroccate del tempio di Giunone e, con un sospiro: "La gente di qui non capiva che i cilindri scanalati e le pietre scolpite appartenevano ai templi greci; si portavano via pezzi di colonna per farsi la casa. O forse fingevano di essere ignoranti…" un altro sospiro, e "vandali erano anche i governanti: quelli sapevano! E fecero buttare in acqua le pietre dei nostri templi per costruire il molo di Porto Empedocle!".

Papà ripeteva quelle parole ogni volta che passava da lì; le sapevo a memoria e mi distraevo guardando i templi. Contavo i turisti che vedevo aggirarsi a due a due, o in fila come formiche, tra le colonne e sul crinale. Superato il tempio di

Giunone, ci avvicinavamo al ponte sul fiume Ypsas. Lì era soltanto campagna, con qualche mandorlo. Nulla sfuggiva all'occhio scrutatore di mio padre: la potatura di un uliveto, un albero sofferente, un orto ben accudito. Lui riconosceva a distanza le varietà di grano seminato e dalla fioritura degli ulivi azzardava una stima approssimata del futuro raccolto. Poi, rivolto a me: "Guarda, il fiume s'è scavato il suo corso nel costone", e rallentava sul ponte. Nel letto dell'Ypsas, ormai rigagnolo, non vedevo traccia di acqua: vi cresceva, rigoglioso, un verde canneto. "Ai tempi dei greci era navigabile fino all'interno dell'isola" commentava lui, con rammarico.

Cambiava marcia e accelerava. Con un boato la Lancia saliva veloce sui due tornanti sulla collina: Papà dava uno sguardo a sinistra, le mani sul volante. "Da quel pizzo inizia la Contrada Mosè" e puntava il dito all'estremità della valle, dove una torretta si alzava dirimpetto al tempio di Giunone.

Ero tutta un palpito: mi sentivo parte della storia del mondo. Sapevo che, dopo la salita, saremmo entrati nella piana coltivata a grano e a un certo punto sarebbe apparsa la "nostra" guardiola di tufo giallo come i templi, corredata di merli e terrazza, con finestre rettangolari sui due piani superiori.

"Simonetta, eccola, la guardiola di Mosè!" Ma io l'avevo già avvistata, e il cuore mi batteva forte. Sapevo che dietro la guardiola, il terreno si piegava in colline coperte di ulivi e più giù, a metà collina, nascosta agli occhi degli automobilisti, c'era la nostra casa. Non vedevo l'ora di raggiungerla. Quello era Mosè.

Un posto "nostro".

Agli inizi dell'Ottocento, Gerlando Giudice, un ricco medico di Favara e trisnonno di Mamma, acquistò da un'Opera

Pia un centinaio di ettari di terreno nella Contrada Mosè, che un tempo faceva parte della riserva di caccia di Federico di Svevia, re di Sicilia: un vasto bosco che copriva le dolci colline tra Agrigento e Favara. Di questa era rimasta soltanto un'imponente torre medioevale con cisterna funzionante, circondata da grandi ulivi. Nel 1843 il bisnonno di Mamma, Giuseppe Giudice, costruì il frantoio e, anni dopo, una casa di villeggiatura per la famiglia, che inglobava la torre antica; ricostruì anche la guardiola e nel 1870 concluse i lavori con l'aggiunta della chiesetta. La casa era completa.

Attorno al fabbricato erano già stati piantati mandorli, pistacchi, carrubi, un minuscolo giardino di agrumi, una vigna e un orto, insomma, tutto quello che serviva per cucinare e mangiare bene. Il mio bisnonno vi passò felicemente parte dell'estate, con figli e nipoti, fino alla morte nel 1882, a ottantasette anni. Da allora i Giudice – nostra madre, Elena, è stata l'ultima proprietaria a portare il nome della famiglia – hanno sempre trascorso le vacanze estive a Mosè. Con una penosa eccezione: durante la Seconda guerra mondiale l'esercito dell'Asse requisì la tenuta. I soldati occuparono casa e fattoria e Mosè divenne un accampamento militare. Nell'uliveto furono costruite postazioni in cemento armato per le mitragliatrici e, lungo il crinale che guarda il mare d'Africa, bunker e posti di vedetta. Nel luglio del 1943 Mosè fu il centro di una battaglia sanguinosa, la prima resistenza all'avanzata degli Alleati in Sicilia. Una bomba cadde nella sala da pranzo e distrusse la scala d'ingresso principale, altre devastarono la cantina. Gli Alleati vittoriosi vi si insediarono per un periodo. Quando ebbero conquistato Agrigento, abbandonarono Mosè lasciando casa e fattoria aperte ai vandali.

La tenuta fu ereditata da Mamma nel 1946. Le piaceva raccontare a Chiara e a me le ragioni di questa attribuzione. Nella divisione delle proprietà del padre, i figli maschi, zio Giovanni e zio Peppino, ebbero le terre di pianura, le migliori, mentre Mosè e Narbone, terre di collina, furono destinate alle femmine, zia Teresa, la sorella maggiore, e Mamma. Fecero a sorte: a Mamma era toccato Narbone, un feudo di montagna. Nella primavera di quell'anno erano andati tutti insieme in gita a Mosè. La fattoria attigua alla casa, corredata di due bagli, piccionaia, mandria e piccola torre di vedetta, era di nuovo funzionante: i Vella, un nucleo di contadini originari di Favara e mezzadri di Mosè, che avevano dovuto lasciare la fattoria e gli animali all'esercito dell'Asse per rifugiarsi in paese, vi erano ritornati dopo l'armistizio.

La fattoria era scampata ai bombardamenti e, lavorando sodo, loro erano riusciti a rimetterla in sesto e a riprendere il lavoro. La casa padronale era in condizioni disastrose. Oltre ai danni causati dalla bomba, era stata saccheggiata: scuri rotti, finestre senza vetri, tubature e pavimenti divelti, mobili bruciati, mura affumicate, carta da parati strappata. Era vuota, tranne la cucina, dove tutta la mobilia era rimasta intatta: forse perché i mobili erano troppo pesanti per essere trasportati o forse, come mi piace pensare, perché anche in guerra si rispetta il posto in cui si prepara il cibo.

Nell'aia spizzuliavano galline e pulcini; le corna a torciglione delle capre girgintane spuntavano alte dallo steccato della mandria. Mamma raccontava che Rosalia, la moglie di Luigi, il campiere, a cui lei e zia Teresa volevano molto bene, aveva offerto loro 'u caffè du parrinu e del pane ancora tiepido, cotto nel forno a legna. Quando erano fuggiti dalla fattoria con i bambini, Rosalia s'era portata la livatina, la pagnottella di pasta lievitata che si conserva ad ogni impastata di pane, per farla inacidire e trasformarsi nel lievito per le successive panificazioni. La livatina di Mosè proveniva da una pasta madre mantenuta in vita dalle femmine della sua famiglia sin dal 1870. Scappando, Rosalia se l'era messa addosso, sotto le vesti, a diretto contatto con il proprio corpo per proteggerla e mantenerla calda. Ma la livatina era morta. Era stata rimpiazzata da un'altra che veniva da una pasta madre regalo di un pastore di Castrofilippo: "Il pane riesce bene ed è buono, ma non è la stessa cosa" aveva concluso Rosalia.

Nel frattempo gli uomini erano andati in giro a cavallo nell'uliveto assieme a Luigi. "Era una bellissima giornata di primavera," ricordava Mamma "il sole caldo era temperato da un venticello rinfrescante; le chiome degli ulivi frusciavano allegre, e la campagna era nel suo splendore, tutta fiorita. Quella passeggiata fece innamorare Papà di Mosè: lo voleva. Me ne parlò quella sera stessa e io chiesi a mia sorella se potevamo scambiarci le campagne."

Zia Teresa volle accontentarla e fu lieta di prendersi in cambio Narbone.

I lavori di ristrutturazione furono lunghi e costosi. C'erano impalcature dappertutto, impastatrici di cemento, operai e muratori. Un magazzino era stato trasformato in falegnameria per Michele, l'anziano falegname di Agrigento che aveva lavorato per i Giudice quasi tutta la vita: lui fece tutte le persiane della casa da solo, a mano. La cucina fu rifatta e i vecchi mobili abbandonati, freschi di una mano di pittura blu e celeste, accolsero tra loro una moderna cucina economica alimentata dal legno della pota degli ulivi.

Il 19 agosto del 1949 celebrammo a Mosè il primo compleanno di Chiara; eravamo accampati al primo piano, insieme alle famiglie di zio Giovanni e zia Teresa. L'illuminazione era data da candele e lampade ad acetilene. Poco alla volta la casa di Mosè rinasceva e si abbelliva, grazie a Mamma e a Melina, la sarta, che cucivano tende, fodere, copriletto, tovaglie, tovaglioli, e alla generosità di parenti e amici che ci mandavano quello che a loro non serviva più, come servizi di piatti e di bicchieri incompleti, o mobili di cui volevano sbarazzarsi: divani e poltrone ingombranti, armadi vecchi, l'intera sala da pranzo liberty e la camera da letto ottocentesca dei nonni Giudice. Malandati e poi tirati a nuovo, questi mobili furono e rimangono molto amati da noi, e continuano ad accogliere nelle stanze ombrose di casa nostra la famiglia allargata, amici e ospiti di passaggio; ci ricordano la solidarietà all'interno delle famiglie e l'affetto di amici generosi. I miei figli, nati a Oxford, sono stati portati a Mosè da neonati, e ci ritornano ogni anno, più di una volta, con i loro bambini e con amici, come facevamo Chiara ed io.

Alla morte di Papà, nel 1985, in fattoria vivevano soltanto Rosalia e i figli maggiori, Lillo e Vincenzo, con le rispettive mogli: ambedue non avevano figli. Lillo era emigrato in Francia per anni; poi era tornato e curava il gregge. Vincenzo, il primo dei Vella a guidare il trattore, era il fattore di Mosè: i tempi erano cambiati e la figura del campiere era diventata desueta.

La posizione di campiere si tramandava tra i Vella di padre in figlio, ed era passata a Luigi, padre di Vincenzo e l'ultimo a ricoprire questo ruolo a Mosè. Il campiere era un uomo di fiducia che andava a cavallo terre terre per controllare i possedimenti del padrone; aveva ancora una funzione importante nella Sicilia del dopoguerra – era suo compito controllare ogni giorno, per conto della famiglia, che non ci fossero scanusciuti, animali altrui, o cani randagi nelle nostre terre, che gli abbeveratoi fossero puliti e in ordine. Inoltre, il campiere, sempre all'erta su quello che succedeva nel territorio, bloccava i tentativi di furti, di incendi e di abigeati.

Vincenzo oggi ha quasi ottant'anni; vedovo, continua a vivere a Mosè e vede come suo erede Luigi, figlio di Totu, il fratello più giovane, che, da pensionato, si è trasferito a Mosè per badare alla *ménagerie* degli animali del figlio – galline, oche, cavalli e un piccolo gregge di pecore e capre – e per aiutarlo nella preparazione dei formaggi e della ricotta.

Chiara, di professione architetto, volle occuparsi della tenuta, che convertì all'agricoltura biologica; ricavò dalle case vuote dei contadini e dalle stalle disuse sei appartamenti che aprono su un baglio trasformato in giardino: fanno parte dell'agriturismo Fattoria Mosè che accoglie ospiti da tutto il mondo. Ora, noi e i nostri amici condividiamo con i turisti il pranzo alla nostra tavola.

Ascoltando la conversazione, sembra che nulla sia cambiato a Mosè.

2

Il vecchio uliveto

La cultura dell'ulivo fu introdotta in Sicilia duemila e seicento anni fa dai coloni greci. Da allora l'ulivo, oltre a dare luce con il proprio olio, dà vita grazie ai propri frutti: le olive sono sempre state nutrimento e companatico, l'olio insaporiva il cibo dei nostri antenati, oltre ad essere apprezzato per le sue virtù medicinali.

Per me l'ulivo rappresenta la Sicilia più di qualsiasi altra pianta.

Gli ulivi di Mosè sono antichissimi e di tante varietà. Li chiamiamo "saraceni" perché spesso, da noi, tutto ciò che è antico o bello si attribuisce agli stranieri che ci hanno dominato da sempre: siamo esterofili, in un senso un po' perverso. È possibile che alcuni uliveti detti "saraceni" siano stati piantati dagli arabi, che conquistarono la nostra isola nell'827. Il califfato mussulmano sviluppò enormemente l'agricoltura, introducendo nuovi sistemi di coltivazioni e prodotti, tra cui gli agrumi e la canna da zucchero. La dominazione araba diede alla Sicilia tre secoli di progresso e civiltà. Molti dei grandi uliveti potrebbero risalire effettivamente a quel periodo. Ma non ne possiamo essere certi, in particolare nel caso di quelli con il tronco cavo.

Una volta accompagnai Papà e un agronomo nella parte dell'uliveto dove si trovano le piante più antiche, quelle dai rami attorcigliati e dai tronchi cavi. Erano enormi, chiome magnifiche, tronchi possenti, radici ampie e contorte, come quelli piantati a valle, sotto casa, che si vedevano dalle finestre delle nostre stanze da letto. A maggio, le foglie verde e argento spiccavano contro le messi che crescevano tra uno e l'altro. In estate, contrastavano maestose contro il marrone rossiccio del terreno arato.

Chiesi quanti anni avessero quegli alberi. Papà azzardò seicento, ma l'agronomo lo corresse subito: "Non lo sappiamo, non possiamo stabilire l'età di questi ulivi con il metodo tradizionale, contando gli anelli che si aggiungono ogni anno al tronco, perché i vostri alberi sono fatti di tanti ulivi fusi insieme". Ma l'agronomo ci spiegò che dalla base del tronco degli ulivi nascono i polloni, cioè i germogli di nuovi alberi. Questi polloni crescono rigogliosi e con il passare del tempo si uniscono e formano una gabbia intorno al tronco originale. Questo gradualmente muore, privato del nutrimento che i polloni gli sottraggono e poi corroso dalla carie del legno.

Ci avvicinammo a uno degli alberi, il tronco era un groviglio di rughe contorte, la corteccia grigia era squamosa. Era stato tagliato all'altezza di circa due metri con un colpo netto. Pareva morto, se non fosse stato per dei rami, ricchi di fronde e di olive, anch'essi nodosi e ritorti, che sembravano essere cresciuti per caso sul bordo. Il tronco era squarciato da un lato; intravedevo l'interno, come uno stanzino con le pareti ruvide. L'agronomo mi fece notare dei vecchi rami, piegati come se fossero stati intrecciati dal vento. "La nuova pianta formata da tanti ulivi è flessibile e il suo tronco, una volta distrutto quello della pianta madre, può piegarsi in tanti modi" e poggiò la mano sul groviglio di ulivo. "Così si sono formati i tronchi che vedi oggi." E così, ogni ulivo secolare che getta polloni che rimangono si crea da solo la propria tomba.

Il nostro uliveto è troppo vecchio per dare una resa commercialmente competitiva, ma rimarrà intatto: gli alberi ora sono soggetti al vincolo della Soprintendenza e non possono essere sradicati; è una bella sfida cercare di far quadrare il bilancio agricolo, ma ci proviamo. Gli ulivi di Mosè sono amatissimi da tutti noi. Nonostante siano alberi vetusti, producono un ottimo olio, e per questo meritano il rispetto degli uomini.

Gli inizi degli anni cinquanta furono tempi turbolenti nelle nostre campagne. Un'estate bruciarono, in un breve periodo di tempo, vari ulivi a Piano Carruba, un posto lontano e fuori dalla nostra vista, vicino all'abbeveratoio dove gli animali della fattoria andavano a dissetarsi. In tutta la Sicilia capitano spesso fuochi naturali, particolarmente nei mesi caldi e dove ci sono arbusti, mucchi di rami secchi, spine e restoppia. Alcuni diventano piccoli o grandi incendi. A Mosè non ce n'erano stati mai. La campagna era tenuta bene e pulita, e Luigi girava in lungo e largo e la teneva sotto controllo.

Mirati soltanto agli ulivi di Piano Carruba, quegli incendi erano opera di scanusciuti, che davano fuoco, una sera sì e una sera no, a un solo albero per volta, tra i più carichi di olive, per dare un "avvertimento" a Papà. A noi fu detto che c'era stato un incendio isolato nelle campagne dei vicini: dei ragazzi scapestrati avevano appiccato il fuoco a paglia e rovi per stanare un covo di vipere e ucciderle a fucilate. Il vento aveva spinto la paglia infuocata sui mandorli vicini, e quelli avevano abbandonato la caccia alle vipere e si erano dati da fare per salvare gli alberi ed estinguere il fuoco. Le vipere s'erano poi messe in salvo, e strisciando strisciando erano arrivate nelle nostre terre. Erano state viste perfino nel giardino davanti casa. Noi bambini avremmo giocato soltanto nel cortile interno e non ci saremmo allontanati da casa fino a quando Luigi non si fosse assicurato che le vipere non c'erano più. Lo accettammo. Ma il giorno seguente, e quello dopo, il vento ci portava un'altra storia: ogni folata carica dell'odore acre di legno bruciato e delle sue braci ancora accese ci diceva che c'era un altro incendio, a Mosè. Papà e Luigi erano cupi. C'era tensione in casa. Non facevamo domande. La sera, in terrazza, tanti occhi guardavano nel buio. A letto, ascoltavamo il silenzio della notte – anche quello, talvolta, "parla".

Ogni pomeriggio, dopo pranzo, riposavamo nelle nostre camere da letto, tranne Papà, che si infossava in una poltrona nel salotto di giù, e talvolta sonnecchiava – senza ammetterlo. Mamma non dormiva: leggeva sdraiata sul copriletto, uno scialle le copriva i piedi nudi. Noi cugini dividevamo la stanza accanto a quella di Giuliana; anch'io non dormivo e spesso mi alzavo in punta di piedi e andavo a bussare alla porta di Mamma. Chiacchieravamo per un poco, poi lei mi rimandava in camera: 'nsamai Giuliana, che era severa, si accorgesse della mia fuga.

In quei giorni Mamma non leggeva e nemmeno si sdraiava sul letto. In piedi dietro le persiane della finestra che dava sull'uliveto, guardava attraverso le stecche gli alberi rigogliosi e carichi di olive ai piedi della collina. Socchiudevo la porta e mi avvicinavo. Il venticello che rendeva Mosè gradevole in estate, ci portava l'odore di bruciato, da lontano. Lei poggiava la mano sulle mie spalle e guardavamo gli ulivi. "Tante belle olive, rovinate," mormorava "tanto olio perduto." Le spuntava una lacrima che non scivolava sulla guancia; rimaneva lì, come la goccia di resina del pistacchio rimane attaccata al tronco. Mamma non pensava a "quegli" ulivi, ma agli altri, quelli bruciati.

Anni dopo, da adulta, le chiesi il perché di quelle parole. Non aveva rabbia contro coloro che ci volevano piegare e imporre su di noi le loro nefandezze? "Gli avvertimenti, le lettere anonime e le minacce della mafia non erano inconsueti, a quei tempi. Tutti, purtroppo, c'erano abituati. Ma distruggere un ulivo, pronto a offrire i propri frutti per nutrire la gente, è un atto di violenza contro la natura. Non si brucia un albero sano e maturo..." e Mamma si fermò. Dopo una pausa riprese, la voce bassa: "Il cibo è sacro, e l'olio in particolare...".

I monconi bruciati sono ancora a Piano Carruba.

Mamma ragazzina.

3

L'ospitalità a Mosè

Mosè appartiene ora a noi due sorelle. Insieme a Silvano, il figlio di zia Teresa e cugino quasi fratello, Chiara è la custode delle tradizioni culinarie di Mamma e zia Teresa, tramandate loro da nonna Maria, madre adorata, morta nel 1946 a cinquantaquattro anni. Noi e i miei figli, Giorgio e Nicola, cerchiamo di mantenerle vive.

Il compito delle donne di famiglia era di badare al marito e ai figli, di essere brave padrone di casa e, quando si ricevevano visite, di occuparsi della felicità dell'ospite, dal momento in cui costui arrivava fino al commiato. Esattamente quello che Mamma e zia Teresa cercavano di fare, rendendo l'ospite, per l'intera durata della sua permanenza, parte della famiglia e della loro vita. Al punto di non chiedergli mai quando sarebbe andato via.

L'ospitalità era, all'interno della famiglia allargata, la particolarità di Mosè, perché a noi genuinamente piaceva avere in casa amici e parenti.

La terrazza della sala da pranzo era il miglior punto di vedetta della casa: da lì lo sguardo vagava dalla stradella di ciottoli bianchi che portava al nostro cortile, fino alla statale 115, che serpeggiava nera lungo la pianura, e alla trazzera pietrosa, a fondo valle, tra le colline di ulivi, verso Favara. Nessuno dei contadini possedeva alcun mezzo di trasporto, a parte il carretto, e dunque tutte le automobili che si inerpicavano sulla stradella erano dirette a casa nostra. Chiara ed io le riconoscevamo a vista; Papà andava oltre: sosteneva di essere in grado di identificarle dal rumore dei motori e perfino di riconoscerne il guidatore dal cambio di marcia.

Il senso di isolamento che ci davano i lunghi mesi estivi passati in campagna si allentava con le visite di parenti e amici. Alcune erano pianificate, altre vagamente "anticipate", altre ancora "attese" senza alcuna data specifica, e altre erano semplicemente a sorpresa. Ogni giorno, dopo la mezza, tenevamo d'occhio la stradella dalla terrazza: non essendoci il telefono a Mosè, amici e parenti arrivavano nella certezza di essere benvenuti e di pranzare piacevolmente con noi. Sapevano che c'era sempre qualcosa da mangiare, perché nella campagna siciliana la casa "padronale", cioè l'abitazione estiva dei proprietari del terreno, era attaccata alla fattoria, da cui si approvvigionava di formaggio, ricotta, uova, carne e pollame.

E noi, inoltre, avevamo l'orto, con un prezioso pozzo fatto scavare da Papà. Tuttora, gli ortaggi provengono dalla nostra campagna che dà vita a una prodigiosa quantità di verdure; uniche assenti le patate, che non crescono bene nel terreno argilloso. Gli alberi donano alla nostra cucina una grande varietà di prodotti, compresi olive – da cui l'olio –, mandorle, pistacchi, noci e carrube, oltre alla frutta e agli indispensabili agrumi. I prodotti che coltiviamo alla fattoria sono per lo più gli stessi che vengono coltivati nel territorio fin dal IX secolo quando i mussulmani introdussero nell'isola le loro avanzate tecniche di orticoltura. Le grandi eccezioni sono il peperone, il fico d'India e il pomodoro. Eccezioni che sono diventate nel tempo parte integrante della cucina siciliana. Soprattutto il pomodoro.

Spesso gli ospiti venivano in convogli di due o tre automobili: allora il conto dei posti a tavola era facile. Una di noi scappava in cucina per allertare le persone di servizio e riorganizzare tavola e pranzo. Non mancava mai il panico dell'ultimo momento: "Manca il prezzemolo!", "Ci vogliono altre melanzane!", "Servono foglie di alloro!", "I limoni bastano?". E si correva ai ripari. Io ero sempre pronta ad aiutare.

Tutti in famiglia eravamo padroni di casa

Tutti in famiglia eravamo padroni di casa, dal più anziano ai bambini. Era nostro compito includere nella conversazione e dare attenzione particolare ai timidi, agli anziani, e ai nuovi venuti, per far sì che ciascuno fosse a proprio agio. Seduti al tavolo della sala da pranzo, che si allungava all'occorrenza fino ad accogliere ventiquattro persone, gustavamo il cibo divertendoci e chiacchierando, senza dimenticare di accudire gli ospiti. Offrivamo loro le varie pietanze, versavamo vino e acqua e porgevamo il cestello del pane, facilitavamo la conversazione e traducevamo nelle lingue parlate dagli ospiti stranieri (francese o tedesco – l'inglese non era ancora lingua franca). Immancabilmente, tutti commentavamo il cibo servito a tavola, spiegavamo la sua provenienza – una voluta infrazione alle norme del galateo, che stupidamente lo vieta – e parlavamo di quello che si sarebbe mangiato l'indomani; si raccontavano storie di altri pranzi, e si discuteva, a lungo, la preparazione delle vivande.

Io, da adolescente immersa negli studi classici, pensavo

che i pranzi di Mosè fossero dei veri e propri convivi – una bella parola ormai desueta – senza triclini e con uomini e donne: un'occasione per un buon pranzo, in buona compagnia, mangiando e bevendo con gusto e moderatamente, dove la conversazione regna sovrana. A un convivio si parlava e si parla di tutto; ciascun ospite si sente in grado di esprimere la propria opinione nella certezza di non causare offesa e di non essere offeso. Il pensiero di ciascun commensale è rispettato e ascoltato, anche da coloro che se ne discostano.

E così erano i pranzi di Mosè.

Il pranzo in famiglia

In passato in tutte le famiglie a ogni pasto si riunivano nonni, figli e nipoti; i giovani non si allontanavano dal paese natale e le famiglie, numerose e multigenerazionali, accoglievano anche i parenti non sposati. Oggi cucinare e mangiare insieme in famiglia è diventato più raro: ci si allontana poco a poco gli uni dagli altri. È un processo che inizia gradualmente: i figli tornano da scuola più tardi; i genitori mangiano fuori perché sono al lavoro; i nonni vivono lontano dai nipoti, hanno una propria vita sociale e da vecchi vengono ricoverati in case di riposo. Si arriva al punto che ci si siede a tavola insieme solo di domenica, e non sempre. In quelle occasioni, la preoccupazione che tutto riesca bene ci rende ansiosi. La libera conversazione e la scioltezza del convivio ne soffrono. Il mangiare in comune, parlando, discutendo, ascoltandosi e divertendosi, a un certo punto scompare all'interno delle famiglie e si manifesta soltanto nelle grandi occasioni, come fidanzamenti, matrimoni, battesimi, prime comunioni, compleanni e feste comandate. Condividere le stesse pietanze, intorno allo stesso tavolo, parlando, discutendo e divertendosi, diventa difficile. In queste situazioni tutto è forzato.

Mamma e zia Teresa ridono a una battuta di Papà.

I pranzi di Mosè mi ricordano che mangiare insieme è una gioia reciproca.

A tavola Mamma e zia Teresa sedevano lontane l'una dall'altra: ciascuna di loro si occupava del benessere dei commensali seduti attorno a lei.

Oltre ad applicare le norme del buon senso – far sì che l'ospite possa mangiare quello che desidera, riprendere una cucchiaiata della pietanza che gli piace di più, avere pane, acqua e vino a sufficienza – e a intervenire discretamente nella conversazione per farla scorrere liberamente su tutto senza offendere nessuno, per inserirvi un ospite silenzioso, e per far sì che tutti i commensali avessero la possibilità di dire la loro, Mamma e zia Teresa seguivano una norma ferrea: l'ospite a tavola doveva sentirsi a proprio agio e mai manchevole in questioni di etichetta. Se per esempio un ospite prendeva una coscia di pollo con le mani, una delle due acchiappava quella sul proprio piatto o se ne serviva apposta per copiarlo. La persona che poggiava il tovagliolo sulla tavola era subito imitata da Mamma, che afferrava discretamente il proprio tovagliolo e lo sistemava accanto al piatto, tenendolo lì per tutto il pranzo. Certuni tagliavano il formaggio e poi lo prendevano con le mani, e Mamma subito faceva lo stesso; senza far notare il fastidio che le dava avere le dita unte e appiccicose, mi guardava per incoraggiarmi a fare altrettanto. Era mio dovere, parte dell'addestramento per diventare una buona padrona di casa, capace di non mettere mai l'ospite in imbarazzo. C'era solo un'eccezione: Mamma non sopportava e non riusciva a imitare chi parlava con la bocca piena: "Una bocca che mastica e parla è disgustosa. Va oltre i limiti, anche dell'igiene," diceva "perché si sputacchia". In quei casi allora tacevamo, attente a non incoraggiare nella conversazione l'ospite che masticava a bocca aperta pronto a parlare. E cercavamo di non sedergli di fronte.

Mamma raccontava a noi bambini la storia di zia Titì Eleonora, una cugina di nonna Maria da noi molto amata, che da ragazzina cantava a gola spiegata, disobbedendo agli ordini della bambinaia. Un moscone volò dritto dritto nella bocca e vi rimase prigioniero: la zia lo inghiottì. "Chi mastica a bocca aperta corre lo stesso rischio!" ci avvertiva Mamma, e aggiungeva: "E peggio ancora, chi mastica e contemporaneamente parla è una potente attrazione per le mosche!". L'orrido incidente accaduto alla zia Titì Eleonora ha avuto un effetto duraturo: nessuno di noi, o dei miei figli, o dei miei quattro nipotini, a cui la storia della disobbedienza della zia è ben nota, ha mai osato masticare a bocca aperta o parlare con la bocca piena.

La signorina Gramaglia

Per noi seguire queste regole e imparare a tollerarne le infrazioni non era un onere. Ci divertivamo, e ci rendeva orgogliose: era il modo di apprendere a essere come Mamma e zia Teresa. Una volta soltanto non riuscii a copiare un ospite. Io non frequentai le scuole elementari; ogni mattina veniva a casa nostra la signorina Gramaglia, una maestra privata, arrivava alle sette e mezzo e vi rimaneva per un'ora. Poi lei andava a lavorare mentre io facevo i compiti e giocavo in casa. Era una zitella molto bassa e grassoccia, si tingeva i capelli di un rosso carota che non le si addiceva, ma ben si abbinava ai soli due abiti che io le vidi addosso per tutti i cinque anni di scuola. Uno di lana marrone con puntini rossi e gialli e l'altro più leggero, per la bella stagione, blu a pois. Erano la sua uniforme di lavoro. Quando presi la licenza elementare, Mamma la invitò a pranzo a Mosè per festeggiarla e ringraziarla. Era una bravissima insegnante a cui devo tuttora l'amore per la storia e il senso del dovere. Chiara, Silvano ed io avevamo avuto il permesso di mangiare nella sala da pranzo con loro, e non nell'anticucina con le bambinaie. Mamma aveva preparato un ottimo pranzo, che si concludeva con le pesche sciroppate, oltre alla frutta fresca. Le scatolette di pesche erano una novità portata dagli americani e un grande lusso; si tenevano nel riposto, da usare per le occasioni speciali. La signorina Gramaglia, seduta alla destra di Papà, era la sola ospite, come è opportuno fare quando si festeggia una persona importante che non conosce gli altri familiari.

Al momento del dolce, la cameriera entrò solennemente nella sala da pranzo con la coppa di cristallo tra le mani: dentro, le pesche sciroppate, gialle e lucide, immerse nel loro liquido zuccherino. La seguivo con l'acquolina in bocca. La cameriera andò dritta dall'ospite e si piegò per permetterle di servirsi delle pesche. La signorina Gramaglia le guardò perplessa, poi prese le posate, ne raccolse una e, decisa, la fece scivolare nel lavadita alla sua sinistra. Noi bambini eravamo tutti occhi, muti. La cameriera, impassibile, passò a servire zia Teresa che prese una pesca e la fece cadere a sua volta nel lavadita. Poi passò a Mamma, che copiò la sorella. Poi agli uomini: zio Peppino e Papà rifiutarono le pesche e presero uva. E infine toccò a noi. La coppetta di panna montata da mettere sulle pesche fu discretamente allontanata da zia Teresa, e rimase abbandonata accanto al centrotavola. Io avevo l'acquolina in bocca, volevo le pesche sciroppate e la panna montata; guardai Mamma pietosa, ma lei non volle raccogliere il mio sguardo.

"Uva, per favore" mormorai alla cameriera, e così fecero Chiara e Silvano, anch'essi desolati. Le tre donne ebbero difficoltà a mangiarsi le pesche: nuotavano nell'acqua, sfuggivano al cucchiaio, al coltello e alla forchetta, che insieme o a solo non riuscivano a immobilizzarle per tagliarle e portarle alla bocca. Bene o male alla fine se le mangiarono tutte, mentre noi continuavamo a infilare acini in bocca, gli occhi sulla coppa di cristallo, ancora piena, che nel frattempo aveva raggiunto la credenza. Quando la maestra se ne fu andata,

Mamma mi redarguì, severa: in futuro si sarebbe aspettata che, come lei, io copiassi la manchevolezza dell'ospite. "Non dovevamo servire le pesche sciroppate. Non è colpa sua se non le ha mai gustate e se le ha messe nel posto sbagliato. Avrei dovuto pensarci prima. Ricordati che una padrona di casa che mette a disagio il suo ospite non è degna di intrattenere nessuno."

Padre Parisi

I nostri insegnanti, il medico, l'avvocato e il "prete di famiglia" – come si chiamava il sacerdote che seguiva un gruppo familiare celebrando battesimi nella cappella di casa, preparando i giovani ai sacramenti, officiando ai matrimoni e impartendo l'estrema unzione – erano ospiti "diversi": non parenti, nemmeno amici, eppure rispettati e amati, perché avevano un ruolo importante nella nostra famiglia. Padre Parisi ci conosceva tutti bene, e con lui Papà si permetteva di scherzare e perfino di prenderlo in giro affettuosamente e con rispetto.

Quando Padre Parisi mi preparava per la prima comunione, veniva a Mosè ogni settimana, preferibilmente di venerdì. Mamma amava stare in casa e non andava a messa ogni domenica. Donna di fede profonda, mormorava: "Il Signore mi conosce e spero che mi perdonerà". Papà invece, educato in Toscana in un collegio degli Scolopi, la Badia Fiesolana, aveva perduto la fede. Nonostante ciò, nei primi anni a Mosè, la messa si celebrava di frequente, non necessariamente di domenica. Dopo la lezione di catechismo e la messa, Padre Parisi rimaneva a pranzo. Noi sedevamo alla tavola dei "grandi". Non più giovane, alto e con una tonaca nera dal bordino rosso lungo l'abbottonatura, Padre Parisi era un bell'uomo. Quando lo vedevo camminare da lontano, con la tonaca svolazzante al venticello di Mosè, la sua figura scura mi sembrava meravigliosa. A quei tempi vivevo di amori impossibili: Charly Gaul, un ciclista lussemburghese vincitore del Tour de France, e un inizio di innamoramento per Marlon Brando, che poi si rafforzò e durò fino alle scuole medie. Padre Parisi, pur nella sua avvenenza, era incapace di spodestare quella coppia dal mio Olimpo dei sensi, perché era molto ingenuo e certe volte ridicolo.

Papà o uno zio andavano a prenderlo ad Agrigento, la mattina. Mamma e zia Teresa preparavano per lui un pasto particolarmente buono. Un venerdì mattina zio Peppino era arrivato da Caltagirone portando il solito bendidio da mangiare: frutta dalla sua campagna, formaggi, ricotta, salami e delle fette di vitello "talmente tenere che si sciolgono in bocca". Queste vennero servite a pranzo come cotolette alla milanese con patatine fritte per contorno: il piatto preferito di Silvano. Mentre ci avviavamo a tavola, zia Teresa ricordò a Mamma che era venerdì, giorno di magro: Padre Parisi non avrebbe gradito le cotolette. Ma era una buona forchetta. Le sorelle decisero di far finta di niente. A tavola, Padre Parisi mangiò la prima cotoletta e se ne prese un'altra, alla seconda passata della guantiera. Ci aveva spremuto sopra il succo di due limoni, e aveva mangiato tutte le patatine fritte. Papà lo seguiva con la coda dell'occhio, muto. Proprio quando il prete aveva infilato in bocca l'ultimo boccone, lui lo redarguì: "Padre, ha dimenticato che oggi è giorno di astinenza?". Per poco Padre Parisi non si affogò. Tossiva, paonazzo, gli occhi disperati. I grandi ridevano, noi bambini mantenemmo il silenzio: non sapevamo se ci era permesso ridere di lui, il rappresentante di Cristo in terra.

"Una frittata!" furono le prime parole che uscirono pasticciate dalla bocca del prete. "Una frittata avreste dovuto darmi!" E si girò, occhi spalancati, verso Mamma. "Di venerdì si mangia di magro!" e poi ancora "Una frittata!", e guardava, ora severo ora implorante, Mamma e zia Teresa. "Mi dovevate dare una frittata, non la carne!" Zia Teresa offrì di farla preparare. "Con le patatine?" Padre Parisi annuì. E non parlò fino a quando non ebbe finito la frittata a forma di pesce con un cappero al posto dell'occhio sommersa da una gran porzione di patatine fritte, che riempivano il piatto. Gliel'aveva portata la cameriera, anche lei ridanzosa e con gli occhietti furbi. Da allora, ogni venerdì, quando Padre Parisi veniva a Mosè, si servivano a tavola cotolette di melanzane. Appena le vedeva arrivare sulla guantiera, si rivolgeva a Mamma: "Di lei mi fido, non c'è carne lì dentro, vero?". E Mamma annuiva. Al primo boccone, il prete masticava lento lento, per capire cosa stesse mangiando. E Papà: "Di nuovo peccato ha commesso, Padre! Filetto ha tra i denti!". Allora, davanti alla costernazione del sacerdote, sempre incerto se prendere Papà sul serio o no, ridevamo tutti, compresi noi bambini. Poi, rivolto a Mamma, ripeteva: "Io mi fido di lei, lei sì che si confessa" e ingoiava mezza cotoletta di melanzana, puntando gli occhi su Papà, l'eretico, con aria di sfida. E poi se ne mangiava un'altra, e un'altra ancora. Zitta zitta io intanto mi servivo di altre cotolette di melanzane; le mangiavo di fretta, per prenderne altre: ero conscia di commettere il peccato della golosità, eppure mi sentivo "ben raccomandata" da Padre Parisi, vorace come e forse più di me, per la clemenza del Signore.

Papà e Chiara il giorno della sua prima comunione, nel giardino costruito sulla cantina bombardata.

Ora che zia Teresa e Mamma non ci sono più, l'atmosfera conviviale continua come prima, e spero continui anche il piacere della tavola per i nostri ospiti. Ci siamo adeguati ai cambiamenti sociali, alle innovazioni agricole e ai nuovi ingredienti che hanno raggiunto i nostri negozi dall'estero. La prima colazione, nella sala da pranzo del secondo piano, è diventata un pasto vero e proprio, con il pane e le marmellate di Chiara, formaggi, tè, caffè e aranciate; la cena è il pasto principale, mentre la seconda colazione, "il pranzo" è decaduto a una tablattè di insalate, formaggi, pane, frutta e i resti del giorno prima, per quei pochi che non sono in piscina o al mare. Continuiamo a cucinare usando quello che c'è nel riposto e quanto di fresco giorno per giorno ci offre la campagna: i prodotti dell'orto e gli animali della fattoria. Compriamo soltanto il necessario. I primi e i secondi sono improntati alla cucina tradizionale siciliana, densa di riferimenti a piatti medioevali e rinascimentali di cui si è quasi perduta la coscienza, come il macco, le caponate e le torte salate ripiene di verdure. I piatti sono semplici, ma possono diventare sontuosi aggiungendo un singolo ingrediente, delle spezie, o seguendo un nuovo procedimento nella preparazione. I dolci provengono dal ricettario di nonna Maria; alcuni non sono siciliani.

Il nostro intento continua a essere quello di preparare pranzi gustosi con ingredienti locali e senza sprechi, creare una tavola in cui la conversazione sia piacevole, e di fare star bene i commensali. Vogliamo che il cibo interessi, ma non monopolizzi l'attenzione, e che rispetti la tradizione della nostra isola. Cucinare è un compito piacevole e importante, ma bisogna prenderlo con un pizzico di umorismo: se si prende troppo sul serio, diventa tedioso. Noi partiamo dalla tradizione e cerchiamo innovazioni e miglioramenti. Introduciamo vecchie ricette con sapori nuovi, e ricette nuove con elementi vecchi. Chiara adopera meno zuccheri e grassi quando prepara ricette tradizionali. Tuttavia, siamo caute nei cambiamenti, memori del fatto che la cucina casalinga è basata sul gusto del conosciuto che si tramanda da generazioni, e che il nostro modo di vivere il cibo e la tavola, creato attorno alle pietanze, deve includere il benessere dei commensali: li osserviamo per prevenire i loro desideri, come ai vecchi tempi.

Il regalo del commiato

Quando gli ospiti di famiglia lasciavano Mosè, si offrivano loro i prodotti della campagna, sempre; come loro, del resto, facevano con noi quando li andavamo a trovare: olio, mandorle, verdura fresca, aromi ecc. Nei riguardi degli ospiti "non di casa", che probabilmente non sarebbero ritornati presto a Mosè perché vivevano lontano, Mamma aveva creato un'innovazione: il regalo del commiato. Lei li osservava attentamente a tavola e registrava i loro gusti. Prima che se ne andassero chiamava una di noi e dava dei piccoli ordini specifici: "Metti dei pistacchi in un sacchetto", "Raccogli delle foglie di alloro e due rametti di rosmarino", "Riempi una guantiera piccola di biscotti ricci, avvolgili nel cellophane con un bel fiocco", "Vai in cucina, prendi una bella manciata di fave fresche e insacchettale", "Vedi se è rimasto pecorino con il pepe, taglia una fetta e mettila in un sacchetto di plastica", "Dacci della camomilla", "Prepara un sacchetto di mandorle". Al momento dei saluti, Mamma aveva a portata di mano il regalo adatto per ciascun ospite. Lo offriva veloce, quasi di sotterfugio, come fosse imbarazzata e non volesse che gli altri se ne accorgessero. Per lei era un momento di intimità. A volte Papà insinuava che quei doni sarebbero stati buttati via da chi li riceveva, perché non avrebbe saputo cosa farne. "Ti sbagli," gli rispondeva lei "io lo so che sono regali graditi, da come loro mi guardano quando glieli do."

Chiara ed io portiamo avanti questa tradizione. Mi piace tagliare i rametti di alloro e di rosmarino, disporre i biscotti sui vassoietti di cartone, avvolgerli nel cellophane e infiocchettarli con nastri di seta riciclati o perfino comprati apposta, riempire i sacchetti con pistacchi e mandorle, facendo attenzione a scegliere soltanto quelli sani, e annodarli per bene, pensando alla persona a cui andranno.

Mi sembra di infilarvi un pezzettino di Mosè.

4

A Mosè eravamo tutti cuochi

Quando si discuteva il pranzo, il primo e il più importante pasto della giornata, a Mosè diventavamo tutti cuochi.

Si andava a tavola non prima dell'una e trenta e non ci si alzava anche fino alle quattro del pomeriggio. Zio Giovanni, fratello maggiore di Mamma e padre di Maria, era un grande affabulatore che amava la conversazione prandiale; quando era incoraggiato a lasciare la tavola per permettere alle persone di servizio di finire il lavoro e riposarsi per il pomeriggio, rispondeva alle sorelle: "A tavola non si invecchia mai".

Il pranzo era un pasto forte, perché gli adulti non avevano mangiato nulla dalla sera prima. Nessuno faceva la prima colazione, tranne nonno, a cui nonna somministrava un bicchierone di cafiata zuccherata – il tufo ribollito del caffè – molto leggera e poco appetitosa, che lui consumava a solo, in camera da letto, immergendovi i biscotti al latte. Agli altri veniva portato un primo caffè in camera da letto, e prendevano il secondo verso le dieci nel salotto del secondo piano, dirimpetto alla sala da pranzo. Mamma e zia Teresa erano immancabilmente in salotto con gli ospiti, ogni mattina. Io ero spesso con loro, mi piacevano quelle mattinate insonnacchiate trascorse con i "grandi". Seduta accanto a Papà, mi facevo mosca e ascoltavo, tutta orecchi. Due erano gli argomenti di ogni giorno: il tempo – non capivo perché questa scelta, visto che il cielo era sempre blu e il sole splendeva fino a sera, quando calava in tramonti estivi meravigliosi – che dava motivo di lamentele e non riceveva mai alcun apprezzamento: era troppo caldo, ventoso, afoso, arrivava lo scirocco, o, peggio, "l'aria era ferma". E poi il cibo. Si dava grande importanza al mangiare e alla cucinata del pranzo; meno ai vini, e poca alla cena, di cui non si discuteva mai: sapevamo che avremmo avuto i resti del pranzo o quelli del giorno precedente, spesso pasta fritta, e poi pomodoro, patate e verdure bollite, formaggi, uova, e acciughe salate, lavate e condite con olio, limone e prezzemolo.

A un certo punto Mamma o zia Teresa, dopo aver sorseggiato il caffè, ponevano la domanda rituale: "Che si mangia oggi?". Ognuno – uomo o donna, parente o amico e perfino l'ospite di passaggio – esprimeva il suo desiderio, o commentava le decisioni che via via si prendevano. Tranne nonno. Lui non mangiava formaggio, e lasciava che la moglie, ottima cuoca, decidesse il suo pranzo. Esile e di bassa statura, nonno era un camminatore instancabile, anche in casa. Andava e veniva dalla camera da pranzo, dopo aver fatto un giro completo attorno alla tavola rettangolare. Si fermava per un attimo, come se volesse ascoltare quanto si diceva, e poi riprendeva il giro.

La discussione sul menù diventava presto vivace, talora persino intensa: aiutati dalla seconda dose di caffeina, i grandi si risvegliavano del tutto. Le maggiori questioni, quasi giornaliere, erano sulla salsa al pomodoro: l'aglio, molto amato dagli agrigentini, era per loro un ingrediente essenziale della salsa, mentre per i palermitani era anatema. La salsa al pomodoro della capitale dell'isola era cucinata con il soffritto di cipolla e con l'aggiunta di un pizzico di zucchero, mai con l'aglio!

Quando il menù era stato concordato, Mamma o zia Teresa chiedevano alla cameriera: "Che hanno portato di fresco dall'orto?". La ragazza recitava solennemente la lista. Se gli ingredienti per le pietanze prescelte mancavano, si ricominciava a discutere di cos'altro cucinare, di buon umore. Ma non sempre.

Una mattina, la proposta di cucinare le melanzane "a quaglia" era stata accettata con entusiasmo universale. Quando la cameriera riferì che in cucina c'erano soltanto melanzane tunisine, Raimondo, un cugino lontano di Papà, sancì: "Le tunisine non sono adatte a essere farcite di aglio e formaggio! Ci vogliono le melanzane nere e piccole".

"Non ne capisci niente!" gli strillava la moglie.

"Che intendi dire?"

"Tu in cucina non ci metti piede!"

"Certamente!" la rispustiò lui. "La cucina non è posto per me! È posto tuo, ma tu non te ne occupi, passi il tempo a fare commissioni in via Maqueda!"

"Non è vero! Non sei mai a casa, non sai quello che faccio!"

"Ciononostante mangio e assaggio come tutti voi, o no?" Raimondo fece una pausa e si guardò attorno, poi: "Allora posso dare il mio parere!".

Gli altri ascoltavano attenti: c'era tanto di non detto in quel battibecco, lo capivo anche io. Ma non zia Checchina, un'anziana zitella indigente che viveva con il fratello e la cognata. Le vicissitudini della vita non le avevano tolto la profonda ingenuità e il desiderio di alleggerire qualsiasi tensione dicendo una buona parola, in genere a sproposito. "Secondo me, le tunisine sono buone anche a quaglia!" e scosse i riccioli tinti nero ebano, guardando gli altri, contenta di aver detto la sua. La zia cercava di essere conciliatoria. Fin qui tutto bene. Peccato che tutti fossero al corrente che non aveva mai cucinato in vita sua, e che di cucina sapeva ben poco.

"Ah sì! Cosa vorrebbe dire, signorina? Che l'una o l'altra soluzione si equivalgono?" la voce di Raimondo era stridula. Poi, con tono canzonatorio: "Mi permetta di non essere d'accordo!".

Mamma e zia Teresa fino ad allora s'erano limitate ad ascoltare. Mamma lo fissò per un attimo: un battito di ciglia mise in fuga l'ombra che le attraversò lo sguardo. Zia Teresa sollevò il capo pronta a far da paciera, ma non ce ne fu bisogno. Nonno si avvicinava, appena appena più deciso, a testa bassa e le mani intrecciate dietro la schiena, senza cambiare il passo. Si fermò e, guardando Raimondo, borbottò: "Polpette di melanzane…". Girò sui tacchi e ritornò verso la sala da pranzo.

"Polpette di melanzane!" esclamò zia Teresa, e ripeté, guardando i volti di tutti, veloce: "Polpette di melanzane!". Poi, rivolta alla cameriera: "Perfetto, va' a dirlo in cucina, facciamo polpette di melanzane!". E con un sorriso smagliante: "Con la salsa normale o di pelato?"; soltanto allora la zia posò lo sguardo carezzevole su zia Checchina, che lo ricambiò, grata e contenta. Tutti parlavano contemporaneamente, ciascuno aveva la sua da dire. Raimondo e la moglie questa volta erano d'accordo: sostenevano che doveva essere con pomodoro pelato e basilico, "Pelato e basilico!" strillava lei. "Pelato, basilico e aglio!" la correggeva lui, guardandola, adesso, benevolo.

"Certo, Raimò, con l'aglio!" e la moglie accennò un sorriso. Così uniti, i due debellarono definitivamente il partito a favore della passata.

Cercavo di ascoltare tutte quelle voci, e mi confondevo. Avrebbero potuto evitare l'intera discussione se avessero chiesto fin dall'inizio che c'era in cucina; inoltre Raimondo aveva ragione: le melanzane a quaglia devono essere piccine. Non lo dissi perché avrei potuto sciupare il divertimento e, forse, la parvenza di riavvicinamento tra marito e moglie: era noto che Raimondo aveva un'altra famiglia nascosta chissà dove.

La saggezza di Jean Anthelme Brillat-Savarin

Credevo che l'amore, l'appartenenza allo stesso gruppo e avere gusti e aspirazioni simili fossero gli elementi che tengono unite le famiglie. Lo sono, ma vengono rinforzati, migliorati e trasmessi alle generazioni seguenti dal condividere un pasto regolarmente, se non ogni giorno, tutti insieme, come si faceva fino a una trentina di anni fa in tutta l'Europa. Adesso quella colla è indebolita, e questo è forse uno dei motivi dell'instabilità dei matrimoni e delle famiglie. Un pensiero che è diventato certezza quando ho letto *Fisiologia del gusto* di Jean Anthelme Brillat-Savarin. "Discutere di cosa si mangia allieta la gente e rinsalda o rappezza i matrimoni" affermava nel 1825 Brillat-Savarin, padre della gastronomia francese, grande giurista e uomo saggio, che però non prese mai moglie:

Infine, il buongusto, quando è condiviso, ha il più spiccato influsso sulla felicità che si può trovare nell'unione coniugale. Due

47

sposi buongustai hanno, almeno una volta al giorno, una piacevole occasione di stare insieme, perché anche coloro che vivono
separati di letto (e sono moltissimi) per lo meno mangiano alla
stessa tavola; essi hanno un argomento di conversazione che rinasce continuamente; parlano non solo di quello che mangiano,
ma anche di quello che hanno mangiato, di quello che mangeranno, di quello che hanno visto alla tavola degli altri, dei piatti
di moda, delle nuove invenzioni culinarie ecc., ecc.; e si sa che i
chiacchiericci familiari sono ricchi di fascino.

5

Mentre lavoro in cucina

Compiango coloro che non cucinano e che non sanno cucinare. Perdono piaceri e occasioni di riflessione molto belle.

In Inghilterra continuo a cucinare esattamente come ho imparato in Sicilia, anche se non era facile agli inizi. Negli anni sessanta gli ingredienti della nostra cucina siciliana erano quasi introvabili. L'olio d'oliva si comprava in farmacia, l'origano, il basilico e il prezzemolo piatto erano sconosciuti e le melanzane erano considerate come una rarità. Nel tempo ho imparato ad adattare i prodotti locali alle ricette di casa, ma non sempre con successo. Trovo impossibile rimpiazzare la ricotta di Mosè con quella *made in England*: ha meno siero, è gommosa e non condisce bene la pasta. Il rimedio c'è: uso formaggi soffici inglesi, il sapore è diverso ma il piatto viene bene.

Ho mantenuto le usanze siciliane nell'apparecchiare la tavola, nel servire il cibo e nel badare agli ospiti: questo mi aiuta a ricreare l'atmosfera conviviale di Mosè a Londra. Il nostro modo di mangiare è da un lato informale (raccogliamo il sugo dai piatti con un pezzo di pane che ci infiliamo in bocca con grande gusto), dall'altro ligio alle formalità (metto il tovagliolo di stoffa e una forchetta per pietanza) e applico automaticamente le norme del galateo di casa: rispetto per i commensali, attenzione alle necessità dei nostri vicini di posto e al benessere di ciascun ospite. Ho introdotto anche qualche abitudine inglese: servo formaggio e biscotti secchi a fine pranzo, con la frutta e un buon vino rosso, e lo prendo con le mani, come fanno gli inglesi.

A Londra invece sento la mancanza di un lavoro umile che mi piace tanto: pulire la verdura. Le mani sono un ottimo strumento di lavoro e, ben lavate, sono perfettamente igieniche. Mi diverte usarle per pulire e tagliare ortaggi, condire le insalate, decorare i piatti di portata. Ora in cucina le uso meno. A Londra c'è tutto, in qualsiasi stagione e dovunque: nei supermercati, nelle drogherie, perfino nelle bancarelle dei mercati. E a buon prezzo. Nei supermercati, carne, pesce e verdure sono esposti già tagliati e puliti in pacchetti di cellophane: sembrano imbalsamati. Io preferisco andare al mercato di Brixton: compro dei grossi sedani, che sanno di terra, folti mazzi di spinaci e cavolfiori sfusi. Arrivata in cucina mi metto a pulirli, prima di riporli nel frigorifero: spero di vedere un vermetto, o una lumachina, ma devo rassegnarmi alla pulizia assoluta. Delusa, scorgo tra le coste verdi solo una piccola traccia di terra rimasta. Mi conforto con la musica, metto il cd di un'opera intensa, sanguigna, una *Carmen* o un *Don Giovanni*.

Pulire e preparare la verdura a Mosè è un lavoro pieno di sorprese e dà spunto a tanti bei pensieri. Data la varietà di ingredienti, non c'è noia che possa assalirci. Passiamo ore a sbaccellare fave e piselli, a togliere il mallo ai pistacchi, a pulire gli ortaggi per la cena, ad affettare melanzane, zucchine e peperoni, a piangere sulle cipolle. I nostri ortaggi sono materia viva e capace di dare vita – sbucciando una cipolla si può vedere il germoglio pronto a spuntare, dagli occhi neri delle patate nasceranno altri tuberi – oltre che materia da cui si possono prendere semi, farli asciugare per piantarli alla stagione successiva – lo facevamo spesso con i peperoni più gustosi e i meloni particolarmente dolci e profumati. Maneggiando le verdure le si conosce meglio e si crea con loro un rapporto che va oltre quello tra ingrediente e consumatore, come per esempio quando si taglia un rametto di rosmarino per piantarlo o si conservano i semi del pomodoro che, essiccati, andranno in un vaso, sapendo che saranno destinati a generare nuova vita: è una relazione di reciproco vantaggio che si instaura tra uomo e pianta. È dunque naturale per me chiedermi da dove vengano i nostri ingredienti, dare una personalità a loro e ai loro parassiti, come fossero amici di famiglia. Il baccello dei piselli "mangiato" da una lumaca mi ricorda un invalido, compiango la cipolla non rotonda, schiacciata da un lato, che probabilmente ha incontrato, nella sua crescita sotterranea, un sasso non spietato dall'ortolano durante la zappatura. Ammiro e considero arditi i vermetti rimasti attaccati alle verdure. I porcellini di sant'Antonio, piccoli e attorcigliati su se stessi tra le foglie di cavolfiore, si rivelano per quello che sono: grandi esploratori. A volte paragono semi, ortaggi e bestioline alla gente che mi sta accanto, do loro voce e sentimenti.

Le melanzane tunisine mi ricordano le donne anziane dai capelli troppo carichi di tintura, quasi violetti, a volte con qualche ciuffo bianco o sfuggito al colore, mentre quelle nere sembrano vedove prosperose con la tintura compatta del parrucchiere. Penso a Papà, quando sosteneva che le vedove rifiorivano dopo un anno di lutto e Mamma se ne dispiaceva.

51

"Che dici… quella poverina è tanto afflitta!" replicava accorata. E lui: "Elena, aspetta l'anno, e poi ne parliamo!". E non lo dimenticava. Alla prima visita dopo la messa dell'anno, Papà osservava la vedova: vestita a mezzo lutto, il viso disteso con un velo di trucco discreto ma luminoso, era pronta al sorriso. Quando se n'era andata, si rivolgeva a Mamma: "Hai visto?".

Mi perdo nei ricordi mentre "monto" le parmigiane. A casa nostra si fanno anche con le zucchine, che abbondano sempre. Il terreno argilloso dell'orto, tanto ostile alle patate, è straordinariamente generoso con le zucchine: basta farne cadere un seme per avere una pianta grande in poche settimane. Argilla e zucchina sembrano fatte l'una per l'altra. Dispongo le fette fritte a disegni geometrici, a zigzag, a spina di pesce, verso la salsa di pomodoro come stendessi pennellate di tempera e spargo il formaggio grattugiato come dovessi seminare prezzemolo. E penso ai quadri di arte moderna.

La gran quantità di zucchine certe volte mi tedia. Mi sconforta pulire ancora una volta quelle lunghe, che si mangeranno bollite e condite di olio e limone, raschiandone la superficie con il coltello a seghetta. Poi penso che in poche settimane non ce ne saranno più, per nove mesi, e riprendo a lavorare contenta.

Quando faccio questi lavori con amici, chiacchieriamo senza rallentare l'attività delle nostre mani. Ben presto il momento delle riflessioni cede il passo a quello delle confidenze.

Mamma, invece, amava i suoi silenzi, soprattutto quando era impegnata in un lavoro complesso. Nulla la assorbiva come la pulizia dei tenerumi, i lunghi tralci della pianta di zucchina, raccolti con i boccioli o al primissimo stadio di formazione del frutto.

Rispondeva alle mie domande, paziente, ma poi mi interrompeva: "Amore mio, ne parliamo dopo, lo vedi che devo pulire i tenerumi" mi diceva dolcissima, e riprendeva il lavoro. Aveva il suo ritmo e sembrava maneggiare trecce di seta, intenta a scegliere i colori per un ricamo. Divideva le foglie in quattro gruppi: quelle danneggiate dai bruchi o dure andavano assieme ai gambi in un secchio poggiato ai suoi piedi – erano destinate a cibo per i maiali o concime per i campi; le foglie grandi e larghe erano ottime per il pastone dei cani; quelle medie per le nostre minestre; e quelle piccole con i boccioli sarebbero state cucinate per la tavola. "Tenerissime sono" mormorava Mamma, le dita che carezzavano le foglioline "saranno ottime, stasera a tavola."

Anche io divento silenziosa, quando penso all'origine del cibo che compro a Londra. Percorrendo le corsie dei supermercati mi accorgo che il ciclo delle stagioni è scomparso quasi del tutto. Tra la carne e il pesce surgelati, occhieggiano dai banchi i pasti bell'e pronti di prodotti che vengono da tutto il mondo, verdure "fresche" che arrivano in aereo giornalmente dall'Africa e da altri continenti ancora più lontani. I supermercati sono enormi, ben forniti e accattivanti. Posso trovare tutto quello che mi serve per preparare qualsiasi piatto, in qualunque stagione. A nonna Maria sarebbe sembrato un miracolo. Per me è un'arma a doppio taglio e motivo di sconforto. La convenienza del mercato globale e l'effetto dell'enorme potere d'acquisto sulla scelta e sui prezzi nei negozi sono ben accetti: il cibo costa poco. Da giovane madre cercavo sempre di risparmiare: sceglievo le offerte speciali e mi lanciavo sui banchi della carne a basso prezzo.

Ora, invece, è esattamente il contrario: mi disturba acquistare a basso prezzo carne, pesce e prodotti agricoli che vengono dall'altro capo del mondo, leggo le certificazioni sull'etichetta ma continuo a farmi venire dubbi. E ciononostante spesso li metto nel carrello, per pigrizia e per risparmio. Poi, a casa, cucinandoli, mi turbo con domande che non hanno risposta: "Che fertilizzanti ci hanno messo?", "Che colore strano, perché?", "Com'è che pomodori, peperoni e melanzane restano duri e lucenti per settimane nel frigorifero?", "Questo animale dove l'hanno allevato?", "E la manodopera?".

Dovunque in Europa oggi si trova tutto e sempre; rimpiango la scomparsa della stagionalità nei mercati e la sua perdita nella dieta. Per settimane a Mosè si mangiano gli stessi prodotti, maturati tutti assieme; si conservano sotto sale, sott'olio, sotto aceto, e si elaborano, si cucinano, si surgelano. Tutto a un tratto sulle piante non ce ne sono più. Altri prodotti prendono il loro posto.

C'è un'antica bellezza nell'aspettare

C'è un'antica bellezza nell'aspettare che inizi la stagione dei finocchi; è confortevole fare pentoloni di marmellata di albicocche pensando che basteranno per l'intero anno, e ha un non so che di sensuale fare scorpacciate di arance, e una panzata di fichi, sapendo che non ce ne saranno altri per più di otto mesi. La scansione delle stagioni, prepararsi al caldo, attendere la pioggia, desiderare tanto un frutto, ricordare il gusto degli stufati di coda di bue invernale e del pesce di stagione sapendo che per sentirlo di nuovo si dovrà pazientare a lungo, mi ricorda che c'è un tempo per tutto. Che bisogna saper aspettare. Nell'attesa, mi conforto con altri cibi, che scompariranno dai campi e dalla tavola dopo la loro stagione.

I saluti dopo le vacanze estive: da sinistra mio marito, Martin Hornby, io, Mamma di spalle, zia Teresa intravista tra Mamma e Chiara.

PARTE SECONDA

6

Dalla tavola di nonna Maria alla nostra

"L'accoglienza dell'ospite" diceva Mamma "inizia dalla tovaglia. Deve essere pulita, senza una piega, e su un buon mollettone." Quando le chiedevo com'era possibile che una tovaglia presa dal cassetto non avesse pieghe, Mamma aveva due risposte: la prima era che una tovaglia ben riposta aveva sempre pieghe impercettibili; la seconda, più pratica e vera, era che una volta stesa sul mollettone sarebbe stata stirata velocemente: il ferro caldo avrebbe allisciato le pieghe. La passata era di rigore la prima volta che si stendeva la tovaglia, si ripeteva quando era stata usata più volte e si era stropicciata.

Stiro sempre le tovaglie di casa mia prima di utilizzarle, perché le pieghe – e io ne faccio tante – mi fanno sentire in colpa: deturpano la bellezza della tavola e insultano l'ospite che si siederà. In realtà non sono una brava stiratrice, ma ho sempre stirato il necessario in famiglia, velocemente e purtroppo male. I miei figli ragazzini, appena mi vedevano prendere il ferro in mano, tiravano fuori le loro camicie dal cesto e mi dicevano: "Mamma lasciala, me la stiro io perché devo andare a una festa e la vorrei senza tante pieghe". La verità è che faccio più attenzione a stirare le mie tovaglie che gli indumenti miei e dei miei familiari.

Nonna Maria (nel 1924).

Odio le tovagliette e i mat

Odio le tovagliette e i *mat* tradizionali e moderni, per non parlare dei sottobicchieri individuali e dei sottopiatti. I *mat*, in genere di origine inglese, sono tavolette di sughero con incollate scene di caccia o composizioni di frutta. Quelli moderni si trovano ormai di tutti i tipi e materiali: stoffa, paglia, plastica, legno, metallo. Mi vien detto che sono pratici, proteggono il tavolo, fanno risparmiare energia e detersivo, perché non si lavano né si stirano. Ma preferirei mangiare sul tavolo nudo, ben pulito, anziché usarli.

Dare a ciascun commensale una zona così delimitata è contrario al principio della convivialità: le tovagliette separano gli ospiti e inoltre tolgono il piacere di ammirare i disegni e i ricami di una bella tovaglia. È come se ciascun commensale mangiasse in un tavolo tutto suo in un ristorante, accanto a estranei.

Aborro l'uso dei tovaglioli di carta e di piatti e bicchieri di plastica, che a casa mia non sono mai entrati. Mamma, da anziana, li tollerava in silenzio, quando c'erano molti ospiti e Chiara decideva di utilizzarli.

Non c'è casa siciliana dove non ci sia una seppur modesta tovaglia sul tavolo in cui si mangia: per rispetto al pane che ci poggia sopra. Ricordo le tovaglie profumate di Rosalia, messe ad asciugare sui cespugli di rosmarino. Le nostre tovaglie, prive di profumo, erano generalmente candide, ricamate bianco su bianco; quelle lavorate da Mamma e zia Teresa, su disegno di Mamma, avevano dei ricami dai colori delicati. Capitava talvolta che perfino la stoffa venisse scelta di un colore tenue, secondo la nuova moda.

Il monogramma di Carlo Dati

Questo maggio apparecchiavo il tavolo da pranzo di Mosè con mia cugina Maria, la nipote più amata da Mamma e zia Teresa, che essendo maggiore di me è la nostra memoria storica. Avevamo scelto una tovaglia di damasco da tablattè e dunque priva di ricami, se non per il monogramma ai quattro angoli e nel centro. Il ricamo era molto bello: bianco su bianco, come sempre, e in ottime condizioni. Avevamo soltanto tovaglie delle nostre famiglie, con una A per Agnello o una G per Giudice.

La tovaglia che avevamo per le mani aveva una C e una D. Eravamo perplesse: da dove veniva? Poi, un'illuminazione: Carlo Dati! Era un coetaneo dei nostri genitori che aveva fatto parte della loro comitiva. Un bell'uomo dai capelli chiari, statura piccola, mingherlino, molto raffinato. Figlio unico e orfano, dopo la laurea in giurisprudenza non aveva voluto lavorare. Aveva dissipato l'eredità paterna in viaggi, abbigliamento, automobili, orologi di marca, *objet d'art* comprati alle aste e una sfilza di "fidanzate". Era anche molto generoso e ospitale con gli amici. Dopo una decina di anni, Carlo aveva dovuto vendere gli appartamenti ereditati per pagare i debiti; quello in cui viveva era stato pignorato dai creditori. Papà e gli zii cercavano di dargli delle dritte quando lui veniva a Mosè. "Voglio vivere come mi piace fino a quando posso. Una volta perduto tutto, ricomincerò da zero" rispondeva lui.

Carlo aveva iniziato a vendere il contenuto della propria casa. Non se ne vergognava, anzi, incoraggiava gli amici a comprare quanto rimasto, a prezzi stracciati, decisi da lui. Voleva disfarsi di tutto in fretta e alcuni ne approfittavano.

In soffitta Carlo aveva trovato dei bauli di biancheria di casa: tovaglie antiche, coperte da letto ricamate, asciugamani di fiandra con le frange lunghissime, tutta roba fuori moda che non interessava alla gente, che preferiva la biancheria moderna colorata e ricamata a riporto. Mamma e zia Teresa, per aiutarlo, comprarono molti asciugamani e tovaglie, tra cui quella.

Povero in canna, Carlo accettò alla fine l'offerta di lavoro di un amico direttore di banca: si trasferì a Roma dove incontrò una donna più giovane che sposò e con cui visse felice. Dopo tutto, Carlo aveva avuto ragione.

Si parlò a lungo delle sue vicende e del suo matrimonio; io ero ragazzina e lo ammirai enormemente. Carlo era diventato un mio eroe! A differenza di tanti altri che avevano distrutto la maggior parte del loro patrimonio e vivevano grazie all'ospitalità e agli aiuti di parenti e amici, lui aveva voluto ricominciare, e ci era riuscito. Maria mi diceva che Mamma e zia Teresa non avevano approvato il suo comportamento, e che era stato fortunato a trovare lavoro e moglie.

Però a questo mondo gli eroi servono: le loro gesta, per quanto incaute, ispirano e danno speranza. Sono eccentrici e spesso un po' pazzi, altrimenti non sarebbero eroi.

Certe volte faccio di testa mia

Con poche eccezioni, ho sempre chiesto e seguito i consigli di Mamma. Ma certe volte faccio di testa mia e non ho ripensamenti. Per esempio non mi creo problemi quando metto in tavola piatti di ceramica e di porcellana spizzicati o rotti, finché lo sono sul bordo e non sul fondo, o tovaglioli di diverse stoffe e colori, purché siano della stessa misura. L'armonia non nasce dall'uniformità, né dal lusso, ma dall'equilibrio. Non trovo importante usare le posate dello stesso servizio se non ce ne sono abbastanza o se non le trovo; però sto attenta a che ogni posto abbia le stesse posate. Tutte le posate sulla tavola devono essere utilizzate, perciò non abbondo mai. Farlo confonde l'ospite. Se sono d'argento bisogna che siano lucidate e poi ben lavate, era uno dei punti fermi dell'arredo della tavola di Mamma.

Una volta da giovane padrona di casa, dopo aver ben lucidato il nostro servizio di posate, dimenticai di lavarlo. Avevamo a pranzo Tim, un astrofisico amico di mio marito. Tim stava mangiando con gusto gli spaghetti e tutto andava bene, quando cominciò a sembrarmi preoccupato, si guardava continuamente le mani, di sotterfugio. A un certo punto posò la forchetta e aprì la mano destra: dita e palmo erano neri. "Non so che mi sia capitato, scusatemi, vado a lavarmi le mani" disse tutto rosso. Mio marito non ci fece caso, continuava a mangiare contento. Guardai le sue dita: anche quelle erano nere. Abbassai le mie mani e le esaminai: erano luride e puzzavano del liquido che avevo usato per pulire l'argento. Decisi di fare finta di niente, come mi aveva insegnato Mamma, e tenni le mani con il palmo in basso, per tutto il pranzo. Quando l'amico se ne fu andato, chiesi a mio marito se si era accorto di avere le mani nere. "Ti sbagli, mi disse, non lo sono" e me le mostrò. Aveva ragione, erano pulite. Rimasi perplessa, fino a che, sparecchiando, mi accorsi che il suo tovagliolo era nero e stropicciato: senza farci caso, le aveva pulite lì. Non dissi altro.

La sala da pranzo di Mosè ci era stata regalata da zio Giovanni. Lui aveva ereditato l'appartamento della casa di

Agrigento che era molto grande, e che era stato interamente rinnovato nell'ultimo decennio dell'Ottocento, per accogliervi nonna Maria andata sposa a nonno Gaspare quando lei aveva sedici anni e lui il doppio, nello stile moderno di allora: il liberty. I mobili erano di acero biondo dal colore mieloso, con maniglie di ottone, e intagli e decorazioni floreali.

Mamma cercava di avere una "tavola ordinata" cioè con posate, piatti e bicchieri appattati e se possibile dello stesso servizio. Era il modo in cui era stata educata, faceva eccezioni quando i piatti tutti uguali non bastavano: allora non c'era scelta, e ne rideva. Ma con l'occhio mesto. Altre volte usava cose scompagnate o brutte per uno scopo ben preciso. Non tutto il contenuto delle vetrine era di mio gradimento. Quando facevamo la pulizia degli scaffali, ogni estate, prendevo un boccale sgargiante, una ciotola tutta protuberanze, delle saliere di ceramica dai colori orribili, e chiedevo a Mamma: "Si toglie?". La risposta inevitabilmente era: "Bello non è, però, amore mio, me l'ha regalato lo zio Ferdinando…" o "Questo no, lo ha scelto apposta per me la signora Maria". Poi con uno sguardo un po' triste diceva: "Riponilo sullo scaffale, in fondo; ci mettiamo qualcosa davanti". E poi mi spiegava: "Questi regali devono essere usati al momento opportuno, belli o brutti che siano". Cioè dovevano esser tirati fuori quando chi ce li aveva regalati veniva a pranzo o in visita. Bello o brutto che fosse.

A differenza di Mamma, io non riesco ad apparecchiare la tavola con quello che non mi piace. Mi sembra un'offesa al cibo e ai commensali. Ogni tanto mi capita di dover usare dei piatti di portata brutti; li ricopro di foglie di fico, di vite, e metto sopra frutta o piattini di salsette. Anche allora sto attenta a che le foglie siano ben disposte, una sopra l'altra, e che non ci sia spazio che riveli il fondo lucido. E uso diversi tipi di posate e vettovaglie nell'arredo della tavola, quelle a cui Mamma ricorreva, dispiaciuta, per necessità, quando le cose non bastavano.

Quanto ai bicchieri preferisco una certa continuità. Si vedono da qualunque posto perché sono alti, e non mi piace notarne tanti diversi, fanno perdere armonia all'insieme. Se però non ne ho abbastanza, appatto due servizi incompleti e alterno bicchieri di colori differenti.

Le saliere e le pepiere mancano sempre e dovunque; io uso contenitori di vetro o di cristallo che compro dai rigattieri, più o meno della stessa misura ma di fattura completamente diversa, per metterne molti che possano essere divisi da due o tre commensali al massimo.

Però forse sbaglio nel bandire da casa mia quello che non mi piace. Certe volte la moda cambia e rivaluta stili e colori di arredi per anni considerati di cattivo gusto: le ceramiche futuriste degli anni trenta, i servizi da tè con sgargianti dipinti floreali arancione e verde, i vassoi di metallo a disegno geometrico, i boccali di vetro dipinto a pois. Dopo un po' l'occhio si assuefà e mi sembrano gradevoli. Eccezionalmente, perfino belli. Altre volte basta conoscere la storia di un oggetto e questo diventa interessante e quasi amato. A Mosè abbiamo delle salsiere di porcellana ottocentesche di casa Giudice con un bordo arancione e oro; come decorazione, due mani che si stringono, anch'esse arancione: brutte, anzi repellenti. Un'amica mi spiegò che le mani erano uno dei simboli della massoneria italiana.

Bastò quello a farmi apprezzare le salsiere: i Giudice erano massoni e dunque progressisti, mentre gli Agnello erano rimasti fedeli ai Borboni.

7
Gli ospiti

Tutti gli ospiti meritano di essere accuditi, anche quei pochi che si comportano in modo sgradevole o imbarazzante, o che semplicemente non ci piacciono. Io faccio del mio meglio per rendere il pranzo gradevole a tutti, compresi costoro. Ho imparato e continuo a imparare modi e tecniche per evitare che la leggerezza del convivio e la conversazione ne soffrano.

L'avido

Non è affamato, ma ingordo. Segue con la coda dell'occhio concupiscente l'ultima cotoletta; quando la guantiera è a portata di mano, come un pescatore alla mattanza del tonno, la arpiona con la propria forchetta. Lo osservo, e appena posso gli porgo la guantiera perché lui se ne serva, e gli passo tutte le pietanze per un'ultima volta. Con un poco di attenzione, l'avido è contenibile.

Il timido

Spesso non parla e si serve di poco; si sente a disagio e mette a disagio gli altri, senza rendersene conto. E soffre. È un circolo vizioso che devo cercare di sciogliere. Preferisco avere i timidi accanto a me. A volte la timidezza si sconfigge con una piccola richiesta – di passare l'insalata o il cestello del pane a qualcun altro, di dare un giudizio sulla quantità di aceto nell'agrodolce – o una domanda diretta, ma fatta con un sorriso.

Il tattile

È iperattivo. Tocca pane e frutta prima di decidere di servirsene. Prende con le dita formaggio, foglie di lattuga, fette di prosciutto, pezzi di pollo. Parlando, tocca il braccio dell'interlocutore. Si può distrarre chiedendogli aiuto manuale: scegliere le arance più mature, tagliare le fette di torta, versare il vino ai propri vicini.

Il loquace

Inarrestabile, se gli si offre spazio. Approfitta del convivio per fare monologhi su di sé, e sui propri successi passati, ingigan\-titi. Intriga all'inizio, e ben presto annoia. Lo lascio parlare, poi lo interrompo con richieste di aiuto: "Mi passi il cestello del pane, per favore?". Lo invoglio a mangiare: "Ti taglio un'altra fetta di torta?". E nel frattempo accendo conversazioni altrove, spiazzandolo. Il silenzio non lo spaventa ed essere tacitato non lo offende. Ciononostante, alla fine del pranzo, prima che lui si serva della frutta, gli faccio una domanda chiave, di quelle per le quali il loquace ha una lunghissima risposta bell'e pronta. Ascolto rapita e infine mi sottraggo. Ma a quel punto il loquace è soddisfatto, di se stesso e del pranzo.

Il comodista

Sconosce o intenzionalmente ignora le basi del galateo. Cerco di neutralizzarlo con una gestione specifica della tavola. Alcuni vogliono tutto ciò che serve a portata di mano: acqua, vino, pane, sale, pepe e oliera; e ci riescono, allungando le braccia e chiedendo agli altri di passare quello a cui non arrivano. Attorno a loro si crea un altarino di bottiglie e cestelli. Preferisco conzare la tavola con boccali, saliere e oliere extra, e metterne davanti al loro posto una fornitura completa. Altri sono voraci di pane, e rimescolano le fette nel cestello, per palparle e scegliere le migliori. A costoro passo io il cestello del pane, con un "Vuoi prenderne alcune? Sono state tagliate dallo stesso filone". E quelli ne acchiappano quante ne vogliono senza toccare le altre.

Il mutangaro

È l'ospite più difficile da integrare nel convivio. Non parla perché non vorrebbe trovarsi a tavola con noi o ha avuto una brutta giornata. Bisogna cercare di dissipare il malumore dell'ospite riluttante coinvolgendolo nella conversazione. Se altro non funziona si ricorre all'adulazione: con quella si riesce. Invece desisto dinanzi a chi tace per fare capire a un altro commensale – in genere il proprio partner, ma non sempre – che intende punirlo rovinando l'atmosfera del pranzo: esibisce il proprio silenzio spavaldo masticando lentamente, sguardo fisso sul nemico.

Il saccente

Ovviamente crede di conoscere tutto lo scibile. Parla delle proprie ricette pronto a insegnarci tutto e di tutto. Si autoelogia. Lettore vorace dei quotidiani, li analizza ad alta voce. Lo lascio parlare. I suoi interventi, seppur eclettici, sono brevi. E lo ascolto attentamente: questo ha su di lui un effetto calmante.

Il noioso

La noia è la nemica numero uno del convivio. Il noioso è ingestibile, come il maleducato, ma si può isolare facilmente, mettendolo tra persone che parlano una lingua a lui sconosciuta. Può anche essere saccente, ma in questo caso è probabile che sia anche molto ignorante. Ama parlare, ma non è il loquace che può essere interessante. Il noioso, se parla, ammorba: non a caso la noia è una vera malattia.

Può rovinare un pranzo, ma solo ai suoi vicini perché fortunatamente il noioso non ha smanie di protagonismo.

La smorfiosa

È in genere una femmina. Si dichiara cagionevole di salute e delicata di stomaco: non mangia questo e quello, le fanno male olio, burro, zucchero, pepe e sale, ma le piace il mangiare saporito. Lascia sul piatto quello che le sembra cattivo, duro, calloso ecc. È insopportabile. Certe volte basta lodarla, e farle complimenti. "Che occhi belli!", "Ottimo gusto!" e non farà più smorfie. Almeno per quel pasto.

Il maleducato

C'è un ospite che non vorrei mai dover gestire: il maleducato. Sono in pochi, ma ne capitano. Indica con il dito il piatto che desidera aver avvicinato, sceglie dall'insalatiera i pezzi che preferisce, non fa attenzione ai suoi vicini, non apre bocca finché non ha riempito il suo piatto e poi mastica voluttuosamente a bocca aperta, guardandosi in giro tutto soddisfatto. Si scola l'ultimo vino della bottiglia, senza pensare di offrirne agli altri. Cercare di coinvolgerlo, di prevenire i suoi gesti, di seguire il suo sguardo e passargli quello che sembra desiderare prima che allunghi il braccio davanti al vicino non ha alcun effetto.

Al momento del placement

Al momento del *placement* più che padrona di casa mi sento regista: devo sentire dentro di me tutti quei caratteri, devo sapere di che pasta son fatti i personaggi che metto in scena. Sistemo vicino a me l'avido, il tattile e il timido. Talvolta, anche il noioso. Distribuisco gli altri secondo le loro personalità, per esempio metto colui che gesticola alla fine del lato lungo del tavolo perché non impicci chi gli siede accanto.

Non colloco mai il loquace a capotavola, si sentirebbe su un pulpito. È metto il comodista a metà del lato lungo così che gli altri possano usare quanto lui si ammassa davanti.

A volte, nonostante le difficili personalità dei convitati, riesco a creare una bella atmosfera a tavola, con l'aiuto dei miei figli, o di un altro commensale, a cui chiedo di badare in modo particolare a uno o due degli ospiti difficili.

Una nota prima dei menù
Dove andremo a finire?

La nostra cucina si fonda su alcuni principi tradizionali e su pratiche manuali a cui restiamo fedeli, in una realtà in cui il mondo intero, inclusa la cucina, hanno subito straordinarie mutazioni e vere rivoluzioni, dovute al progresso e alle nuove tecnologie, spesso, ma non sempre, benefiche. Mi piace ricordarli come se fossero un decalogo. Ma si tratta, come si vede, di un decalogo fuori asse, fatto di undici – non dieci – buoni suggerimenti.

Lo si prenda con simpatia e leggerezza: ciascuno di noi è in grado di creare un proprio decalogo, basta pensarci su. Il mio parte da un principio fondamentale: basiamo ogni pasto sul piacere del mangiar bene e in buona compagnia, nel rispetto della natura, del cibo e delle persone.

Da qui, i miei consigli:

1. consumiamo cibo stagionale e del territorio;
2. evitiamo, quando possiamo, di comprare cibi pronti e pietanze precotte o surgelate;
3. limitiamo l'acquisto dei surgelati ai prodotti di base (piselli e pasta sfoglia);
4. evitiamo lo spreco di cibo ed energia;

5. conteniamo le spese, anche per un buon pranzo, creando "falsi" di pietanze costose;

6. commettiamo senza timore infrazioni alla tradizione;

7. cambiamo le norme di comportamento adeguandole ai tempi, sempre rispettando gli altri e il cibo;

8. non dimentichiamo mai che la cucina è anche divertimento, evitiamo di prenderla troppo sul serio;

9. introduciamo fantasia e innovazioni nell'apparecchiata della tavola;

10. coinvolgiamo gli ospiti nella cucinata e condividiamo le nostre ricette;

11. occupiamoci sempre della felicità dei nostri commensali.

PARTE TERZA

Un compleanno in famiglia

Paté di lattuga
Anelletti al forno
Cotolette di melanzane
Insalata di pomodori, carote e capperi
Torta al caramello
Da bere: acqua, vino rosso, spumante

Per le ricette rinvio il lettore a pagina 153.

La celebrazione di una nascita

A me non piacciono le feste di compleanno, a meno che non siano di bambini, o dei miei figli, che rimangono bambini nel mio cuore. Preferisco festeggiare l'onomastico, una festa soltanto cattolica che gli anglicani non celebrano – hanno pochi santi e anche quei pochi sono dimenticati –, che ha il vantaggio di essere noto a tutti. Ma nessuno si è mai ricordato di San Simone.

Il compleanno è una cosa intima, da celebrare fino ai diciotto e dopo gli ottant'anni. Il festeggiato ha diritto di fare quello che vuole per tutto il giorno, di invitare gli amici a casa e soprattutto di decidere il menù.

Oggi si festeggia e ci si festeggia costantemente: esiste il giorno della mamma, quello del papà, quello dei nonni, quello delle donne (ma non quello degli uomini), quello dei gay, quello degli innamorati, quello dei single. In America si chiamano "*Hallmark Holidays*", dalla più grande ditta di biglietti di auguri, che non ha mai avuto sentore della crisi economica. Anche noi dunque ci siamo adeguati e continuiamo a festeggiare i compleanni di tutti i membri della famiglia.

Dolce e delicata come sempre, Mamma ci raccontava il giorno della nostra nascita: descriveva la reazione dei parenti – alla mia, sgomento dei nonni che avrebbero desiderato il nipote maschio – e la sua gioia nel conoscerci, poi commentava la bravura del medico. Non parlava mai del travaglio. Anch'io racconto ai miei figli e ai nipoti il giorno in cui sono nati: è stato il nostro primo incontro. Da piccoli ne erano forse imbarazzati, ma ascoltavano con attenzione sentendosi amati e "speciali". Credo che ora a volte si annoino, ma non ne sono sicura. Quest'anno il compleanno di Nicola, il mio secondo figlio, nato prematuro, è caduto in una giornata di lavoro, così l'ho chiamato in ufficio: "Tanti auguri!" gli ho detto, e non ho aggiunto altro. Lui non ha risposto subito, è rimasto interdetto: "Mamma, ma non mi racconti più com'ero? Con i tubicini nelle narici, è vero?". Faceva quarantadue anni.

Il menù del compleanno è deciso dal festeggiato, senza badare a spese. L'unica scelta prevedibile è quella del dolce: la torta al caramello. Solo d'estate, qualche volta, capita che si scelga il babà di Agorà, la pasticceria del Villaggio Mosè, la preferita dei miei figli. Il primo, che io ricordi, è sempre una pasta, mentre il secondo varia in base al periodo in cui cade il compleanno – pesce d'estate, carne d'inverno, oppure uno dei "finti" siciliani: le cotolette alla milanese, ma con belle fette di melanzana al posto della carne.

Nicola e Giorgio bambini con Chiara.

La tavola del compleanno ha sempre una tovaglia pulita e ben stirata, senza pretese. Piatti, posate e bicchieri sono quelli di ogni giorno. Il *placement* mette il "compleannato" al centro dell'attenzione, seduto dove preferisce; in genere a capotavola, ma non sempre. A me piace per esempio sedermi sul lato lungo, in posizione centrale, per poter parlare con più persone. Noi diamo poca importanza a vini e liquori. Essendo Papà astemio, Mamma si disamorò del vino. Per i compleanni abbiamo sempre uno spumante; siamo talmente contenti di festeggiare l'occasione che basta la truzzata, il brindisi, a inebriarci.

Giorgio ha scelto come primo gli anelletti al forno, da noi chiamati la "pasta al forno". Non ce n'è altra per i palermitani e non ci sarebbe bisogno di specificare. Ma abbiamo ceduto all'unità gastronomica italiana imparando a definirla con precisione. È un timballo di pasta che da almeno sei secoli onora le tavole domenicali di Palermo. Mio figlio, mezzo siciliano, è fedele alla tradizione di sua madre. Per secondo, Giorgio ha voluto le cotolette di melanzane, una leccornia di stagione, ottima e poco costosa. E infine la nostra torta al caramello. È un menù tradizionale, che tiene conto del fatto che per i compleanni le mamme cercano di passare meno tempo in cucina e di godersi la famiglia riunita al momento dell'apertura dei regali, che è sempre la mattina, per poi riposarsi.

Quest'anno abbiamo avuto due torte al caramello, una preparata da me e l'altra da Silvano: ambedue dalla ricetta di nonna Maria – chiamata nel libretto "torta buona di Marisa"–, ma di mano diversa. Io sono più pasticciona, mentre Silvano è metodico e preciso. In questo caso, al centro della tavola ho messo qualcosa di semplice e poco ingombrante, che affiancasse la torta senza metterla in ombra: bicchieri colorati decorati con fiorellini di campo.

Una novità di Chiara

Il paté di lattuga è una salsetta che si prepara frullando pangrattato, sale, pepe, olio, aceto, acciuga, capperi e le foglie esterne e dure della lattuga, che in genere si usano nelle minestre o, più frequentemente, si gettano. Nasce come *dip* degli aperitivi. È piuttosto piccante e viene da un'idea di Chiara, che l'ha introdotta nella nostra cucina. Si presta a molti usi: si consuma come aperitivo con fettine di pane duro o bastoncini di carote e sedano, come salsa di accompagnamento del pesce lesso, come condimento di tonno e pesce blu bollito, affumicato o in scatola, e con il lesso di carne, in sostituzione della salsa verde.

Giorgio lo ha voluto come accompagnamento delle melanzane a cotoletta, caldissime.

La pasta al forno

La pasta al forno è amatissima da noi tutti. Di origine rinascimentale e tipica della nostra isola, si prepara spesso con un giorno di anticipo. È dunque molto adatta per il pranzo di compleanno: basta metterla nel forno e tirarla fuori dopo una mezz'ora abbondante. Deve riposare qualche minuto, per far sì che gli ingredienti, consumata la cottura, tornino alla loro fragrante individualità. Solo allora fa il suo ingresso trionfale. Ogni città siciliana ha la sua pasta al forno, ma la procedura di base è la stessa.

È un piatto complesso e laborioso, ma non necessariamente costoso: è fatto per lo più di resti. Il ripieno si può preparare con il ragù rimasto, pezzetti di provola piccante, di pecorino col pepe e di tutti i formaggi saporiti che si hanno in casa. Un consiglio: non tritate il formaggio in una macchinetta, è meglio sminuzzarlo con il coltello, così da ottenere pezzetti diversi che diano a ogni cucchiaiata un sapore tutto suo.

A Palermo si adoperano esclusivamente gli anelletti, una pasta a forma di piccole fedi nuziali, con i bordi tondeggianti. Un tempo si trovavano solo da noi, ora invece si comprano anche dai grandi pastifici nazionali, che appaltano la manifattura a quelli siciliani, vicino a Palermo.

Il "falso" per eccellenza

Le cotolette di melanzane sono il "falso" siciliano per eccellenza. Quando ero piccola ne mangiavo tantissime, al punto da farmi venire il mal di pancia.

Il segreto della loro riuscita sta nella preparazione: vanno passate prima nella farina e poi "ammaccate", come diceva Mamma, cioè pigiate perché si infarinino bene, poi immerse nell'uovo sbattuto e infine passate nel pangrattato. E lì bisogna premerle di nuovo con grande cura. Dopo la frittura, è bene asciugarle poggiandovi un pezzo di carta da cucina per togliere l'olio in eccesso e condirle con una spruzzata di limone prima di portarle in tavola, proprio come si fa con le cotolette alla milanese. Certe volte è davvero difficile distinguerle da quelle di carne.

L'insalata va preparata ad arte

Le cotolette di melanzane si maritano a meraviglia con un'insalata asciutta di capperi, pomodori e carote, e con il paté di lattuga di Chiara: ambedue portano colore sul piatto. Non sempre oso, ma quando le carote sono fresche e ben lavate non tolgo la buccia. Noi ormai la togliamo automaticamente a tutto, ma è come denudare una bella persona e scoprire che bella non è. A volte quando si è coperti, si fa una figura migliore. Sciolgo sempre il sale per l'insalata nell'olio e nell'aceto di vino perché sia poi uniforme. Mi piace mescolare l'insalata con le mani; pulite con cura e asciugate, sono lo strumento migliore per amalgamare gli ingredienti. L'insalata del compleanno è stata arricchita da me, in onore di Giorgio, con l'aggiunta di scorza d'arancia e di limone, e foglioline di menta.

La torta buona di Marisa

La torta al caramello ha la forma rotonda della pasta al forno e le medesime dimensioni perché viene preparata nelle stesse teglie. Teniamo separati i cucchiai, i mestoli e le spatole di plastica tra quelli per il piccante e quelli per il dolce, ma non le teglie, che costano care e che sarebbe assurdo non usare indistintamente, se ben lavate.

La torta al caramello era chiamata in famiglia anche la torta di Marisa, una cuoca trevisana che aveva lavorato a casa Giudice nel primo decennio del secolo scorso. A differenza di tutte le altre cuoche, gelosissime delle proprie ricette, Marisa quando tornò nel continente regalò a nonna Maria tutte le ricette dei dolci di cui era golosa.

Eravamo convinti che questa torta fosse veneta e ognuno di noi aveva le sue fantasie sul paese da cui proveniva: io me la facevo veneziana e pensavo che il rosso ambrato del caramello fosse il rosso dei capelli delle modelle di Tiziano. Ci rimasi male quando Giuliana, nata in Ungheria, dichiarò che era una torta del suo Paese. Nessuno però fu d'accordo con lei: zia Teresa in particolare era chiarissima, quella era la torta di Marisa, nata e vissuta a Treviso, che lei aveva conosciuto personalmente. Ogni tanto Giuliana cercava di interessarci all'origine ungherese della torta, ma senza successo. Negli anni settanta mio marito mi portò in un ristorante ungherese, il Gay Hussar, nel centro di Soho a Greek Street, e come dessert scelsi la torta nazionale ungherese: mi fu servita una versione della *nostra* torta al caramello, più brutta. Gli strati erano spessi, il cioccolato troppo burroso e il caramello grosso e duro.

Incuriosita, feci delle ricerche. Scoprii che la torta al caramello aveva una data di nascita, il 1884, un creatore, József C. Dobos, cuoco e imprenditore, e uno scopo: affermare la potenza dell'impero austro-ungarico.

Tante sono le pietanze che nel tempo hanno contribuito allo sviluppo del nazionalismo europeo: questa torta divenne il simbolo dell'impero austro-ungarico e fu presentata all'Esposizione universale di Budapest, dove ebbe un tale successo che Dobos mise su una fabbrica da cui mandava le torte bell'e fatte all'estero, in un contenitore termico, tra i primi al mondo. Altri chef crearono piatti che si identificavano con uno Stato o un personaggio famoso, tra gli altri la torta Savoia, le Madeleines, i biscotti Garibaldi, la torta Battenberg, il gelato Napoletano, tanto amato nell'Inghilterra degli anni sessanta, e la pizza Margherita.

"È un dolce molto elaborato" diceva Mamma, ignara di tutto ciò, "e costosissimo", e ci elencava gli ingredienti contandoli sulle dita: nove uova, un intero panetto di burro, una tavoletta e mezza di cioccolato nero a non meno del 75% di cacao. E poi ci spiegava la preparazione. Si fa un pandispagna molto leggero che bisogna cuocere a strati, mai meno di quattro. Il ripieno è una crema al burro con quattro ingredienti soltanto: uova, zucchero, cioccolato e tanto burro.

Sull'ultimo strato di pandispagna – il più bello e liscio tra quelli pronti, messo prima da parte – si sparge lo zucchero caramellato, facendo attenzione a farvi dei piccoli fori per inserirvi le candeline. Il caramello è difficile da fare, sapevamo tutti che solo a zia Teresa riusciva bene, meglio di chiunque altro. Quando era pronto, lo spargeva sulla torta con pochi colpi sicuri: veniva dritto e piatto come uno specchio. Noi aggiungiamo una variante tutta nostra: applichiamo pistacchio tritato ai bordi della torta. Questo la rende bellissima, perché i lati sono di un verde intenso e non marroni. Il caramello è dorato e lucidissimo e lo si taglia facendo attenzione, con piccoli battiti del coltello sulla superficie per romperlo senza creare schegge. Poi si poggia la fetta sul piatto, la torta gode del suo momento di splendore: i segmenti di pandispagna giallo alternati al marrone scuro della crema dicono "mangiami", e il caramello lucido e l'intenso colore del pistacchio echeggiano a turno "mangiami", "mangiami".

Non ho imposto la torta al caramello ai miei nipotini nati a Londra e soltanto per un quarto siciliani. La assaggiavano ai compleanni dei loro Papà, e l'hanno apprezzata: me la chiedevano a ogni loro compleanno. Una volta soltanto Lola, di nove anni, non la volle: desiderava un dolce decorato con la pasta di zucchero esposto in una pasticceria di Brixton. La accontentai. Il compleanno successivo, due mesi dopo, era quello di suo fratello, Oliver, di sei anni. "Che dolce vuoi?" gli chiesi. E lui rispose, guardandomi con i suoi grandi occhi castani: "Well Nonna, I think it would have to be *the traditional*. La torta al caramello!". Da allora io chiedo sempre, ma conosco già la risposta di tutti e quattro i nipotini.

Dopo che le candele sono state spente, racconto ai miei figli e ai nipotini il nostro primo incontro, appena nati. È un bellissimo ricordo, per me, e spero che sia gradito anche a loro. È il mio modo di coccolarmi, quando tutte le attenzioni sono, a buon motivo, per il festeggiato.

9

Un pranzo in piedi

Arancine
Paté di melanzane con bastoncini di carota e sedano
Pizza rustica
Verdure in pastella
Spiedini di frutta tagliata
Da bere: due limonate (in bottiglie di vetro trasparente),
acqua, vino bianco e rosso

Per le ricette rinvio il lettore a pagina 161.

Un pranzo tutto di donne

Aspettavamo per un pranzo in piedi una ventina di amiche della Fidapa (Federazione Italiana Donne Arti Professioni Affari), che mi dicono sia stata la prima organizzazione di donne lavoratrici in Italia.

Le abbiamo ricevute nel cortile davanti casa, dove ci sono tre tavoli su cui si può mangiare e allestire una tablattè, per quattro motivi. Il primo, di cortesia verso le ospiti: alcune sarebbero rimaste per poco – avevano altri impegni – e dunque era educato permettere loro di mangiare quello che le allettava e poi andarsene in sordina senza l'imbarazzo di lasciare un posto vuoto a tavola. Il secondo, il tempo: era una bellissima giornata di primavera e avrebbero gradito sedersi dove volevano, formare gruppi, passeggiare intorno alle aiuole, godersi il clima mite e il cielo di maggio. Il terzo, di ordine pratico: Chiara ed io ci saremmo occupate da sole della cucinata e del servizio; preparare il cibo e intrattenere le ospiti sarebbe stato più comodo nel cortile, in cui avevamo già disposto i divani e le poltrone di vimini e di legno che vi sarebbero rimasti fino ad autunno inoltrato. Il quarto, legato al cibo: volevamo offrire i fritti. La nostra anziana friggitrice addimora tutta l'estate sul ripiano di marmo lungo il muro che dà sul cortile, e avremmo potuto adoperarla senza allontanarci dalle nostre ospiti, porgendo loro il fritto caldo caldo.

Zia Teresa in campagna, a un picnic.

I preparativi per la cucinata del pranzo in piedi

Prima di cucinare per un pranzo in piedi si prepara la tavola; è possibile che la cucinata si dilunghi e che gli ospiti arrivino mentre siamo ancora ai fornelli: possono raggiungerci lì e chiacchierare, aiutarci, spilluzzicare. Chiedere loro di darci una mano nel portare il cibo a tavola e nel riempire i piatti di portata può essere gradevole, ma accettare le offerte di aiuto nel conzare la tavola crea confusione, perché ogni padrona di casa ama conzare la propria tavola a modo suo e io ci tengo molto. Preferisco farlo da sola e prima: è un lavoro che mi piace. Chiara ed io avevamo disposto sulla tavola da cui le ospiti si sarebbero servite bicchieri a disegno triangolare, pile di piatti, posate e tovaglioli a raggiera, acqua, vino rosso, limonata, sale, pepe, e cestelli di pane e grissini. All'ultimo momento avremmo aggiunto i piatti di portata, il vino bianco, freschissimo, e versato cubetti di ghiaccio nell'acqua e nella limonata.

Avevamo già, tra avanzi e roba da cucinare per cena, quasi tutti gli ingredienti: occorreva solo prepararli, friggerli e disporli sulla tablattè.

Quando tutto è pronto e bisogna soltanto mettersi a friggere penso a me stessa e mi coccolo: è quello il momento di prendermi una tazza di acqua e alloro, che ristora e lascia un senso di benessere che fa star bene a lungo.

La fattura delle arancine

Le arancine piccole, quelle che si possono mangiare in uno o due bocconi soltanto, sono chiamate con affetto "arancinette", come se avessero una loro identità.

La cucina dei bocconcini usa molto i resti. In particolare, le arancine possono essere preparate utilizzando tutto quello che è rimasto: risotto avanzato o persino riso bollito da altri pranzi, aggiungendo, se necessario, burro, formaggio e un uovo sbattuto come collante. Per il ripieno bastano un ragù o fette di carne cotta da riciclare con i resti di qualsiasi tipo di formaggio spezzettato – tranne quello blu – piselli e pochissima *béchamel*, per legare gli ingredienti. Per un ripieno vegetariano sono sufficienti resti di melanzane fritte a cui si aggiungono salsa di pomodoro ristretta e formaggio. In realtà, qualsiasi resto saporito muore bene nel cuore di un'arancina e rinasce glorioso dopo la frittura.

La fattura delle arancine è un'arte, a cui si approda dopo anni di tirocinio, iniziato da piccini. Uno dei nostri primi "compiti" in cucina da bambine era quello di modellare con i resti della velata minuscole palline, da mangiarsi in un boccone, e poi arrotolarle in pistacchi tritati, o nella polvere di cacao. Le palline possono essere anche di pasta reale, anche quelle poi avvolte nei pistacchi o nel cacao: ambedue si servono con il caffè.

Il secondo stadio ci portava a fare palline di pasta lievitata da friggere e servire con miele sciolto, per merenda o come dolce.

L'ultimo stadio era quello dell'umido: prima imparavamo a modellare le polpette piatte di carne o di melanzane, che andavano impanate, passate nell'uovo e nella mollica di pane – così si chiama da noi il pangrattato –, prima della frittura. Poi i crocché di patate, cilindrici e ripieni: si poggiava nell'impasto schiacciato sul palmo della mano un bastoncino di tuma o di primosale, e poi si ripiegavano i lembi dell'impasto e si modellava il crocché. Raggiunto quel livello di bravura, si era pronti ad accedere alla fattura delle arancine, che contengono un ripieno vero e proprio. Alla soglia dei dieci anni sono stata "promossa", e tuttora, per me, preparare le arancine è ritornare un po' bambina e giocare.

L'arancina si prepara con le mani appena bagnate, per evitare che il riso si attacchi ai palmi durante la lavorazione. Con la mano prendo un grosso uovo di riso, lo manipolo per farlo amalgamare bene in una palla, poi apro la mano e con indice e medio formo un incavo nella palla di riso, come a creare un nido, lasciando circa un centimetro e mezzo di spessore. Vi inserisco con un cucchiaino da tè una noce di ripieno, ricopro il tutto e chiudo la palla di nuovo, dolcemente, facendo attenzione che il riso circondi bene tutto l'impasto. La forma finale dell'arancina cambia a seconda del ripieno, se classico è sferica, se vegetariano è ovale. Infine le passo nella farina, nell'uovo sbattuto con un po' di latte e pepato, e nella mollica di pane. Le arancine devono riposare per qualche ora prima di friggerle. Altrimenti corrono il rischio di spappolarsi durante la frittura.

Sono una pietanza ideale quando ci sono molti invitati, perché si mantengono calde a lungo.

Ode alla calunniata frittura

Quando si frigge è saggio friggere molto, perché farlo costa calore e olio. La frittura deve essere del calore giusto. Non avendo termometri in cucina, per controllare la temperatura noi gettiamo un pezzo di pane nell'olio: se si trasforma in *croûton* immediatamente, l'olio è pronto. Ci mangiamo il *croûton* e iniziamo a friggere.

Noi serviamo quasi tutte le verdure di stagione fritte con la pastella, che crea un involucro uniforme e permette di prenderle con le mani. La mia pastella preferita consiste di acqua, farina e un po' di uovo sbattuto. Chiara non mette sale nella pastella, a differenza di me. Lei sparge il sale dopo la frittura, con il risultato che ogni boccone è una sorpresa, salato in modo diverso. Il miglior fritto è quello di cavolfiore, sempre in pastella. Il più raffinato è quello di fiore di zucca, farcito con un bastoncino di pecorino e un pezzetto di sarda salata, poi passato in pastella e fritto: un piatto insolito e prelibato. Il fiore fresco e tenero si apre per accogliere il ripieno, lasciandosi quasi violare per il piacere del nostro palato.

Il fritto è adatto ai pranzi con ospiti numerosi – sarebbe uno spreco riscaldare l'olio per friggere quattro cosuzze. Inoltre la pastella forma un involucro che trattiene il calore.

Friggere è il modo più pratico di cucinare: velocissimo, fa risparmiare energia, e l'olio si può riutilizzare. Rimpiango che la frittura sia diventata ora il paria della cucina mediterranea. Se ne dicono centomila di cose brutte su di lei: fa male, è cancerogena, ingrassa, è unta, è volgare… Sono opinioni spesso esagerate o addirittura false. E snob. In realtà la frittura, del salato e del dolce, presa con moderazione, non fa male, è nutriente e decisamente squisita.

C'è di più: la frittura è un potente antidoto contro la tristezza. È impossibile essere tristi mangiando una triglia fritta, un dolce di pasta avvolto in zucchero e cannella o un bastoncino croccante di melanzana fritta!

Un centro per la tablattè

Non si può offrire agli ospiti un pasto di soli bocconcini. Serve una pietanza bella, corposa e solare, che faccia da centro della tablattè, da condividere e che si possa tagliare e mangiare a pezzi, con le mani, senza sporcarsi. Che non faccia sentire l'ospite trascurato e solo. Chiara ha voluto preparare la pizza rustica.

La pizza rustica a base di ricotta ha un significato speciale per me: nei miei ricordi è il primo piatto che Mamma ragazzina aveva cucinato da sola, dall'inizio alla fine. Almeno così credevo che lei mi avesse raccontato più di una volta. Chiara un giorno mi ha rivelato che sbagliavo: il piatto di cui Mamma aveva sempre parlato era il gattò di ricotta e non la pizza rustica. Dunque avevo confuso le due pietanze! Ma ormai la pizza rustica nella mia memoria era associata indissolubilmente all'immagine di Mamma adolescente nella cucina della casa di Agrigento. Non posso più ritornare alla verità storica, tanto più che sempre di ricotta si tratta, e ricordando mi concentro su altri aspetti della storia di Mamma. Lei ci raccontava che da bambina riceveva da sua madre quella che chiamava "educazione domestica". Una volta alla settimana, dopo pranzo, doveva fare l'intera lavata di piatti e pentole della famiglia sotto lo sguardo severo di nonna Maria. "Così impari che significa lavorare e sarai una brava padrona di casa" le spiegava. Pian piano nonna Maria iniziò a insegnarle a cucinare le torte e gli sformati. Mamma ne era talmente orgogliosa che, appena arrivava la ricotta, si presentava in cucina pronta a preparare la "sua" torta. Certe volte le era permesso di usare tutta la ricotta, con grande sdegno di suo fratello Peppino, maggiore di sette anni, a cui sarebbe piaciuto mangiarsi la ricotta fresca. "Ma la nonna continuò a permettermelo. Forse ero un po' viziata da Mamà, essendo la più piccola" concludeva Mamma perplessa. E poi con un sorriso: "Ma per Peppino cucinava le cotolette alla milanese, e gliele serviva con la Worcester, una salsa inglese che non si trovava più nelle drogherie perché il governo fascista aveva imposto l'autarchia e c'erano le sanzioni contro le importazioni inglesi".

La pizza rustica non ha niente della pizza come la si intende normalmente. La parola "pizza" nacque nel Medioevo per indicare un cerchio di pasta fatta di acqua e farina, e pochissimo grasso, modellato a forma di piatto e poi cotto al forno; ai pranzi dei ricchi si usava proprio come un piatto: verdure e altre pietanze, alcune ricoperte di pasta, vi poggiavano. A fine pranzo le pizze venivano distribuite ai servitori e, quando questi si erano sfamati, ai poveri. Erano gustose perché inzuppate dei sughi delle pietanze (la pizza napoletana, con pomodoro e mozzarella, è del tardo Ottocento).

La nostra pizza rustica altro non è che una torta salata foderata di pasta frolla dolce, con dentro ricotta, salame e tutto quello che c'è in casa di salato e di formaggio. "Ogni figateddu 'i musca fa sustanza": ogni fegatino di mosca è nutrimento, dice un bel proverbio siciliano. Chiara vi aggiunge talvolta la *béchamel* rimasta e il risultato è eccellente. Lei preferisce decorarla in modo più "grezzo", e ha abbandonato la tradizione del reticolo di pasta frolla sull'intero ripieno, come si faceva nel Medioevo e come faceva Mamma con precisione certosina: disponendo le strisce tagliate a zigzag sulla torta e unendole ai bordi alti un centimetro per creare un rosone. Era un lavoro accuratissimo e geometrico. Chiara invece piega i lembi di pasta frolla sul ripieno, a caso, e poi li "cuce" con strisce di spessore diverso, come un rammendo grossolano.

Non mi dispiace per niente, la decorazione di mia sorella è moderna.

I paté di Chiara

I paté sono una specialità di Chiara. Lei li ha introdotti a Mosè e ne ha inventati molti. A casa nostra non si offrivano aperitivi e nemmeno salatini o antipasti. Si servivano limonata, acqua e zammù, cioè l'anice, o spremuta di arancia, quando era il periodo. Talvolta c'erano mandorle tostate. A tavola si doveva andare con un pizzico di fame e con un appetito opportunamente stimolato.

Chiara ha iniziato a preparare i paté ed è bravissima. Dapprima si è cimentata con quelli tradizionali, di pomodori secchi, di ceci – imitando l'hummus del Medio Oriente –, di melanzane, e poi ha sperimentato i paté di scarti: il migliore è quello fatto con le foglie esterne della lattuga. I paté sono accompagnati da pane fresco, grissini, o pane duro affettato e messo in forno per diventare croccante. Oppure da bastoncini di sedano e carota, per i salutisti. Serviamo i paté anche a tavola, quando siamo in tanti; li trattiamo come una pietanza.

Niente briciole ai pranzi in piedi

Ai pranzi in piedi non offriamo dolci. L'alternativa sarebbero biscotti o dolci secchi, ma è quasi impossibile evitare di fare briciole, odiose alla vista e difficili da raccogliere. Prepariamo un *plateau* di frutta che si può mangiare a bocconi: uva, fragole, ciliegie. Oppure frutta tagliata, spellata e infilzata su stecchini poi piantati su un'arancia o su una patata. Scegliamo frutta che non sia troppo umida, come le pesche, o che non macchi le dita, come i gelsi. Al pranzo in piedi abbiamo servito stecchini di melone d'inverno, bianco, e melone Cantalupa, color salmone, inficcati su arance – una bella macchia di colore.

La padrona di casa a una tablattè mangia poco o niente, ha troppo da fare per intrattenere gli ospiti: li incoraggia a servirsi, conversa, sta attenta che nessuno sia isolato o sembri a disagio, soccorre il malcapitato nelle grinfie di un logorroico, o del solito noioso, presenta le persone che non si conoscono e forma piccoli gruppi di conversazione, sorridente e disponibile. Non serve gli ospiti, ma si offre di riempire un bicchiere vuoto e incoraggia gli invitati a tornare alla tablattè e vedere se c'è qualcosa che stuzzica il loro palato. Se si serve di qualcosa, lo mangia a piccoli bocconi, per potere intervenire nella conversazione velocemente, se il suo intervento è richiesto.

La limonata, regina tra le bevande

La limonata è una bevanda preziosa e dissetante. Non è certo un segreto che si ottiene spremendo il limone e aggiungendo acqua e zucchero. Mi meraviglio sempre che la limonata oggi venga offerta raramente nelle case dei siciliani. Io faccio bollire in un poco di acqua la buccia di un limone che poi aggiungo alla limonata che assume un bel colore giallo. Dissetante, gradevolissima e sana, costa poco e fa bella figura sulla tablattè.

Nei lunghi pomeriggi caldi sulla terrazza, noi bevevamo limonata; si accoglievano gli ospiti a qualsiasi ora con una bella caraffa. Quando eravamo malati, Mamma ci portava la limonata calda a letto – più alta era la febbre, più zucchero lei ci metteva.

A me piace preparare la limonata all'antica, aggiungendo lo zucchero nel pentolino in cui si fa bollire la buccia del limone. La offro soltanto a chi la desidera perché ormai lo zucchero è escluso per motivi di dieta da tanta gente, che però non esita a riempirsi di bibite bell'e fatte di dubbia origine. Se soltanto leggessero gli ingredienti.

Giorgio ne prepara una più raffinata, davvero squisita, molto diversa dalla mia. Scioglie dello zucchero di canna con poca acqua in un pentolino, e lo porta a caramellare: appena diventa biondo, aggiunge altra acqua. Poi fa riposare il tutto per dare il tempo al caramello di sciogliersi. Quando è pronto, lo versa sul succo di limone e diluisce con acqua a piacere.

Assente dalla maggior parte delle tavole, la limonata è stata soppiantata dalle bibite confezionate e assai dolci, decisamente meno sane e più costose, che si comprano al supermercato. A casa mia queste bevande non hanno il permesso di entrare, anche se portate dai miei nipotini.

10

Les beaux restes di Mamma

Il mio pranzo preferito

Cucinare i resti era una ricorrenza frequente e molto amata a casa nostra. La famiglia, gli ospiti e il personale di casa mangiavano le stesse pietanze. Non si buttava niente e dovevamo utilizzare quello che c'era, inclusi i resti.

Mamma era francofona, e le piaceva chiamarli *les beaux restes*, come diceva la sua governante, Mademoiselle, che le rimase accanto fino al fidanzamento. Con i resti Mamma preparava i migliori pranzi di casa. Erano pasti cucinati con immensa cura e tanto amore.

Quando c'erano più denari in famiglia, compravamo prosciutti particolarmente buoni e tagli di carne pregiata, che a me non piacevano molto: sapevano di ricco in modo quasi volgare, poiché non c'era lavoro nel portarli in tavola, non c'era la cura di una preparazione attenta, come quella dei *beaux restes*, di cui abbiamo i ricordi più belli di nostra madre in cucina.

Il risparmio diventava puro godimento gastronomico.

Io e Chiara su un ulivo di Mosè.

I pranzi creati con quello che è rimasto dai giorni preceden-
ti, i cosiddetti piatti di recupero, continuano a essere i miei
preferiti per molte altre ragioni:

- sono gradevoli da preparare: richiedono manipolazione
e dunque le mani e le dita godono;
- richiedono immaginazione perché si trasforma una cosa
in un'altra;
- contribuiscono al risparmio della spesa di casa, dandomi
grande soddisfazione;
- rispettano la natura: utilizzando i resti non si butta quello
che altrove andrebbe nella pattumiera – oggi neanche nelle
ciotole dei cani, ormai abituati a mangiare cibo cucinato o
comprato già pronto apposta per loro;
- sono ottimi: non soltanto i resti hanno il loro gusto, ma
prendono quello di ciò che si usa per legarli.

La mia predilezione per i resti è aumentata nel tempo, tro-
vando giustificazione non solo nella mia "oculatezza", ma
anche nelle statistiche secondo le quali un terzo di tutto il
cibo prodotto del mondo occidentale viene gettato, mentre
la metà della popolazione vive affamata: uno sciupio inde-
gno, di cui ciascuno di noi deve sentirsi responsabile nella
sua pur minima parte.

*La mia tavola dei resti deve essere particolarmente bella e
colorata*

La tavola dei resti deve essere particolarmente bella e colorata,
perché un pasto di resti è un pranzo modesto, di poca spesa. E,
mentre sappiamo tutti che ciò che "costa" è molto apprezzato

e trattato con cura particolare, i resti corrono il rischio di essere sottovalutati. Bisogna dunque estendere ai resti lo stesso rispetto offerto alle pietanze rare e costose, per incoraggiare i commensali ad apprezzarli: la presentazione deve dare il messaggio che il pranzo di resti è un pranzo speciale e raffinato.

La mia tavola dei resti è colorata e preferibilmente blu: blu la tovaglia, semplice, con ricami di margherite fatti da Mamma, blu i piatti di ceramica inglese con disegni floreali, e blu i bicchieri. Un centrotavola blu sarebbe lezioso. C'è necessità di staccare. Per esempio lo si può scegliere rosso: i gerani di Mosè, che fioriscono anche nei mesi di siccità e calura, sono i fiori più indicati.

I medaglioni di carne: la pièce de résistance

I pasti di resti consistono nell'amalgamare quello che si trova in casa o nel frigorifero con altri ingredienti e cuocerli di nuovo, in padella o nel forno. Quelli siciliani sono preferibilmente fritti: il modo più veloce e gustoso per farli rinvenire. Tra i fritti, i medaglioni di carne a Mosè erano la pietanza principale quando arrivavano ospiti a sorpresa e c'era soltanto il tempo per raccattare quel che era rimasto e trasformarlo in un pasto. Si preparavano di fretta, pregustando il piacere di mangiarli a tavola con gli amici appena arrivati.

I medaglioni si possono fare con la carne rimasta – i miei preferiti – o anche di magro, adoperando le verdure. Pezzi di ragù tritato o rimasugli di prosciutto sono amalgamati da una *béchamel*, il migliore e il più economico dei collanti, arricchita di piselli e pezzetti di formaggio, poi aromatizzati. Si può scegliere un aroma "antico" come la cannella, la noce moscata, lo zenzero, il chiodo di garofano o lo zafferano – la spezia più costosa. Oppure "moderno", ad esempio timo, salvia, prezzemolo, basilico, erba cipollina. Le spezie appartengono all'antica cucina medioevale e poi rinascimentale, mentre le erbe fresche, a quei tempi chiamate "droghe", sono state introdotte dalla *nouvelle cuisine* francese del Settecento, come risposta, anzi ribellione, francese alla supremazia inglese sul mercato delle spezie.

Noi compriamo il pane due volte al giorno. Quello che avanza diventa pangrattato, ma non tutto. Talvolta tagliamo i filoni di pane raffermo in fette di un centimetro di spessore, per usarle in caso di emergenza, cioè di ospiti a sorpresa, come base per i medaglioni e di altri piatti di recupero. I medaglioni si preparano imbevendo ogni fetta nel latte o in acqua tiepida, facendo attenzione che il pane si inumidisca ma non al punto di rammollarsi, e poggiando su ognuna un ovulo del ripieno prescelto. Si lavora ogni medaglione con le mani, come fosse un'arancina, amalgamando bene pane e ripieno; poi si immerge nuovamente nel latte brevissimamente, e si modella di nuovo a forma di mezzo uovo e si poggia sulla farina. Quando tutti i medaglioni sono stati modellati, si inizia l'impanatura tradizionale: prima si passano nella farina, poi nell'uovo sbattuto, e infine nel pangrattato. Si fa e a volte si rifà, perché l'uovo e il pangrattato devono coprire totalmente la superficie infarinata del medaglione: altrimenti durante la frittura il composto, tragicamente, si smembra. È fondamentale che il pane usato sia duro quanto il legno, perché poi va ammorbidito nel latte. Se è troppo molle, corre il rischio di spappolarsi mentre si preparano i medaglioni o, peggio ancora, mentre si friggono. Non sono difficili da preparare, ma bisogna "averci la mano". Si impara osservando chi li sa fare.

Fritti, i medaglioni sembrano piccole cupole, timballi dorati. In ciascun boccone il forte gusto del ripieno è attutito dal pane ammorbidito nel latte. I medaglioni possono avere anche un ripieno vegetariano: funghi, broccoli, piselli. Tutto legato dall'insostituibile *béchamel*.

Uova alla romana

Le uova alla romana si preparano in genere quando c'è abbondanza di uova fresche, o quando ne rimangono di dure dalla cena, oppure se ci sono avanzi di *béchamel* da smaltire.

Chiara ed io credevamo fosse una ricetta di Roma, ma zia Annamaria, che era romana, ci disse di non averle mai assaggiate. Da dove venga questo "alla romana" rimane per noi un mistero, e aggiunge un non so che di esotico alla pietanza.

L'uovo alla romana è un piatto sontuoso, perché l'interno ricco è una sorpresa. Diventa bellissimo quando all'impasto si aggiunge prezzemolo tritato: tagliandolo, la crosta dorata si apre a rivelare la base candida di albume coperta del soffice ripieno giallo con puntine verdi.

Non è difficile preparare questi fritti di resti, purché si sia arditi nel ripetere il procedimento preparatorio della frittura: non bisogna temere di ripassare nell'uovo sbattuto e nel pangrattato quello che non è venuto bene la prima volta. La frittura, come sempre, dev'essere nell'olio d'oliva. Il pangrattato che avanza dall'impanatura non viene gettato. Lo passiamo al colino e poi lo conserviamo con le foglie di alloro. Quando avevo solo cinque anni e andavo in cucina chiedendo "Posso aiutare?", Mamma non poteva farmi far nulla, se non porgere le cose. Passare la mollica di pane era l'unico vero compito che mi affidava perché, se non era ben fatto, potevo rifarlo. Mi piaceva moltissimo. Osservavo il pangrattato che, scendendo dal colino, sembrava pioggia di luce.

Frittella "alla palermitana"

Questa "frittella" non ha nulla di fritto. Nessuno in famiglia sa da dove prenda il nome. A Mosè la chiamiamo "alla palermitana" per distinguerla da quella di Agrigento, preparata senza l'agrodolce e dunque un po' scipita.

È un piatto assemblato. Fave, piselli e carciofi vanno cucinati separatamente, perché ciascuno ha il proprio tempo di cottura. Sono uniti poi da un agrodolce leggero, che li lega ma non li amalgama.

È una pietanza invernale, che continua nella primavera perché da noi i primi carciofi, piselli e fave a volte maturano proprio a dicembre. Le prime frittelle dell'anno scolastico erano servite da zia Teresa a Palermo al pranzo della vigilia di Natale. La aspettavamo con gioia: è un piatto pregiato quanto il miglior pesce. Ora la cuciniamo anche in estate, ma soltanto per farla gustare ai miei figli, che ne sono ghiotti. Chiara conserva per loro nel freezer i piselli, le fave e i carciofi dell'orto.

La frittella non è un contorno ma una Signora Pietanza: dunque non ha bisogno di decorazione alcuna, nemmeno di prezzemolo tritato o mollica di pane tostata, e va servita a solo su un piatto di portata grande, possibilmente ovale.

Bello è far seguire a ogni boccone di carciofo un sorso d'acqua; in bocca rimane un sapore dolce, squisito. Mangiare la frittella, accompagnata da un buon pane e da sorsi d'acqua è un'esperienza di alta cucina. Così, almeno, la pensiamo noi.

Arance con cannella e un filo di zucchero caramellato

La frittura è saporita, e bisogna attutirla con un dolce semplice e facilmente digeribile. Le arance sbucciate e affettate con cannella, zucchero e qualche foglia di menta sono il dolce adatto ai *beaux restes*. Si possono rendere più profumate con il chiodo di garofano, che si marita perfettamente alla cannella. A me piace impreziosirle con un filo di zucchero caramellato, che forma ghirigori sulle fette e rende il piatto bellissimo. È straordinario cosa si possa fare con lo zucchero caramellato. Quando ci sono bambini, ne conserviamo un po' da far cadere a grandi gocce su un piattino. Il liquido si indurisce e forma caramelle che sembrano pietre preziose. Ai bambini piacciono moltissimo.

In assenza di arance si può ricorrere ad altra frutta lavata e tagliata da prendere con le mani. Spesso la camuffo da centrotavola, così da non servirla: la mangia solo chi lo desidera. Le fragole sono perfette a questo scopo, tagliate a metà e disposte in una fruttiera dal piede a calice. Altrimenti espongo fette di frutta a giro su un piatto rotondo (mele, pere, pesche lisce, albicocche, prugne, banane, mango), come se fossero la decorazione di una crostata, poi verso del caramello a cerchi concentrici: il risultato finale somiglia a una torta al caramello, solo di frutta.

11

Un pranzo di dolci

Cassata
Biscotti ricci di mandorle
Fette del cancelliere
Cous cous di pistacchio
Finocchi
Da bere: acqua e Marsala dolce

Per le ricette rinvio il lettore a pagina 171.

Un nonnulla di dolce ogni giorno fa bene

Siamo una famiglia golosa di dolci di tutti i tipi. Passerei una brutta giornata se non mi fosse possibile mangiare qualcosa di dolce, anche piccolo.

In inverno a Palermo, Mamma e zia Teresa cucinavano torte e biscotti leggeri, per accompagnare il tè del pomeriggio. In estate a Mosè, oltre a quelli per il pranzo, preparavano dolci al cucchiaio in coppette singole, da offrire a chi veniva in visita, accompagnati da tè freddo o limonata. Con l'avvento del freezer questi dolci estivi furono rimpiazzati dai gelati fatti in casa, con la panna e le uova, o dai sorbetti. Chiara, Silvano ed io eravamo costanti visitatori in cucina quando Mamma e zia Teresa si mettevano alla preparazione dei dolci.

A differenza del piccante, la manifattura dei dolci attraeva gli uomini di casa. Papà e zio Peppino erano un pubblico fedele e "vocale": offrivano commenti, suggerivano varianti ed erano pronti ad assaggiare tutto. Papà sapeva cucinare bene certi dolci. Soffriva di osteomielite e durante i mesi di malattia, costretto a casa, si dilettava in cucina. Zio Peppino non cucinò mai, mentre Silvano è un vero grande cuoco sia di dolci sia di piccante.

Silvano Comitini, mio cugino.

Il dolce si gode a pancia vuota

Il modo migliore per assaporare il dolce è a stomaco vuoto, preferibilmente a metà mattina. Prepariamo i dolci preferiti e quelli "importanti" – come la cassata, che si serve a Pasqua e a Natale – in dosi maggiori del necessario lasciandone una buona parte per l'indomani, quando il resto del dolce non sarà servito a tavola ma verrà mangiato nella mattinata o nel pomeriggio, se ne viene la voglia, anche da soli. Nel caso sia un dolce asciutto rimane sul tavolo da pranzo, coperto da un velo di tulle per proteggerlo dalle mosche. Altrimenti va nel frigorifero. Chi passa e ne ha desiderio prende piattino e forchetta, ne taglia una fetta e lo mangia seduto, assaporandolo boccone per boccone, senza fretta. Quando si mangia a pancia vuota, il dolce scivola lento e risveglia lo stomaco. Prima o poi passa sempre qualcuno che si unisce al buongustaio solitario, ma non è necessario: il dolce del giorno prima si gusta bene anche mangiandolo da soli, "a tu per tu".

Zia Teresa e la torta di ciliegie

Un pomeriggio di scirocco, tanti anni fa, leggevo delle carte di lavoro in soggiorno, a Mosè. Ero sola, tutti gli altri riposavano in casa o nelle amache del giardino. Avevo piena vista della sala da pranzo: lì le imposte socchiuse davano una parvenza di frescura. Regnava il silenzio. Una falce di sole cadeva sul tavolo da pranzo e di tanto in tanto la fissavo, ammaliata dalla luce. Poi, il ticchettio delle scarpette di zia Teresa: si era rassettata i capelli, aveva inumidito i lobi delle orecchie con il suo profumo e indossato il vestito da pomeriggio con la collana di perle grosse. Mi sarei aspettata che Mamma, con cui divideva la camera da letto, fosse con lei. Guardai l'orologio: erano le tre e mezza, l'ora del riposo. La zia stava già diventando vaga: chiaramente s'era svegliata prima del tempo e, delicata come sempre, s'era lavata quatta quatta e vestita senza svegliare Mamma. Non mi mossi; la seguivo con la coda dell'occhio, non vista.

"Che c'è da fare per me?" chiedeva la zia entrando in cucina, certa di trovarvi qualcuno. Era tornata nella sala da pranzo, interdetta. Guardava il tavolo. Al centro, in bella mostra, lasciata a raffreddare sotto un velo di tulle, c'era la torta di ciliegie, cotta nel forno con il gattò di patate che avevamo mangiato per pranzo.

"Vediamo che c'è di buono lì sotto!" La zia aveva sollevato un lembo del tulle: "Che squisitezza!" e poi, come se chiedesse il permesso a qualcuno, "Ne potrei tagliare una fettina…" e si era girata. S'aspettava Mamma dietro di lei. Era sola. Un attimo di confusione, e poi, decisa, aveva preso un piattino dalla cristalliera, coltello e forchetta dal cassetto della credenza, e si era seduta a tavola davanti alla torta. Si godeva la sua fetta a bocconi piccini, guardando la torta intensamente. Poi l'aveva ricoperta con il tulle e aveva portato piatto e posate in cucina. Sentivo lo scroscio dell'acqua. Zia Teresa lavava il piattino, lo lasciava scolare e lo asciugava. Allora soltanto lavava anche coltello e forchetta e li strofinava con cura nel panno asciutto. Poi li poggiava sul piattino e riappariva in sala da pranzo. Andava a riporre il piatto asciugato e le posate lucide ai loro posti, chiudeva la cristalliera e il cassetto, e si girava: cercava Mamma. Lo sguardo le cadeva di nuovo sulla torta. "Vediamo che cosa c'è qui sotto!" e sollevava il velo di tulle.

Ripresi a leggere le mie carte. Girai una pagina e sbirciai una figura: la zia seduta a tavola mangiava una seconda fetta di torta. Riportava piatto e posate in cucina. Un altro scroscio d'acqua, un'altra lavata di piattino e posate, un'altra asciugata, ed eccola di nuovo nella sala da pranzo, piatto e posate in mano. Stavolta non si dirigeva verso la credenza. Fissava avidamente il telo di tulle. Si sedeva, e si mangiava, a piccoli bocconi, un'altra fetta di torta, più sottile di quella di prima. Di nuovo andava in cucina a lavare piatto e forchetta, ritornava in sala da pranzo, si accostava al tavolo, sollevava il velo, "Vediamo che c'è qui sotto!". Tagliava e mangiava fettine sempre più piccole di torta, e continuava il ciclo: cucina tavola dolce, cucina tavola dolce. Masticava con gusto, zia Teresa, anche se le fette erano diventate filiformi. Non volli interromperla: godeva.

Alle quattro Mamma apparve in sala da pranzo, la cercava. "Elenù, è buonissima, ne vuoi una fetta?" La zia le fece cenno di sedersi accanto a lei, poggiò la forchetta sul suo piatto e si alzò a prenderne uno per la sorella.

I Signori Dolci

Un sorbetto, una crema, una mousse, qualcosa di leggero e delicato va bene dopo un pranzo sostanzioso, ma non un "vero" dolce, non una torta al caramello! Seguito per di più da *petit four* e frutta. È irrispettoso relegare il dolce a fine pasto. In questo devo dissentire dal riverito Jean Anthelme Brillat-Savarin. I Signori Dolci meritano di essere apprezzati soli nel loro splendore. Quanto al detto: "Dulcis in fundo", se riferito al pranzo, non sono d'accordo.

Ogni tanto è bello dedicare un pasto intero ai dolci. Nel nostro menù tutte le portate sono siciliane. Questo non significa che ci piacciono solo i dolci siciliani, al contrario: le ricette delle torte di casa sono state date per la maggior parte a nonna Maria da Marisa, la cuoca veneta, e siamo ghiotte di tutto ciò che si trova nelle pasticcerie di Palermo, quasi sempre di origine svizzera e che il ricettario di nonna Maria non cita. A Palermo li compravamo e li gustavamo, senza mai pensare di copiarli. Il nostro preferito in assoluto era la torta Savoia di Caflisch.

Palermo è una città golosa

Palermo è una città golosa, ricca di gelaterie, confetterie e pasticcerie, molte dai nomi stranieri; appartenevano a svizzeri o austriaci che vendevano ai palermitani abbienti i loro dolci. Nel 1895, la panna montata, sconosciuta ai siciliani, fece il suo ingresso trionfale nella nostra cucina. Quell'anno Vincenzo Daneu, un antiquario di Opicina, vicino a Trieste, e il professor H. Ross, direttore dell'orto botanico, inaugurarono il primo stabilimento caseario di tutta la Sicilia, che produceva latte sterilizzato, burro e panna da montare. Nello stesso anno Cristiano Caflisch, discendente del Luigi Caflisch che nel 1835 aveva aperto la prima pasticceria svizzera a Napoli, ne aprì una nel centro di Palermo, e comprò gran parte della produzione dello stabilimento per usarla nelle decorazioni e come ripieno dei pasticcini di pasta frolla, dei cornetti di pasta sfoglia zuccherata e dei babà: tre dolci che oggi consideriamo a pieno titolo parte della nostra cucina. Caflisch esiste ancora e Palermo ha mantenuto il titolo di capitale gastronomica dell'isola.

La panna tardò a diffondersi nel resto della Sicilia. Ad Agrigento, fino agli anni sessanta, arrivava solo una volta a settimana, esclusivamente alla pasticceria Pedalino. Era raccolta in un'ampolla sigillata, inserita in una bolla di metallo che conteneva ghiaccio secco. Ogni mercoledì la bolla viaggiava in treno da Palermo ad Agrigento, accompagnata da un commesso che se ne prendeva cura. Ad Agrigento la panna andava a ruba e non era mai abbastanza: dovevo affrettarmi, se arrivavo da Pedalino di pomeriggio la brioche con gelato e panna era già finita.

La cassata è più buona il giorno dopo

Tutti noi, prima Mamma e zia Teresa, poi Chiara, Silvano ed io, abbiamo imparato a preparare i dolci dal libretto di nonna Maria. Nonna era molto precisa nell'indicare gli ingredienti, nella preparazione meno: le indicazioni erano semplicemente un *aide-mémoire*, per il resto bisognava cavarsela da soli. Zia Teresa era la migliore nei dolci e Silvano, che ha imparato da lei, è certamente più bravo di noi due.

L'ingrediente fondamentale della cassata è la ricotta. Fresca, viene messa nello zucchero e "passata" con l'aiuto di un cucchiaio attraverso un setaccio fitto. Oggi se ne trovano di rete sintetica ma a Mosè ne usiamo uno di seta, l'ultimo che Mamma e zia Teresa sono riuscite a trovare. Si avverte subito la delicatezza del tessuto contro il cucchiaio. E mentre la si passa il profumo della ricotta sbummica di nuovo. Una volta pronta è lucida e bellissima, quasi per incanto si è trasformata.

Altrettanto magico è il processo chimico che crea la velata, lo strato superiore fatto di zucchero e acqua. Non ho mai capito cosa succeda, e non voglio capirlo perché il suo mistero mi affascina. Si mettono zucchero e acqua sul fuoco per una decina di minuti. Se ne controlla poi la consistenza con le dita: se sono bagnate in acqua fredda, non ci si brucia. Poi con una paletta si sparge il contenuto su un piano di marmo disegnando cerchi veloci. Il liquido, d'un tratto, diventa bianco, pastoso e lucido. La velata è pronta.

La cassata, tra i dolci siciliani, è il più amato in famiglia. A noi piace mangiarla in tarda mattinata. Seduti al tavolo ancora non conzato, la serviamo nei piatti da frutta, come per farci perdonare il nostro cedimento alla golosità. La accompagniamo con un bicchiere d'acqua. Chi passa è invitato a unirsi a noi, in questa trasgressione comune. Quando prepariamo la cassata da servire a tavola, adoperiamo la forma più grande che abbiamo per avere dei resti sostanziosi e lasciarne una buona parte per il giorno dopo: sappiamo tutti che la cassata è più buona dopo qualche giorno.

Il nostro menù di dolci non può certo avere un altro primo. Spesso, oltre alla cassata mia e di Chiara, arriva quella di Silvano. Le differenze sono visibili e fondamentali. La cassata di Silvano è tradizionale e riporta subito alla memoria quelle di zia Teresa e di Mamma. Chiara invece ha apportato delle innovazioni alla ricetta di nonna Maria: meno zucchero nella crema di ricotta e nella pasta reale, e l'uso delle mandorle intere nella pasta. Quella di Chiara ha un ottimo sapore, ma è rossastra e dunque non si può colorare di verde, come la pasta reale della cassata è da che mondo è mondo.

La decorazione della cassata di Silvano è semplice e bellissima – soltanto amarene sciroppate, come quelle che zia Teresa e Mamma preparavano ogni anno. Alla nostra invece aggiungiamo la zuccata, la zucca candita, tagliata a strisce sottili e disposta a festoni. Quella di Silvano è la più buona, quella di Chiara ha un gusto più moderno e delicato, meno dolce. A me piacciono ambedue.

Nessuno di noi tre ha mai adoperato per decorazione la frutta candita usata dalle pasticcerie: è scenografica e sontuosa, ma il gusto troppo sciropposo fa a pugni con tutto il resto e in particolare con la ricotta.

Le amarene sciroppate di zia Teresa

Le amarene sciroppate sono ingrediente essenziale del ripieno delle crostate e dei pasticciotti di frolla da noi amatissimi e che si facevano tutto l'anno. E si usano per decorazione dei gelati fatti in casa e soprattutto delle cassate. Le amarene non crescono bene a Mosè, con gran dispiacere di tutti. I fruttivendoli locali le espongono raramente sui loro banchi perché sono acidule, e bisogna chiedere a quello di fiducia di comprarle al mercato generale, ma soltanto se sono sode e mature. Zio Peppino a volte le portava da Caltagirone: erano ottime.

La preparazione delle amarene, lunga e laboriosa, dura diversi giorni. Bisogna innanzi tutto avere delle giornate di caldo non umido, perché la cottura delle amarene snocciolate avviene naturalmente, al sole, in bacili bassi e larghi di smalto bianco con i bordi blu, coperti con veli di tulle per allontanare mosche e vespe: "I contenitori migliori per avere un'ottima amarena" dicevano Mamma e zia Teresa.

Durante il giorno le sorelle sorvegliavano a turno la cottura delle amarene, ma era zia Teresa che le accudiva con maggiore dedizione e otteneva i migliori risultati. Le "guardava" regolarmente: sollevava il tulle e le toccava appena con la paletta, poi decideva se rimescolarle o no. Quando le rimescolava, muoveva la paletta di legno delicatamente, per non romperle. Zia Teresa controllava con il dorso della mano la temperatura, perché i bacili dovevano essere ritirati prima del tramonto, al primo accenno di raffreddamento e di umidità. Le sorelle scolavano insieme le amarene e le facevano riposare, asciutte, nei rispettivi bacili fino all'indomani. Il giorno seguente, quando il sole era a picco, le amarene, nei loro bacili, ricoperte con il liquido scolato e bollito, erano esposte di nuovo al sole. Alla fine venivano messe in burnie di vetro, nel loro sciroppo, pronte per l'uso.

Le amarene di zia Teresa erano insuperabili, sembravano rubini cabochon: rosso scuro, la forma di una perla perfetta e lucidissima.

Sulla cassata le ottime amarene sciroppate preparate da Chiara fanno la loro figura, sono disposte a disegno geometrico, con una o due varianti, ma immancabilmente punteggiano il bordo della pasta reale.

Fette o "felle" del cancelliere

La seconda portata è un dolce monacale, le fette del cancelliere. La ricetta proviene dal libro di nonna Maria e, a differenza di quanto prevedono altri ricettari, non è particolarmente ricca di uova. Come la cassata, è un dolce assemblato con vari ingredienti preparati separatamente e in tempi diversi. Dapprima si prepara un impasto di pistacchio tritato con zucchero, uova, e un po' di farina, cotto in un paiolo come se fosse una crema. È squisita. Assaggiarla appena pronta è un godimento. Io assaggio sempre, fa parte del mio gioco con il cibo, del seguirlo fino a quando non diventa perfetto. A volte sbaglio, metto troppo sale per esempio, allora aggiungo una patata lessa, la soluzione migliore per togliere il sale alle minestre, alle mousse, ovunque. Mamma mi permetteva sempre di leccare le posate alla fine della cucinata e io ne ero felice. Se non potessi assaggiare mentre preparo una pietanza, non credo che cucinerei.

Quando l'impasto raffredda, lo si modella a forma di uovo e si frigge nell'olio d'oliva ad alta temperatura: il risultato, una formella ovoidale scura e brutta, si trasforma in una pietanza bellissima quando è conzata. Ogni uovo di pistacchio, raffreddato, è aperto a metà come una brioche e rivela il proprio interno verde brillante. Gli ovuli si farciscono con un ripieno di crema di latte bianca e dolce, profumatissima, e diventano fette del cancelliere. Socchiusi, sono disposti in fila sulla guantiera, e coperti da una pioggia di zucchero a velo. Il colore scuro del fritto, il verde brillante dell'interno, e il bianco candido della crema sono un godimento per gli occhi. Il gusto è celestiale.

La ricetta viene da Canicattì, la città di nonna Maria. A Palermo lo stesso dolce è la specialità di uno dei numerosi monasteri che c'erano un tempo nella capitale dell'isola. Ciascun monastero aveva una propria specialità dolciaria, e ne teneva segreta la ricetta. Nei conventi di Palermo abbondavano novizie e monache di sangue blu, per motivi dinastici che nulla avevano a che fare con la vocazione: la dote monacale era semplicemente di molto inferiore a quella necessaria per un matrimonio. Nel diciottesimo secolo le monache palermitane, e non solo, facevano baldoria nei loro conventi, con preti e frati. Si dice che il nome originale del dolce fosse "Felle" – cioè natiche – del cancelliere, ovvero l'economo del convento. È meglio non soffermarsi sull'origine di questo nome. Fatto sta che il dolce è squisito.

Una volta, in una pasticceria di Palermo, zia Teresa fu affiancata da un professionista noto. Voleva da lei conto e ragione sul perché avesse la ricetta delle fette del cancelliere, sostenendo di esser certo che sua moglie, e lei soltanto, ne fosse la depositaria esclusiva. La zia, educatissima, gli rispose che la ricetta veniva dal quaderno di sua madre. E senza aggiungere altro girò sui tacchi e se ne andò. Da allora, zia Teresa e Mamma aggiunsero la ricetta a quelle che incoraggiavano le parenti e le amiche a provare.

Biscotti ricci delle monache di Favara

I biscotti ricci, sono un altro dolce monacale. Cettina, madre di Luigi e Linda, e nuora di Rosalia Vella, ci ha insegnato a prepararli. Semplicissimi di fattura, sono un dolce tipico delle campagne siciliane, dove i contadini coltivano i mandorli. È un impasto di uova, mandorla, zucchero, limone grattugiato e null'altro. Si dispongono su una teglia come fossero dei fiorellini e poi, quando si tirano fuori dal forno, sembrano proprio dei riccioli dorati. Sono squisiti e si conservano a lungo.

"Cuscus" delle monache di Santo Spirito

Non lo abbiamo mai preparato in casa. È un dolce che sempre compriamo dalle monache del convento di Santo Spirito ad Agrigento, un luogo molto bello in cui ogni volta ci rechiamo con piacere. Situato nella parte vecchia della città, in un'area di degrado abitata per lo più da immigrati nordafricani, custodisce tra le sue mura questa antica ricetta che prende spunto proprio da un piatto magrebino. Mi chiedo se i giovani immigrati sanno che la tradizione del loro cibo è stata preservata in quel grande edificio con le inferriate alle finestre, quasi una prigione.

Il convento è povero, e la vendita dei dolci aiuta a sostenere le monache. Papà forniva loro i pistacchi, facendo attenzione a darne il doppio di quanto richiesto, per far guadagnare alle monache un poco di più. Lui, che si dichiarava ateo, amava andare al convento e flirtare con la monaca dietro la grata: "Sorella dolcissima, ma lo ha fatto proprio lei con le sue mani questo dolce del paradiso?" e quella rispondeva con un risolino: "Eh sì, proprio con le mie mani".

Cosa offrire alla fine di un pranzo di soli dolci?

In un pranzo di dolci non è facile decidere cosa offrire a fine pasto. Qualcosa di piccante? Abbiamo deciso che delle fettine di finocchio, tenute per una mezz'ora in una bacinella di acqua fredda, sono l'ideale: bianche, fresche e croccanti, lasciano in bocca un senso di ristoro e sono digestive.

Tutto sommato un pranzo di dolci una volta l'anno si può fare, anzi si *deve* fare. Ha un non so che di liberatorio. Dà goduria, e anche leggerezza, perché servendoci piccole porzioni assaporiamo ogni boccone e ci alziamo da tavola sazi ma non satolli, lo stomaco per nulla appesantito e la bocca pulita, fresca di finocchio. Inoltre il fatto che siano dolci siciliani e monacali rende ogni volta preziosa questa esperienza: come fare un tuffo nel passato della nostra storia ed entrare nei chiostri dei monasteri di clausura.

12

Le caponate

Caponata di melanzane barocca di Aurora
Caponata con le mandorle tostate
Caponata al cioccolato
Caponata di casa Agnello
Tuma all'argentiera di Chicchi
Palline di pasta reale
Da bere: acqua e vino rosso e bianco

Per le ricette rinvio il lettore a pagina 179.
Questo pranzo è vegetariano, anzi vegano: esclude uova, burro e latte.
Raccoglie le ricette di casa nostra e di quattro care amiche.

La prima vegetariana a Mosè: Liz

Non conoscevo persone che fossero vegetariane per principio e convinzione fino a quando non sono andata all'estero a diciassette anni. A Cambridge c'erano molti indiani di fede indù. La mia grande amica Darshana di fede jainista è vegetariana, ma non ho mai cucinato espressamente per lei: Darshana si è sempre accontentata di formaggi e insalate.

Un'estate arrivò a Mosè Liz, la ragazza alla pari dei miei figli. Da quando Chiara ed io invitavamo a Mosè tanti stranieri di altre culture, Mamma aveva preso l'abitudine di inserire sempre nei nostri pranzi almeno una pietanza vegetariana a solo, oltre ai contorni, per non mettere in imbarazzo eventuali ospiti vegetariani.

Liz era una studentessa universitaria molto attraente. Ci annunciò, all'arrivo in campagna, che lei era vegetariana. E lo disse anche a Vincenzo e a Rosalia, sua madre: "Non mangia carne!" ripeteva Rosalia "Poverina, dev'essere molto malata". E le portava ogni giorno le uova fresche che metteva da parte per i bambini, gli anziani, e Liz. A volte quando mangiavamo all'aperto, Vincenzo, anche lui giovane e attraente, passava con sua madre e altri fratelli e sorelle. Si fermavano a osservare Liz che si riempiva il piatto d'insalata. "Poverina, mangia solo erba" sospirava Rosalia. "Eppure è così bella, bionda e con le carni rosa, anche se è malata." Io le spiegavo che non era malata, che quella di non mangiare carne era una sua scelta. Vincenzo scuoteva la testa: "Nonsi, una bella picciotta che non mangia carne deve essere malata!". Liz era coccolata da tutti i Vella, non soltanto per la sua gentilezza e avvenenza, e nemmeno per le minigonne che facevano sognare i giovani contadini, ma soprattutto per la sua stranissima malattia.

I contadini amano gli animali che allevano e amano mangiarli. Era difficile spiegare a Liz l'atteggiamento di Rosalia; certe differenze culturali sono troppo grandi per essere assorbite. La gente di Mosè però ha accettato la scelta di Liz, anche se tutti sono sempre rimasti convinti che non fosse affatto una scelta, ma una questione di salute che lei non voleva svelare.

Noi continuiamo a essere molto attente ad avere cibo a tavola che dia l'opportunità a un ospite vegetariano di fare un buon pasto escludendo carne e pesce. Non è difficile, perché nella cucina siciliana tradizionale le verdure abbondano.

Un pranzo di due portate

C'è un motivo per cui questo pranzo ha due sole portate, caponata e tuma – le palline di pasta reale sono solo un assaggio per addolcire la bocca: oggigiorno si servono spesso troppe portate, e abbondanti. I padroni di casa si sentono in dovere di offrire sempre più del necessario. Bisogna invece avere il coraggio di affermare che "poco è meglio di troppo". Ma si ha paura di essere criticati. E si mettono pietanze su pietanze in tavola, continuando a scusarsi della propria inesperienza e scarsa abilità. Ci si agita, invece di godere della compagnia e pensare che l'ospite sia semplicemente contento di mangiare come noi, e che la conversazione e l'accoglienza siano più importanti della ricchezza del cibo e della sua abbondanza.

Per un pranzo semplice come questo, soprattutto se gli invitati sono amici cari e di lunga data, è bene che la tavola sia allegra e informale: tovaglioli colorati e un centrotavola di fiori campagnoli. Per ravvivarla si possono aggiungere cestini di pomodori rossi, che diano vivacità.

In occasioni simili, prendo sempre posto sul lato lungo del tavolo, all'angolo vicino alla cucina, per potermi alzare senza disturbare i commensali e la loro conversazione.

La caponata, il cibo più siciliano che io conosca

Quando si parla dell'origine della parola caponata non si è mai d'accordo. Alcuni dicono che venga dalle "capone", le osterie frequentate dalla gente più povera, altri invece le attribuiscono origini arabe. Ogni città della Sicilia ha la propria caponata. Si è fedeli alla caponata del luogo di nascita quanto lo si è alla salsa al pomodoro. Se ne discute a tavola e fuori tavola, come se fosse un argomento di grande importanza. E lo è, per noi. La caponata è il cibo più siciliano che io conosca, più della cassata, più delle arancine, perché la mangiamo più spesso. A Mosè si prepara in grandi quantità almeno una volta alla settimana e si serve a tavola per due o tre pranzi consecutivi, tanto piace sempre. Si conserva bene, anzi i sapori si amalgamano meglio e il gusto diventa più pronunciato dopo qualche giorno. Preparare la caponata è come realizzare un'opera d'arte, un lavoro di mani e di colori che, ovunque io mi trovi, mi riporta agli odori e ai sapori di casa mia. Il gusto dell'estate per me è inscindibile da quello del sughetto che rimane sul piatto dopo l'ultimo boccone di caponata, quel misto di olio, zucchero e aceto che, raccolto con il solito pezzo di pane, lo profuma e, imboccato, dà gioia al palato.

La nostra caponata, quella di Palermo e di Agrigento, esclude totalmente carne e pesce. Abbiamo cercato di cucinare la caponata al coniglio del ragusano, e perfino una volta quella con il pesce, ma non ci piace. La caponata dev'essere vegetariana e con i pochi consueti ingredienti: melanzane fritte, l'ingrediente principe, cipolla soffritta, aglio soffritto, pezzettini di sedano, olive e poco pomodoro. Tutte le varietà di melanzane nostrane vanno bene. L'importante è che siano sbucciate, come ci ha insegnato Mamma, a strisce – in modo da lasciare la giusta quantità di amaro, ma non troppo – e tagliate a tocchetti uguali, perché è dai tocchetti che si riconosce la mano della caponata. I tocchetti vanno salati e lasciati scolare. Chiara mette sempre un coperchio sullo scolapasta in cui si mettono a scolare le melanzane tagliate e salate, e lo appesantisce di pesi: le melanzane così premute perdono tutta l'acqua salata. I nostri "pesi" sono esagoni di marmo, probabilmente parte del pavimento a mosaico della torre federiciana. Li abbiamo trovati intorno alla casa quando da bambini andavamo in giro a scavare, con tanto di carriola e vanghe e trovavamo di tutto: pietre, cocci, resti greci ed etruschi, nonché reperti della Seconda guerra mondiale.

Qualunque sia la preparazione della caponata – un piatto nato come popolare, ma in realtà sofisticato – è l'agrodolce, che rende questo misto di melanzana fritta a immersione e successivamente soffritta al tegame una poesia per il palato. L'agrodolce, che entra ed esce dalle cucine europee, in Sicilia è sempre rimasto. Quella della caponata è una miscela di aceto e zucchero squagliato che dà un liquido dorato. Non saprei dare una ricetta per l'agrodolce: tutto dipende dall'aceto e ogni aceto è diverso, per questo la sua preparazione è un continuo lavoro di assaggi fino a ottenere le dosi giuste.

Dopo la degustazione di caponate, servo tuma all'argentiera ad Avia, Cristina e Aurora.

Caponata di Aurora

Aurora, un'amica siciliana, artista e cuoca appassionata, vive a Milano e non ama per niente il colore scuro della caponata tradizionale. La sua, arricchita di peperoni e altri ingredienti, è visibilmente diversa dalle altre: si presenta come un arcobaleno di colori a macchie vistose – pezzi decisamente non piccoli di peperoni rossi e gialli, carota, sedano, pomodoro, capperi e olive, e fiori di finocchio, piccoli e giallissimi. A prima vista sembra una magnifica insalata colorata; solo assaggiandola si scopre che è un'ottima caponata, ricca e gustosa. Più un piatto unico che un companatico, questa caponata "di fuori" merita di entrare nell'Olimpo delle varianti della caponata siciliana.

Caponata di Avia

Avia, amica di Chiara dalle scuole medie e nostra ospite frequente con la sua famiglia, è figlia di una signora toscana; ha imparato a cucinare molte pietanze siciliane a Mosè, ma non la caponata, che era stata insegnata a sua madre da nonna Elettra, la suocera sicula. A questa ricetta Avia ha apportato le proprie modifiche. La sua caponata non è dunque dissimile da quella di Mosè: tagliata a pezzi piccini e ben amalgamata, con poca salsa di pomodoro. Ma ha un gusto diverso: Avia usa meno aceto e la sua aggiunta – mandorle tostate tagliate grossolanamente – rende necessario masticare bene ogni boccone. Basta questo, assieme al sapore inconfondibile della mandorla, per distinguerla dalla nostra. In bocca si assaporava ogni ingrediente, uno alla volta.

Caponata di Cristina

Cristina, nata e vissuta in Toscana fino all'adolescenza, prepara una caponata alla palermitana, di solito con l'aiuto di una parente siciliana. I tocchetti di melanzana sono più grossi dei nostri, ed è forte il gusto del pomodoro. Cristina vi scioglie del cioccolato quasi amaro, ad alta percentuale di cacao, e poi decora la caponata con scaglie dello stesso cioccolato. L'aceto usato nell'agrodolce acquista un non so che di aromatico e dolciastro. Il risultato: la salsa è ricca e vellutata e ogni boccone ha un gusto meravigliosamente ambiguo.

Caponata di Mosè

La nostra caponata è fatta con melanzane fritte leggermente; la sua caratteristica distintiva sono l'assenza di salsa al pomodoro e gli ingredienti tagliati a pezzettini molto piccoli, in modo che ogni forchettata contenga tutti i sapori. Chiara preferisce un agrodolce leggero e le piace lasciare il sughetto abbondante perché a casa nostra si crede fermamente che la caponata sia un companatico e non una pietanza a sé.

La tuma di Chicchi

Dopo il sapore forte della caponata bisogna mangiare qualcosa di leggero e delicato, e la tuma all'argentiera è quello che ci vuole. Fette del primo formaggio, fresco, non ancora primosale, tagliate con lo spessore di un centimetro sono rosolate delicatamente in una padella con l'olio. È un piatto che si prepara con grande velocità, ma per farlo ci vuole sapienza: bisogna capire quando le fette vanno girate, in modo da lasciarle croccanti e morbide, mai disfatte. Appena formata la crosta si girano dall'altro lato e poi si aggiungono un pizzico di origano, aceto, sale e pepe e si fa rosolare per uno o due minuti soltanto. Si servono immediatamente, il centro è tenero e filante, e la tuma si scioglie in bocca. Anche la tuma si mangia con abbondante pane. Io raccolgo sempre quel che rimane sul piatto con il pane, sostengo che sia fondamentale, per dare la giusta soddisfazione al palato; chi dice che è maleducato sbaglia.

Chicchi, la mia prima amica, e figlia di una straordinaria donna, la signora Ersilia, amatissima amica di Mamma, mi racconta che il nome viene da una storia bizzarra, che si racconta a Raffadali. Un argentiere era caduto in disgrazia e non voleva che gli altri, in particolare i vicini di casa, lo scoprissero. Mangiare carne era un indizio di ricchezza, e l'argentiere, in tempi migliori, si faceva preparare ogni giorno belle bistecche di carne in padella, arrotolate nell'olio con un po' di cipolline, condite con sale, pepe e uno spruzzo di origano. Quando di carne in casa non ne entrava più, per ingannare i vicini, faceva cucinare allo stesso modo modeste fette di tuma: l'aroma del fritto e dell'origano gabbavano tutte le malelingue.

Dolci quanto basta

Abbiamo conservato parte della pasta reale preparata per la cassata: dura bene per settimane, se coperta. Se ne possono fare palline, che arrotolate sul cacao, sul pistacchio tritato, sulle mandorle e sullo zucchero brillantato formano disegni geometrici sul vassoio, molto belli. E il gusto è dolce quanto basta. Una singola pallina è sufficiente a sciacquare la bocca dal sapore della tuma e dare un senso di dolce benessere.

13

Otto mani in cucina

Macco di fave di Antonio
Sarde a beccafico
Tortino di carciofi e patate
Babà di Justin e Giorgio
Da bere: acqua, vino rosso, vino bianco

Per le ricette rinvio il lettore a pagina 183.

È bello invitare amici e preparare il pranzo insieme. Ognuno porta una propria ricetta e, chiacchierando, si cucina. Uno dei più riusciti è quello organizzato la scorsa estate a Mosè. Era un pranzo a otto mani: di Chiara, le mie e quelle di Antonio e Justin, due amici di famiglia. Ci è sempre piaciuto avere amici e bambini in cucina, e Justin era un ragazzino quando da Londra venne per la prima volta a Mosè. Compagno di classe e migliore amico di Giorgio dai tempi del Dulwich College, è il padrino di sua figlia Elena.

Imparare in cucina

A Mosè ero sempre bene accolta in cucina. Mettevo il mio grembiulino con tanto di tasche, importantissime per nascondervi pistacchi, frutta, pezzi di formaggio che avrei poi sgranocchiato da sola, e ci passavo ogni mattina. Era una fucina di lavoro: si preparava il pranzo per una trentina di persone, e c'era un via vai di cameriere, garzoni che portavano mazzi di prezzemolo, uova, legna per la cucina moderna, brocche di acqua potabile.

C'era sempre qualcosa di nuovo e di interessante, e spesso rimanevo a dare una mano. Mi cimentavo in tutto, dal pulire il ripiano di marmo ogni volta che si sporcava, alla stricata delle pentole con la sabbia, a spennare un pollo, in un angolino – mi tenevo le penne più belle per scrivere e dipingere –, a scegliere e lavare la frutta da portare in tavola – mi facevo squisite abbuffate della frutta troppo matura –, a lavare la verdura e gettare dal balcone le lumachine e i vermetti più tenaci, ancora attaccati alle foglie; dal tritare la cipolla sul tagliere di legno con la mezzaluna, ad asciugare pentole e piatti puliti; oltre che nel cucinare vero e proprio, che mi veniva insegnato da Mamma e zia Teresa.

Da loro imparavo a mescolare la crema pasticcera nel paiolo, disegnando il numero otto sul fondo con il cucchiaio di legno, a fare i pasticciotti ripieni di amarena, a battere sulla balata di marmo l'impasto per la brioche e a decorare i dolci prima di portarli in tavola. Aiutavo Mamma anche in un compito per niente delicato: nei primi anni, quando non c'era elettricità e la ghiacciaia era spesso rotta, si comprava la carne di vaccina una volta la settimana, uno o due chili di sfasciatura avvolta in un grosso foglio di carta gialla, la parte interna leggermente cerata. Mamma mi aveva insegnato a pulire la carne: la prima pulizia toglieva membrane e grasso, la seconda i nervi. Poi la dividevo per i vari usi: la carne tenera per cotolette, scaloppine o involtini, quella con nervetti e membrane da tritare per ripieni e polpette, e i pezzi peggiori per brodo o lentissimi stufati. Le ossa e i calli insaporivano il pastone di resti e tozzi di pane raffermo cucinato per i cani.

Anni dopo, quando i miei bambini erano piccini, la cucinata a Mosè fu semplificata grazie agli elettrodomestici: avevamo un freezer e le fruste elettriche per montare velocemente uova e zucchero e la panna. La carne arrivava dal supermercato tagliata e poggiata su un vassoio di polistirolo, avvolta in una pellicola trasparente. Per il resto, la cucina di Mosè era cambiata di poco, c'era meno personale ma si cucinava sempre in compagnia: cucinavamo con i bambini per insegnare loro attraverso l'esempio, e per divertimento.

Mamma è stata la grande maestra di cucina di Mosè. Grazie a lei e a zia Teresa, Chiara ed io siamo diventate cuoche. Ma c'è di più. Se i miei figli sono diventati abili cuochi, e bravissimi nel pulire l'intera cucina (pavimento, forno, lavelli) il merito va a Mamma, con cui passavano le vacanze: lei è stata il loro punto di riferimento culinario e non solo. Quando erano all'università, Giorgio a Bristol e Nicola a Edimburgo, la chiamavano al telefono se non erano sicuri di come preparare scaloppine, polpette, salse e perfino sformati, e cucinavano seguendo quanto la nonna diceva in telefonate interminabili. E dispendiose. Chiara ed io ce ne lamentavamo. "Sbagliate," ci redarguiva Mamma "non è mai uno spreco insegnare a cucinare il buon mangiare di casa." E a me: "Dovresti essere fiera dei tuoi figli: hanno la voglia di imparare". Poi, a solo, mi diceva: "Fai lo stesso con i tuoi nipotini: io non ci sarò per seguire la loro cucinata".

In famiglia siamo ligi alla tradizione, ma anche curiosi e dunque innovativi; ci basta ascoltare un amico che descrive una minestra insolita, un dolce nuovo, una variante di un'antica ricetta, per sentire l'acquolina in bocca. Chiara ed io abbiamo voluto includere nel pranzo improvvisato due pietanze scelte da amici, appunto per imparare nuove ricette da inserire nei nostri menù, godere del cibo preparato da loro e divertirci.

Il mio lettore

Antonio, pediatra di Canicattì e mio "lettore di fiducia", è l'autore del macco alla canicattinese. L'ho conosciuto grazie al mio mestiere di scrittore. Nel 2004 ero stata invitata a presentare *La zia marchesa* alla scolaresca del liceo di Canicattì frequentato dalla figlia di Antonio. Lui venne a prendermi a Messina, e durante le quattro ore di viaggio parlammo di tutto e di più. Antonio aveva provato a cucinare "u tagamu", un piatto siciliano descritto nel mio romanzo, e con successo! Gli confessai che nessuno a casa nostra aveva mai osato cimentarsi nell'impresa. Parlammo anche dei nostri rispettivi lavori, io avvocato dei minori e lui pediatra, e di letteratura.

"Vorrei che lei fosse il mio autore," mi disse a un certo punto "che ne pensa?"

"Che significa?" chiesi, colta alla sprovvista. Lui ci aveva pensato molto: era un appassionato lettore e desiderava avere un rapporto letterario con uno dei suoi autori preferiti. Non era una richiesta fatua. Cercavo di tirarmi indietro, l'idea di diventare l'autore "di qualcuno" mi metteva a disagio. "Almeno tentiamo" propose lui. E aggiunse: "Magari potremmo parlare di cibo e scambiarci ricette, io faccio ottime marmellate e conserve di verdure". Sapeva che il cibo mi interessava: "Mi piacerebbe fargliele assaggiare" insistette. Mi stava prendendo per la gola, e alla fine abboccai. Dopo averlo tempestato di domande – Aveva cercato di "avere" altri autori? Come mai gli era venuto questo desiderio? –

cedetti al suo: "Tentiamo per qualche mese, almeno". È da dieci anni che io sono il suo autore e lui è il mio lettore di fiducia. Ci vogliamo davvero bene. So di averlo deluso con i miei troppi no, ma Antonio mi ha dato preziosi consigli. È entrato a fare parte della nostra famiglia, è diventato amico di Chiara, e Mamma era molto contenta quando lo invitavamo a cena.

Quel pomeriggio Antonio era venuto sul presto, portandosi pentole, ingredienti e un inizio di macco cucinato la sera prima, per fare più in fretta. Chiara ed io avevamo già preparato i secondi: sarde a beccafico e pasticcio di carciofi e patate. Chiara seguiva nel cortile la preparazione del babà di Justin, con Giorgio, mentre io ero nella cucina grande, con Antonio.

Il macco alla canicattinese di Antonio

Il macco – un pasto povero antichissimo, che risale ai tempi dei Romani – consiste in fave secche cotte e stracotte, ammaccate in una pappa sostanziosa, a cui si aggiunge, al momento di servire, quando non è più caldissima, un filo di olio d'oliva. Può risultare pesante e privo di odori – se non quello pastoso delle fave –, ma si nobilita e diventa subito un piatto eccellente della cucina ricca con l'aggiunta di odori freschi e di un pezzo di lardo o di pancetta. È un esempio di come una minestra un po' insapore possa trasformarsi in un primo piatto fragrante e vivace. La sapiente aggiunta di erbe, odori o di un rametto di foglie d'alloro fa la magia.

Il macco, che un tempo ci si vergognava di portare in tavola, oggi in Sicilia ha infinite varianti. Quello di casa nostra, che a noi è sempre piaciuto molto, è semplice: fave fresche cotte e un filo d'olio. Quello di Antonio è più ricco: insaporito da piante selvatiche, incluse le foglioline di cappero, dal *bouquet garni* alla siciliana e da pancetta. Leggerissimo e fragrante, è il migliore che io abbia mai assaggiato.

Un filo d'olio sul macco di Antonio.

Sarde a beccafico, un "finto" palermitano

Chiara ed io abbiamo scelto di preparare come secondo le sarde a beccafico e il pasticcio di carciofi e patate. Il pesce era cucinato secondo la ricetta di casa e il pasticcio, inventato da Chiara tempo fa, l'annata in cui l'orto offrì un'abbondanza straordinaria di carciofi, ormai è un classico della cucina di

Mosè. Le sarde a beccafico, capolavoro della cucina povera e dell'inventiva siciliana, copiano i beccafichi ripieni delle tavole dei nobili angioini che colonizzarono la Sicilia nel Medioevo: freschissimi e carnosi. Il ripieno di uva passa, mollica, prezzemolo e pinoli le alleggerisce, e il limone di cui si irrorano quando sono cotte lascia un retrogusto leggermente salato, molto ben equilibrato dalla dolcezza del carciofo e delle patate. Mi piace prepararle e siccome non è un lavoro gradito a Chiara finisco sempre per farlo io, con grande gioia. È bello lavare le sarde allinguate – cioè già aperte e pulite –, metterle in ordine sul tagliere, la parte interna in alto, dividere il ripieno con un cucchiaino perché vengano della stessa misura e poggiarlo su ognuna; poi avvolgerle e metterle in fila sulla teglia, separate da una foglia di alloro. È come creare un collage. Io vado veloce, mentre Mamma e zia Teresa erano lente. Si trattenevano a lungo in cucina, facevano tutto con calma. Se per esempio Mamma si accorgeva che nel ripieno di una sarda erano finiti pochi pinoli la riapriva e ne aggiungeva altri. Ogni sarda doveva essere un piccolo universo perfetto.

Gli sformati e i tortini di Chiara

Chiara è diventata maestra nel preparare sformati e tortini che in origine non erano parte delle pietanze di Mosè, dato che non avevamo un buon forno. Per anni si utilizzò un forno portatile, una gabbia di ferro nero che si poggiava su un fornello a gas.

I suoi tortini sono leggeri, poco oleosi, e profumati: lei usa tante erbe. Potrebbero essere una pietanza a sé.

Devo la mia prima ubriacatura a Rageth e Koch

Rageth e Koch era la mia pasticceria preferita di Palermo. Ormai scomparsa, a lei devo il mio primo incontro con l'alcol, all'età di sei anni. Mi ci portava Papà, per mangiare il montblanc. Un giorno a mio padre venne voglia di babà e lo ordinò. Volli imitarlo e ordinai il babà anche io. A forma di fungo, immerso in un bagno di acqua, zucchero e rum e poi sgocciolato, il babà era servito su una coppetta di carta che raccoglieva il liquido lucido e dorato, con un bel ciuffo di panna sopra. L'aroma intenso del rum mi riempì le narici prima che il cameriere poggiasse con sussiego il piattino davanti a me. A ogni boccone mi sembrava che il babà si gonfiasse fino a riempirmi tutta la bocca. Il profumo del rum, potente nelle narici ma dolce e leggero in bocca, aveva un effetto mai provato prima. L'insieme di queste sensazioni mi dava un senso di benessere avvolgente: avevo in bocca tutto quello che c'era di inebriante e squisito nel mondo. Tuttora considero il babà come un dolce "trasgressivo", l'equivalente dell'assenzio servito da un oste della Parigi *fin de siècle*.

Il babà con panna è rimasto per noi un dolce importato dalla Svizzera, diventato prima palermitano e poi, grazie alla diffusione della refrigerazione, anche siciliano. In più ha qualcosa di misterioso: nessuno in famiglia saprebbe prepararlo in casa. I miei figli lo adorano; da piccoli credevano che fosse la specialità di Agorà, la pasticceria del Villaggio, che lo vende conzato alla siciliana: il fungo di pasta, dopo l'immersione in sciroppo di zucchero e rum, è suggellato dalla glassa di albicocca su cui posa una generosa cucchiaiata di panna montata e zuccherata. Quest'ultima aggiunta è rifiutata dai "puristi" del babà: sostengono che appesantisca la consistenza soffice della pasta lievitata. Secondo loro non c'è bisogno di fronzoli per apprezzare questo dolce squisito. Se non è buono nudo, non c'è panna o decorazione che possa rimediare.

Nel corso delle ricerche per questo libro, Giorgio e Justin mi hanno rivelato che il babà non era svizzero. Parente del *Gugelhupf,* un dolce della Lorena tedesca, fu la fortuita invenzione di un re polacco, Stanislao Leszczyński. Sconfitto dallo zar Pietro il Grande, ricevette a parziale risarcimento il ducato della Lorena. Si dice che il re esiliato amasse la buona tavola e il bere, e che fosse molto esigente riguardo al mangiare. Un giorno gli fu portato un dolce lorenese, il *Gugelhupf,* piuttosto spugnoso e privo di gusto: dimostrando una natura irascibile e assenza di buone maniere, il re spinse con forza il piatto, mandandolo a sbattere contro una bottiglia di rum che gli faceva compagnia in mancanza del prediletto tokai, suo conforto nell'esilio. L'acquavite della Martinica si rovesciò sul dolce, che la assorbì tutta. Incuriosito, il re volle assaggiarlo. Ne fu ammaliato. Si mangiò l'intero *Gugelhupf* imbevuto di rum e gli cambiò il nome in *babka,* "vecchietta" nelle lingue slave – non saprei dire perché, immagino che a quel punto Leszczyński fosse completamente ubriaco.

Il babà di Justin e Giorgio

La scelta di Justin, preparare il babà, ci aveva lasciate perplesse. A Mosè eravamo addirittura sprovviste della teglia adatta, quella a ciambella: Giorgio dovette chiederla in prestito ad Agorà.

Contavo su Justin per un buon dolce inglese. Contrariamente a quanto pensiamo – sviati forse dal gusto alla zuppa inglese, che sembra non possa mancare sul banco di ogni gelateria che si rispetti, normalmente in seconda fila e spesso, giustamente, il meno scavato – la pasticceria britannica è molto buona.

Ma Justin era irremovibile: avrebbe preparato un babà. Lui e Giorgio si erano scambiati ricette e addirittura qualche foto dei babà che ciascuno di loro aveva preparato nella propria cucina. La settimana precedente Justin era andato a cena al Manoir aux Quat'Saisons, il ristorante francese dell'Oxfordshire. Lì aveva parlato con Raymond Blanc, il famoso cuoco stellato che gli aveva dato la propria ricetta e insegnato personalmente a preparare il babà. Le sue istruzioni erano dettagliate: dalla percentuale di glutine nella farina (alta, preferibilmente la Manitoba 00) al metodo per mescolare la pasta (lentamente, per dieci minuti fino a quando l'impasto diventa elastico). La ricetta era stampata su un pezzo di carta con annotazioni e macchie direttamente dalla tavola di marmo del pasticcere.

Justin aveva ragione. Il suo babà è stato eccezionale. Anziché essere appesantito dall'alcol, era leggero e profumato; l'odore di menta, unito a quello dell'alcol, aleggiava su tutta la tavola. Non avrebbe potuto fare una scelta migliore! Da allora nessuno di noi ha avuto il coraggio di emularlo.

Il babà di Notting Hill

Anche se ormai ne conosce la storia, per Giorgio il babà continua a essere legato a doppio filo alla città di Napoli, dove lo mangia ogni volta che gli capita di passare. Per la maggior parte delle persone, inclusa me, l'anima culinaria di Napoli risiede nei forni a legna per la pizza della città vecchia, dove gli antichi Greci fondarono Neapolis e portarono la loro pita dall'altra sponda del Mediterraneo. Per lui invece si esprime nelle morbide bolle, nella soffice cupola e nei dolci fumi alcolici del babà. E non è l'unico a pensarla così. Nonostante la tecnologia moderna e l'abbondanza di ingredienti nella dispensa londinese, i connazionali che abitano nella mia seconda città sono ben lieti di pagare l'equivalente di sei euro per un singolo babà fatto a Napoli, volato a Heathrow e infine venduto alle persone in coda davanti a un piccolo negozio di specialità italiane a Notting Hill. Inutile dire che io non sono una di loro. Giorgio invece sì. Di quando in quando, il ripiano più alto del frigorifero di casa sua è occupato da una piccola scatola di plastica trasparente con dentro un solitario babà sovrastato da un ciuffo di panna montata e mezzo acino d'uva. Tutto il resto è stato spostato sui ripiani inferiori e la luce del frigorifero crea intorno al dolce un alone mistico da altare sacrificale. Un tempo per mio figlio era un piacere solitario, ora deve condividerlo con Elena e Francesco, i suoi bambini. A loro passa subito la cucchiaiata di panna, e così tutti e tre sono contenti: lui con mezzo babà nudo e loro con un quarto a testa, nascosto sotto una nuvola di dolcezza candida.

Un sabato mattina andai a trovarlo. Era in giardino. Seduto da solo, con un caffè e un piattino sul quale troneggiava un bel babà, assaporava ogni cucchiaiata con un sorriso stampato in faccia che soltanto in parte ne ammortizzava il costo indecente. A mio avviso, solo la soddisfazione di un orgoglioso napoletano che sente nostalgia di casa la notte di

San Gennaro – e non quella di un golosone anglo-siciliano – può giustificare il prezzo del babà londinese. Mi fermai, non vista, per rispettare quel momento di intimità tra un goloso e il proprio dolce preferito.

EPILOGO

L'albero delle fragole

Elena e Francesco, i figli di Giorgio, hanno trascorso tutte le loro estati a Mosè, come i loro cugini Lola e Oliver. Francesco in particolare è goloso di pistacchi come anche io ero alla sua età e ancora sono. Nel soggiorno, Chiara tiene sul tavolino davanti al camino un cesto di pistacchi dal guscio spaccato, facili da aprire, anche con le unghie, e una ciotola di pezzi di pistacchi sgusciati, quelli scartati quando si preparano i sacchetti da vendere che devono contenere frutti interi. I miei nipoti attingono da ambedue costantemente. Durante la raccolta, ai primi di settembre, vanno e vengono dal pistacchieto per prendere dall'albero i frutti maturi e rosati, che tutti adorano. Francesco, più degli altri tre, se ne faceva enormi scorpacciate, e si avventurava nel pistacchieto anche da solo.

Quando Francesco aveva sette anni e sua sorella Elena quasi nove, Chiara li portò a fare una passeggiata in campagna. Insegnava ai nipotini le varie colture e cercava di interessarli all'agricoltura con domande semplici, come nostro padre aveva tentato di fare con me, senza alcun successo. Nel pistacchieto i grappoli di frutti acerbi erano rossi e duri, non ce n'era nessuno che avesse cambiato colore nel rosa pallido del frutto maturo. Chiara racconta di aver puntato il dito verso un albero particolarmente carico chiedendo a Francesco: "Che sono?", esattamente la domanda che Papà ci poneva nelle nostre passeggiate terre terre.

Francesco aveva riferito poi a suo padre che non era riuscito a ricordare la parola italiana; aveva aggrottato la fronte e, strizzando gli occhi per vederci meglio, aveva azzardato una risposta: "Strawberries!", cioè fragole. "Giufà!" aveva risposto Chiara "sono pistacchi! Quelli che ogni anno ti mangi a non finire!" Francesco era arrossito e i due fratelli erano scoppiati a ridere: conoscevano bene le fragole perché crescevano nel giardino della nonna inglese. Forse Francesco aveva pensato che nella fertile e solatia Sicilia le piante di fragole crescessero grandi e alte e si trasformassero in alberi. O forse l'imbarazzo di non saper rispondere lo aveva spinto ad aggrapparsi a un frutto qualsiasi purché fosse di colore simile a quelli davanti a loro. Ignorante sì, ma stupido no.

Dal seme allo scaffale

Oggi proliferano i programmi di cucina, le riviste specializzate e ci sono letteralmente milioni di prodotti in vendita nei supermercati e attraverso internet, eppure pochi di noi si interrogano sulla provenienza degli ingredienti. Nemmeno i bambini chiedono più da dove viene il latte e se le zucche di Halloween pendono dagli alberi. Siamo più interessati al prodotto finale, quello che mangiamo, e meno al suo iter dal seme allo scaffale del supermercato. Siamo felicemente inconsapevoli dell'origine di quello che ci mettiamo in bocca, ma ne conosciamo le calorie, le proteine, il contenuto di sale, perfino i tipi di grassi. La nostra cultura è cambiata e non ce ne siamo accorti: non ci interessa sapere da che pianta e da che animale viene il nostro cibo quotidiano, come crescono e come vivono.

L'episodio di Francesco, un bambino sensibile e curioso, mi ha reso chiaro che la conoscenza del cibo e della sua provenienza, acquisita da me bambina senza rendermene conto, in campagna, nelle botteghe dei fruttivendoli, nelle pescherie e nelle macellerie, oltre che in cucina e a tavola, non è più accessibile alla generazione dei miei nipoti. Esistono le *farm* metropolitane e le fattorie didattiche, ma le visite in questi posti sono equiparate nella mente dei bambini a quelle allo zoo. E non possono sostituire la mancanza di insegnamento all'interno della famiglia, che avviene attraverso il cucinare insieme, in allegria, parlando, sbagliando, bruciando, scuocendo.

Cucinare non è mai una perdita di tempo. Quando compriamo i cibi già cotti accettiamo qualcosa di estraneo a noi, non sappiamo bene come sono fatti, quando e da chi. Perdiamo la nostra identità se viviamo solo di ciò che è bell'e pronto, preparato da estranei. E perdiamo anche la nostra umanità, l'uomo è l'unico animale al mondo che pianta, alleva, cuoce e cucina il cibo di cui si nutre.

Cucino ogni giorno a casa mia, anche se poco, per abitudine e perché mi piace. A paragone di mia sorella Chiara e Silvano, sono la cuoca peggiore della famiglia; preferisco dedicarmi alla conzata della tavola e a ricevere gli ospiti, i due primi compiti che mi furono insegnati da Mamma. Ma non me ne faccio un cruccio: l'importante è che io cucini. Cucinare è un modo di accudire me stessa, anche di pensare, mentre tocco e odoro il cibo: di sentirmi viva. Non esistono "giusto" o "sbagliato" in assoluto, anche se la cucina dei dolci lascia meno spazio all'originalità, per le reazioni chimiche che avvengono tra ingredienti, soprattutto nella cottura al forno. Nella cucina del salato si può improvvisare ed errare con maggiore disinvoltura. Alcune delle mie minestre e dei miei stufati più apprezzati sono il risultato della sostituzione di un ingrediente fondamentale – secondo la ricetta – che però non avevo nel riposto.

La cucina e l'apprezzamento del cibo sono universali e democratici: siamo tutti esperti in qualcosa, sia pur semplice – spargere lo zucchero a velo, fare il caffè, condire l'insalata – e ogni essere umano ha la capacità, vecchio o bambino, uomo o donna, ricco o povero, intellettuale o "povero di spirito" di dare un giudizio su quello che mangia.

Il pranzo di Mosè

Durante le riprese del programma *Il pranzo di Mosè*, ci siamo resi conto ancora una volta che cucinare è anche rispettare la materia prima che si mangia. Vegetale o animale. La fecondità delle piante è diventata oggetto di ricerca e di lucro: sono state rese più resistenti ai parassiti e i loro semi trasformati in sterili per ottenere i profitti necessari alle spese di ricerca e produzione. Con due risultati: la diminuzione delle varietà delle piante e la dipendenza dei produttori – contadino, imprenditore agricolo e grande azienda alimentare – dalle multinazionali che vendono semi.

Le domande che ci siamo poste Chiara ed io e quelle che ci sono state fatte quando ci preparavamo per il programma erano molte: di alcune non avevamo la risposta e abbiamo dovuto consultare libri, amici o internet. Tuttora, sappiamo poco del cibo e della sua origine sia vegetale che animale. Dovremmo saperne di più.

La vera scoperta di quei giorni, dominati dal cucinare e dal mangiare sotto il mirino delle macchine da presa e gli occhi della troupe e della gente di Mosè che ci stava a guardare, è stato l'interesse per il cibo che ci univa agli ospiti dei nostri pranzi, a Cristiana e Riccardo Mastropietro e ai loro colleghi di Pesci Combattenti. Come per ogni altro argomento di conversazione, pensavamo che l'interesse sarebbe diminuito con il passare del tempo. Invece, la curiosità non scemava: ogni giorno c'era una nuova scoperta. Nessuno di noi si sarebbe aspettato di sentirsi raccontare – e per di più da un inglese – che il babà "napoletano" deve la sua origine a un sovrano polacco esiliato nella Lorena. L'origine degli ulivi "dal tronco cavo" ha sorpreso tutti, tranne Chiara e me. Ogni novità era discussa e commentata. E così le pietanze che Chiara ed io preparavamo: ci era sembrato normale cucinare in abbondanza per condividerle con coloro che lavoravano con noi. E mangiando, dimenticavamo i nostri rispettivi ruoli: attore, assistente in cucina, cameraman, contadino, ospite, padrone di casa, producer, regista: ciascuno aveva da dire la sua e la diceva, mentre gli altri ascoltavano attenti. Scivolavamo in un convivio spontaneo. Imparavamo insieme. La consapevolezza di quello che mangiavamo aumentava il piacere. E ci divertivamo. Non ho mai riso tanto in tutta la mia vita.

Auguro lo stesso al gentile lettore: un buon pranzo in un'atmosfera conviviale.

LE RICETTE DEI MENÙ DI CHIARA

Menù
del compleanno in famiglia

Paté di lattuga

INGREDIENTI PER 6-8 PERSONE

150 g di foglie di lattuga (quelle esterne più dure e senza la costa bianca)
100 ml di brodo fatto con un pezzetto di dado vegetale
1 spicchio di aglio o un mazzetto piccolo di erba cipollina
3 cucchiai da minestra di aceto balsamico
il succo di mezzo limone
mollica di pane (3 fette di circa 1,5 cm ciascuna)
100 ml di olio d'oliva
sale e pepe

PREPARAZIONE

Lavare e ripulire della costa bianca le foglie della lattuga, spezzettarle grossolanamente e metterle nel bicchiere del mixer.

Aggiungere l'olio, il brodo, l'aglio (o l'erba cipollina), il sale e il pepe e frullare fino a ottenere una crema fine e omogenea.

Aggiungere anche l'aceto balsamico e il succo del limone, frullare ancora e unire la mollica del pane fino a ottenere una crema sostenuta, tanto da potervi intingere i bastoncini di carota o di sedano.

Anelletti al forno

INGREDIENTI PER 8 PERSONE

1 kg di pasta (anelli siciliani)
150 g di piselli
1 cipolletta
100 g di parmigiano grattugiato
100 g di pecorino tagliato a dadi piccolini
1 litro di salsa di pomodoro
pangrattato
olio d'oliva
sale e pepe

PER IL RAGÙ

200 g di trito misto di maiale e di vitello
1 carota, 1 cipolla media e 1 costa grande di sedano tritati finemente
1/2 bicchiere di vino rosso
2-3 cucchiai di passata di pomodoro
2 cucchiai di olio d'oliva
sale e pepe

PREPARAZIONE

Per preparare il ragù mettere in una terrina capiente 2 cucchiai di olio extravergine di oliva, quando è caldo aggiungere gli odori tritati finemente. Fare colorare e poi aggiungere il trito di carne; fare ben rosolare, aggiungere sale e pepe, sfumare con il vino e completare con la passata di pomodoro. Fare cuocere a fuoco basso per circa 20 minuti.

In un pentolino piccolo mettere i piselli, una cipolletta tritata finemente, un filo d'olio, sale, pepe e 2 cucchiai di acqua. Cuocere per circa 10 minuti.

Cuocere la salsa di pomodoro.

PER LA SALSA DI POMODORO

In casa Agnello abbiamo le idee molto chiare sui parametri di una buona salsa: con l'aglio, e tanto densa da macchiare il pane di un rosso intenso, e non dolce.
Ecco le due varianti da noi accreditate.

● *Salsa di pomodoro pelato*
2 kg di pomodoro pelato
4 cucchiai di olio d'oliva
8 spicchi di aglio
sale, pepe e basilico

Mettere sul fuoco una pentola di media grandezza piena a metà di acqua, portare a ebollizione e immergervi i pomodori. Farli cuocere fino a quando la buccia non si spacca. Spegnere il fuoco, mettere i pomodori sotto l'acqua fredda e pelarli, quindi tagliarli a pezzetti e togliere il più possibile i semi. Mettere nella pentola di cottura l'olio e l'aglio tagliato a pezzi grossi. Appena comincia a dorare versarvi il pomodoro, condirlo con sale, pepe e qualche foglia di basilico e cuocere a fuoco vivo per una decina di minuti mescolando ogni tanto.

● *Salsa di pomodoro passato*
1,5 litri di passata di pomodoro
4 spicchi di aglio
4-5 foglie di basilico
3 cucchiai di olio d'oliva
1 cucchiaino da caffè di sale

Versare l'olio nella pentola, aggiungervi l'aglio tagliato a pezzi grossi e accendere il fuoco.
Non appena l'aglio comincia a imbiondire versarvi la passata di pomodoro, aggiungere il basilico e il sale e mescolare bene. Cuocere a fuoco vivace per circa mezz'ora mescolando

di tanto in tanto. La salsa deve passare da un colore rosso scuro a un arancione intenso, dev'essere densa e, provata su un pezzo di pane, deve colorarlo.

Quando tutti gli ingredienti sono pronti, il parmigiano è grattugiato e il pecorino è tagliato a dadini mettere sul fuoco la pentola con l'acqua.

Quando l'acqua bolle versarvi la pasta e il sale. Cuocere per la metà del tempo di cottura (in genere è non più di 7-9 minuti, su un totale di circa 14 minuti di cottura) perché poi la pasta continua a cuocere nel forno. Prima di scolarla tenere da parte un pentolino di acqua di cottura.

Durante il tempo di cottura della pasta, oliare una teglia e passare il pangrattato sul fondo e sulle pareti.

Scolare la pasta e rimetterla nella pentola di cottura, condire con la salsa di pomodoro, 1 o 2 cucchiaiate di ragù, un po' di piselli e ammorbidire con qualche cucchiaio di acqua di cottura.

Mettere uno strato di pasta così condita nella teglia, una metà del ragù, una metà dei piselli, il pecorino a dadini, il parmigiano grattugiato e un po' di salsa di pomodoro. Ricoprire con qualche cucchiaiata di pasta, condire di nuovo con il resto e infine ricoprire con la pasta rimanente. Spolverizzare con un po' di parmigiano e con il pangrattato.

Pressare la superficie della pasta con la mano, condire con un filo d'olio e infornare per almeno 40 minuti a 180 °C.

Cotolette di melanzane

INGREDIENTI PER 4 PERSONE
2 grandi melanzane tunisine a polpa bianca
farina
2 uova
pangrattato
olio per friggere

PREPARAZIONE
Lavare le melanzane e togliere la parte del picciolo. Con un coltello affilato togliere anche una parte della buccia, lasciando la melanzana a strisce (è una regola ferrea, ma non so se serve a dare un po' di consistenza – non troppa – alle fette che si taglieranno poi, oppure a complicare la vita a chi cucina!), poi tagliarle a fette alte 1 cm circa.
Passare le fette prima nella farina, poi nell'uovo sbattuto e infine nel pangrattato, quindi friggerle in olio bollente.
Sono buone sia calde che fredde.
Impanate, ma non fritte, si possono surgelare e poi friggere dopo averle scongelate lentamente.

Insalata di pomodori, carote e capperi

INGREDIENTI PER 6 PERSONE
2-3 grossi pomodori maturi
2 carote
1 cucchiaio medio di capperi sott'aceto o sotto sale
1 cucchiaino di aceto di vino bianco
la buccia grattugiata di un limone e di un'arancia piccola
5-6 foglioline di menta
3 cucchiai di olio d'oliva
sale

PREPARAZIONE

Togliere i semi dei pomodori, tagliarli a dadini e versarli nell'insalatiera. Aggiungere le carote, spellate e tagliate a rondelle sottili, e mescolare tutto.

Preparare una miscela uniforme con l'olio, l'aceto e il sale e versare sull'insalata.

Aggiungere metà della scorza degli agrumi. Mescolare bene e poi aggiungere la scorza degli agrumi rimanente e i capperi. Decorare con le foglie di menta.

Torta al caramello o Torta buona di Marisa

INGREDIENTI PER 8-10 PERSONE

Per la base della torta
130 g di zucchero
5 uova
80 g di farina

Per la crema al burro
240 g di burro
150 g di zucchero
4 uova
150 g di cioccolato amaro
1 tazzina da caffè di pistacchi tritati finemente

Per il caramello
100 g di zucchero
acqua qb

PREPARAZIONE

Mettere in una ciotola i tuorli d'uovo e lo zucchero e sbatterli bene, fino a quando lo zucchero è completamente sciolto.

Aggiungere la farina e infine le chiare montate a neve. Mescolare delicatamente e dividere il composto in quattro parti. Foderare la base della tortiera con un foglio di carta da forno, mettervi 1/4 della pasta, livellare bene e infornare a 180 °C. La pasta cuoce in pochi minuti.

Quando è pronta togliere dalla tortiera e mettere su una grata a raffreddare (se si hanno due tortiere delle stesse dimensioni cuocere gli strati due alla volta e, comunque, la cottura dei quattro strati dura in tutto non più di mezz'ora). Mentre gli strati raffreddano preparare la crema al burro. Sbattere il burro (lasciato fuori dal frigo almeno una mezz'ora prima per ammorbidirlo) con lo zucchero e montarlo bene. Poi, sempre sbattendo, aggiungere 2 uova intere, i 2 tuorli, il cioccolato precedentemente sciolto a bagnomaria e infine le 2 chiare montate a neve. Mescolare delicatamente e mettere in frigo.

Scegliere tra i quattro strati già cotti quello più compatto e metterlo da parte per adoperarlo come ultimo strato della torta.

Mettere sul piatto di portata uno degli altri strati. Spalmarvi sopra 1/3 della crema, livellare bene e sovrapporre il secondo strato.

Ricoprirlo di crema, mettere il terzo strato e il resto della crema (tenerne però da parte una mezza tazza da tè per la decorazione) e infine coprire con l'ultimo strato.

Con un coltello piatto spalmare la crema rimasta sul bordo della torta e spolverizzarlo con i pistacchi tritati.

Mettere la torta in frigo e tenercela per almeno mezza giornata.

Un'ora prima di portarla in tavola, preparare il caramello con zucchero e poca acqua (quanto basta per inumidirlo).

Mettere in un pentolino zucchero e acqua, fare cuocere a fuoco basso: lo zucchero si scioglie e inizia a formare dei grumi bianchi, poi, a poco a poco, questi iniziano a sciogliersi e a caramellare. Mescolare sempre fino a quando è tutto caramellato.

Versarlo sulla torta spalmandolo molto velocemente con un coltello a lama piatta.

Menù
del pranzo in piedi

Arancine

INGREDIENTI PER CIRCA 28 ARANCINE

1 kg di riso Arborio (o altro adatto a risotti)
un battuto di carote, sedano e cipolla (vedi ricetta degli Anelletti al forno a pag. 154)
1,5 litri di brodo vegetale per il risotto
1 tazza da latte di ragù di carne mista (vedi ricetta degli Anelletti al forno a pag. 154)
1 tazza di piselli (vedi ricetta degli Anelletti al forno a pag. 154)
40 g di parmigiano grattugiato
mezza tazza di pecorino a dadini (circa 40 g)
1 uovo
olio per friggere
sale e pepe

Per la panatura
2 uova
farina
pangrattato

PREPARAZIONE

Fare un risotto esattamente come si fa un risotto alla milanese, ma avendo come base un finissimo battuto di sedano, carota e cipolla che si fa dorare con un filo d'olio; versare poi il riso, farlo tostare e cuocere piano piano aggiungendo a poco a poco brodo vegetale tenuto in caldo. Quando è cotto versarlo in una ciotola grande per farlo raffreddare. Quando è abbastanza tiepido da poterlo lavorare aggiungere un uovo intero e amalgamare bene.

In una ciotola mescolare il ragù, i piselli, il pecorino a dadini e il parmigiano grattugiato.

Su un piano di lavoro grande e sgombro mettere la ciotola con il riso, la ciotola con il ragù condito, una ciotola con acqua per bagnarsi le mani, tre vassoi con la farina, l'uovo sbattuto e il pangrattato, e un vassoio grande spolverizzato di farina per poggiarvi le arancine già pronte per la frittura. Bagnare le mani e prendere una cucchiaiata abbondante di riso, metterlo sul palmo della mano e farne una coppetta. Al centro mettere un cucchiaino di impasto e richiudere la coppetta formando una pallina (aggiungere del riso se necessario).

Compattare bene la pallina e passarla nella farina, poi nell'uovo sbattuto e infine nel pangrattato.

Adagiarla sul vassoio spolverizzato di farina e poi formare un'altra pallina fino a esaurire il riso. Coprire con un canovaccio pulito e lasciare riposare per qualche ora. Poi friggere in olio abbondante.

Paté di melanzane
con bastoncini di carota e sedano

INGREDIENTI PER 8 PERSONE
4 melanzane (1-1,3 kg)
4 cucchiai da minestra di olio d'oliva
il succo di 1 limone
2 spicchi di aglio
20 foglioline di menta
4 carote
3 coste di sedano grosso
sale e pepe

PREPARAZIONE

Tagliare il picciolo alle melanzane, lavarle, fare un taglio a croce nel punto in cui era il picciolo, disporle in una teglia e infornare fino a quando non sono completamente cotte (impiegheranno circa un'ora e mezza a una temperatura di 190 °C).
Quando sono fredde, sbucciarle e versarle nel bicchiere del mixer, aggiungere l'aglio, la menta, l'olio, il succo di limone, sale e pepe e lavorare fino a ottenere una crema liscia.
Assaggiare e aggiustare di sale, olio o limone a piacere. Mettere in una ciotola e tenere in frigo.
Quando è il momento di consumare il paté, pelare e tagliare a bastoncino delle carote e del sedano. Oppure tostare delle fettine di pane da servire insieme.

Pizza rustica

INGREDIENTI PER 8-10 PERSONE

Per la pasta frolla
500 g di farina
200 g di zucchero
200 g di burro
1 tuorlo d'uovo
2 cucchiai di latte

Per il ripieno
800 g di ricotta fresca ben asciutta
1 uovo
1 tazza da caffè di salame tagliato a dadini
100 g di parmigiano grattugiato
sale e pepe

PREPARAZIONE

Mettere la farina sul piano di lavoro, al centro unire il burro già ammorbidito e spezzettato, lo zucchero, il tuorlo d'uovo, il latte e impastare velocemente. Formare una palla liscia e farla riposare in frigo per circa un'ora.

Per preparare il ripieno è importante che la ricotta perda molta della sua acqua, quindi è meglio metterla in frigo su un vassoio e con sopra un piattino capovolto, in maniera che perda il suo liquido, per almeno un giorno.

Versare quindi in un mixer la ricotta, aggiungere l'uovo, il formaggio grattugiato e raffinare tutto per qualche minuto: deve risultare una crema liscia e morbida.

Versare in una ciotola e aggiungere il salame a dadini.

Mettere una metà della pasta frolla sul piano di lavoro infarinato e stenderla col mattarello fino ad avere un foglio spesso circa 4-5 mm. Foderare con questo la teglia apribile e versarvi la ricotta.

Mettere la pasta frolla rimasta sul piano infarinato, stenderla e tagliarne delle strisce di circa 2 cm da sistemare sulla ricotta a formare dei quadrati o dei rombi o un disegno a piacere. Infornare a fuoco medio per circa 40 minuti. Quando la pizza è pronta, la parte a vista della ricotta risulterà molto colorata e la pasta frolla di un colore più pallido.

Verdure in pastella

INGREDIENTI PER 6 PERSONE

1 cipolla media
12 fiori di zucca
12 bastoncini di formaggio (caciocavallo o pecorino) di 0,5 x 2 cm
12 pezzetti di acciuga
6 cimette di cavolfiore già sbollentato
olio per friggere

Per la pastella
300 g di farina di grano duro
350-400 ml di acqua tiepida
6-8 cucchiai da minestra di olio extravergine di oliva
sale e pepe

PREPARAZIONE

Tagliare la cipolla ad anelli di circa 6 mm. Aprire i fiori di zucca, riempirli con il formaggio e con i pezzetti di acciuga e poi richiuderli.

Mettere in una ciotola la farina di grano duro, un po' di sale e di pepe (se piace) e versare lentamente l'acqua sbattendo con una forchetta e intercalando con l'olio.

Sbattere sempre fino a quando non si raggiunge la consistenza di una crema. Immergendovi una forchetta e sollevandola
deve essere fluida, ma non troppo!

Mettere abbondante olio in un pentolino largo circa 20 cm
e a bordo alto (o nella friggitrice). Quando l'olio è ben caldo
immergere nella pastella le verdure una a una e poi metterle nell'olio (probabilmente 4-5 pezzetti per volta a seconda
della larghezza del pentolino).

Quando le verdure sono fritte, scolarle bene e metterle su un
piatto con della carta che ne assorba l'olio in eccesso.

Spiedini di frutta tagliata

INGREDIENTI PER 6 PERSONE
1 melone bianco
1 melone Cantalupo
2 mele
2 pere

PREPARAZIONE

Tagliare la frutta a pezzetti di 3 x 3 cm e infilzarli in uno spie-
dino alternando i diversi tipi di frutta. Servire gli spiedini
poggiati su un piatto oppure infilzati in un melone ancora
integro.

Menù
dei *beaux restes*

Medaglioni col ragù

INGREDIENTI PER 6 PERSONE
12 fette di pane raffermo
150 g di ragù di carne
1 tazza da tè di piselli
50 g di parmigiano grattugiato
1 tazza da tè di *béchamel*
1 tazza da tè di latte
olio per friggere

Per la panatura
farina
pangrattato
2 uova

PREPARAZIONE
Mettere in un piatto fondo il latte. Inumidire le fette di pane
con il latte e strizzarle bene. Metterle su un vassoio.
In una ciotola mescolare il ragù, la *béchamel*, il parmigiano
e i piselli in modo da ottenere un impasto consistente.
Mettere una cucchiaiata di impasto su ciascuna fetta di pane
e farne una cupoletta.

Versare la farina in un piatto piano, in un altro il pangrattato e sbattere leggermente le uova in un piatto fondo.

Passare le fette con l'impasto nella farina, poi nell'uovo sbattuto e infine nel pangrattato. Sistemarle tutte su un vassoio infarinato e poi friggerle in olio bollente.

Uova alla romana

INGREDIENTI PER 4 PERSONE
6 uova sode
300-350 ml circa di olio per friggere

Per la panatura
farina
1 uovo
pangrattato

Per la béchamel
300 ml di latte
1 noce di burro
2 cucchiai di farina
una grattatina di noce moscata
1 cucchiaio di parmigiano grattugiato
un pizzico di sale e uno di pepe

PREPARAZIONE

Per preparare la *béchamel* mettere in un pentolino una noce di burro e farla sciogliere a fuoco medio. Quindi togliere dal fuoco e aggiungere la farina, mescolare bene fino a ottenere una pasta morbida e priva di grumi (è un'operazione molto veloce). Aggiungere lentamente, a filo, il latte freddo e amalgamare bene alla pasta di farina e burro, sciogliendola a poco a poco nel latte. Dopo aver versato tutto il latte, rimettere il pentolino sul fuoco basso (così la farina cuoce) e, sempre mescolando, portare avanti la cottura fino a raggiungere la consistenza desiderata (deve essere comunque abbastanza densa e ci vogliono circa 15 minuti). Quindi, aggiungere sale, pepe, parmigiano e noce moscata.

Sbucciare le uova sode e tagliarle a metà nel senso della lunghezza. Togliere i tuorli e metterli in una ciotola, dopodiché schiacciarli con una forchetta e aggiungervi a poco a poco la *béchamel*. L'impasto deve risultare abbastanza sodo.

Con un cucchiaio, riempire il vuoto lasciato dal tuorlo nelle mezze uova e ricreare la forma dell'uovo sodo intero. Dopo aver riempito tutte le mezze uova, passarle a una a una prima nella farina, poi nell'uovo sbattuto e infine nel pangrattato. Scaldare l'olio in un pentolino di almeno 15 cm di diametro, a bordo alto. Friggere le uova a due a due e, quando sono ben dorate, metterle a scolare su un foglio di carta assorbente. Sono buone tiepide, forse ancora meglio fredde.

Frittella e sua variante in agrodolce

INGREDIENTI PER 8 PERSONE
600 g di fave fresche
800 g di piselli freschi
600 g di carciofi freschi
2 cipollette
100 ml di olio d'oliva
sale e pepe

PREPARAZIONE
Sgranare i piselli e le fave, pulire i carciofi e tagliarli a quarti. Cuocere in pentolini separati perché i due legumi e i car-

ciofi hanno tempi di cottura diversi. Condire tutti con sale, pepe, cipolletta fresca tagliata finemente, un po' di olio e 3 cucchiai di acqua.

Mettere i pentolini sul fuoco a temperatura media. Controllare la cottura e aggiungere, se necessario, ancora acqua o olio. A fine cottura, unire tutto nella pentola più grande, mescolare e scaldare un po'. Servire caldo.

La variante in agrodolce si fa spesso con la frittella che rimane dopo il pranzo e si serve completamente fredda.

Riscaldare in un pentolino un mezzo bicchiere da vino di aceto di vino bianco con 2 cucchiai medi di zucchero, non appena lo zucchero è completamente sciolto versare sulla frittella fredda e mescolare un po'.

Arance con cannella

INGREDIENTI PER 6 PERSONE
5 arance fresche
2 cucchiai da tè di zucchero
2 cucchiaini da caffè di cannella e chiodi di garofano ridotti in polvere

PREPARAZIONE

Pelare le arance a vivo (senza la parte bianca della buccia) e tagliarle a fette di circa 6 mm. Poi disporle nel piatto di portata. Se non sono molto dolci condirle con lo zucchero e poi spolverizzarle con la cannella e il garofano.

Oppure decorare con il caramello (vedi ricetta della Torta al caramello a pag. 158).

Menù
del pranzo di dolci

Cassata

La cassata è fatta da 4 preparati diversi: il pandispagna, la pasta reale (il marzapane), la crema di ricotta e la velata. Tutti vanno preparati qualche giorno prima. Il pandispagna deve essere fatto almeno 2 giorni prima così si compatta meglio.

INGREDIENTI PER 10-12 PERSONE

Per il pandispagna
6 uova
200 g di zucchero
150 g di farina

Per la velata
300 g di zucchero
acqua (un bicchiere da vino, pieno)
qualche goccia di limone

Per la pasta reale (marzapane)
1 kg di mandorle sgusciate e spellate (circa 3,5 kg di mandorle in guscio); oppure 1 kg di farina di mandorle
4 mandorle amare
2 litri di acqua
600 g di zucchero

Per la crema di ricotta
1 kg di ricotta fresca e ben scolata
600 g di zucchero
150 g di cioccolato amaro tagliato a dadini

PREPARAZIONE

Per preparare il pandispagna: separare i tuorli dalle chiare. In una ciotola, sbattere bene i tuorli e lo zucchero; quando lo zucchero è completamente sciolto e il composto è bianco, gonfio e spumoso aggiungere, a poco a poco, la farina.

Quindi, montare le chiare d'uovo a neve ferma. A questo punto unire a poco a poco le chiare al composto di uova, zucchero e farina.

Dal momento che questa ricetta non prevede lievito, la sua riuscita dipende dalla fermezza delle chiare sbattute a neve e dal modo in cui le si amalgama al composto: non mescolando con forza ma incorporandole con un movimento lento dal basso verso l'alto, cercando di mantenere la consistenza delle chiare il più a lungo possibile.

Imburrare e spolverare di zucchero una tortiera apribile (del diametro di 25 cm). Versare il composto nella tortiera, infornare e cuocere a 180 °C per circa mezz'ora.

Quando il pandispagna è gonfio e dorato, forarlo con uno stecchino: se esce asciutto, il pandispagna è pronto.

Per preparare la velata: versare lo zucchero e l'acqua in un pentolino, metterlo su fuoco basso e mescolare con un cucchiaio. Non appena lo zucchero si trasforma in un liquido denso e quasi trasparente, immergere pollice e indice in un bicchiere di acqua fredda; quindi, con il cucchiaio, lasciar cadere sulle dita bagnate una goccia del liquido bollente, quando comincia ad avere una piccola consistenza sarà pronto.

Versarlo lentamente su un ripiano di marmo e "lavorarlo" con una paletta di legno, disegnando come dei cerchi; aiutarsi con un coltello per raccogliere il liquido mentre si spande. In una decina di minuti, si trasformerà in un composto sempre più consistente e non più trasparente, che infine diventa una glassa compatta e bianchissima, pronta per essere staccata dal marmo con la lama di un coltello e raccolta in una ciotola.

Prima dell'uso, mettere la quantità desiderata di velata in una tazzina, aggiungere qualche goccia di limone e mescolare con un cucchiaio fino a ottenere la consistenza voluta.

La velata si spalma con un pennello duro e si indurisce velocemente.

Per la pasta reale: mettere sul fuoco una pentola con circa 2 litri di acqua (quella della pasta va benissimo). Appena bolle, versarvi le mandorle e spegnere.

Dopo circa 5 minuti, scolare le mandorle con un colino e cominciare a togliere la pellicina. In genere è un'operazione facile, veloce e gradevole. Se la pellicina resiste troppo, rimettere le mandorle in acqua e lasciarle a mollo ancora un po'.

Una volta spellate, disporre le mandorle in uno strato non spesso, su uno o più vassoi, e lasciarle asciugare all'aria per almeno 5 giorni. Quando le mandorle sono ben asciutte, tritarle nel mixer fino a ottenere una farina fine.

Versare in una pentola lo zucchero bagnato con l'acqua, accendere il fuoco, mescolare ogni tanto finché lo zucchero non è completamente sciolto (circa 10 minuti a fuoco basso) – "a cileppo" diciamo noi, cioè leggermente denso.

Aggiungere nella pentola la farina di mandorle, mescolare velocemente finché il composto non si stacca dal fondo e versarlo su un ripiano di marmo, allargandolo un po' e facendolo raffreddare.

Quando – dopo circa 5 minuti – la pasta è abbastanza fredda da essere lavorata con le mani, iniziare a impastarla per amalgamare bene farina e zucchero e raffinarla.

Durante questa operazione è utile usare un po' di farina per dolci (2 o 3 cucchiai da minestra) per poter assorbire l'olio prodotto dalle mandorle e rendere più facile la lavorazione. Dopo circa 5 minuti, la pasta reale risulterà liscia, senza grumi e compatta.

Farne un panetto e conservarlo su un piatto nella credenza. *Anche la pasta reale si conserva molto a lungo, un mese e più. La si può avvolgere nella carta oleata o nella pellicola per alimenti. Se si indurisce troppo, basta lavorarla di nuovo sul marmo con pochissima acqua appena tiepida.*

Per la crema di ricotta: lasciare scolare la ricotta per almeno un giorno, poi passarla in un setaccio fine oppure metterla in un mixer con lo zucchero, deve diventare una crema molto fine. Incorporare il cioccolato alla ricotta e metterla in frigo.

Un giorno prima del pranzo prendere la forma della cassata e spolverizzare con un po' di farina per dolci. Lavorare la metà della pasta reale fino a formare un rotolo, spianare poi col mattarello formando una striscia larga circa 6 cm e lunga quanto si può e dello spessore di circa mezzo centimetro. Appoggiare la striscia al bordo inclinato dello stampo per cassata e rivestirlo completamente. Formare poi con la pasta rimasta un rotolino di circa 1 cm di diametro e lungo quanto si può e schiacciarlo lungo il margine inferiore della striscia precedente. Tagliare il pandispagna in fette di circa mezzo centimetro di spessore con cui coprire il fondo dello stampo, inumidire con un po' di acqua leggermente zuccherata.

A questo punto versare la crema di ricotta e ricoprire tutto con il resto delle fette di pandispagna. Mettere in frigo.

L'indomani capovolgere nel piatto di portata e staccare dallo stampo. Pulire con un pennello della farina in eccesso e ricoprire con la velata sciolta leggermente con un po' di zucchero.

Biscotti ricci di mandorle

INGREDIENTI

1 kg di mandorle sgusciate e pelate
800 g di zucchero
3 uova
1 bustina di vanillina
la scorza di 1 limone

PREPARAZIONE

Tritare finemente le mandorle bene asciutte, versare in una ciotola capiente, aggiungere tutti gli altri ingredienti e mescolare bene con le mani. Lasciare riposare per una notte.

L'indomani, usando un imbuto a stella a sezione molto larga, fare i biscotti, tondi o allungati, direttamente in una teglia e infornare a 180 °C.

Cuocere per circa 20 minuti, fin quando non diventano dorati.

Fette del cancelliere

INGREDIENTI PER 10 PERSONE
1 litro di latte
450 g di semola
250 g di zucchero
250 g di pistacchi tritati finemente
1 uovo
olio per friggere
zucchero a velo

Per la crema "biancomangiare"
300 ml di latte
50 g di zucchero
30 g di amido

PREPARAZIONE

Versare il latte in un pentolino, aggiungervi a poco a poco la semola e lo zucchero e, mescolando sempre, a fuoco medio, farlo addensare come una crema. Questo procedimento dura non più di 8-10 minuti.

Quando è denso toglierlo dal fuoco e aggiungervi i pistacchi tritati.

Rimettere sul fuoco e fare addensare fino a raggiungere una forte consistenza per 5 minuti ancora.

Fare raffreddare l'impasto.

In una ciotolina sbattere leggermente una chiara d'uovo e, con le mani bagnate dalla chiara, fare delle grosse polpette ovali da friggere in abbondante olio.

Per preparare la crema "biancomangiare": mettere in un pentolino il latte, lo zucchero e l'amido. Mescolare bene. Accendere un fuoco medio e, mescolando sempre, fare

cuocere fino a quando la crema comincia a divenire densa.
Provare con il mestolo a tracciare un segno sulla crema: se
questo è visibile, la crema è pronta.
Spegnere e fare raffreddare.
Quando anche le polpette sono fredde, aprirle a libro, riem-
pirle con un cucchiaino di biancomangiare e spolverizzare
con lo zucchero a velo.

PRANKING PARADISE

The Whoopee Wagon is the place where Hubble Trouble's pranks are born. Full to the brim with tricks and pesky pranks, this silly spaceship is bursting with fun. It has even got its own slime blaster which will be grreat for distracting other space cadets during the race.

Remember to watch out for oodles of silly booby traps and be 'chair-ful' not to sit on any whoopee cushions when on board — the place is full of them!

PLAY TIME

Living in space isn't all work in their free time astronauts like to watch movies, tease their crew mates, play music and work out! They even have a high tech gym on board.

HUBBLE TROUBLE

RACE CARD:
2/12

SPACESHIP:
Whoopee Wagon

SUPER SKILL:
Ability to blow contestants off course

BEST GADGET:
On-board slime blaster

WATCH OUT FOR:
Space junk, it could burst the whoopee!

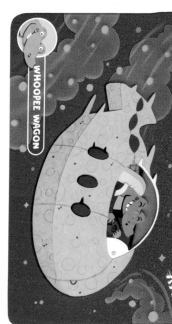

WHOOPEE WAGON

BEAR'S SPACE RACE

Menù
di caponate

La caponata di casa Agnello

INGREDIENTI PER 6 PERSONE
800 g circa di melanzane
1 tazzina da caffè di sedano tagliato molto fine
200 g circa di cipolla
2 cucchiai di capperi
1 tazza da tè di olive verdi col nocciolo
3 cucchiai di passata di pomodoro
1 bicchiere da acqua di aceto di vino
1 cucchiaio di zucchero
400 ml circa di olio per friggere

PREPARAZIONE

Lavare, togliere il gambo e qualche striscia di buccia alle melanzane. Tagliarle a fette spesse 2-3 cm e poi tagliare le fette a dadini.

Friggere i dadini di melanzana in olio bollente fin quando prendono un bel colore dorato e metterli in una ciotola sopra un foglio di carta assorbente per eliminare l'olio in eccesso.

Tritare molto finemente (nel mixer, oppure con la mezza-luna sul tagliere) la cipolla, il sedano, i capperi e le olive prima denocciolate. Scaldare in una padella 4 cucchiai di olio, versarvi il trito e far cuocere a fuoco vivace fin quando la cipolla non imbiondisce, quindi aggiungere la passata di pomodoro e far cuocere per altri 5 minuti.

Spegnere il fuoco e aggiungere metà dell'aceto e dello zucchero, mescolare e far riposare per 5 minuti.

L'altra metà dell'aceto e dello zucchero va tenuta da parte: l'agrodolce ha sempre un gusto molto particolare e personale e se ne realizza appieno il sapore una volta che tutti gli ingredienti sono freddi e "riposati" da almeno un'ora.

A questo punto condire i dadini di melanzane già fritti e scolati dall'olio con il trito già aromatizzato con l'agrodolce. Far riposare per almeno un'ora. Poi assaggiare e, se necessario e gradito, aggiungere tutto o parte dell'aceto e lo zucchero tenuti da parte.

Si può surgelare o mettere in barattoli di vetro da sterilizzare.

Caponata di melanzane barocca di Aurora

INGREDIENTI PER 6 PERSONE

2 melanzane viola
mezzo peperone rosso
mezzo peperone giallo
30 g di olive verdi
30 g di olive nere
30 g di capperi dissalati
30 g di fiori di finocchio selvatico
50 g di pinoli
2 cipolle medie rosse
3 spicchi di aglio
10 g di cannella in polvere
70 g di coste di sedano verde sottile

20 ml di aceto di vino bianco
700 ml di pelati, o pomodori tagliati a dadi
10 g di zucchero
olio di semi di girasole per friggere
sale

PREPARAZIONE

Togliere la buccia delle melanzane per 3/4, tagliarle a dadi di 2 cm, mettere in un colapasta, salare e coprire con un piatto pesante. Lasciare scolare il nero, premerle leggermente e poi friggere in olio di semi di girasole.

Tagliare il sedano a pezzetti di circa 1 cm, sbollentare per ammorbidirlo e metterlo da parte.

Tagliare i peperoni a quadri di 2 x 2 cm, le cipolle, l'aglio, e soffriggere in olio di semi.

Mescolare al soffritto di cipolla, aglio e peperoni, il sedano ammorbidito, i capperi, le olive verdi e nere e i pinoli.

Unire anche il pomodoro fresco pelato e tagliato a pezzi e le melanzane fritte, aggiungere lo zucchero, sfumare con l'aceto di vino, aggiustare il gusto alla fine se manca di sale.

In ultimo aggiungere i fiori di finocchio e una spolverata di cannella.

Tuma all'argentiera di Chicchi

INGREDIENTI PER 4 PERSONE
8 fette di tuma fresca
1 cipolletta tritata finemente
2 cucchiai di aceto di vino bianco
una manciata di origano
2 cucchiai di olio d'oliva
sale e pepe

PREPARAZIONE

Versare in una padella antiaderente l'olio e fare soffriggere la cipolla, quando è pronta aggiungere le fette di tuma e farle friggere.

Girare dall'altra parte le fette, salare leggermente e sfumare con l'aceto.

Infine aggiungere sale, pepe e origano. Servire caldo.

Palline di pasta reale

La ricetta della pasta reale è uguale a quella della Cassata a pag. 171, con l'unica differenza che le mandorle non sono pelate, il marzapane viene più scuro ma con un sapore più forte e il colore, che non è bello, viene poi coperto con le granelle. Con mezzo chilo di mandorle si ottengono molte palline, in genere questo "dessert" viene preparato quando "rimane" del marzapane.

INGREDIENTI

pasta reale (si veda ricetta della Cassata a pag. 171)
zucchero brillantato aromatizzato con polvere di cannella
granella di pistacchi tritati non troppo finemente
cacao amaro

PREPARAZIONE

In tre piatti piani diversi mettere lo zucchero brillantato, la granella di pistacchi e il cacao amaro.

Con la pasta reale formare delle palline di circa 2 cm di diametro e passarle nelle 3 granelle in modo da avere gusti e colori diversi nello stesso piatto.

Menù
a otto mani

Il macco di fave di Antonio

INGREDIENTI PER 6 PERSONE

500 g di fave secche (messe ad ammollare in un litro e mezzo di acqua
24 ore prima, poi scolate e sgusciate una a una)
4 cipollotti
3 o 4 gambi di finocchietto selvatico, un mazzetto piccolo di cicoria, uno di
mazzareddri selvatici (se possibile) e uno di cavolo nero (o cime di rapa)
2 coste di sedano
un mazzetto di cime di capperi
50 g di pancetta tagliata a dadini
4 cucchiai di olio d'oliva
sale e pepe

PREPARAZIONE

Per preparare il brodo, mettere a bollire in un litro e mezzo
di acqua 3/4 di sedano, finocchietti, cicoria, mazzareddri
selvatici, cavolo nero (o cima di rapa), 2 cipollotti e le cime di
capperi, tagliati grossolanamente, per circa un'ora e mezza.
Scolare e conservare brodo e verdure separatamente.
Passare alla preparazione del macco: mettere a soffriggere in
una capiente pentola di coccio (in cui sarà cotto e poi servito a

tavola il macco), con un cucchiaio di olio extravergine di oliva, 2 cipollotti tagliuzzati finemente e la pancetta tagliata a dadini. Quando saranno dorati aggiungere le fave sgusciate, mescolare e soffriggere leggermente. Aggiungere le verdure del brodo scolate e soffriggere un po'. Mescolare e coprire il tutto con qualche mestolo di brodo.

A quel punto inizia la lenta cottura del macco, a fuoco basso, che bisogna rimescolare ogni 20 minuti, aggiungendo, piano piano, tutto il brodo.

Controllare la cottura del macco. Dopo 3 ore e mezzo le fave dovrebbero essere quasi spappolate e cotte. Aggiungere allora il quarto di verdure tagliate grossolanamente tenute da parte e completare la cottura, per circa 30 minuti.

Quando il macco è pronto spegnere il fuoco e lasciare sul fornello; aggiungere sale, pepe e 2 cucchiai di olio e mescolare. Fare riposare per 30 minuti.

Prima di portare in tavola aggiungere un cucchiaio di olio senza mescolare.

Sarde a beccafico

INGREDIENTI PER 6 PERSONE
3-4 sarde a persona (diliscate e aperte a libro)
100 g di pangrattato
un mazzetto piccolo di prezzemolo
5 acciughe sott'olio
100 g di pinoli e uva passa
foglie di alloro tante quante sono le sarde
1 limone (sia il succo che la scorza grattugiata)
olio d'oliva
pepe

PREPARAZIONE

Lavare le sarde e metterle a scolare su un piatto capovolto.

In un padellino mettere 2 cucchiai d'olio, le acciughe e, a fuoco basso, farle sciogliere lentamente. Spegnere il fuoco.

Mettere in una ciotola il pangrattato, aggiungere le acciughe sciolte con il loro olio, il pepe, il prezzemolo tritato, l'uva passa e i pinoli, il succo e la buccia grattugiata di mezzo limone. Amalgamare tutto, aggiungere un po' di acqua se l'impasto è troppo secco.

Mettere le sarde su un piano di appoggio, spalmare su ciascuna un po' di impasto e formare un rotolino.

Sistemarle nella teglia da forno fino a riempirla con i rotolini di sarde ben allineati.

Inserire tra ogni rotolino una foglia di alloro, condire tutto con un filo d'olio e una spruzzata di limone.

Coprire con carta da forno e infornare a 180 °C per circa mezz'ora.

Tortino di carciofi e patate

INGREDIENTI PER 6 PERSONE

3-4 sarde a persona (diliscate e aperte a libro)
700-800 g di patate
12 carciofi
50 g di caciocavallo
mezza tazza da tè di capperi sotto sale
1 cipollotto (o 2 spicchi di aglio)
3 cucchiai da minestra di pangrattato
60-80 ml di acqua
50 ml di olio d'oliva
pepe

185

PREPARAZIONE

Preparare una teglia rettangolare di circa 30 x 16 cm.
Sbucciare e tagliare le patate a fette spesse circa mezzo centimetro.
Pulire i carciofi delle foglie esterne e tagliarne il cuore a fettine sottili (anche il gambo è buono e va anche questo tagliato a rondelline).
Dissalare i capperi. Tagliare il formaggio a dadini piccolissimi.
Tritare molto finemente il cipollotto o l'aglio (se preferito).
Versare un filo d'olio sul fondo della teglia, mettervi uno strato di patate e condire con pepe, una spolverata di formaggio, una di pangrattato e qualche cappero. Ricoprire con uno strato di fette di carciofo e condire nello stesso modo, ma con l'aggiunta di un filo d'olio. Andare avanti così fino all'ultimo strato di patate, aggiungere una metà dell'acqua e coprire con la carta da forno.
Infornare a fuoco medio per circa 40 minuti.
Dopo 20 minuti controllare il livello di cottura e, se necessario, aggiungere l'acqua rimanente.

Babà di Justin e Giorgio

INGREDIENTI

250 g di farina Manitoba
15 g di lievito di birra sciolto in acqua tiepida
3 uova
15 g di zucchero
un pizzico di sale
la buccia grattugiata di un limone
100 g di burro

Per lo sciroppo
1 dl di acqua
200 g di zucchero
il succo di 1 limone
1 bicchierino di rum

PREPARAZIONE

Per preparare la pasta: mettere in una grande ciotola gli ingredienti asciutti (farina, zucchero, sale, buccia di limone); aggiungere il lievito già sciolto e poi le uova una a una.
Mescolare con le mani e poi lavorare energicamente con le dita per 5 o 6 minuti fino a quando la pasta non è liscia ed elastica. Oppure utilizzare un'impastatrice elettrica a velocità media per lo stesso tempo. Quando il burro è morbido aggiungerne 80 g sull'impasto, mettere il tutto in un posto tiepido e coprirlo con un canovaccio pesante. Lasciare riposare per circa un'ora (meno se il posto è caldo, un po' di più di un'ora se è freddo).
Quando l'impasto lievitato è raddoppiato, versarlo in uno stampo abbastanza grande, imburrato e infarinato, da riempire per metà.
Coprire con il canovaccio e attendere altri 30-45 minuti fino a quando la pasta non lieviterà di nuovo e riempirà tutto lo stampo.
Infornare per 25-30 minuti fino a quando il babà diventa dorato e asciutto.
Togliere immediatamente il babà dallo stampo (la crosta sarà fine e scura) per prevenire la condensa.
Nel frattempo preparare lo sciroppo: mettere gli ingredienti (tranne il rum) in un pentolino sul fuoco fino a ottenere uno sciroppo non denso, poi aggiungere il rum.
Quando il babà è freddo immergerlo in un piatto largo dai

bordi alti in cui è già stato versato lo sciroppo; fare gocciolare lo sciroppo sul babà per far sì che il babà sia del tutto imbevuto e abbia assorbito interamente lo sciroppo.
Sollevare e disporre sul piatto di portata.

APPENDICE

Agli inizi dell'Ottocento, Gerlando Giudice, trisnonno di Mamma, acquistò un centinaio di ettari di terreno nella Contrada Mosè.

Da cinque generazioni la nostra famiglia trascorre qui le vacanze.

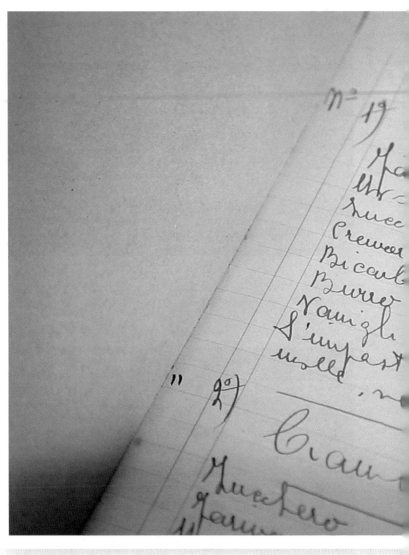

Tutti noi, prima Mamma e zia Teresa, poi Chiara, Silvano ed io, abbiamo imparato a preparare i dolci dal libretto di nonna Maria.

Dolci

...ine al burro

...li)   gr.   800
                        4
...taro "   200
...di soda   30
          gr.   15
          gr. 2 ov
...nico
...latte nè teppu
...ppa dura

Cuciniamo usando quello che c'è nel riposto e quanto di fresco giorno per giorno ci offre la campagna.

I piatti sono semplici, ma possono diventare sontuosi aggiungendo un singolo ingrediente o seguendo un nuovo procedimento nella preparazione.

*Partiamo dalla tradizione e cerchiamo innovazioni e miglioramenti. Intro-
duciamo vecchie ricette con sapori nuovi, e ricette nuove con elementi vecchi.*

*Ora, noi e i nostri amici condividiamo con i turisti il pranzo alla nostra ta-
vola. Sembra che nulla sia cambiato a Mosè.*

Gli ulivi di Mosè sono antichissimi e di tante varietà. Enormi, hanno chiome magnifiche, tronchi possenti, radici ampie e contorte.

Luigi Vella, fattore di Mosè, ogni giorno ci porta i prodotti della terra e si prende cura della campagna, come faceva un tempo suo zio Vincenzo.

La melanzana fa parte della cucina povera siciliana da ormai trecento anni. È l'ingrediente principale dei nostri piatti più amati.

*Noi serviamo quasi tutte le verdure di stagione fritte con la pastella, soprat-
tutto quando abbiamo pranzi con ospiti numerosi, in cui ci si serve in piedi
e con le mani.*

*La nostra anziana friggitrice addimora tutta l'estate sul ripiano di marmo
lungo il muro che dà sul cortile. Possiamo servire il fritto caldo caldo agli
ospiti che riceviamo all'aperto.*

Gran parte dei mobili che arredano la nostra cucina risalgono a prima della Seconda guerra mondiale, furono gli unici a rimanere intatti durante l'occupazione prima tedesca poi alleata.

Vincenzo, il primo dei Vella a guidare il trattore. Con lui condivido preziosi ricordi della mia infanzia a Mosè.

È bello cucinare chiacchierando con amici. Ben presto il momento delle riflessioni cede il passo a quello delle confidenze.

Chiara, Silvano ed io eravamo costanti visitatori in cucina quando Mamma e zia Teresa si mettevano alla preparazione dei dolci. Oggi continuiamo a prepararli come loro ci hanno insegnato.

Come Mamma, confeziono per gli ospiti piccoli regali con i prodotti della campagna, da offrire loro al momento del commiato.

205

*Ho mantenuto le usanze di famiglia nell'apparecchiare la tavola: "L'acco-
glienza dell'ospite" diceva Mamma "inizia dalla tovaglia. Deve essere pulita,
senza una piega, e su un buon mollettone".*

Seguire la tradizione nell'apparecchiatura della tavola mi aiuta a ricreare l'atmosfera conviviale dei tempi di Mamma e zia Teresa.

Al momento del placement *più che padrona di casa mi sento regista.*

Cerco sempre di creare una bella atmosfera a tavola, con l'aiuto dei miei figli, o di Chiara, a cui chiedo di badare in modo particolare agli ospiti più difficili.

Ogni pranzo a Mosè mi ricorda che mangiare insieme è una gioia reciproca.

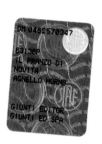

Stampato presso Giunti Industrie Grafiche S.p.A.

Stabilimento di Prato

RŌNIN

A JOHN MILTON THRILLER

MARK DAWSON

rōnin

noun, historical

Landless or masterless peasant soldiers or samurai who
through dishonour or the loss of their masters were forced
to wander Japan until some other lord would accept their
services.

Oxford English Dictionary

PROLOGUE

Miyasato Nishimoto clutched the straps of the bag a little tighter as he negotiated the crowds around the Sensō-ji Temple in Asakusa. It was the day of the Sanja Matsuri festival, and the streets were busy with people. He saw women in traditional kimonos, schoolkids with their parents drinking smoothies from paper cones, and a handful of tourists who looked bemused at the spectacle. He saw men wearing nothing but *fundoshi*, thongs that left little to the imagination, as they hauled *mikoshi*—portable shrines—on their shoulders, stopping every few steps to clap their hands and chant to the spirits of their ancestors who were reputed to live within the palanquins.

He made his way to the Ishibashi bridge and a long line of market stalls that sold street food and local delicacies. The stall he wanted specialised in *matcha kakigori*—shaved ice topped with matcha syrup atop red bean paste—and he found it at the end of the line. He shared a glance with the man who was in charge and waited as he said something to his teenage assistant.

Miyasato watched as the kid dashed back into the building behind the stall, returning after a short pause to gesture that Miyasato should follow. The boy led the way through the crowd, going into and then passing through a restaurant and emerging in an alleyway on the other side. A large man, almost big enough to be a sumo, blocked the way ahead. He approached Miyasato and frisked him, then gestured that he should continue along the alley to a folding table where an al fresco meal was in progress.

Satoshi Furokawa was sitting at the table. He was an important man, the leader of the Chinese Dragons, yet he was not interested in the ostentatiousness that characterised some of his peers who had recently found infamy with their arrest, trial and imprisonment. Furokawa was cannier than that. He dressed simply, without wishing to draw attention to himself with clothes that were obviously expensive. He did not wear jewellery, and it was only the extensive tattoos that were visible between the folds of his simple robe that identified him as a gangster.

Miyasato took a deep breath to compose himself and waited for Furokawa to look up from the bowl of *udon* that he was eating.

"Come," he said, beckoning him with his fingers.

Miyasato approached the table and waited for an invitation to sit in the empty chair. Furokawa smiled at him and gestured again. Miyasato sat.

"Nishimoto-*san*," he said, "how are you?"

"I'm well."

"Your wife?"

"She's well."

"And your son? It is Yamato—yes?"

"That's right," Miyasato said, his mouth dry.

Furokawa smiled benignly. "He just had a birthday."

Small talk with a man as ruthless and dangerous as Furokawa was not pleasant. Miyasato knew that he was making a point: I know *everything* about you and your family.

"He did," Miyasato said.

"How old is he?"

"Five. He's five."

Furokawa put his chopsticks together and rested them in the empty bowl.

"What does he like?"

Miyasato started to sweat. "Sorry?"

"What does he like to play with?"

"Godzilla. Power Rangers. Wrestling."

Furokawa smiled, his leathery skin crinkling at the corners of his thin, mean lips. He dispensed with the small talk now, revealing by doing so just how inconsequential he considered it.

"Do you have it?"

"Yes." Miyasato indicated the bag. "I do. In here."

"Was it easy?"

It *had* been easy—ridiculously so—but Miyasato did not think it was in his interest to say that. Furokawa was paying him well, and Miyasato knew there was value in his encouraging the misapprehension that the item he was so keen to have had been difficult to acquire. In reality, all Miyasato had had to do was wait for his father to go to sleep and then take the item from the wall in his apartment where it was displayed. It had taken less than a minute, and the fact was not lost on Miyasato that those sixty seconds would change his life beyond all recognition.

"Not easy," he lied.

Of course, the fact that it had been easy to remove the item was neither here nor there. He was being well paid because of *who* he had stolen from. His father would not tolerate thievery, and his rage would not be tempered by the fact that the thief was his son. There would be a reckoning, and Miyasato had arranged to be remunerated well enough to avoid it. He didn't just plan to take his family out of Tokyo; he planned for them to be out of the country entirely.

Furokawa leaned forward, his eyes gleaming. "Show me."

Miyasato took the bag and set it on the table. He opened the zip and, with careful hands, withdrew the bundle from inside. He had wrapped the item in newspaper, but, before he could uncover it, Furokawa held up his hand and indicated that he wanted to do it himself.

"Do you know the story of Yoshida Shōin?" he asked as he peeled back one corner of the sheet.

"Not really."

"He was born in 1830. The Americans arrived when he was twenty-three, and he looked at their fleet and their guns and then at what Japan had to offer in return, and decided that we were lacking. They say it was at that moment that he decided that the old ways—the ways of the samurai—were no longer relevant. That they held Japan back. What is a sword to a gun, after all? Shōin tried to stow away on one of the American ships so that he could visit their country and learn from them, but he was found before they could set sail. He was imprisoned, yet he still made his case for reform. They executed him for it. He was just twenty-nine when they decapitated him. A tragedy. If he had lived for another nine years, he would have seen the changes for which he had campaigned come to pass. The end of the Tokugawa shogunate. He didn't know it, but Shōin was one of the last samurai."

Furokawa opened the newspaper slowly and reverently,

peeling the leaves away to reveal what was hidden beneath. It was a *tantō*, a blade not quite long enough to be considered a sword yet too long to be a dagger. It was double edged, around thirty centimetres in length and with inscriptions on the hilt.

Furokawa held it up and turned it so that the light caught on the dull metal blade. "It is a *shinshinto*," he said. "You know anything about them?"

Miyasato shook his head. He didn't and wasn't interested in learning. He wanted to get his money and go. The longer he waited to collect Sakura and Yamato, the better the chance that his father would find out what he had done. But he couldn't insult a man as prone to offence as Furokawa. He had to hear him out.

"A samurai would carry a *katana* while on the battlefield and a *tantō* for close work. This blade would have been ceremonial for Shōin. And the most ironic thing of it all? Shōin never had the chance to go to America, but his *tantō* did. No one knows how it got there, but it was found in the attic of an academic in California. The inscription here, on the *nakago*"—he turned the sword so that Miyasato could see the hilt core—"confirmed that it was his." He held it up. "This sword symbolises the moment that Japan changed, the moment we looked outwards rather than inwards. It is progress. That is why I want it."

And it will look very nice on your wall, Miyasato thought.

"Now," Furokawa said. "You need to be paid."

Furokawa looked over to the big man, who was observing from the other side of the alley, and gave a shallow nod of his head. The man disappeared into the restaurant, and when he returned, he was carrying a small sports bag. He brought it over to the table and set it down in front of Miyasato.

"Your turn, Nishimoto-*san,*" Furokawa said. "Open it."

Miyasato took hold of the zip and pulled it toward him, opening the mouth of the bag as he did so. He looked inside: the bag was full of banknotes. He had agreed to a fee of ¥10 million—around $100,000—and he hoped it would be enough to get him and his family to the United Kingdom and then set them up there.

"I've given you a little more than you asked for," Furokawa said. "You've taken a risk for me, and I believe in rewarding those who take chances. There's another million yen there. I give it to you with my thanks."

"Thank you," Miyasato said. "I'm grateful."

Furokawa bowed his head. He took the *tantō*, admired it for a moment, and then gave it to his bodyguard. "Take it back to the house."

The man bowed, took the sword, and walked away.

Furokawa smiled at Miyasato. "Are you sure I can't tempt you with a glass of sake to celebrate a job well done?"

"That's very kind," Miyasato said, "but I'd rather be on my way."

"Of course. You'll be leaving the city, I expect. Your father will be unhappy when he finds out what you've done."

Miyasato fought his nerves, stood, bowed his head respectfully, and took his leave. Unhappy? That was an understatement. He would be *murderous*, but that didn't matter. Miyasato did not intend to be anywhere near the old man ever again.

Miyasato hurried back through the festival crowds to the parking lot where he had left his car. He looked over his shoulder as he made his way through the busy streets, convinced that he would see someone that he knew following him. He knew that his father would find out that he was responsible for taking the sword and, when he did, his reaction would be violent. The only thing that kept him going, and put strength in his legs, was the thought of returning to Sakura, collecting Yamato and then heading straight for Narita and the ANA flight that would deliver them to their new life abroad.

He opened the driver's side door, tossed the bag of money into the footwell of the passenger seat, and got in. He started the engine and pulled out. Traffic was heavy, just as it usually was at this time of day, and it took him thirty minutes to negotiate it. He slowed down as he ran into congestion and, trying to save time, he took out his phone and called his wife.

She picked up on the second ring. "Where are you?"

"Five minutes away," he said.

"How did it go?"

"It went well. I'll tell you later. Have you seen your father?"

"Yes," she said. "He wouldn't talk to me."

"I'm sorry, Sakura."

She didn't reply. Her relationship with her father, Hachirō, had soured after their marriage. Hachirō and Takashi were brothers and Takashi was father to Miyasato and Katsuro. There had been a time when Hachirō and Takashi had got along, but then Hachirō had suffered a crisis of conscience that stemmed from his role in the family business, and a fissure had developed between them.

Miyasato had agreed with Hachirō's decision to step away, but felt that his uncle's refusal to give his blessing to his marriage to Sakura made the old man a dreadful hypocrite. Hachirō might have forsworn the yakuza now, but that had not always been so. He had been *wakagashira*, or first lieutenant, just as Takashi had been. Miyasato had chosen a different path when he had decided that he could not stomach the things that he was asked to do. Takashi had not suffered the same qualms and had risen to the top.

The choices made by Miyasato and *his* own brother, Katsuro, mirrored those of the two old men. Katsuro was all-in with the yakuza, determined to impress his father and rise to the top of the clan. But Miyasato had rejected them, just as Hachirō had rejected them. Miyasato wished that Hachirō would approve of him, if only to prevent Sakura from having to choose between her father and her husband, but, on reflection, he supposed that it didn't matter. She had chosen.

"Where are you?" he asked her.

"Ogikubo," she said. "Outside Otaguro Park."

"On my way."

"Be careful, darling."

"I will. We're nearly there."

They had been planning their escape for a month, but had only felt confident enough to make the final preparations—packing their cases and purchasing their flights—yesterday. Miyasato was fearful—and rightly so—that his father or brother would find out what he had done, and had insisted that there must be nothing in their lives that would provide any evidence to back up their possible suspicions. That meant they could not leave packed cases around the apartment in Hiroo on the off-chance that anyone else from the clan might visit and see them. It was only now, when the die had been irretrievably cast, that he had told Sakura to get started.

He pulled up outside the entrance to the park and saw

that Sakura was waiting for him. He reached over, opened the door and pushed it back for her.

"Well?" she said. "Did you get it?"

"Open the bag," he said with a grin, nodding to the bag in the footwell.

She sat down in the seat, hoisted the bag up onto her lap, unzipped it and looked inside. "Oh, my goodness."

"That's what our new life looks like. It gets us away from here, away from my father, your father, my brother—all of it."

She leaned over and kissed him. "I can't believe it."

"Did you transfer our savings?"

"I did."

"But you left a little for emergencies?"

She said that she had. They had a little money themselves, and, rather than lose it, they had agreed to move it into a Swiss bank account, where it would be difficult to trace. It felt like another definitive step on the way to their departure, the severing of one of the final ties to Tokyo and their old lives.

Miyasato put the car into drive and pressed down on the accelerator.

They just had one more thing to do.

MIYASATO REVERSED the car into the space that came with their nanny's house and turned off the engine.

"We need to be in and out," he said. "No delays. We get Yamato, pay Ichika and go."

"I know," Sakura said. "You don't have to remind me."

"I know I don't." Miyasato leaned across the car so that he could kiss his wife. He held his palm against her cheek and looked into her eyes. "Nearly there. This time tomorrow, we'll be in London."

She nodded and smiled at him. He could see the uneasiness in her eyes and couldn't really blame her for it. He was uneasy too, but, he reminded himself, the worst of it was over. The transaction was done, he had the money they needed, and now they just needed to collect their son and get to the airport.

He got out of the car and waited for Sakura before they both walked quickly to the front door. He wondered, again, whether he should have suggested that Sakura take Yamato to the bank with her, but then discounted it as fruitless second-guessing. They had talked about it, and Sakura had argued that she would be much faster without him. She was probably right, he thought, although it was difficult not to think that they could be on the way to Narita now if Yamato had been with her. Never mind.

Miyasato opened the door and stood to the side so that Sakura could go in first.

"Ichika? We're here. Where—"

Sakura screamed.

Miyasato stepped to the side so that he could look around her.

Their nanny, Ichika, was lying face down on the carpet in the middle of the living room. Blood had gathered around her head and shoulders, and Miyasato could see from the bloody furrow beneath her chin that her throat had been slit.

He reached for his pistol just as he became aware of movement behind him. He was too slow to prevent the crushing blow that caught him just above his left ear, and he stumbled forwards, his head ringing, and fell to his knees. He put out his hands to break his fall and looked back to see

Katsuro standing there. His brother had been waiting in the bathroom for them to come inside. He had a pistol in his hand and he pointed it at Miyasato's head.

"Stay down," he said, a spiteful leer on his lips.

"You don't have to do this," Miyasato said.

"Where's my son?" Sakura said, panicking. "Where's Yamato? What have you done with him?"

"He's safe," Katsuro said. "He's with his grandfather."

"No," Sakura said. "No, no, no…"

"Too late for that," Katsuro said, grinning at her. "You should have thought of that before you allowed my idiot brother to do something as *stupid* as steal from our father."

"Please," she begged. "Katsuro, *please*."

"Be quiet."

Katsuro took a step forward and booted Miyasato in the ribs.

"Where's the *tantō?*" Katsuro barked.

"I don't know what you're talking about."

"Yes, you do. You took it. Father wants it back."

"I would never do that," Miyasato said, although he knew that it was hopeless.

There were footsteps at the door and Miyasato turned his head, painfully, to see two other men step inside. He recognised them: Tsukasa and Wakabayashi, both of them *shatei*—little brothers—foot soldiers who were loyal to Katsuro. They made their way to Sakura; Tsukasa forced her hands behind her back while Wakabayashi secured them with a cable tie.

"Leave her alone," Miyasato said. "She has nothing to do with this."

"She has *everything* to do with it," Katsuro said. "It's her fault. You were never like this before you met her. You would never have thought about leaving."

"I've wanted to leave for months. It's nothing to do with her."

Katsuro smirked again. "You can say that if you want, but I know better. It's Sakura's fault. She'll pay for her actions, just as you will."

Miyasato felt a bloom of anger that quickly became rage, and, fists clenched, he started to his feet. But before he was halfway upright, Katsuro kicked him flush on the chin. It was a hard blow; the ringing in Miyasato's ears intensified, and darkness gathered at the edge of his vision. He fell onto his face and stared into the unblinking eyes of their nanny, at her blood smeared across the carpet, just inches away.

Katsuro knelt down and leaned in close enough to hiss into his brother's ear, "She's *ruined* you, brother, and now you're both going to pay for what she made you do."

PART I

SUNDAY

1

J ohn Milton ran his fingers across the roof of the car, down the windshield and across the hood. It was a 1970 Pontiac Le Mans, specified as a two-door convertible with an interior from the Luxury Le Mans but with the front seats swapped out for Strato buckets. She was painted in royal blue with a big V8 engine that had been a joy as it had eaten up the miles.

The man who was interested in buying the car sucked his teeth. "She's a beauty."

"She certainly is," Milton agreed.

He had placed an ad on eBay when he arrived in Panama, and the very first offer had been at the asking price. The prospective buyer—a man called Durán—was the owner of a used car dealership specialising in American cars, and Milton had driven the Le Mans across town this morning to close the deal. The business was not quite as grand as the website would have had him believe, but there were some nice cars in the lot of a similar vintage to the Pontiac. That had given Milton some encouragement. He knew that it was foolish, but he had grown fond of the car during the long drive, and he was pleased that it might be going to a purchaser who would appreciate it.

Durán scratched his chin. "And you've driven down from where?"

"Mexico."

"Like—a road trip?"

"That's right."

"How many miles did you put on the clock?"

"Quite a few. And I didn't have a single problem."

That was the truth. Milton had driven over four thousand miles during the last three weeks, and, in that time, the car had behaved perfectly. It had started every time he turned the key, and had not complained as he navigated the mountain switchbacks through Guatemala and Honduras, then down through Nicaragua, Costa Rica and, finally, into Panama.

"I didn't know you'd come so far," Durán said. He winced. "I'm not sure I can offer quite what I said in the email."

"I gave you the mileage when we spoke," Milton replied patiently. "I actually overestimated it by ten miles. It's a perfect runner. And the price is the price—take it or leave it. If you don't want it, someone else will."

Durán exhaled, feigned reluctance, and then—after seeing that Milton was not going to budge—he caved in. "Fine. Twenty thousand. Come through into the office and we can sort out the paperwork."

Milton gave the Pontiac a final wistful look. He was going to miss it. He had given some thought to continuing the trip all the way down to Argentina, but didn't want to press his luck. He had made an appointment with an old acquaintance in Bali, and, given that he had two long flights ahead of him—to Istanbul and then to Denpasar—he wanted to get going. He had been travelling as John Smith, and that was now a lot more precarious than it had been before. His old legend would serve him one final time, and then it would be retired. Milton intended to be someone else from now on.

The dealer indicated that Milton should follow him. Milton tapped the hood of the car—a final thank-you for a journey well done—and made his way to the hut where the transaction could be completed.

MILTON TOOK a taxi back to the hotel. He opened the window and let the warm air blow over him. The last month had been a balm. He had allowed himself the luxury of unplugging from the world, forgetting what had happened to him in Colombia and then Kansas City, where his fears—that Group Fifteen had resumed the hunt for him—had been confirmed. He had planned to take a road trip across America from coast to coast, but had recalibrated his itinerary on the basis that it would be much harder to locate him in South America than it would have been if he had stayed north of the border.

His choice had been more than vindicated. Apart from the anonymity that it had afforded him, the trip had been rewarding. He had stopped at San Cristobal de las Casas, the heart of the Mayan culture, and had taken a boat trip to the ruins at Yaxchilan. He spent two days in the frontier town of Frontera Corozal and had diverted to observe the waterfalls of Agua Azul. He visited the ruins at Tikal, drove through the volcanic Cerro Verde national park, and toured the canyons around León. The dislocated shoulder that he had suffered in Kansas City had healed without complication.

He had eaten well, had run every morning and swam when he could, and, as a result, he felt better than he had in years.

But all good things eventually come to an end, and he was at the end of the road. His flight to Turkey was at ten o'clock tomorrow morning. He had one more night to enjoy himself.

2

M ilton awoke late after a deep and restful sleep and looked around the small hotel room. The sunlight streamed in through the curtains, highlighting the threadbare patches and stains in the material. The room in the República was not luxurious by any stretch of the imagination, but it had suited his needs well. He had wanted somewhere quiet, cheap and anonymous. The small room had met all three of his criteria.

He showered and dressed in loose clothing that would be comfortable while he was travelling. He satisfied himself that he had left nothing behind, picked up the gym bag that contained his small collection of clothes, his books and his toothbrush, and left the room. He would not be coming back. His next stop was Istanbul, and then he would take a second flight to Bali.

The fact that he had to travel to the island was no inconvenience at all. Milton had been there once before to deliver justice to the unconvicted mastermind of a bombing that had murdered twenty people in 2005. It had been a typical working trip for him—in and then out within the space of a few hours—but he had found the island to be beautiful and had always intended to return. The circumstances of this visit were not quite what he would have preferred, but it was what it was.

He shut the door behind him and made his way down the undecorated but functional fire escape of the hotel, stepping over the piles of laundry that littered the stairwell. The elevator was unreliable and he had a plane to catch. He did not want to miss it because he was trapped in a metal box.

He walked out into the foyer of the hotel and saw the elderly man who staffed the desk. The man was arguing with a couple of backpackers whom Milton had noticed yesterday afternoon. Milton stood behind the two youngsters and gathered that they were debating the cost of the room. The male backpacker—an American—was trying to negotiate a discount because the room he and his female companion had stayed in was—he said —"crawling with lice." His girlfriend scratched herself a couple of times to make the point. Her companion grew angrier and angrier with the elderly concierge.

Milton stepped forward. "How much is the room?" he asked the man behind the desk.

The elderly man shook his head. "You paid already."

"Their room?"

"Thirty-five dollars."

Milton dug into his pocket and pulled out four tens and placed them down on the counter.

"We don't need your charity," the male backpacker said with a forced smile.

Milton frowned at him. "It's not charity. Your parents probably spent more on your teeth than this man earns in a year. Why not just say thanks and go on with your day?"

The backpacker's girlfriend stifled a laugh before

crossing her arms over improbably firm breasts. "Come on, Casey," she said, her voice nasal. "We're done here."

Casey fixed Milton with a hard stare. Milton could almost hear his brain working as he tried to come up with a reply that would enable him to save face in front of his girl. Milton returned the stare with interest until the young man thought better of it. He snorted derisively and turned around.

Milton turned his attention back to the elderly concierge.

"Can you get me a taxi to the airport?"

"Of course."

"A proper taxi. I know what the fare should be—don't send someone who thinks they can take advantage."

"No problem." The man pulled a mobile phone from his pocket, and a moment later was barking into it in rapid-fire Spanish.

THE TAXI that arrived a few minutes later was an almost-new Toyota Prius. It rolled to a halt outside the hotel with a quiet electric whir. Milton was waiting outside the hotel, sweating in the sticky heat, and the taxi driver jumped out with a broad smile to greet him.

"Luggage, mister?"

Milton raised his hand to show him the small gym bag before he put it on the rear seat and climbed inside. The interior of the taxi was blissfully cool, and Milton settled into the seat, grateful for the relative comfort. The driver got in and turned to look at him over his shoulder.

"Where to?" he said, grinning and showing off a set of

yellowed teeth. The man was older than Milton had first thought. "You want to go have some fun?"

"Airport, please."

"You sure? I know lots of good places."

"Airport." The driver's smile slipped a little as he turned back around and flipped the small red sign in the corner of his windshield down to show that the cab was occupied. "Okay, okay. Seventy dollars. Very good price."

Milton stared pointedly at the meter sitting in the centre of the Toyota's dashboard. "The *right* price."

The two of them spent the rest of the journey in silence. It took half an hour to get from the hotel to the airport, not helped by an accident just before the start of the bridge over Rio Juan Diaz. The congestion eased as the driver accelerated onto the Pan-American Highway, and, for the rest of the journey, Milton watched the city whizzing past him in a blur of brand-new buildings and wide-open spaces.

They reached Tocumen International Airport with three hours to spare before Milton's flight. The driver pulled up into a bay reserved for taxis. The terminal was a sleek, futuristic building with a tall control tower that reached into the azure sky. The sculptured gardens were full of well-trimmed topiary, tended by bored gardeners. Milton checked the meter. It read thirty-eight dollars. He peeled off two twenties from the small roll in his pocket and handed them to the driver. He held up his hand to decline the change, grabbed his bag and stepped out into the humid evening.

3

The interior of the airport terminal was not as cool as the inside of the taxi had been, but it wasn't as uncomfortably humid as it was outside. Milton made his way through the entrance and past the armed police whose only job seemed to be to keep the street traders out.

He looked around for the nearest restroom and went inside. He found an empty cubicle, undid his gym bag and ran his fingers over the hidden compartment in the material that made up one side of the bag. He found the concealed zipper, undid it and pulled out the bundle of passports held together with a fraying elastic band. They were all in the name of John Smith, but issued by a number of different countries: the United Kingdom, the United States, Canada, Australia, New Zealand. He leafed through the documents until he found the one that he had used when he booked the ticket before he stepped on the bowl of the toilet, lifted up one of the ceiling panels overhead and hid the others in the void above it. He was done with John Smith and, after this flight, he would never use the legend again. Refreshing his cover was the reason that he was making this trip, but he had one more risk to run before he could relax in the comparative safety of a new identity.

Milton flushed the toilet and, after washing his hands, made his way back into the main terminal building. He stood for a few seconds, watching the hundreds of people rushing about, all eager to be anywhere but where they were. He found the Turkish Airlines check-in desk and joined the queue. Milton was apprehensive as he waited in line. He had grown out his beard and was wearing clear glasses to break up the geometry of his face, but he had always been reluctant to submit his details to electronic retention, and that edginess was heightened to the point of neurosis today. He had read *Catch-22* for the first time during his trip and he had been amused by one line in particular: "Just because you're paranoid doesn't mean they aren't after you."

Milton knew, for a fact, that they *were*. And the people who were searching for him did not have his continued well-being in mind.

"Sir?"

The check-in clerk was ushering him forward.

Milton stepped up. "Good morning."

"Flying to Istanbul?"

"That's right."

"Passport and ticket, please."

Milton laid the documents on the counter and waited as the woman scanned them. He was aware that well-equipped and well-funded IT experts in London were engaged in the effort to locate him, and that the details remitted by airlines and airports would be among the first things to be searched. That was the main reason he had dropped off-grid over the course of the last few weeks, paying for everything in cash and avoiding anywhere where his details might be taken. This was the most exposed he had been since he had left Kansas City, but there wasn't really an alternative if he wanted to move on.

"It all looks in order," the woman said. "Are you checking anything into the hold?"

"No, thanks," Milton said. "I'm travelling light."

"Very good, sir. Enjoy the flight."

PART II

MONDAY

4
_____

There were no direct flights from Panama City to Bali, so Milton had plotted a slightly circuitous route. He flew Turkish Airlines to Istanbul and slept on a bench in the arrivals hall while he waited for the Garuda Indonesia flight that would depart later that day.

He freshened up in the bathroom and made his way to the check-in. There were two staffed counters: one for first- and business-class passengers, and one for everyone else. The only difference between the two desks was the long queue that snaked back from the latter. Milton joined the end of that line and relaxed. It didn't matter to him how long he would have to wait. He was in no rush.

He passed the time people-watching. It was a habit that had been drummed into him and refined over his career, both in the military and in Group Fifteen. It wasn't enough just to notice a person. You had to _see_ them. See who they really were. He concentrated on a young family a few places ahead of him. They had a small child and all the accoutrements that came with taking an infant on an airplane. There were toys, wet wipes, bottles of milk. Milton looked at the faces of the parents. Children also came with fatigue, frustration and unqualified love, or so he had been told. He wondered for a moment why anyone with a toddler would consider long-haul travel. The faces of the other passengers nearby all mirrored his own emotions; there was curiosity, sympathy for the ordeal that the family was about to endure, and fear that they might be seated close to them. Milton was hoping for the chance to grab a little extra sleep, and hoped that he might have a few rows between him and them to insulate him from any disturbance.

There was a minor commotion behind him. Milton turned to see a small procession making its way down the empty waiting area for the first-class check-in desk. Leading the procession was an airport orderly, the old man trying his best to manoeuvre a trolley that had been piled high with designer suitcases. It looked as if one of the trolley wheels was broken, because the whole edifice jerked to the side every few feet. The orderly pushed the trolley past Milton and, right on cue, it gave its most significant wobble yet. The suitcase at the top of the pile slid forwards, toppled over the edge and crashed onto the floor at his feet.

Milton bent down to retrieve it. He picked it up, surprised at how light it was, and placed it back on top of the pile. The orderly smiled at him in gratitude and muscled the trolley back onto its original course. Milton straightened up and noticed that a woman was also smiling at him.

He stared at her, aware—but too late to preserve any pretence of nonchalance—that his jaw had dropped. The woman was wearing a simple, thin navy-blue lace dress decorated with coloured flower prints that did little to hide her figure. Milton could not help but look, something that he had in common with every other man within twenty yards. He saw the mother with the child staring hard at her partner as he ignored the toy that the infant had dropped to the floor.

The woman smiled at Milton and changed course so that she was heading for him. She was *hāfu*—half-Japanese and half-European—and looked to be in her late twenties. The effect of her mixed-race heritage was stunning. Her long black hair fell down to her mid-upper arms and was halfway between mussed and styled. She was wearing a pair of large dark sunglasses, which she pushed up onto her head as she drew nearer, revealing deep brown eyes that complemented the fine structure of her cheekbones and elfin oval face perfectly.

"Thank you," she said in accentless English, widening her smile.

He smiled back. "My pleasure."

She walked on toward the first-class desk. She had a swing to her hips that, either intentionally or accidentally, attracted the attention of every man old enough to have facial hair. The orderly parked the trolley next to the desk and Milton watched as two male Garuda Indonesia employees fell over themselves to book the woman into her flight. One of the two clerks tried to shoo the orderly away, but the woman held out a perfectly manicured hand to stop him. She opened a small clutch purse and pulled out a note. The porter's eyes widened as he looked down at it: she had given him two hundred lire, and, as the orderly tucked it away in his uniform pocket, he clasped his hands together as if in prayer before bowing at the waist to thank her. Milton wasn't surprised. The tip was generous.

The staff took no time at all to process the woman through the check-in gate, making short work of her suit-cases. She walked toward a frosted glass door engraved with the words First Class Passengers Only, but then paused and turned. Her eyes ran down the ragtag queue of passengers until they found Milton. She smiled again, raised a hand in acknowledgement, slipped her round sunglasses back over her eyes, and turned to walk through the door.

"Bloody hell, mate." Milton turned to see a sunburned middle-aged man standing behind him in the queue. He sounded Australian. "Think you pulled."

"Just being helpful," Milton said.

He shrugged it off and turned back to face the slow-moving queue.

5

The man at the check-in desk regarded Milton carefully, his eyes flicking between the passport photograph and Milton's face.

"Flying to Bali, Mr. Smith?"

"I am."

The scrutiny didn't concern Milton overmuch; the photograph on the passport was of him, complete with the scar on his face. The member of staff, dressed in a simple black tunic with a zippered front and the airline logo on his left breast, closed the passport with a practised flourish and handed it back to Milton.

"Any hold baggage?"

"Just carry-on."

"Could you just read this for me, please?" The man pointed at a laminated sheet of paper on the desk in front of him as he tapped at his computer keyboard. Milton looked at the sheet. It was a standard list of do's and don'ts regarding what he could—and could not—pack in his luggage.

"I've read it."

"And you packed your bags yourself?"

"I did."

Milton found his thoughts drifting to the woman who had smiled at him while he'd been queuing. It wasn't just that she was attractive; there was something enigmatic about her. He pushed the thoughts to the back of his mind. The chances were that he would never see her again. He knew that was the reality, but it did not stop him from being ever so slightly disappointed.

The man directed him to security and Milton set off, groaning a little as he saw he had another long queue to negotiate. He settled in, removed his belt and unlaced his shoes, and took advantage of the pause to think about what he wanted to achieve when he arrived at his destination.

Uppermost on the list was a visit to see Victoria Carmichael. She had worked for Group Eight as an operational support officer. She was what was known in the trade as a cobbler: a very specific kind of forger, with a particular talent for creating legends for field agents and then 'papering' them. She provided the official documents that would ease their passage across borders and legitimise their presence in the locales where their targets could be found.

Milton had first met Carmichael as he prepared for an operation that took him into Texas. He had been given the file of a local official who was proving particularly tenacious in his investigation of an oil spill in Galveston Bay following the collision between a British-flagged tanker and a barge. Milton had been impressed with Carmichael's ingenuity and thoroughness; she had provided him with a set of perfectly aged passports, a driver's licence and even pocket litter—receipts and tickets and the like—that painted him as a lowly functionary who worked for the owner of the tanker. Milton had entered the country without issue, eliminated his target and then exfiltrated, all without exciting the attention of law enforcement.

Milton had assumed that would be the extent of their contact until—to his surprise—he had seen her in a meeting of Alcoholics Anonymous that he'd attended in Kensington one Saturday morning. Carmichael was fresh in the Fellowship, and Milton saw all of the doubt and struggle that he remembered when he had started to attend. Milton had stayed at the back and listened to her share her story, and saw—with absolute certainty—that she had no chance of staying the course without assistance. Although he hated the idea of being her sponsor, he was compelled to make the offer. Once Carmichael had got over the shock of seeing a Group Fifteen agent in her meeting, she had accepted Milton's proposal and, over the course of the next six months, they had attended meetings together. They had grown close and, perhaps unsurprisingly, had embarked on a short-lived and, in the end, unsatisfactory affair. While their desultory fling had not been the best idea, Carmichael had managed to stay off the drink and, just before Milton had gone AWOL, she had told him that she credited his kindness for her continued sobriety.

Milton had asked Ziggy Penn to track her down, and he had reported that she had married and taken her French husband's name—Deschamps—and was now living in Bali. It appeared that both she and her husband were working at the Hilton Hotel in Nusa Dua. Ziggy had provided access to Deschamps's Facebook profile, and Milton had seen photographs of what was evidently a very enjoyable life. It looked as if she had finally found the peace that she had been searching for, a contentment that had always eluded Milton.

Milton would have preferred not to bother her, but he

knew that his John Smith legend was burned. The Group was looking for him and he was going to need a new persona—perhaps more than one—if he was going to continue to stay off their radar. Victoria Deschamps was his best option, and Milton knew that she would consider that her sobriety formed a debt between them that had never been repaid. Milton had wondered about the good sense of contacting her in advance—David Tanner had demonstrated what fear of the Group could lead to when he had betrayed him in Kansas City—but he had concluded that their shared history meant that she would not betray him. He had called her and, after the initial shock at hearing from him after so long, she had invited him to come and visit.

6

Sakura Nishimoto stood by the window of the small first-class lounge. She had a view of the 787 that would take her and her fellow passengers to Bali; the airbridge was being hustled into place so that boarding could begin. She thought of the man who had helped with her suitcase and realised, with a wry smile of self-awareness, that he had made an impression on her. They had barely shared a word, yet there was something about him that she'd found calming. He had a presence—a *competence*—that had been reassuring. And she needed reassurance. She was anxious, just as she had been the last time she had been here to meet the Gülenist mercenaries, and the time before that. She wondered whether she would see him again.

She was tired, and, as she looked at her reflection in the glass, she saw the fatigue on her face. It had been a long night with not nearly enough sleep. She had arrived in Istanbul yesterday evening and had been driven out to Silivri, a town to the west of the city. She had met her usual contact and had spent an hour preparing herself for today's journey. It was the usual unpleasant and demeaning experience, but she had no choice but to do what she had been told, just as she had done all the times before.

"Sakura?"

She turned.

"Oh my God—Sakura, it *is* you!"

A flight attendant dressed in the distinctive brightly coloured pastel uniform of Garuda Indonesia was walking toward her with a broad smile.

Sakura found a smile. "Amber?"

The woman's smile grew even broader as she reached Sakura. The two hugged, air-kissed, and then hugged again.

Amber took a step back, leaving her hands on Sakura's shoulders. "You look fantastic."

"You too. You're flying for Garuda now?"

"They offered me a better job."

Sakura glanced at the badge that Amber wore on her lapel. "Head Purser. My goodness."

"I know. Going up in the world."

"I'll say. When did *that* happen?"

"Months ago. How long has it been since I saw you?"

Sakura frowned, trying to remember. "Six months. Might be a bit more."

"Nearer a year," Amber corrected. "We were crewing the flight down to Brisbane—do you remember?"

"I do," Sakura said, although she wasn't sure that she did.

"We had the worst turbulence ever. We'd just served dinner. The cabin was like landfill by the time we got out of it." Amber grinned at the memory. "Time flies. What are you doing now?"

"I'm still in Tokyo," Sakura said.

"Really? With your husband?"

"That's right," she said.

"And how's your son? He must be, what, five?"

Sakura's smile faltered. "Yes."

"What's his name? I know I should remember, but—"

"Yamato," Sakura cut over her. "He's in England. With his aunt."

"And he's doing okay?"

"He's fine. He's just having a little holiday. Like me."

"Obviously," Amber said. "First class to Bali. Goodness. I saw your name on the manifest, so I thought I'd come and say hi." She grinned, showing Sakura a perfect set of straight white teeth. "You must be doing all right if you can afford to turn left."

"I'm doing okay," Sakura said, determined to change the subject from the lies about her husband and her son. "What about you? What are you up to?"

Two men in navy-blue suits and white-topped peaked hats walked past them to the door. The pilot and co-pilot. Amber glanced at the one with four gold rings on the cuffs of his jacket.

"Not much," she replied.

Sakura followed her eyes, saw the pilot give Amber a wink, and realised what was going on.

"Amber!" she hissed playfully. "That is *such* a cliché. Are you serious?"

"For the moment? Yeah. Why not?"

"Is he married?"

"Probably. I've never asked."

They both laughed. Sakura realised that this meeting, although it was by chance, had presented her with an opportunity. Amber had been something of a party animal when they had been crewing together for All Nippon, and there had been more than one occasion when Sakura had rescued her from a sticky situation into which her drunkenness had deposited her. One, in particular, stood out: a man they had met in a bar in Phuket had offered to buy them both drinks. Sakura had immediately pegged him as a creep and had declined, but Amber—who had been drunk—had said yes. She went from mildly pissed to helplessly paralytic within fifteen minutes and had been about to go home with the man when Sakura stepped in and stopped her. She suspected that the man had doped her drink, and it had been a shock—although not a surprise—when, upon their next visit to the bar, a waitress had told them that the man had subsequently been arrested for rape. There had been other incidents, too, and Sakura knew that, with those in mind, Amber would likely be predisposed now to helping her out.

"What is it?" Amber asked her.

"Sorry?"

"You're a million miles away."

"It's nothing," Sakura said. "Look—actually, there is something. Could I ask you for a tiny favour?"

7

Milton's patience was wearing thin and the plane hadn't even left the gate. The co-pilot had welcomed passengers to the flight over the PA and explained that there would be a slight delay before they took off. The flight attendants circulated with bottles of water and complimentary magazines, but Milton wasn't particularly interested in either. He just wanted to get going.

He leaned his head to one side and looked down the aisle toward the front of the plane. All the passengers were seated and only the crew were moving about. He watched as they checked seatbelts, secured bags in the overhead bins, and fussed about the cabin. One flight attendant walked down his aisle, glancing from left to right. She was looking for someone. The woman caught his eye, paused and looked at him for a long second or two. He saw her pause as she noticed his scar—it was a reaction to which he was accustomed—before she swept past him and continued down the cabin. She returned a few seconds later and swished past again. There were two men sitting in the seats immediately ahead of him, and Milton noticed as the man directly in front of him leaned out and followed her progress. Milton overheard the man and his friend egging each other on, their accents giving them away as Australian.

"Look at her," the man said. "She's gorgeous."

"How do you turn a fox into an elephant?" his friend asked.

"Yeah, I know—marry it. Very funny."

The two continued in the same vein, making no effort to hide their lecherousness or their lack of respect.

The flight attendant disappeared through the curtain that separated economy from business, closing it behind her. The curtain was reopened a fraction later and Milton saw someone peering through it. It closed again as the co-pilot announced that they would shortly leave the gate. Milton closed his eyes and tried to ignore the screams of the small child for whom he had given up his window seat so that the family could sit together. He knew from experience that the minute the flight took off, the screaming would get even louder. He would put his earbuds in as soon as they were up, and listen to some music. He was wondering what he would play—Queens of the Stone Age or The Jesus and Mary Chain—when he noticed the flight attendant had returned to stand next to him.

"Excuse me, sir?"

She had squatted down next to him and was leaning in close to his ear. He could smell her perfume and the mints on her breath.

"Is everything okay?"

"Oh yes," she said. "I'm very sorry to disturb you." She spoke in perfect English, with only the faintest trace of an accent. "I'm afraid there has been a mix-up. Could you come with me?"

Milton looked at the woman's badge. Her name was

Amber, and, according to the badge she was wearing, she was the chief purser.

"Of course. Where to?"

"You're supposed to be in a different seat," she replied with a faint smile. "I'm ever so sorry for the error, but I'll take you forward if that's all right?"

Forward? Milton decided not to press too hard and got to his feet, using the seat in front of him to help himself up. He made sure that he pulled back on it as hard as he could so that he rewarded the Australian for ogling the flight attendant. It was petty, but that was fine; Milton could do petty. He collected his bag from the overhead bin and stared down at the man before following Amber down the aisle; the man tried to hold his eye but lost his nerve and looked away.

8

Sakura looked at her reflection in the bathroom mirror. She blew her breath out through her cheeks before putting a hand to her sternum. Her heart was racing. She took another breath and held it for a count of five. Just like Katsuro had told her to do when she had first started to work for Takashi.

Inhale.

Hold for five seconds.

Exhale.

Pause.

Repeat.

It didn't work. The exercises were a waste of time. Her heart was thudding just as quickly again as soon as she stopped. She turned the tap on and splashed lukewarm water over her face before patting it dry with a soft paper towel. With a final look at herself in the mirror, Sakura pushed the button on top of the cistern and opened the door.

SAKURA RETURNED to the first-class cabin and noticed the man who had taken the empty space next to her. The cabin was configured in a 1-2-1 layout, with the two seats in the middle separated by a privacy divider. There were just eight seats in the cabin; each was luxurious and could recline all the way back to make a bed. Each seat had its own entertainment system, complete with a large flatscreen and complimentary headphones, with a fold-down table that could easily have accommodated a small family, let alone a single passenger.

The man got to his feet to check his bag and then saw her. "Hello again," he said, surprised.

"Hello," she said with a smile.

They both sat down. Sakura looked at him as she fastened her seatbelt, never once taking her eyes from his face. She had found him distinctive when she had seen him earlier. It wasn't just his eyes that had caught her attention, although they were very striking. He had a full beard, but it did not completely hide the scar that extended from his right eye to the corner of his mouth. It didn't look as if it had been caused accidentally, and Sakura suspected that he was someone who at the very least had experienced violence. He looked fit and strong and capable, and, if her initial assessment of him was correct, he was used to delivering a sound beating when required.

He looked at her with an uncertain smile. It was a reaction with which Sakura was familiar. She knew that she was beautiful. Her parentage—a British mother and a Japanese father—was a genetic lottery with excellent odds. Sakura had got more numbers in that draw than most.

"Are you English?" Sakura asked.

"Why do you say that?"

"The accent."

"Is it that obvious?"

"A little."

She pretended to study the menu as the noise of the engines increased.

"Have they offered you champagne yet?"

"I just sat down."

"They're carrying two today: Billecart-Salmon 2006 Vintage Brut and Billecart-Salmon Brut Rosé. They're both good."

"I don't drink."

"Not at all?"

He shook his head. "Not at all."

"*That's* a shame. Not even for a special occasion?"

"What would that be?"

"Getting upgraded."

The man laughed. One of the other flight attendants came by with a glass of orange juice and carefully placed it down on the table attached to his seat. The man took it and sipped. His movements were economical and considered.

Sakura asked for a glass of the Brut Rosé and then gestured back toward economy. "It'll be a lot more comfortable up here than back there."

"Much more."

"Good," Sakura replied, warming to him. "I'm Sakura, by the way."

The flight attendant returned with a flute and a bottle of champagne. She showed Sakura the label, removed the cork, and then poured. The man raised his glass, and Sakura leaned across the lowered privacy screen to touch her flute against it. She took a tiny sip. She knew that she couldn't have too much, but she didn't want anyone to notice her abstinence.

"Can I ask you a question?" he said, placing his glass down.

"Of course."

"Is my being up here anything to do with you?"

"Why would you say that?"

"I don't know—it just seems very coincidental after what happened at check-in."

She paused before answering, determined to make sure she pitched her reply correctly. After a few seconds, she decided to be honest, or at least after a fashion.

"You were very chivalrous. Everyone else just stood there watching. I thought that was nice of you, so I called in a favour."

"The porter would have picked it up."

The aircraft lurched back, causing their glasses to slide an inch.

"But he didn't. *You* did." Sakura anchored her champagne, desperate to pick it up and drain it although she knew that she could not. "I've always thought that one good turn deserves another. Don't you think?"

She gave him a grin as the aircraft settled and reversed into position.

"You got me an upgrade because I picked up your case?" He sounded dubious, but, at the same time, a smile played across his lips.

She shrugged.

"Well, it's very generous. How did you manage it?"

"I used to fly myself," she said. "I can still pull the odd string."

"Well, whatever you did, thank you."

She offered her hand for him to shake, leaning across the privacy screen.

"I didn't catch your name?" she said, twitching the corners of her mouth in a way she knew men appreciated.

"I'm John," he replied, shaking her hand. His grip was firm, but gentle at the same time. Measured and reassuring. "John Smith."

Milton relaxed in his seat as the 787 lumbered along the taxiway. The next few hours promised to be more comfortable than he had expected. Amber was folding the demonstration life jacket away after concluding the safety demonstration at the front of the cabin. She stowed it in one of the overhead bins, glanced down the aisle, and gave Sakura a wink that Milton noticed before taking her place in the jump seat.

"I take it that's who you called a favour in from?"

Sakura grinned, showing off perfect white teeth. "Guilty as charged. I used to work with her."

"You were air crew?"

"I used to be."

They paused for a moment as the engines roared, the plane racing down the runway and climbing into the air.

"What were you doing in Istanbul?" she asked once they were aloft and it was a little quieter. "Holiday?"

"Just transiting," he replied. "I flew in from South America yesterday."

"Really?"

"I took a road trip. I started in Mexico, then headed south and ended up in Panama."

"That sounds fun."

"It was."

"And Bali?"

"I'm going to visit a friend. She works at a hotel there."

"Which one?"

"The Hilton."

"In Nusa Dua?"

Milton nodded.

"It's gorgeous. You'll love it."

The airplane turned slowly, and out of the window Milton could see the steel-framed airport below with the sun glinting off the glass-domed roof. They spent the next fifteen minutes enjoying a casual chat while they waited for their food to be prepared. There was a member of the crew in chef's whites supervising the preparation of dinner, and the smell of garlic quickly filled the cabin.

Milton saw that Sakura had some red lines in terms of what she was content to discuss with him. That was fine—so did he—but it made him curious. She told him she was from Miyazaki Prefecture, about an hour and a half by plane from Tokyo, and that she had lived with her grandmother—a woman she referred to as Oba-*chan*—and her father after her mother had died when she was young.

"What about now?" Milton asked. "Are you married?"

He had noticed that she did not wear a ring, but he wasn't sure what the customs were in Asia. Her face fell as he asked the question, and he caught a flash of pain. It lasted for only a split second before her expression hardened again, but it was long enough for him to notice.

"No," she said quietly. "I was. But not anymore."

"I'm sorry," Milton said. "It's none of my business."

"No," she replied. "It's not."

There was a fresh steel to her tone that took Milton by surprise. She stared at her hands clasped in her lap. Milton was wondering whether he should apologise again when Amber arrived with their meals.

"Thank you," Sakura said as the woman put a china plate down on her table and fussed with the cutlery. "That smells lovely."

She waited for Amber to leave before she looked over the divider at Milton again.

"It's I who should say sorry. My husband—Miyasato—died not that long ago. It's still..." Her voice trailed off, and she cleared her throat before continuing. "It's still very difficult to talk about it, and I wasn't expecting your question."

She met his eyes; Milton saw that they were damp. She looked away and there was another moment of silence. Milton could see that the memory of her loss was still raw, and, rather than probe any deeper, he changed the subject.

"So, what do you do now that you don't fly?"

She took a sip of her refilled champagne. "I'm an executive for an import-export company in Tokyo. They're always looking for new markets, and they send me to find them. Istanbul looks interesting, so I've been digging around there for the last week."

"And Bali?"

"The same. They export a lot of rice. I have a meeting with a producer to see whether we can agree to a deal to bring some of it to Japan."

She said it with an expectant face, almost as if she was asking him for approval for what she did. He smiled at her. This was turning out to be an unexpected journey. He relaxed in his seat. It wasn't all that long ago that he had been sitting in economy, concerned about the child who he knew was going to cry, and irritated with the lecherous boor in front of him. Now he was sitting in a first-class suite, next to a beautiful woman who seemed—for reasons he couldn't quite fathom—to have taken an interest in him.

10

Sakura poked at her chicken with her fork, moving it around the plate. It wasn't that she wasn't hungry—she hadn't eaten for hours—but that she was feeling a little unwell. She told herself it was just the nerves. The alternative was not worth thinking about.

She looked at Smith and saw that he was shovelling *pad kee mao* into his mouth as if it were his first meal in days. She felt bad about snapping at him when he'd asked whether she was married. She was being honest when she had said that she wasn't expecting the question, and it was still a difficult subject for her to talk about. Everyone who asked the question wanted to ask a natural follow-up: *how* had Miyasato died? The truth—that he had been murdered by his brother at the behest of his father—was not something that she could share.

"How's the chicken?" Smith asked.

"Very good," Sakura said. "The sauce is delicious. And the rice?"

Smith held up his empty bowl. "It was okay," he said with a self-deprecating smile. "Maybe I was hungrier than I thought. Eat when you can, sleep when you can. That was drummed into me a long time ago."

"Drummed into you where?"

"What?"

"The phrase? What is it? Military?"

He paused before replying. "That's right," he said. "Eat when you can, sleep when you can. Because you never know when you'll be able to do either again."

"Is that what you do, then? You're in the military?"

"Not anymore. Once. A long time ago."

"You're full of surprises," she said, pushing the table away from her chair. Sakura picked up her clutch purse in one hand and stood up. "Would you excuse me for a moment? I just need to pop to the bathroom."

SAKURA FELT PROGRESSIVELY WORSE. It had started with mild nausea, a feeling in the pit of her stomach that she was going to be sick, and the feeling became more acute until she had hurried to the bathroom to be sick, only to find that all that came up was acrid bile.

Her next trip to the bathroom an hour later was more productive, with the salty white cheeses, tahini and molasses that the Gülenists had given her for breakfast splashing down into the bowl of the toilet. She returned to her seat. The cabin lights had been dimmed, and most of the other passengers were sleeping, their seats reconfigured as beds. Amber had taken care of her seat, folding back the duvet so that the seat belt was visible. Sakura braced her arm on the armrest and lowered herself onto the thin mattress. She felt weak and was beginning to feel dizzy. She glanced across the divider, hoping for a word with Smith, but saw that he was asleep; he had been watching one of the films on the in-flight entertainment and had nodded off as the credits rolled up the screen. She felt a twinge of disappointment. He had an assuredness about him that had been consoling, and she would have appreciated some of that comfort now.

The nausea came again and then passed. It was strange and unpleasant, a combination of biliousness and drowsiness. She lay down, closing her eyes against a sudden swell of disequilibrium. Maybe she was tired. Sleep would help. She checked her watch. They had another five hours to go. She would try to pass the time in sleep and, when she woke, they would nearly be there. The thought of reaching her destination reminded her of who would be waiting for her.

Katsuro.

She tried to erase him from her dreams, but his image was persistent, like a stain that would not be wiped clean, and, as sleep finally came to take her, she saw his face: leering, derisive, expectant.

11

Milton woke up as the captain made an announcement that they would be landing in thirty minutes. He unclipped his belt and pushed the moveable TV screen out of the way. He had been watching the new Christopher Nolan film and had drifted off toward the end.

He looked over the divider and saw Sakura. She was sitting up and she looked dreadful.

"Hi," she said. Her voice was weak.

"Are you okay?" he said. "Are you sick?"

"Don't... don't feel well."

"How do you mean? Are you drunk?"

She gave a little shake of her head. "Not drunk."

He believed that. She had pretended to drink, but had only been sipping at the champagne in her glass. "Have you taken something?"

She nodded, then took a deep breath. "Swallowed."

Milton looked at her eyes. Her pupils, which had been so dark and languid, were now little pinpricks. "What have you swallowed?"

"Drugs," she said.

"What?"

"Heroin. Condoms. Lots and lots of little condoms."

He swore under his breath. This was *ridiculous*. He should have guessed that his good fortune would not be quite as auspicious as it had appeared. Why wasn't it possible that he could enjoy a surprise upgrade and the company of a good-looking girl who appeared to like him without being dragged into yet another moral quagmire? He had known it was too good to be true. Good things didn't happen to him. Not for a long time. He'd long since chalked that up to karma.

"That's why you were in Turkey?"

She nodded. "Not for money. Don't have a choice."

"You *always* have a choice."

"I don't. They've got my son. If I don't do what they say... I'll never see him again."

"Who has your son?"

"Takashi."

"Who?"

"Takashi Nishimoto. Yakuza." She took out her phone. "Look."

She opened the album and swiped clumsily through the photos. She found the one she wanted and held it up so that Milton could see it. It was a picture of a young boy; Milton wasn't the best judge of a child's age, but he guessed he was five or six. He was looking into the camera with a glum expression on his face. The background to the shot was what looked like a squalid bedroom: Milton saw the bars of a cot, dusty naked floorboards and a scattering of cheap-looking toys.

"That's your son?"

She nodded. "They sent that yesterday, before I..." She

paused, but Milton knew what she was going to say: *before I swallowed the drugs.* "They send me pictures to remind me... to tell me that I have to do what they want. So you're wrong. You're *wrong*, John. I don't have a choice. I *don't*."

This wasn't good, he told himself. Not good at all. The yakuza were blackmailing her into a career as a mule. As a body packer. She would smuggle their contraband across the border inside her stomach and then deliver it once it was safe to do so. It was exceptionally dangerous, and not only— as appeared to be the case here—if one of the packages leaked. The Balinese authorities took drug smuggling seri- ously. *Very* seriously. He remembered reading about a middle-aged British woman who had been arrested with cocaine in her suitcase; she was still on death row, waiting for her appointment in front of the firing squad. Sakura would face a similar fate. There was no way that she would be able to get through immigration without help.

Milton had no time for drugs, but he was not about to abandon her.

"I'll help," he said. "But you have to do exactly as I say. Understand? *Exactly.*"

She nodded.

"I'm going to say that you're drunk."

She shook her head. "Only had a sip of champagne."

"They won't know that on the ground. I'll say that we met on the plane and that you were knocking them back."

He tried to work out his own risk. He thought that he was safe enough. He didn't know Sakura. He had begun his journey in Panama, and Sakura had started in Turkey. There was nothing to connect them save the chance encounter in the queue. If he was asked, he would tell the truth: he didn't know her, she had arranged for him to be upgraded, and he had gratefully accepted. He would say that he thought she was drunk. How would he know what the real reason might be?

He would help her get into the country, and then he would get her some help.

After that?

He would wait and see. One step at a time.

Milton looked out of the window as the 787 descended. As the wings shuddered up and down, he caught glimpses of green fields, a highway with a long line of red lights, and a dense residential area. The wheels touched down with a soft jolt, and the engines roared briefly as the pilot applied reverse thrust. The plane came to a halt, and Milton undid his seatbelt as soon as the pilot turned the light off. It was very civilised in first, and, not for the first time, Milton couldn't help but compare what it was like here with what he knew would be the case in economy. It would be a scrum now as all the passengers tried to get their bags from the overhead bins at the same time.

"Here, sir," Amber said, handing Milton his carry-on bag.

"Thanks." He pointed at Sakura. "I don't suppose you could get hers as well, could you?"

Sakura was in her seat, her eyelids drooping. The flight attendant looked over at her quizzically.

"She's had a little bit too much to drink," Milton explained.

"I didn't think she..." Amber started, then let the sentence drift away.

She turned to Milton, a frown on her face, and he realised what she was thinking: she knew that Sakura had not been drinking heavily, yet here she was, apparently drunk. She must have wondered whether Milton had dosed her drink with something. Milton thought that she was going to say something, perhaps that she would take care of Sakura and that he did not need to concern himself, but, with a little shrug, she gave Milton a thin smile.

"Of course, sir."

Milton walked around the cabin until he was next to Sakura. He looked down at her. Her face was ashen. The realisation of what she had done, and what she was going to have to do now, must have broken through the narcotic fugue. She looked up at him with a fearful expression.

"I'm going to help you," Milton whispered as he leaned down to her.

Her eyes were wide and unfocused. "I don't feel good."

"I know you don't. Remember—you've been drinking. Say it."

"I've been drinking," she repeated.

He held out his hand and helped her to her feet. She took a step toward him and stumbled. Milton grabbed her by the elbow and held her up. There was perspiration on her forehead, and she looked more ill than drunk. He had his work cut out for him.

"Come on," Milton said. "We just need to get you through immigration."

She found the strength to stand. "I can do it," she mumbled.

Milton wasn't sure if he believed her, but helped her as she slipped her arm through the crook of his elbow.

Amber wheeled Sakura's case over to them. "Here you are," she said.

"Thanks."

She looked at Sakura with concern and then at him with suspicion, but, once again, she held her tongue and stepped aside so that Milton could help Sakura to the door. He slung his bag over his right shoulder and pulled Sakura's case with his right hand, his left hand looped around her torso. She was able to walk, but just barely, and he suspected that she would fall without his support. They reached the door and the cabin crew thanked them as they disembarked. An airbridge had been pushed into place against the exterior of the 787, allowing them access to the main terminal. Milton looked down through the windows to see the passengers from economy descending a portable stairway to the tarmac of the airport. They didn't have the luxury of the air-conditioned walkway, and several fanned their faces in the late afternoon heat.

Milton helped Sakura cross over the uneven join between the airbridge and the terminal. The other passengers from first were heading toward passport control. The fastest had already formed a loose queue in front of a counter where an official was getting ready to check their credentials.

"Sakura," Milton said.

Her eyelids were heavy again. Milton paused and pinched her on the underside of her arm, just above her elbow. She gasped and winced, her eyes snapping open.

"You need to stay awake. Have you got your passport?"

She looked at him with vacant eyes, her mouth open and her bottom lip trembling. "I don't feel well."

No kidding.

The cabin crew overtook them, walking together in a group. Milton saw Amber, but she took no notice of either of them as she and her colleagues diverted toward a door in the side of the corridor marked Cabin Crew Only.

"Where's your passport?"

Sakura didn't answer; instead, she closed her eyes and swayed forward. Milton anchored his arm around her slim hips to keep her upright. She was getting worse. There was no way that she would be able to answer even the most rudimentary question from the official, and he doubted that he would be able to speak for her. He shook his head. He couldn't risk it, but if trying to get her through immigration was off the table, what next? She needed medical attention, but he knew that if he alerted the locals to her predicament, she would be in serious trouble as soon as she recovered. Life in prison, if she was lucky.

So he couldn't do *that*, either.

So what *could* he do?

He looked around, assessing his options.

He was going to have to be creative.

13

M ilton stiffened his arm to keep Sakura upright and looked up. The official in the booth had been joined by a colleague, and now they were processing the passengers more quickly than before. Milton saw two policemen just beyond the booths. They were both carrying medium-frame revolvers attached to their belts with lanyards.

He looked around and assessed again. They were effectively in a tunnel, trapped between the airplane behind and the security checkpoint in front. They couldn't go back, and they couldn't go forward, so, with just one other option, Milton diverted to the door that the cabin crew had just used. It was on a sticky mechanism and was closing just slowly enough for Milton to catch it before it shut. Sakura moaned at the sudden movement, but Milton held her up and guided her toward the door. He pushed it with his shoulder, manhandling Sakura through as he glanced down the corridor at the policemen.

Milton took in their new surroundings. The interior of the corridor they were now in was functional rather than aesthetic. Areas like this, where paying clients were not supposed to be, did not need decoration; it was just the same in hotels and restaurants. Milton observed the bare walls and the industrial piping that ran along the ceiling as the door closed behind them with a resounding *thunk*. There was another door ahead of them and it was about to swing shut. It was too far away for Milton to reach, especially with Sakura in tow, but, just before it closed, someone stopped it and looked back through the gap.

It was Amber.

Her face fell. She turned to say something to whoever was in front of her and then walked back through the door to where they were standing.

"What are you doing in here?" she hissed, any trace of her earlier friendliness gone. She looked at Sakura and then at Milton, her brow furrowed. "What's going on?"

"We need to get out," Milton said. "She's not well."

"I can see that. And I *know* she wasn't drinking. So what did you give her?"

"I didn't give her anything," he said. "She's swallowed packets of drugs. I think one of them has split."

She was aghast. *"What?"*

"That's what she told me."

"Why would she do something as stupid as that?"

"She said she's been forced to do it. Someone has her son."

"My God." Amber's mouth fell open. "If she gets caught here..."

"I know," Milton said. "That's why I'm trying to help."

"You need to get her to a doctor. If they catch you helping her..." Fear flashed across her face. "If they catch *me*..."

Milton heard the sound of someone pounding on the

door that they had just come through. He set off toward the second door, hauling Sakura with him. Amber followed. Milton grabbed Sakura's arm, pulling it around his shoulder to give himself a more secure grip.

"Help me," Milton said. "Help me get her out of here."

"Are you *nuts?* They shoot drug smugglers here. I'm taking a risk even talking to you."

"Fine," he said. "I'll do it. Get out of the way."

Milton looked over Amber's shoulder, down the corridor through the second door, and saw a sign that indicated a fire exit. Milton shouldered through the door and helped Sakura to the exit.

"You can't go through there," Amber said.

"Why not?"

"It's locked," she said, gesturing to the padlock that secured the handle. "I know it shouldn't be, but—"

Milton ignored her, drew back his foot and drove his heel into the door, striking it just above the handle. The door flew open with a crash of splintering wood, and a rush of humidity swept into the corridor.

"Now it's not."

14

K atsuro Nishimoto was known to some as Popeye, on account of a muscular build that stood in contrast to his small stature. His beefy arms and powerful shoulders, combined with a technique that had been rendered perfect by hours of repetition, meant that he could hit a golf drive almost three hundred yards in the right conditions. His love of golf had also furnished him with another story that had coloured his notoriety: he had once beaten a man to death with a driver on the eighteenth hole of the Fan Ling course in Hong Kong. The story had it that the man Katsuro killed had wandered across the approach line between his golf ball and the hole. Not only was this a grievous infringement of the rules of golf, but the indentation of the man's shoes on the green had spoilt Katsuro's putt. The story was apocryphal, but Katsuro was happy to let it stand uncorrected. The reality was that the man he had killed—a businessman on Hong Kong Island—had owed a great deal of money to Katsuro's father, Takashi. Several polite requests for repayment had been made, all of them rebuffed. Katsuro was sent to sort the problem out. Takashi did not murder people on a whim, only when there was a serious message to be delivered. This message—that it was not acceptable to renege on your debts—had been deemed sufficiently important, and Katsuro had been dispatched.

Katsuro was waiting in the arrivals terminal. He was surrounded by hopeful-looking people waiting for family members, and bored drivers sweating in cheap suits as they held up signs advertising the names of the passengers they had been sent to collect. Katsuro had moved to the front of the throng to make sure that he didn't miss Sakura.

He resisted the temptation to scratch the scar that meandered from just below his left ear to his neck. It was a reminder of his first task when he'd joined the family business. Even though his father was the *oyabun*, Katsuro had still needed to be initiated when he came of age to become a *kobun*. It was his first kill, and he had been badly underprepared. The *kobun* from the Watanabe-*kai* had seen him coming, and there had been a struggle, during which the man had swiped at him with a blade. That Katsuro had fought him off and then killed him had gone some way to ameliorating the shame he felt from his injuries. The scar was a reminder that a slovenly attitude to preparation was dangerous, and he had never made the same mistake again. Katsuro clenched his teeth to distract himself from the itching, exacerbated by the humidity that even the powerful air-conditioning units in the foyer couldn't completely ameliorate. The fine woollen suit that he was wearing was not helping matters, but he was here on business, and appearances were important.

And—although he didn't like to admit it—he wanted to look good for Sakura. He hadn't seen her since the last run, and he had been looking forward to being reunited.

He looked to the automatic double doors that separated the arriving passengers from the main terminal building. They opened and closed every few seconds, and Katsuro peered through them, scanning the row of security booths. He could see a line of passengers beyond them, slowly funnelling between the booths as their passports were checked. He frowned. There was no sign of Sakura.

This was an easy job for Katsuro. He had refined his skills since his almost fatal initiation and was now highly adept. His repertoire went all the way from babysitting—the reason he was in Bali—to wet work when his father needed it. Takashi had made Katsuro responsible for developing the relationship with the *premans* on the island, and all of the first runs had been successful.

The job before this one had been more personal. Katsuro had murdered his own brother, Miyasato, after he had brought down disgrace upon himself by stealing from their father. Takashi blamed Sakura for turning her husband's head, and Katsuro had suggested that she be punished by working as their mule to smuggle the heroin that the *premans* wanted. His father had agreed, and Katsuro had set the plan in motion. It had gone well. Sakura was a beautiful and regal-looking woman, and, as Katsuro had suspected, a passenger like her—fresh from first class—did not fit the usual template for a body packer. The arrangement had been easy and a little boring, but he didn't mind. He was being paid well and took satisfaction in earning his father's respect. And, more than that, he was able to spend time with Sakura. She had been resistant to his advances at first, but it had not taken him long to remind her that it would be unwise to say no to him. There was her son to consider, he had said. And it wasn't as if she was indispensable. There were other good-looking women they could use.

Katsuro shifted on his heels. He was becoming impatient. His car was outside and he needed to take Sakura to the hotel. The process was simple: meet Sakura, take her to the hotel to shit out the heroin, then ensure that the drugs were delivered to the Laskar Bali gang. The relationship with the *premans* was fledgling, but potentially lucrative. Takashi had agreed to half a dozen runs as a demonstration of their efficiency and trustworthiness, and after the first five had gone well, this final delivery—if handled as smoothly as the others—could presage a more permanent relationship.

The doors slid open again. He glimpsed a woman in a navy-blue dress with a coloured flower pattern being supported by a Western man. It was too far away for Katsuro to see much detail, but he could tell that the man was white and of medium build, and that he was holding the woman up.

Sakura.

He heard raised voices from the immigration booths and then heard heavy footsteps behind him. He turned to see two policemen running toward the booths. Katsuro craned his neck to see what was going on, but Sakura and the man were out of sight now. He cursed under his breath, reminded himself to stay calm and objective, and considered his options. He could call his father and let him know that there was an issue, but that ran the risk that the old man would decide that he wasn't up to the task and had called for help.

That was not acceptable.

The other option—the only one—was to deal with this himself. He couldn't go further into the terminal; he had no ticket, so they wouldn't let him pass through immigration, and besides, he wasn't about to tell the authorities that he was here to meet a woman whom he knew to be carrying seven hundred grams of heroin inside her stomach.

He would need to regroup and consider his options. He turned on his heel and walked to the exit. Something had happened to Sakura, and he was concerned that the local police would get to her before he could.

There was no way he could let that happen.

15

Milton helped Sakura through the splintered fire door and out of the terminal building. She was barely conscious. He checked around him: although they were outside the terminal, they were still inside the perimeter wire of the airport. In front of them was a security fence, ten feet high and all business. Atop the fence, and angled away from the interior, was a concertina of razor wire. It was designed not to keep people inside the perimeter, but to keep people out. It didn't matter. It would still be impossible to scale, especially with Sakura in such a bad way.

Milton knew that they had been spotted. He could not be sure how long it would take the authorities to mount a proper response, so he set off across the tarmac as quickly as he could manage. He saw the tall red-and-white metal air traffic control tower, a rotating semicircular dish atop it. In the tower's shadow was a two-storey red-brick building, and beyond the fence to the left was a two-lane highway that was lined with black and white kerbstones.

He saw what he was looking for outside the red-brick building.

Vehicles.

There was a large white SUV with tinted windows and a bright orange Bajaj, a small three-wheeled vehicle that stood with its engine still running.

Milton reached the vehicles just as he heard shouting behind him. He looked back to see the two policemen from the security desk stepping through the broken fire door. The older one of the two was barking out orders in Indonesian. Milton had hoped to have an opportunity to hot-wire the SUV, but there was no time for that now. He went to the Bajaj and examined it. The vehicle was not much more than an adapted motor scooter with a bright orange frame around it to provide some protection from the elements. The original single rear wheel had been replaced by two wheels side by side, with a bench across the top for seating and an aluminium alloy monocoque chassis that provided a body of sorts. The Bajaj looked as if it was used to move staff around the airport. It wasn't luxurious, nor did it look particularly quick, but, Milton reflected as he pushed Sakura into the rear seat, the little engine was already running.

Once Sakura was safely stowed in the back—or as safely as was possible, given the open sides—Milton tossed their luggage in, then performed a rapid three-hundred-and-sixty-degree assessment. The policemen were running toward them, but they were still a decent distance yards away. One had drawn his weapon and was sprinting with it raised in the air. He would have to be a hell of a shot to put a round within twenty feet of the Bajaj from where he was, but Milton did not intend to stick around to let him chance his arm. He could see a young man waving at him through the smoked-glass window of the adjacent building. The man was frowning and shaking his head, and Milton guessed that he must have been responsible for the vehicle. Milton disregarded him and looked beyond the building to the access gate to the terminal compound.

It was slowly retracting to allow a blue sedan to roll inside.

It was a chance.

He got into the front of the Bajaj and saw that the controls were almost identical to the ones on the moped he used to ride when he was younger: in the centre of the driver's compartment was a set of handlebars with the gear selector on the left-hand side and the accelerator on the right. Milton gripped the accelerator handle and rotated it toward him. The engine burbled happily, its quiet chugging becoming a frantic but faintly asthmatic grumble complete with a billow of filthy smoke that was belched out of the exhaust. He tried to rotate the left-hand grip to select first gear, but nothing happened.

"Hey! Mister? *Stop!*"

Milton heard the shout over the racket of the engine. The man he had seen inside the building was on his way out. Milton saw the two policemen—both now with weapons drawn—less than fifty yards away. The gate that had opened to let the sedan into the terminal was closing.

Milton tried to engage first gear again, but the handle wouldn't move. He saw a gleaming silver pedal on the floor of the vehicle.

"Clutch," he muttered as he pulled back on the accelerator again and pushed his foot down on the pedal. He twisted the gear selector, and the engine clicked into first. "It's got a bloody clutch."

He eased up on the clutch and the Bajaj jerked forward.

He twisted the handlebars to the right to avoid the SUV, but, even with a narrow turning circle, the Bajaj was not quite going to make it. They sideswiped the vehicle with a loud crunch that set off the car's alarm. Milton opened up the accelerator to its stops and hammered the Bajaj toward the terminal compound exit, racing between the closing gates with just inches to spare.

16

Milton swung the Bajaj onto the main road outside the airport terminal. The two policemen who had been chasing on foot had given up, staring helplessly at them through the chain-link fence. The road headed back toward the terminal, and, although Milton wanted to go in the other direction, the central reservation was constructed of large cinder blocks that separated the carriageways. The blocks were painted black and white, and, as he pushed the Bajaj into its third and highest gear, they flashed by in a blur. There was no opening that would allow him to cross onto the lane that led away from the airport.

He looked over his shoulder at Sakura and saw, with relief, that she was still breathing, huddled on the seat where he'd put her. He could hear sirens behind them. Police. The officers had called for help. Milton needed to turn around, get them heading away from the airport and onto quieter streets where it would be easier to hide. Quite apart from what would happen to them in the event that they were caught, Sakura needed to see a doctor. Milton had a phone call to make to arrange that, and the sooner he made it, the better.

The terminal fence flashed by on the left. Milton was concentrating so hard on weaving in and out of the slow-moving traffic that he almost missed the break in the cinder blocks to his right. He saw his chance, angled the handlebars to the left, and gripped the brakes hard. The Bajaj slid into the turn, and Milton felt the high-sided vehicle begin to lean as one of the rear wheels lifted into the air. He compensated, leaning to his left so that he could shift weight across. He got the Bajaj back onto all three wheels just inches before striking a minibus taxi that had pulled up at the side of the road. He swept through the opening and rejoined the road, headed in the opposite direction. He opened up the accelerator, relieved that he could finally head away from the airport.

Milton saw the flashing lights of the police cars on the opposite carriageway. There were two of them, and they both slowed as Milton approached. The cruiser nearest to the central reservation turned sharply toward it and stopped and, as Milton sped past, he could see the driver glaring at him through the windshield. The blocks were at least eight inches tall, and Milton doubted that the car would be able to get across them without being grounded.

He eased off the accelerator, happy that—for the time being at least—the police were thwarted. The Bajaj was unstable, and driving it at high speed took concentration, especially given that the road was busy with traffic in both directions. He kept a close eye on the left-hand side of the road, looking for a way to get into the side streets, but all he could see were businesses and workshops in yards that bracketed the carriageway. It was possible that he might be able to find a way through and into the city itself, but Milton was not prepared to chance it. The last thing he wanted was to be caught in a dead end.

He glanced back over his shoulder and saw, to his dismay, that one of the police cars was halfway across the central reservation. An officer had stepped out of the vehicle and Milton guessed that he had moved the blocks by hand to create a way for the cruiser to get across. The driver hit the sirens as the car crossed the central verge. The second car turned in behind it.

Damn it.

Milton turned the accelerator back to its stops and held on as the Bajaj picked up speed.

17

K atsuro had been fortunate: the airport's short-stay lot was next to the arrivals area and, as he had hurried to his car, Katsuro had seen Sakura and the Westerner exiting the building. He watched as the man had loaded her into the orange Bajaj and then observed as it had raced out of the compound.

Katsuro drove out of the lot at speed and joined the carriageway in an attempt to locate the Bajaj so that he could follow it. He had been frustrated; the Bajaj was on the opposite carriageway and he had been helpless as it had raced by. He drove on until he saw a police officer moving the barricade that divided the road so that the two cruisers that were waiting could cross over and give chase. Katsuro did not see how he would be able to follow without giving himself away.

What could he do? There were CCTV cameras set at regular intervals along the road, and a large black rental bumping over the central reservation would only attract attention. Katsuro did not like attention of any sort, least of all from the authorities. He had *some* contacts in the Balinese police force, but they were all low-level functionaries. They were good for tidbits of information in exchange for a few rupiah, but not senior enough to bail him out if he had a problem.

He had no choice. He would have to wait and trust that he could pick up the scent.

He knew, with a sickening feeling in his gut, that he needed to alert his father. He found a parking spot and pulled over, then opened the door and stepped out into the heat. He walked a few steps away from the car, turned his back on it, and reached into his pocket for his phone. He dialled the number.

"*Otōsan*, it's me."

"Katsuro?"

"We have a problem."

"That doesn't sound promising."

"Our friend has left the airport."

"With you?"

"No, Father. With a Westerner. A man."

"I don't understand," Takashi said. "Why?"

"I can't say."

"Why are you telling me this? Find her."

"I will. And then?"

"The goods must be delivered. This is a valuable opportunity. We must show them that we can be trusted."

Katsuro bit his lip; his father made no effort to disguise his exasperation, and disappointing him was something that Katsuro could not tolerate. "I understand, *Otōsan*."

"Don't let me down, Katsuro-*chan*."

Katsuro pressed his lips together into a thin smile, ignoring his father's childlike suffix. He waited for more, then realised that he was listening to a dead line. He put his phone back in his pocket and turned to walk back to the car.

He decided to wait for a while to let things settle. The local police would either catch Sakura and her companion, or they would not. There was nothing he could do to influence what happened, but he would be ready to adapt to whatever fate allowed. He dropped into the driver's seat and tapped out a quick text to one of his contacts. He told him that there had been an incident at the airport and that he needed as much information as the man could provide. The quicker the update, he said, the more generous the reward.

18

Milton moved the Bajaj into the left-hand lane, ready to swerve into the first suitable turning that they reached. They sped past a low red-brick building with a tiled roof, a two-storey white house with a bicycle balanced on a veranda, and then a collection of other buildings separated from the road by a low wall with a crumbling façade. The sirens from the two police cars grew louder. He glanced in the wing mirror and saw that the leading car was gaining on him rapidly. The Bajaj was not fast, and the cruiser was only about a hundred yards away and closing quickly.

Milton saw an opening on the left and moved over to the right-hand lane to give himself the best chance of making the turn. He eased up on the accelerator to prepare for the manoeuvre and, after taking a quick glance to his left, he grimaced as the lead police car closed to less than twenty feet. The driver was preparing to undertake them on the inside lane.

Milton leaned to his left and jerked the handlebars in the same direction. The Bajaj started to tilt, more dramatically than the last time, but two of the wheels held the road and he made the turn.

Almost.

A small green and yellow cart with two large bicycle wheels on either side was right in front of them. A stove was lashed to the cart with a strap, and a selection of bottles had been arranged in the back. The cart's owner—an elderly man dressed in flip-flops and a white shirt over a traditional sarong—stared at him with wide eyes before realising that Milton's Bajaj was heading directly for him and his cart. The scooter caught the cart a glancing blow with a loud, splintering crash. The cart was upended, the bottles and the stove scattering across the road and sidewalk. The owner hopped out of the way with a sprightliness that belied his age and shook his fist as Milton wrestled the Bajaj back on course and raced down the narrow road that was now in front of him.

There was a screech of brakes from behind him. The police car had adjusted to the sudden change in route, and, as Milton looked in his mirrors, he saw that it was right up behind him again. The alleyway was much narrower than the main road, so narrow that the police car lost one of its wing mirrors to a metal fence as it continued the pursuit. Milton felt more confident, but it was still not ideal. He needed somewhere even more difficult to negotiate, somewhere he could go but the police cars could not.

He raced to the end of the alleyway and, to his annoyance, saw that it opened out into a wide parking lot. He looked left and right, scouring the space for an escape route. He saw a dark sliver between two buildings on the other side of the space, half hidden behind two large industrial bins. He angled the Bajaj toward the opening and twisted the accelerator all the way around. The police car flew out of the alleyway, its blue and red lights reflecting off the walls of the neighbouring buildings and the whoop of the sirens echoing loudly.

Milton had no idea what was at the other end of the passage. It might be a dead end, and, if it was, he and Sakura would be spending the rest of the day at the local police station, and what would happen after that would be anyone's guess.

No time to worry about that.

He aimed for the space between the bins.

The police car rammed the back of the Bajaj, causing it to veer wildly to the left and then the right. Milton grappled with the handlebars, keeping the front wheel lined up with the opening of the passage. He knew what the driver was trying to do: spin the Bajaj so that it toppled over. The *vehicle* clipped one of the industrial bins, the impact helping Milton to reorientate it and line it up for the passage. They leapt forward, disappearing into the passage a moment before the tyres of the police car squealed as it was brought to a sudden stop.

The alleyway was only just wider than the scooter, and Milton eased up on the accelerator. There was no way that the police cars could follow them now, so he risked a glance over his shoulder and saw, to his relief, that Sakura was still nestled on the rear bench, held in place by the seatbelt across her lap.

19

M ilton manoeuvred the Bajaj to the end of the alleyway before bouncing across a road and following the alley on the other side. He took a series of turns through the backstreets until he reached a small parking space at the rear of a run-down office block. There were only a few cars parked there, and he slotted the scooter between two of them, neither of which looked as if they had moved for a while. One of them—a venerable dark blue Nissan Skyline—had a thin film of dust across its bodywork.

Milton got out of the Bajaj, grateful to stretch his legs, and then checked on his passenger. Sakura was unconscious. She was pale, and, when he pressed his index and middle fingers to her neck, he could feel that her pulse was slow. He patted her cheek, but she did not stir, then he carefully pulled one eyelid open and saw that her eyes had rolled to the back of her head.

She was in a bad way.

Milton pulled his phone from his pocket. He had not even had the chance to turn it on since he had arrived in the country. He held down the button and waited for it to power up. The screen woke and the phone buzzed with two text messages welcoming him to Bali. He ignored them and opened his contacts, scrolling down until he found the name he wanted.

Victoria Deschamps.

Milton tapped her number.

"Hello?"

Milton could hear the sound of excited children in the background.

"Victoria? It's John."

"Hey," Victoria said. Milton could hear the warmth in her voice. "You made it. Fantastic. I'm by the pool. You at the airport? Want me to come and pick you up?"

"It's not quite as simple as that."

"What's up?"

"I need your help."

"Wait a minute." The children's voices grew quieter as, presumably, Victoria moved away from them. "What is it?"

"I need a safe place for a while."

"Right," she said. "Not what I expected."

"And a doctor."

"Are you hurt?"

"No. It's not for me. I'm fine."

"So?"

"I've got a woman with me. She's sick and needs treatment, but it needs to be discreet. Do you know anyone?"

"Possibly. Where are you?"

Milton glanced around the deserted parking lot.

"I've got no idea. A couple of miles from the airport. I can ping you my location."

"Have you got transport?"

Milton looked through the scratched windshield of the elderly Nissan. "I think so."

"I'll text you the location of a hotel. Drive there and go around to the rear. Someone will meet you there. This woman? How did she get injured?"

"She's not injured—she's sick. She's a drugs mule. I'm not an expert, but I'd put money on a bag splitting inside her."

Victoria cursed. "For fuck's sake, John. You know they don't play around with drug smuggling here!"

"I know. You don't need to worry—it's got nothing to do with me, and nothing will blow back on you."

"So why is she with you?"

"Because she's been blackmailed into smuggling the drugs and she needs my help."

Victoria exhaled. "Right—okay. We can figure it out later. Get to the hotel. There's a man I know who used to be a doctor in London before... Well, he's colourful. I'll tell you about him afterwards. I'll get him to meet you there."

"Thanks."

Milton killed the call. He looked around the parking lot and again at the Nissan before grabbing the Bajaj's radio aerial and snapping it off. He bent the thin end of the aerial into a hook and crossed to the Skyline. He peeled back the rubber weatherproof strip at the top of the driver's door and pulled hard on the top of the window frame, bending it open just enough to feed the aerial inside. He used the hook to pull the lock open and, knowing that a car this old would not have an alarm, he opened the door. He reached inside and pulled the plastic cowling from underneath the steering wheel to expose the ignition wires. He found the ones that he wanted, stripped them with his teeth and touched the bare ends together. He had no idea whether the Nissan would have fuel, but, as the ignition sparked, the engine coughed twice and then grumbled into life.

He lifted Sakura from the rear seat of the Bajaj and felt his phone vibrate in his pocket. Ignoring it, he arranged her as comfortably as he could on the back seat of the car, making sure that she was on her side and that her airway was clear, before getting into the driver's seat. He pulled out his phone and read the text message from Victoria. The hotel was called the Bayt Kapoki and, according to the pin that dropped onto Milton's map, it was only about ten minutes away. He opened the glove compartment of the Skyline and found a pair of dusty sunglasses. He cleaned them off on the tails of his shirt and slipped them on. It was a terrible disguise, but it would have to do. At least he would not be driving around the city in a bright orange motorcycle taxi. The Nissan would be far less conspicuous.

He glanced over his shoulder at his unconscious passenger before putting the car into gear, releasing the handbrake and rolling toward the exit.

20

The drive to the hotel was, to Milton's relief, uneventful. It took longer than ten minutes, and he was sure that the app on his phone had not taken him by the most direct route, but at least they were undisturbed. He passed several police cars and motorcycles on the way down the Ngurah Rai bypass and into the Kuta area of the island, but the change of vehicle meant he was able to drift by without incident.

He pulled up to the kerb opposite the hotel and checked that he was in the right place. The building was two storeys high, with the upper level clad in dark wooden planks. On one side of the frontage was a halal restaurant with a line of mopeds parked outside. To the other side was a narrow road that led around to the rear of the building. Milton swung the Nissan around and followed the road.

They reached the rear of the hotel. A young Balinese man was sitting on an upturned bucket, smoking a cigarette. He leapt to his feet as Milton pulled to a stop, and flicked the cigarette away.

Milton opened the door and got out.

"Mr. John?"

"That's right," he said.

"You need help?"

"I do."

Milton nodded at the back seat of the car. The young man looked inside, but, other than frowning for a moment, he did not react to the sight of Sakura slumped across the rear seats.

"Where can I take her?" Milton asked.

"I have room for you."

"Could you grab the bags for me?"

Milton opened the car door, scooped Sakura into his arms and lifted her out, one arm around her back and the other beneath her knees. Her head lolled against his shoulder as he adjusted his grip. She was lighter than he had expected: one hundred and ten pounds, perhaps, certainly no more than one twenty.

The man took their bags and hurried over to a set of double doors that led into the hotel. He pushed them open.

"This way, Mr. John."

Milton carried Sakura into the corridor, blinking his eyes to readjust to the gloomy light. The interior of the hotel was clean, but tired. The floral wallpaper on the walls was peeling away in places, and the carpet had a well-worn threadbare strip down the middle. Milton waited as the young man walked past him and down the corridor. He reached a door, pushed it open and indicated that this was where Milton was to go.

Milton turned sideways so that he could carry Sakura inside without bumping her legs against the frame of the door. The room matched the corridor in terms of decor, with the very same pattern of wallpaper, also peeling where the walls had grown damp. Milton did not care about luxury. He just needed somewhere quiet and out of the way where Sakura could be treated. He gently laid her on the sagging double bed in the middle of the room, turned her on her side once more, and pushed a strand of hair away from her eyes. She didn't stir.

The young man deposited their bags on the floor. "Doctor coming," he said.

21

The doctor was not at all what Milton had been expecting. He was a Westerner in his mid-sixties with a clump of white hair and a bulbous nose that was lined with prominent blue veins. It was still stiflingly hot, but, despite the temperature, the man was wearing a dark brown three-piece suit, complete with a claret-coloured waistcoat. He brushed past Milton with an officious air and assessed the room beyond.

He gestured to Sakura. "This is who I'm here to see?"

"That's right."

The medic put his bag down and crossed to the bed, where Sakura was snoring softly. He put two fingers to her neck to take her pulse.

"Not wonderful," he said. He opened one of her eyelids and examined her eye. "Opiates?"

"I don't really know her. She told me she'd swallowed condoms filled with heroin."

"Silly girl."

The doctor picked up the leather briefcase and undid it, rummaging inside to find what he wanted.

"I'm John, by the way."

The doctor did not acknowledge him as he removed a series of medical supplies and dropped them on the sheet next to Sakura. Milton saw a needle, a syringe and a clear ampoule.

"And you are?"

"Edwin," the doctor muttered. "Let's keep it vague, shall we? I don't want to know anything more than is absolutely necessary."

He took out an alcohol wipe and opened it with his teeth, spitting the torn packet onto the floor. He ripped open the sterile packets containing the needle and syringe and assembled them. He snapped the top from the plastic ampoule with a well-practised twist of his hand and held it up in front of his face as he pierced the seal with the needle and filled the syringe with the liquid from inside.

"What's that?" Milton asked.

"Naloxone." He turned his attention to Sakura and, to Milton's surprise, lifted up her skirt to expose her thigh. "It's an antidote to opiates." He squeezed the flesh of her thigh with his fingers and then clucked his tongue. "Too thin." He raised her skirt even higher so that one of her buttocks was exposed. He drew an imaginary cross on her skin before swabbing it with the alcohol wipe.

Milton recalled the annual training he had done in the Regiment. The gluteus maximus was the best place for an intramuscular injection. His training had been the opposite of this; he had been shown how to get morphine *into* someone's body, not how to counteract it.

Edwin worked quickly and with obvious skill. After he had injected the naloxone into Sakura's buttock, he placed an intravenous port into her forearm and secured it with tape.

"See this," he said, nodding down to Sakura's arm. "They used to call it the houseman's vein."

"Really," Milton replied, not sure what else to say. "What's a houseman?"

Edwin flushed the cannula with saline. "A baby doctor, back when I was doing my medical training. That's why it's a houseman's vein—it's easy to get a line into it."

"You learn something every day."

Edwin was filling another syringe from an ampoule and missed Milton's gentle sarcasm. He connected the syringe to the cannula and slowly injected its contents into Sakura's vein. "Another shot of naloxone. The jab in her backside will take a while to kick in, but this should wake her up a bit quicker."

That proved to be something of an understatement. Sakura's eyes started to flicker within seconds. A minute passed and then she sat bolt upright and stared around her.

"Nice and easy," Edwin told her.

Her eyes were wide and she blinked rapidly at him. "Who are you?"

"You need to relax. You've been very unwell."

She looked from Edwin to Milton. He could see that she didn't recognise him, either.

Her voice was dry and scratchy. "What the hell happened? Where am I?"

She looked as if she was about to get off the bed. Milton stepped around the doctor, sat down next to her and rested a hand on her forearm, careful not to dislodge the cannula.

"Do you remember me?"

She looked at his face and blinked slowly.

"I'm John," he said. "We met on the plane. You upgraded me."

"Shit," she said. "Shit, shit, shit."

"It's okay," he said as reassuringly as he could. "Yo
safe."

"But where am I?"

"In a hotel."

"Where?"

"Bali." He nodded at Edwin. "This is Edwin. He's a
doctor."

Sakura looked at the medic with wild eyes. "Why do I
need a doctor?"

"You told me you were feeling unwell on the plane. And
then you collapsed."

Edwin put his medical equipment back into his bag. "I'm
just going to get more supplies," he said. "I'll be back soon."
He looked down disapprovingly at Sakura. "We're not done
just yet, young lady. But I think the two of you need to have a
chat. I won't be long."

Edwin closed his briefcase, then turned away and left
the room, closing the door quietly behind him.

"I collapsed?" Sakura said.

"You did. Just before we were due to go through immigration."

"So... I don't get it. How..."

"How did you get here? I had to be creative—let's leave it
at that for now."

She shook her head. "I've not been feeling well for the
last few days, to be honest. Not been eating properly. I was
starting—"

Milton cut over her. "I know what happened. What you
did. You told me."

She bit her lip. "I did?"

He nodded.

"And you still helped me?"

"You told me about your son," he said. "You said that the

o are using him to force you to smuggle drugs
one called Takashi. Is that true?"

away and nodded.

ıou were in a bad way. I could have left you, but you wouldn't have got out of the airport. And I'm sure you know what they do to drug smugglers here. You would have been locked up for life, and that's only if you were lucky and had a friendly judge. You could have got the firing squad." He angled his face so that he could look into her eyes. "I don't approve of drugs. I've seen what they can do to people. But if you're telling the truth—"

"I *am*," she pleaded.

"Then there are extenuating circumstances. And maybe I can help."

Sakura smiled weakly at him, and he saw her lips were dry.

Milton got to his feet. "I'll get you a glass of water. As long as you promise not to run away."

"I promise," she said.

"And then you can tell me again what's going on."

There was a plastic cup on the bathroom sink, and Milton peeled off the shrink-wrapped cover and filled it with water from the tap. He looked in the mirror and took a moment to confirm to himself that he was doing the right thing. It was possible that Sakura was lying to him—God knows he'd been fooled by pretty girls before—but he didn't think so this time. She had been out of her mind on the plane, in no fit state to spin a false tale. He was not prepared to take everything that she said at face value, and he would have questions for her that she would need to answer, but, for now at least, he was prepared to stick around.

"He wanted to be an accountant," Sakura said as Milton handed over the plastic cup.

"Who did?"

"Miyasato. My husband." She took a sip of the water and then licked her lips. "Thank you."

"Miyasato was your husband?"

She took another sip and put the glass down on the bedside table. "Yes. He died last year."

"I'm sorry to hear that. What happened to him?"

She paused, perhaps choosing what she would tell him and what she would keep for herself. "They killed him."

She looked at Milton, her brown eyes damp and full of pain. Her voice caught in her throat, and when she reached out for the glass on the table, her hand was shaking.

"Who did?"

"His own family. His father gave the order; his brother, Katsuro, did it."

"This is to do with the yakuza?"

"The Nishimoto-*kai*."

The name was unfamiliar, but Milton knew what the suffix denoted. *Kai* meant 'group,' and, when combined with a family name, it signified a criminal clan.

"I've been to Tokyo before," he said, thinking back to when he had helped solve one of Ziggy Penn's problems that had, he recalled, also involved a pretty woman. "I know a little about the yakuza."

"The Nishimoto-*kai* used to be powerful. Takashi and Hachirō Nishimoto were in charge. Takashi is the father of Miyasato and Katsuro. Hachirō is my father."

She made herself comfortable on the bed, examining the cannula in her arm with a frown as she did so. Milton frowned; why was the daughter of one of the clan leaders being forced to be a drug mule?

"Miyasato and I had always been close, ever since we were kids. We started to see each other—as a couple, you know—when we were in our late teens. We kept it quiet. His father and my father had fallen out by then. My father didn't want anything to do with the things that Takashi was getting them into. I don't know all the details—my father wouldn't tell me—but I think Takashi wanted to move into drugs, and my father was against it. Anyway—he got out."

"And did what?"

"He set up a sushi restaurant," she said.

"And he was unhappy that you were seeing Miyasato?"

She chuckled bitterly. "Disapproving of us was the one thing they still had in common. Takashi said I would take Miyasato away from his responsibilities with the family, and my father thought Miyasato was a bad influence on me."

"What happened to Miyasato?"

She sighed. "He decided that he wanted to break away from them. Katsuro had done something really bad—Miyasato never told me what it was—and Miyasato said it was the final straw. We started to plan how we could do it. There was no way that Takashi would have let him leave. It had already happened with his own brother, and that was bad enough, but this was his *son*. Takashi was always desperate to leave a legacy, and Miyasato was the one he thought would take over. Katsuro's frightening and brutal, but he's not smart. Miyasato was—he was always the clever one. Takashi knew the family business was finished unless Miyasato agreed to take it over, but Miyasato didn't want to. We wanted kids and a normal life, not..." She waved her hand in front of her, distaste on her face. "Not *that*."

"So he was killed for what—for leaving?"

Sakura laughed, a sound with no humour at all. "No—not that. Takashi was still trying to persuade him to stay. He killed Miyasato because Miyasato stole from him. He took a sword. A very expensive sword that was the pride of Takashi's collection." She reached for the water glass and sipped again. "I told him it was crazy, but he said that he could sell it for enough money that we could leave the city and go somewhere else. Ten million yen. Enough to leave the country. Enough to start again." Her voice cracked. "Far away from Tokyo, somewhere they'd never find us. I told him I didn't want him to do it, that there had to be a better way—a safer way—but he stole it anyway. He sold it to Satoshi Furokawa."

"Who is?"

"The leader of the Chinese Dragons. It's another gang— they recruit their members from the children of the Japanese families who were left in China after the war. They say there were ten thousand kids who didn't get out. They were raised by Chinese families until the Japanese government identified them and brought them home in the eighties and nineties. The kids were grown by then and had their own families—the government said that they could all settle here. It wasn't as easy as that. There was discrimination and racism, and many of the younger ones found that it was difficult to find jobs and make money. They did what all similar people do in those circumstances—they fed themselves and their families with the proceeds of crime."

"And the yakuza?"

"Yesterday's news. They were prosecuted by the government, broken up and driven underground, and now they're all getting old. The leaders are dying, and no one is taking over from them. Gangs like the Dragons and the *hangure* are taking their place. Men like Furokawa are younger, more dangerous, and don't care about *Jingi*—the code of ethics— that the yakuza have always followed. Furokawa hates everything they stand for."

"Miyasato stole the sword to order, then?"

She nodded. "And then Takashi found out. Katsuro killed Miyasato, and now Takashi wants me to pay back the value of the sword. That's bullshit, though. It's not the money. He wants to humiliate me. He blames me for what happened to Miyasato."

The tears in her eyes overflowed and ran down her cheeks.

"And this is how he's humiliating you? By making you run drugs for him?"

"Yes. Most of the Nishimoto-*kai* is gone. They're dead, arrested, or just quit. All that's left is Takashi, Katsuro and a few diehards. Takashi has an old arrangement with criminals in Turkey, and now he makes his money buying their dope and selling it to others. People like me move it from one to the other. There's a gang here—the Laskar Bali—and he's trying to come to an agreement with them. He's using me to prove that he can deliver what they want. I've been going between Istanbul and Bali every month for five months. This was supposed to be the last load. I've got to get them to Katsuro. And if I don't..."

Her voice choked and her shoulders shook.

"Your son?"

"He's their guarantee. If I don't do what they want, if I don't pay back the debt they say I owe... I... I..."

She stopped, unable to go on.

Milton sat on the bed, thinking hard. He had no business being here. He had brought Sakura to a place of safety, or at least safety of sorts. The doctor seemed competent enough, although what he was doing working on the sidelines in Bali was anyone's guess. If Victoria was using him because he was *discreet*... well, if that was the case, then Edwin was certainly operating in the margins.

Milton knew that he had other options. He could get up, leave Sakura in the doctor's care, and let everything else work itself out.

He knew it was no good trying to fool himself. He was involved now whether he liked it or not.

"What's your son's name?"

"Yamato."

"And where is he now?"

"Tokyo. And if I don't do what they tell me to do, I'll never see him again."

akura watched as Smith sat in silence on the bed, evidently considering the story that she had just told him. He looked as if he was wrestling with his own thoughts. At least they had that in common; Sakura was struggling with hers.

She had been honest with him. Takashi had insisted on keeping Yamato as security, and she believed him when he said she would never see her son again if she let him down. Sakura had pleaded for clemency; she pleaded that Yamato was only a child, and that the son should not be punished for the sins of the father. She had used what little knowledge she had of the yakuza's codes of behaviour. Miyasato had explained the *Jingi* to her, and she had argued that to harm a child would be dishonourable. All her efforts had done was to whet the edge of Takashi's anger, and to reinforce his hatred of her for turning his son against him. He had reminded her that Yoshida Shōin's *tantō* was priceless, and that she was lucky that he had offered her a debt that she might one day be able to repay. He had considered murdering her and Yamato, he said, or forcing her to work in a 'black jail'—a brothel—for the rest of her life, but he had seen the value of clemency. *That* was honourable, he argued, not the bastardisation of *Jingi* that she had tried to rely upon. She had been lucky that he was an ethical man.

She had begged again and again, and Takashi had ignored it all. Sakura would carry to her death the sight of Yamato's tear-streaked face pressed against the rear window of the car as he was driven away. She would get him back— she would do *everything* that Takashi asked—or she would die trying.

She glanced over Smith's shoulder at the rest of the room. She couldn't be here. She had to follow through on what she had promised and deliver the packages. Katsuro was waiting. Yamato needed her to do it. Perhaps it wasn't too late.

Smith got to his feet and excused himself. He walked into the small bathroom and closed the door behind him. Sakura heard the taps being turned on and the splash of water. Knowing that she had only moments, she looked around the small hotel room for her things. There was a single chair in the corner with her clutch bag lying atop it. Her phone would be in the bag; she could just leave and find somewhere else to hide until Katsuro could come and get her.

She got to her feet, careful not to bump the cannula, stood unsteadily for a few seconds until the room stopped spinning, and then picked up the bag. She opened it to confirm that her phone was still inside, and then, with a glance over her shoulder at the closed bathroom door, she crossed the room and opened the door as quietly as she could.

24

The bathroom was a tiny room, with a shower cubicle, a toilet and a sink. There was a narrow window with a cracked pane of glass and, as Milton looked through it, he saw that it offered an uninspiring view of the roof of the building beneath, together with a collection of wheezing air-conditioning units. There was an alley between the two buildings that looked as if it was used as a place to smoke and chat by members of the hotel staff. A man in chef's whites was leaning against the wall while a porter emptied a trash can of rotten food waste into a large industrial bin.

He looked at his reflection in the mirror, a jagged crack in the glass almost lining up with the scar on his face, and breathed out. What a day. He would have said that he was surprised that trouble had found him again, but he was not. It always did. It made no difference where he was or what he was doing; it always found him. He stared at his reflection and wondered whether that was right. Did *it* find *him*, or did *he* find *it*? It didn't matter. He'd been presented with a problem, with someone out of her depth and in need of his help,

uld do what he could to bring her justice. It was
e for the blood in his past, his own debt, one that
ervice but never truly repay. He had grown to
accept that, and almost found comfort in the certainty that
this would be his life until he found a problem that even he
could not fix.

Perhaps it would be this one.

He opened the door and went back into the bedroom.

Sakura wasn't there.

He chuckled to himself as he looked around the dingy
room. The only thing she had left behind was the indentation on the bed where she had been sitting. He pulled his
phone from his pocket and called Victoria.

"John?" she said. "All okay? The doc sort you out?"

"He did. Is he really a doctor?"

"He *was*. Struck off a few years ago. Got into a relationship with a patient, by all accounts."

"Unwise."

"Especially when they're seventeen. All consensual, or so
the patient said. The police weren't interested, but the
General Medical Council took a dim view. As did his wife."

"I'm not calling about him," Milton said. "I have a
problem."

"Another one?"

"The woman Edwin was treating..." He went over to the
window and looked out onto the scrubby hotel grounds. "I
appear to have misplaced her."

"You..." She paused. "I'm sorry, what?"

"I was in the bathroom. She left when I wasn't looking."
He shrugged. "Forget it, never mind—it's her choice. I can't
force her to accept my help. How much do I owe you?"

"What for?"

"For the room and the doctor." Milton glanced around

the dilapidated space. It couldn't be much, but that wasn't the point. He always paid what he owed.

"Don't be daft," Victoria said. Milton could tell from the tone of her voice that she was smiling. "A dodgy hotel room and the services of an even dodgier doctor? I think I can cover that."

"We'll talk about it later."

"No, we won't," she insisted. "Look—are you coming over?"

"I was just—"

Milton was interrupted by the door to the stairwell opening. Sakura came through first, closely followed by Edwin. The doctor had a hand tight around her upper arm and looked distinctly unimpressed.

"Will you help me explain to this young lady just how stupid it would be to leave before she's treated?" the doctor asked him.

"I'll call you back," Milton said and killed the call.

Edwin was angry. His face was even redder than before, and the veins on his nose were darker. He pushed Sakura toward the bed, not particularly gently, and she stumbled a little before sitting down hard on the edge.

"Easy," Milton said.

Edwin ignored him. "If you leave," he said to Sakura, "you'll die. I'm not speculating about that. It's not a guess. It's not a prediction. It's a *spoiler*. Do you understand?"

"I feel fine," Sakura complained. "That injection you gave me? It's worked."

"Do you have any idea what the half-life of naloxone is? When it stops working, which it will, soon, you'll be right back where you were before, but this time there won't be anyone to help you. You need regular doses, and I need to get the *meracuni* inside you out."

at?"

son, my dear. The heroin."

aw that Edwin had a carrier bag in his hand. It was bright orange with a distinctive red-and-white chequered logo emblazoned on the side beneath the word GUARDIAN in large white letters.

The doctor took a deep breath, and some of his anger seemed to dissipate. "You need to take this seriously," he said, but this time his voice was calmer. "I'm sorry—I shouldn't snap at you. But you need help. Otherwise?" He shrugged. "Otherwise, I promise you that you will die."

"Think of Yamato," Milton suggested.

"Who do you think I'm thinking of?" Sakura snapped, then dipped her head and began to sob.

"Edwin?" Milton said. The doctor turned to look at him, his eyebrows raised. "What can I do to help?"

"Nothing," Edwin replied, his face creasing into a weary smile. "I have a nurse on the way. She works with me sometimes, and we'll leave them to it." He raised his hand with the carrier bag in it. "I've just cleared out their entire laxative supply." He gave a wry nod of his head. "I'm afraid this is not going to be pretty."

Milton took a deep breath as he walked out into the parking lot at the rear of the hotel. He was pleased to be out of the room, pleased to be away from Edwin and the nurse who had arrived ten minutes after the doctor had frog-marched Sakura back into the room. The nurse was a hard-faced Filipina, all business from the minute she had arrived and saw what needed to be done. She had a deep frown and an inscrutable face, and she had shooed both Milton and Edwin out of the door.

Declining Edwin's invitation for a quick drink—the look on the medic's face clear evidence that he wouldn't be having just one—Milton had excused himself. Edwin told him to come back to the hotel at midnight, so he had a few hours to kill. He texted Victoria to see if she was free for him to visit, and quickly received a response.

Of course, the text said. *Come to the Hilton in Nusa Dua. I'll meet you at the restaurant.*

Milton went to the parking lot and walked over to the Skyline that had brought them here. He doubted that it would have been reported as stolen, but he couldn't be sure. He decided to move the car somewhere a little way away from where Sakura was being treated; ten minutes later, the Nissan was stowed in an otherwise deserted lot to the rear of another even more anonymous hotel.

Milton made his way back to the main road and stood for a moment to take in downtown Kuta. The street was loud with a barrage of competing sounds. Taxis crawled along the kerbs, drivers leaning on their horns to attract passengers. Hookers strutted up and down the sidewalk, seeking a different type of client. Cicadas provided an ever-present accompaniment to the man-made racket.

Milton stood by the kerb and waited until a blue taxi approached him. The car stopped and the driver's window jerked down.

"Where you go?"

Milton found himself looking at a middle-aged man with buck teeth and an optimistic but enthusiastic comb-over. He had to raise his voice to make himself heard over the *gamelan* music that was blaring from the radio. Milton ignored the incomprehensible—to his ears, at least—mixture of metallophones, drums, gongs, and bamboo flutes.

"Nusa Dua. The Hilton?"

"Of course. How much you pay?"

Milton peeled a twenty-dollar bill from the roll in his pocket. "You take dollars?"

The driver's smile broadened, his misshapen teeth evident despite the poor light inside the car. "Everyone take dollar. Get in."

Milton climbed inside, and the driver pulled out into the heavy traffic along Ngurah Rai before muscling his way into the outer lane, ignoring the blasts of horns as he did so. He made no effort at conversation, seemingly content to just nod his head in time to the music.

Milton watched the streets of Kuta pass by. He saw street vendors selling everything from magazines to motorcycles, with a different stall every few metres, the traders sheltering in the shade of the palm trees that lined the road. The driver slowed for a bottleneck that had formed in the run-up to a bridge, and Milton noticed an elaborate temple on the banks of the river. They cleared the bridge, and the road gave way to the Nusa Dua road; the driver accelerated toward Bualu. The journey took another fifteen minutes, and then the driver pulled up outside the entrance to a private road. A large block of stone divided the road ahead, HILTON inscribed on it. The road proceeded beneath a stone archway that was laden down with purple frangipani and hibiscus.

The driver edged up to the archway and stopped in front of a lowered barrier. A uniformed security guard approached, a Glock stowed in a holster that was clipped to his belt. He spoke to the driver in Indonesian.

"You stay here?" the driver asked, turning to Milton.

"No," he said. "Tell him I'm here to see Victoria Deschamps."

The guard caught that. "You said Deschamps?"

"That's right."

"Your name, please?"

"John Smith."

"Very good, Mr. Smith. She called and said to expect you."

The guard spoke to the driver again and went to open the barrier. The driver continued through the arch and followed the road to the main hotel complex. Milton had checked the hotel website during the journey and had seen that it had been built on a cliff overlooking the ocean. The reception was actually at the hotel's fifteenth floor, with the rest of the property descending to the beach below.

The driver pulled up and Milton's door was opened by a porter. Milton paid the cabbie and got out into the sweltering heat. He looked around and admired the manicured gardens. The entrance to the hotel sat beyond a wooden pagoda that sheltered two sofas arranged around a small fountain. Milton asked the porter for directions to the restaurant and was encouraged to follow along as the man took him to an elevator and pressed the button that would take him to the foot of the cliff. Milton tipped the man with a dollar and turned to admire the view of the darkening horizon as the elevator dropped down.

The hotel was huge, stretching out in both directions. This was a very different part of Bali than the area he had just left. This was for foreign money. He wondered how many tourists ever ventured beyond the fringes of these kinds of establishments, impressive yet anodyne and disinfected, and saw the real Bali, the country that people lived in rather than just visited.

The elevator slid to a halt and the doors opened.

"John!"

Milton turned to see Victoria striding toward him, a broad grin on her face. She ignored the hand Milton extended and pulled him into an embrace. Milton was not keen on outward shows of affection, but he remembered that she had always been something of a hugger, especially after she had conquered the bottle. She was wearing a crumpled linen sundress and a pair of sandals that might have been described as shabbily chic. Her face was deeply tanned, and when she smiled, her white teeth stood out against the nutty brown.

"There's a sight for sore eyes," Victoria said. "How long?"

"Years."

"I know exactly how many," she said. "I last saw you when I got my six-month chip. And that was six years ago. Actually, six years, two months and thirteen days."

"Not that you're counting," Milton said.

"You know how it is," she said.

Milton *did* know. Recovering alcoholics gave thanks for every day that they shunned the next drink. He had originally likened it to a convict scratching the passing days into the wall of a cell, but now he saw the good sense in keeping track; the more days that had been accumulated, the more there was to lose.

"You're still sober, then?"

"Couple of wobbles here and there," she said, "but I managed to stay the course. You?"

Milton nodded. "Same."

Victoria slapped him on the shoulder. "It's good to see you. You're looking relaxed."

Milton knew that she was being kind; he looked *anything* but relaxed. It had been a long two days of travel and he hadn't changed clothes since his layover in Istanbul. He needed a shower and, at the very least, a clean set of underwear.

"I don't feel it," Milton replied, watching her easy grin playing over her face.

"Maybe a little frazzled around the edges. Where's your stuff?"

"I left my bag at the hotel."

"Come on through," she replied, turning and taking a few steps toward the restaurant entrance. "I'll show you where you're staying. You can grab a shower, and I'll head home and grab you some clothes from my other half." Milton followed, grateful that Victoria had seen his need without him having to say anything. "Then we'll have a drink and you can tell me all about this mysterious woman you've met."

26

Sakura groaned as another painful cramp rolled across her abdomen. The nurse—who was anything but caring—gave her a dour and unsympathetic stare.

"You got more?" the Filipina asked, gesturing to the door to the bathroom.

Sakura had no interest in spending any more time in that foul little room. More than that, she just wanted the nurse to leave her in peace. What had happened over the last hour had been embarrassing—*demeaning*, even—and, although Sakura had known from experience what she would have to do to retrieve the drugs, she had hoped to do it in private and without needing the help of a very large dose of laxatives.

"More?" the nurse asked again.

"No."

She held her hand to her stomach. She was telling the truth. She had counted the small packages in, and then she had counted them out. They were on the floor in the bathroom: twenty-five small condoms with knotted ends, freshly washed and full of pure heroin. One of them had split, and some of the contents had leaked out. That had been the cause of her illness.

"You sure?"

"I'm done. You can go now if you want."

"I stay for doctor," the nurse replied. "Make sure you okay."

"Maybe I could get some fresh air?"

The nurse walked to the hotel room window and cranked it open. The air that drifted in was warm and humid. "There," she said. "Fresh air."

Sakura moaned as another wave of cramp hit her. She just wanted the woman to leave so that she could go and find Katsuro. He and his father would not accept the loss of the consignment, and she had to deliver the packets as she had promised.

"I need *fresh* air," she protested. "Outside."

The nurse started to pack her supplies away, and then she sat down on the chair, folded her arms across her ample chest, and glared at Sakura.

"Wait for doctor."

27

V ictoria brought two glasses and a plate with slices of fresh mango laid out in a crescent. She gave Milton one of the glasses and put the plate down on the table.

"You won't taste fresher than this," she said, taking a slice and holding it up. "On the tree thirty minutes ago. Unbelievably juicy."

They were on a sun deck in front of the restaurant. The deck was large, with a series of tables and chairs that had been arranged to take advantage of its chief virtue: a stupendous view of the ocean. The sun was just starting to set, and the sky was coloured with kaleidoscopic reds and oranges and yellows. Tiny sparks of light caught against the gentle waves that lapped onto the white sand of the beach that curved away from them in a lazy crescent.

Victoria had put Milton up in one of the small beachside villas that belonged to the resort that the restaurant served. He had freshened up with a shower, and now he had the benefit of the clean clothes that Victoria had delivered. She explained that they belonged to her husband, Jean-

Michel: a linen jacket, a crumpled linen shirt, and a pair of linen shorts. Milton thought they made him look like a middle-aged beach bum trying too hard to hold onto what was left of his youth, but, not wishing to insult Jean-Michel's taste, he said nothing.

"The villa's nice?"

"Too nice. I really don't need anything as grand as that."

"It's off season," Victoria said, waving off his objections. "It's empty anyway, and the manager's fine about you staying as long as Jean-Michel and I clean it afterwards."

"I'm still getting my head around the fact that you're married," Milton said.

"Three years. You'll like him."

"I'm sure I will."

Milton thought back to when he and Victoria had grown close. He remembered the brief fling that had developed as they realised that they had a lot of baggage in common: two drunks, both new in admitting their addictions, both slaves to their compulsive behaviours. It was not unusual for addicts to fall into ill-advised relationships, but Milton's role as Victoria's sponsor had raised the eyebrows of those perceptive enough to notice. He had wondered whether he would feel awkward coming here and seeing her again, but, so far at least, there had been none of that. She had an earthiness about her that he had always found attractive, and the fact that they had slept together was not something that she was going to be sensitive about. She had been refreshingly open and honest during their affair; she had made the first move and she had ended it, too. Milton had known that they had reached the end of the road, but had been too much of a coward to say anything. She didn't have his hesitation, and the matter-of-fact way that she had sat him down and told him what she had decided had meant that they had been able to stay friends, and had cauterised any possibility of rancour. The clean break meant that there was no awkwardness now, too, and Milton was grateful all over again for her straightforwardness.

Milton clinked his glass against hers and took a sip of his drink. The liquid was white and ice cold and very sweet.

"This is lovely," he said, peering at the glass. "What is it?"

"It's called *kopyor*. Made from mutant coconuts."

"Intriguing." Milton laughed.

"Jean-Michel will explain it to you properly." Victoria's phone buzzed on the table between them. She picked it up and squinted at the screen. "His ears must be burning." She read the text and frowned.

"Everything okay?"

"He's working late. I was hoping he might be able to come and say hi, but maybe not."

"Tomorrow, then?"

"For sure."

"I'll be here for a few days. There'll be plenty of time."

The two of them sat in companionable silence for a few moments, both content to watch the blood-red sun slip below the horizon. A beam of orange light reflected on the surface of the ocean like a shining path that led straight to them.

"Can I ask you a question?" Milton said.

"Sure."

"What is it exactly that you're doing here—for work, I mean?"

Victoria paused for a moment, then—perhaps remembering Milton's own history—she shrugged and smiled. "I'm a fixer. If there's a problem in the resort that needs sorting out, they ask me."

"What kind of problem?"

"Maybe we have a guest who gets into trouble with the police. Someone doesn't pay and does a runner—I'll go and track them down and persuade them that they need to settle their debts. Or maybe there's an issue with Laskar Bali."

"Which is?"

"The Balinese gangsters."

"They have gangsters here?"

She smiled at his faux naivety. "They call themselves *premans*—means 'free men.' They do some legitimate work —security, mostly—but most of the time it's extortion, prostitution, drugs. All the usual highlights. It might not be glamorous, and it's sometimes a little grubby, but the way I see it, we used to do grubby work when we were at the Firm, and this pays better than it did back then. They've given me a nice truck and I can live rent-free. Everything I could ever want is here."

Milton saw a look of contentment pass across his friend's face, and he felt a momentary pang of envy.

The two spent the next hour catching up. Victoria told Milton story after story about life in Bali and the work she did for the hotel. She told him about Jean-Michel, about how he had had a problem with coke when he had worked as a sous-chef in Paris and how both of them being in recovery meant that they were perfect for each other. Milton side-stepped her questions about what he had been doing since they had last spoken, preferring instead to keep things vague. Victoria knew enough of Milton's past to know not to push too hard, and Milton was relieved that he was allowed to skim across the surface of things.

Victoria eventually moved the conversation around to Sakura. Milton told her everything that had happened, from the meeting at the airport to his unexpected upgrade, from her sudden sickness to her confession and how he had helped her to get into the country.

"What are you going to do with her now?"

"I don't know," he said.

"You saved her life already."

"She still has problems that she doesn't know how to solve."

"But you do?"

He shrugged. "Maybe. I don't know."

Milton took a slice of mango and ate it. The flesh was succulent, full of juice and delicious. He took another.

"Good, right?"

"Very."

Milton leaned back and ate the mango. He looked out at the pool, at the children who were still frolicking with inflatables, and imagined what life might have been like if he and Victoria had stayed together. It was a fool's errand, and he knew it; he dismissed the thought.

"So," she said, as if sensing his momentary discomfort. "Your new legend."

"Have you had a chance to prepare it?"

"Of course. I've spent the better part of three days on it." She grinned. "Not that I want to pat myself on the back, but it's some of my best work. You'll have everything you need: a new name, new papers, new backstory. Everything. It was good to get back into the swing of things again. You remember the first one I did for you?"

"I don't," Milton said. "I was drinking then. They blend into one another."

"John Smith," she said.

"That was you?"

"It was."

"Then you've been helping me out ever since I left the Group. I've been Smith ever since."

"But no longer."

Milton took out his passport and held it up. The old document was battered, the cover ripped in places and creased in others. He opened it and flipped through the pages. They bore stamps from dozens of countries all around the world. He tried not to think about it too much; many of those stamps memorialised the assignments that he had been given, the red-ribboned files that had landed on Control's desk and been passed to him to action.

Thinking of that nudged Milton to do something impulsive. He took out his lighter, thumbed a flame and then held it underneath the passport. The pages caught first, the dry paper quickly consumed by fire. The stiffer covers took a little while to burn; they smouldered at first, then blackened, and then they were alight. Milton held it by the edge until it was completely alight and then dropped it into the ashtray and watched it burn.

Victoria held up her glass.

"Rest in peace, John Smith."

Milton felt odd. His legend was nothing more than a fiction, a cloak that he put on to glide into the shadows, but he realised—as stupid as it sounded—that he had grown attached to his alter ego and was sad to see him go.

THEY STAYED AND CHATTED, catching each other up, both of them leaving the uncomfortable territory deliberately unexplored. Eventually, Milton looked at his watch. It was ten.

"Shit," he said. "It's later than I thought. I need to get back to the hotel. Where's the best place to grab a taxi?"

"You don't need a taxi," Victoria replied, getting to her feet. "You know how to ride a scooter, right?"

Milton thought back to the bright orange Bajaj. "I can manage."

"Come with me—I've got one you can borrow for as long as you need."

"I don't have a licence," Milton replied. "Or insurance."

"Don't be a dick," Victoria replied with a chuckle as they walked. "You don't need those. This is Bali."

28

M ilton adjusted the strap under his chin to make the crash helmet as comfortable as possible. Victoria had led him to a small thatched garage near the hotel that had a dozen scooters lined up, explaining that the resort rented them out to guests. She had given Milton a quick lesson in what to do if the police pulled him over; being a foreigner, Victoria explained, meant that he would almost certainly be stopped at some point. He was to ask for a ticket, then, when that didn't work, to ask for a superior. If *that* didn't work—and, according to Victoria, it probably wouldn't—then a small contribution to the policeman's back pocket would grease the wheels and he would be good to go.

Milton kept the scooter at a steady pace as he navigated his way back to the bridge over the Gulf of Benoa, grateful when the potholed and unlit roads around the hotel gave way to the modern two-lane carriageway. The road was busy despite the late hour, with cars and buses and trucks vying for space. It was loud, too, with the whine of the scooter's engine and the sound of nearby horns mixing into a discordant racket. Although a six-foot-tall Westerner on a tiny scooter could not help but stand out, he tried to keep himself within a gaggle of younger riders. One of them would peel off from the group every once in a while, only to be replaced by another. None of them seemed to mind the fact that Milton had muscled his way into the shoal, and they shouted loudly at each other across him. A young woman on the back of one scooter gave Milton a broad smile and waved at him.

He was only a few moments away from the hotel in Kuta when he saw the first flashes of blue lights in his mirror. He risked a glance over his shoulder and saw three police cars in the distance, their roof bars casting a blue wash under the overhanging leaves of the *thika* palm trees that lined the road. Milton looked left and right. The same black and white breeze blocks that had slowed the police down earlier that day lined the road here, too, but beyond them on both sides were deep storm drains and concrete walls that extended as far ahead as Milton could see. There was no reason to think that the cars were after him, but the sight of them made him nervous in any event.

The scooter slowed as it ascended the upward slope of the underpass, just as the leading police car drew level. Milton could see that he wasn't going to make the turning; it was still a couple of hundred metres in front of him. The driver of the cruiser—a young man in his early to mid-twenties—was gripping the steering wheel hard and staring straight ahead. He didn't even look across, keeping his foot down and speeding ahead. The second car and then the third followed, all three of them accelerating up the ramp from the underpass, their lights and sirens receding into the distance.

Milton leaned back a little, his shoulders bunched with

tension. *Paranoia*, he told himself. They hadn't been looking for him. For now, at least, he was in the clear.

29

"Jean-Michel?" Victoria called out as she opened the door and stepped into their villa. "I'm home."

Her husband's whites had been tossed over the back of the chair, and his Crocs had been left with the other shoes by the door. He heard her call and put his head out of the kitchen door.

"Tea?"

Victoria slipped off her sandals. "Yes, please."

She walked into the kitchen and gave Jean-Michel a hug. That had been their ritual every evening for years. No matter how busy a day it had been, no matter how tired they both were, it was always the same. Getting back to him was the part of the day that she looked forward to the most.

"I'll make it," she said. "You go and sit down. You look bushed."

"Long day," he admitted. "The fish was delivered late— Gopinath lost his shit and I had to get it fixed."

"But you did?"

He nodded. "I went down to the dock with Nyoman and

picked up everything we needed. It was okay—just took a couple of hours I couldn't really spare."

She took some ginger and a small chopping board, slicing the root into matchstick-sized slivers. She flicked the switch on the kettle and, as she waited for it to boil, she de-stalked and chopped lemon grass.

"I saw you with your friend," he said. "How is he?"

"Seems good," Victoria replied, pouring the steaming water into two cups before throwing in the ginger and lemon grass. "Honey?"

"Go on, then. And, if we're being indulgent, look in the fridge. I made something for you."

She opened the fridge and saw that Jean-Michel had prepared a plate of *pias*. They were her favourite: sweet pies with golden crusts, a creamy lemon centre and topped with baked cheese. She put the glasses of tea and two *pias* onto a tray and joined Jean-Michel in the sitting room.

"So," he said, "is your friend in the villa?"

"His name is John," she said, "and no, not yet. I lent him a scooter to get back to his hotel."

"Hotel?" He frowned. "I thought he was staying here."

Victoria explained how Milton had called her, needing help. She left some parts of the story out, such as the request for a medic and the reason one was needed, preferring instead to concentrate on the fact that Milton was helping the woman.

"Who is she?"

"John said he met her on the plane."

"And he doesn't know her?"

"Not before that."

"So why is he helping her?"

"Apparently that's what he does now. He helps people."

"And that's a change for him?"

Victoria nodded and bit into one of the pies. She knew that Milton hadn't always been that way. She knew that for a fact, and that—indirectly, at least—the work she had done while she was employed by the Firm had enabled him and the other headhunters of Group Fifteen to do what they did. She had never told Jean-Michel about her work, explaining instead that she had worked as a civil servant in London before quitting and coming to the island. Complete honesty was not necessary in this case. It would lead to difficult questions, and, although she did not like being economical with the truth with her husband, there were some subjects —ancient history now—that would lead to difficult conversations that they did not need to have.

"He helped me," she said. "I don't know if I'd be here, with you, if it weren't for him."

Jean-Michel pulled Victoria back into another hug, wrapping his arms around her and holding her tight. He had never known Victoria when she was a drunk. They would not have met without the changes that she had been able to make to her life, and Victoria knew that she had Milton to thank for that. He had made an effort with her in the first few days after she had admitted to herself that she had a problem. She had been white-knuckling her recovery back then, and the nervousness that she had felt as she waited outside the church hall for her first meeting had been almost insurmountable. There had been shame, too, a cutting self-disgust with the state that she had allowed her life to get into. Milton had helped her to work on that shame, and had shown her how she could find relief and peace of mind just by sitting at the back of the room, drinking cheap coffee in paper cups and listening. He had chivvied her to get to meetings, one a day for the first thirty days. He had even told Victoria his real name as a gesture of trust. Victoria knew that Milton worked for the Group, and that he was a killer, but there was something in him—something inherently *good*—that gave her a reason to believe that he might have her best interests at heart.

"You okay?" Jean-Michel said.

"Sorry."

"You look like you're a thousand miles away."

"Just thinking back to how it was before I met him."

"Times change. People change. You're different now."

"I love you," she whispered in his ear as she pressed herself against him.

S akura stood with her arms folded over her chest, staring at the nurse. "No," she said firmly, looking at the syringe in the woman's hand. "I don't need it."

The nurse's phone had rung just a few moments earlier, and the woman had had a terse conversation with whoever it was on the other end of the line. She guessed it was the doctor. Sakura could not understand what they were talking about, but, from how the nurse kept gesturing, it had obviously been about her.

The nurse held up the syringe.

"I don't need another injection."

"Dr. Edwin say you do. He say you get very, very sick without it."

"But I feel *fine*."

The nurse took a step toward her, a determined expression on her face. It was evident that she was not going to take no for an answer.

"I don't want a needle," Sakura said.

"No needle," the nurse replied, pointing at the cannula

in Sakura's forearm. "It go in there. The drugs you swallowed, they last long time. You get sick again. Dr. Edwin says so."

Sakura swallowed a mouthful of acrid bile. What the nurse said made sense, and the last thing she wanted to do was to get ill again. She needed to call Katsuro; she needed to speak to him so that he could come and collect the drugs.

"I need some fresh air first," she said. "Let me go outside for a few minutes. Then you can inject me with whatever Dr. Edwin says I need." Sakura expected that the woman would say no, like before, but, this time, she relented.

"I come too," she said. Her expression made it very obvious that it wasn't a suggestion.

"Fine."

Sakura picked up her clutch bag, opened the door to the hotel room, and walked out into the corridor. She glanced left and right and, seeing a fire door at the end, headed toward it, the nurse close behind. There was a small parking lot behind the fire door, with a couple of beaten-up old cars illuminated by a single orange street lamp. Sakura saw two white plastic chairs next to a large catering tin that was full of sand and cigarette butts. She sat on one of the chairs and took out her phone. There were several text messages and missed calls. She thumbed out a text to Katsuro. She had seen the name of the hotel on a half-used notepad inside the room, so she entered that now with a message for him to come and pick her up as soon as possible.

"Do you smoke?" Sakura asked the nurse, hoping to play for some time outside in the fresh air. The hotel room had been stifling, and the odours from the bathroom hadn't helped. The nurse shook her head emphatically. Sakura didn't smoke, either—she had quit when Yamato was born

—but she would have lit one up if it had meant she could stay outside for a bit longer.

Her cell buzzed. She glanced at the screen to see an incoming text.

Stay there. I'm coming.

She got to her feet and turned to the nurse.

"Okay."

The two women went inside and walked back down the corridor to the room. Sakura hoped that Katsuro would be quick. Smith would be back at some point, she knew, if only to collect his bag. It wasn't that she was ungrateful to him for helping her, but she didn't want him to get involved any more than he already was. If he turned up at the same time as Katsuro, it was possible that things could get complicated. Katsuro had a temper, and he had taken pleasure in telling her some of the things that he had done for his father.

She would just have to hope that the paths of the two men did not cross.

"On the bed," the nurse said as they re-entered the room.

Sakura did as she was told, even offering up her forearm with the cannula. The nurse inserted the needle into the thin tube and injected another dose of the opiate antidote. She was brusque and efficient, noting down the time on a small notepad.

Sakura felt a sudden billowing of nausea, and for a second, she thought she would vomit. She made to sit up, but the nurse laid a meaty hand on her shoulder and pushed her back into the bed. Everything was strange. The nausea passed as soon as it had arrived, but an over-whelming lassitude took its place. Sakura's eyelids grew heavy; she tried to keep them open, but knew that it was a struggle that she would not win. The room spun around her, noises blended into one another, and Sakura gave in and let her eyelids close.

Her final thought as she passed into unconsciousness was that whatever had been in that syringe, it was not an opiate antidote.

31

Milton crested the slight incline and emerged from the underpass. The police cars had pulled out to half a mile ahead of him and, as he watched, their brake lights flashed red and they turned off the road. It took him a few moments to catch up with them and, as he closed in, he saw that they had stopped in the parking lot at the rear of the hotel. Milton took the off-ramp and turned into the lot himself. He brought the scooter to a halt, turned off the ignition and raised it onto its stand. He made his way to a small clump of *kelapa* trees that would allow him a little cover while he watched what was happening.

A small crowd of hotel staff and guests had gathered outside the building, no doubt attracted by the arrival of the police. Several of them had their phones aloft, filming whatever was happening. The small crowd turned as the main doors to the hotel opened. A uniformed officer strode through, gesturing angrily with his hands that they should move out of the way; the crowd shuffled back, but no one left. Milton watched the policeman. It was the driver he had seen before; he was young and lean and had a pistol holstered at his hip.

Milton turned his attention to the doors of the hotel. He could see movement inside. Two officers were carrying someone to the door. Milton saw the navy-blue flowered dress and knew that the person being removed was Sakura.

The policeman in front was holding onto her ankles, and the man behind had his hands underneath her armpits. Her arms hung loose and her head lolled back. What had happened to her? Surely the naloxone would have worked on the opiates by now; had she had some sort of relapse? And where was Edwin? Where was the Filipina nurse whom the doctor had summoned to help? One of Sakura's shoes came loose, unnoticed by the policemen, and dropped to the sidewalk as the officers hauled her toward the nearest cruiser. They opened the door at the back and dumped her inside.

A fourth policeman came out of the door to the hotel, followed by one of the hotel employees, who was arguing furiously with him. The policeman turned and said something to the employee. The man shrank back with his hands in front of him in supplication.

Two of the policemen got into the front of the first car, the remaining men heading for their own vehicles. The small convoy set off, their blue lights still flashing.

Milton heard the low rumble of thunder from a distance away.

32

Milton emerged from behind the trees, unnoticed by the crowd that was now beginning to disperse, and walked down the alleyway to the rear of the hotel. The fire door that he had used earlier was propped open by a bright red fire extinguisher, and he made his way through it and along the corridor to Sakura's room.

Milton wrinkled his nose as he walked in: the room smelled fetid. It was just as he remembered it earlier, except that now it was empty apart from his bag, which was still in the corner where it had been left earlier. He picked it up, relieved at the policemen's incompetence or lack of interest. The bag held a change of clothes, some toiletries and the twenty thousand that he had made from selling the car in Panama. The bag also had his most recent copy of the Big Book. He could get a replacement easily enough, but this copy held all his notes, the thoughts and reflections that he had scribbled into the margins. He didn't want to lose it.

He glanced at the wrinkled bedspread and, leaning in,

g black hairs on the white pillowcase. The

rt hair; these must have been from Sakura.

k in the bathroom. The smell was stronger

.. the room was empty apart from the wrappers of medical supplies that had been dropped into the bin.

He went back out into the corridor just as an employee approached. It was the man whom he had seen arguing with the policeman outside. He was in his sixties, with salt-and-pepper hair and a leathery face, and he was wearing a simple white robe with sandals.

"Hello," Milton said.

The man scowled at him.

"Do you speak English?"

"Little."

"The woman who was in this room—the police took her."

"Yes."

"Where have they taken her?"

The man shrugged. Milton took his bankroll from his pocket and peeled off a ten. He held it up.

"Jimbaran," he said, staring at the bill. "Police station. They say she bring drugs here—yes? Is not allowed."

"There were a doctor and a nurse here," Milton said. "Where are they?"

The man shook his head. "No doctor. No nurse."

"How do I get to Jimbaran?"

The man reached for the money, but Milton pulled it back.

"Where is it?"

"Wanagiri," the man said.

"How far?"

"Ten minutes, maybe fifteen."

Milton gave him the note and left him outside the room.

MILTON HURRIED BACK to the scooter. He took out his phone and called Victoria.

"You okay?" she said. "You sound breathless."

"Do you know Wanagiri?"

"In Kuta Sel?"

"No idea," Milton said, straddling the scooter. "It's somewhere near the hotel you found for us."

"Why? Is there a problem?"

"That girl I told you about? She's in trouble."

"More than before?"

"I think your doctor has sold her out to the police."

"Edwin?" Victoria replied. "I doubt that very much."

"He's not here now," Milton said. "And she's just been taken away by the police."

"I can't see him doing that. I know him. He can be an arse, but he's not a bad guy."

"They found her somehow," Milton said. "Maybe it was the nurse. Or someone at the hotel. It doesn't really matter."

"What can I do?"

"I need someone with local knowledge."

"Where on Wanagiri have they taken her? The police station?"

"Yes," Milton said.

There was a silence that lasted for a few seconds while Victoria thought. "I know it. There's a motorcycle shop about a hundred metres to the north of the police station. You can't miss it. Just past it is a lay-by. Meet me there. I'll head out now."

Milton thanked her, inserted the key into the ignition of the scooter and started the engine. A light rain started to fall. He pushed the scooter off its stand as a jagged flash of lightning split the sky on the horizon. He heard the boom of thunder as he pulled away from the kerb.

33

K atsuro had been outside the police station at Wanagiri for ten minutes. He had parked on the other side of the road from the building, the car partially hidden behind a stand of *lontar* palm. It had been a frustrating evening. He had received Sakura's text, telling him that she was at a hotel in Kuta. He had hurried to the car and made his way across the island, arriving at the hotel only to see a crowd of people outside the doors and the policemen bringing her out.

They had driven her away; Katsuro had followed.

The police cruisers had parked at the front of the building, next to a rank of motorcycles that single officers would use to get around the island. Katsuro peered at the station through the rain that was hammering against the windshield of his car. The building was behind a substantial cream-coloured wall, with access in and out through a gate. The building itself was reasonably large and constructed in the local style: yellow-painted walls and a steeply sloping red tile roof. The Indonesian flag hung limply from a flag-pole, the pennant drenched by the rain. Katsuro had examined the satellite image on his phone and saw that there were another two buildings in the complex, with a small courtyard laid out between them.

Sakura was in there somewhere.

Katsuro turned round and picked up his bag from where he had left it in the well behind the driver's seat. He pulled out the Glock 17 pistol that he had collected from the long-term storage locker he rented in Seminyak. He pulled down on the slide lock lever and it did not budge, confirming it was installed in the proper orientation. He pulled the trigger and cycled the slide quickly, satisfying himself that the reset was working properly and that the trigger safety had engaged. He pulled the trigger again, holding it to the rear of the pistol before cycling the slide to check the reset again. He went through the rest of his checks, making sure that the firing pin was safe and that the recoil spring didn't need replacing. The pistol was old, and he couldn't vouch for the reliability of the man from whom he had purchased it on the island the first time he had visited to deliver Sakura's drugs; he would be especially thorough. His final task was to take a fully loaded magazine and slot it into the pistol.

He took out his phone and composed a message to his father.

I have her.

It wasn't entirely true, but that was just temporary. It would be true soon enough.

The phone buzzed with a reply.

The packages?

Katsuro paused for a moment before replying, considering his best response.

Not seen.

He was composing a follow-up with a request for instructions when the phone buzzed again.

Find them and deliver them.
He nodded.
And then?
His father's reply came quickly.
Clean up your mess, Katsuro-chan.

34

Sakura knelt on the bare concrete floor, bent at the waist with her arms wrapped around her midriff. A drain was just in front of her face, set into the centre of the cell. It was at the lowest point of the floor, with the concrete angled toward the grate to make it easier to hose down. She retched again, but, apart from a small amount of bile, there was nothing left in her stomach to vomit up.

Hoping that the nausea had passed, she struggled to her feet and, bracing herself with an outstretched arm against the wall, she made her way to the concrete slab that passed for a bed. It was bare, too, just like the floor. The cell was ten feet by ten feet. There was the bed, a forbidding metal door, and a bare bulb inside a wire cage on the ceiling. On the opposite side of the wall from the door was a barred window that was not much more than a narrow slit. There was no toilet; she guessed that the drain in the floor was used for that.

Sakura listened to the rain slamming down outside and felt tears welling at the corners of her eyes. She had been in a first-class cabin just a few hours ago. And *now* look at her.

She thought of Yamato. He was the only reason she had agreed to Takashi's demands and Katsuro's degradations. Her job as a parent—her *only* job as a parent—was to keep him safe. To provide him with an environment where he could grow into a man and make his own way into the world. She had failed. The tears overflowed and streamed down her face.

She sat on the bed, shuddering with sobs that seemed to run up and down her body, and then heard a noise at the door of the cell. She looked up to see the access hatch slide open and a pair of dark eyes peering through.

"I need to speak to a lawyer," she said.

"No lawyer."

"I don't even know why I'm here."

The man chuckled. "Drugs, lady. You know."

"Could I have a drink, then?" she asked. "Please?"

The hatch slid shut and, a few seconds later, the door was unlocked. It swung open. A policeman stood in the corridor outside. He was in his early twenties, well built, and dressed in the standard uniform of the Balinese police: a beige shirt with breast pockets and navy-blue trousers held up with an elaborate belt. Above his right breast pocket was an embroidered badge with his name—Nugraha—and above the other pocket was a gold metal shield. Epaulettes with a single stripe completed the uniform.

"I'm thirsty," Sakura said. "Please could I have something to drink?"

Nugraha did not reply, and Sakura felt her skin crawl as his eyes wandered up and down her body. She shuffled back along the concrete bed; his eyes hardened as he took a step toward her.

Another policeman came to the open door. He was older, rounder, and had more stripes on his epaulettes. He

barked something in Indonesian and the first officer—
perhaps chastised—sneered at Sakura in response. She
thought he was about to spit at her, but, instead, he glared
before turning on his heel and leaving her cell.

The older policeman took his place.

"He get you water," the policeman said.

"Thank you."

The man regarded Sakura with a look that could not
have been described as friendly, but was not hostile,
either.

"What's going to happen to me?" Sakura asked.

The policeman paused before replying. "You in big trouble, lady. Drugs not allowed here." He shook his head sadly
from side to side, his face softening. "You tell me where they
are and maybe I help you?"

Sakura thought quickly. If the police did not have the
drugs, then where were they? The only explanation was that
the nurse or the doctor had taken the packages after drug-
ging her in the hotel room, then reported her to the police to
get her out of the way. Or perhaps someone at the hotel had
called them?

"I don't know what you mean," Sakura replied, her voice
breaking.

"We find one packet," the man said. "But there are more
—yes?"

That was smart: whoever was responsible had left a little
of the heroin to incriminate her and then taken the rest. Her
thoughts went beyond her immediate difficulties, severe
though they were, and on to how Takashi and Katsuro
would react. How was she going to get Yamato back if she
didn't deliver the consignment? Takashi had a reputation for
making people disappear—*especially* people who had
crossed him—and if he thought that she had taken the

packages herself, then he would surely kill her son and then her.

Sakura felt fresh tears. "What's going to happen to me?"

"Tomorrow, you in court for charge and sentence. Then, prison." The policeman's face had hardened, any trace of sympathy disappearing when he realised that Sakura wasn't going to tell him anything about the location of the narcotics.

Sakura's voice quivered as she tried to assert herself. "Lawyer," she whispered before repeating herself in what she hoped was a more confident voice. "Lawyer. I want a lawyer."

The policeman laughed. He left the cell and slammed the heavy metal door behind him.

She pulled her legs up onto the concrete bed and curled up into a ball, wrapping her arms around her knees. She couldn't stop thinking about her son: the party they had thrown for his third birthday, when Miyasato had given him a wrestling figurine that he had ordered from America. Sakura had had no idea who the comically muscular figure was, but, from the look of utter joy on Yamato's face when he'd opened the present, she had seen that he was special in some way to him. The memory triggered others—Christmas, reading to him before he went to sleep, pushing him on the swings at Higashi-Shinagawa Park—and fresh tears fell down her cheeks.

She jumped as the hatch in the door snapped open. She looked up to see an arm extended through it, a plastic cup of water in its hand. She got to her feet, still dizzy, and started to walk across the cell to take it when the hand turned over and poured the contents of the cup onto the floor. Sakura watched the water run toward the drain. A cruel laugh came through the hatch before it was slammed shut.

35

M ilton was soaked to the skin by the time he found the motorcycle shop on Wanagiri. There was a lay-by beyond the tin-roofed shack that passed for the shop. The shack looked to be held together by the rust on the metal slats. Leather straps held the roof to the rest of the structure. The wind had worked beneath one panel and was lifting it up and dropping it back down, the sound of the metallic slaps ringing out through the howl of the weather.

The lay-by marked the entrance to a network of dirt roads that led into what looked to Milton like run-down residential areas. Ragged signs advertising local hotels fluttered in the wind, and a pack of stray dogs stared at him from underneath a wooden lean-to shelter. The downpour had cleared the streets of most foot traffic, with only a few hardy souls braving the wet. Milton sloshed through rain-filled potholes before dismounting and pushing the scooter to the end of the line of mopeds that had been arranged outside the shop. He jogged over to a car that had been covered with a tarpaulin and sheltered as best he could under a canopy of palm fronds while he waited for Victoria.

KATSURO COULDN'T STOP THINKING about the consequences of letting his father down. Their relationship went beyond the familial; the Nishimoto-*kai* was a shadow of what it once was, but Takashi was the head of the family, and Katsuro's standing within it would not insulate him from the consequences of failure. His father was traditional to a fault, and the notion of being discredited filled Katsuro with dread. Would his father make him apologise in the traditional way? Katsuro knew that he would. *Yubitsume*—the removal of a fingertip—would be painful, but the pain would pass.

The shame would not.

He reached down for his bag and pulled out a small folder full of individual sheets of paper that were, in turn, protected by plastic sleeves. He leafed through the papers until he found the one he wanted. Across the top of the sheet were two crests: the first had a building within a circle, surrounded by laurel leaves with a black banner underneath, and was the official crest of the Hong Kong Police Force; the second crest belonged to Detachment 88, the much-feared counter-terrorism unit of the Indonesian police.

The text of the letter introduced Katsuro to whoever was reading it as a senior member of the Hong Kong Police Force. According to the text—in both English and Indonesian—Katsuro was seconded to Detachment 88 on an important national security mission and was to be afforded every professional courtesy available. It was complete fiction, but the letter looked official enough to pass muster by a local policeman, particularly when it was accompanied by the excellent forged identity card that Katsuro had in his wallet. He knew that he could pass for Chinese, and the chances of meeting anyone who spoke Cantonese better than he did were rare, especially here. He wasn't fluent in the language, but when he was younger, he had studied in Hong Kong for a semester. Good enough.

His plan was simple: he would walk into the police station and take Sakura into his custody. The chances of a local policeman having the gall to question a Detachment 88 order were slim, but, in the event that he was unfortunate, he had his Glock. Either way, he would be leaving with her this evening. And then he would find out what she had done with the shipment.

He had just reached for the door handle, ready to turn it and step out into the rain, when a white Toyota Hilux rumbled past. The truck pulled off the road, emptying the potholes as it splashed through them. It came to a stop perhaps fifty feet away and, as Katsuro watched, a white Western man—six feet tall, bearded, dark hair plastered to his scalp by the rain—stepped out from next to a corrugated metal shack and walked over to the truck. Katsuro didn't recognise him, or the vehicle into which he had climbed, but there was something about the incongruence of it that gave him pause. Why was a Westerner waiting outside the police station in the rain? It was curious, and he wondered whether he could have anything to do with Sakura.

And then he remembered what he had seen at the airport. Sakura had been assisted by a dark-haired, bearded Western man of around the same height. The visibility in the rain was such that it was impossible to say that this might be the same man, but it didn't seem as if it was such a stretch.

Katsuro reached for his Glock. He would watch for a moment. Perhaps he had been fortunate and found a way to redeem himself in his father's eyes. He would find Sakura, murder whoever it was who had involved himself in family business, and deliver the drugs to the *premans* as arranged.

Perhaps he would be able to absolve himself of blame after all.

36

M ilton wiped the rain from his face. The driver's window slid down and Victoria looked out.

"Hop in," she said.

Milton made his way to the passenger side and pulled the door open, climbing gratefully into the cab.

"It's torrential," he said.

"That's Bali for you. It'll be glorious tomorrow."

"Thanks for coming out."

"I should be in bed with my husband," she said. "Not only that, but you smell like a wet dog. How about you tell me what's going on?"

Milton explained what he had found when he returned to the hotel.

"How did they find her?" she asked, her forehead creased with a deep frown.

"I don't know."

"Shit," Victoria said. "Maybe it *was* Edwin."

"It doesn't make much difference now. What's done is done."

"What about the drugs?"

"Gone," Milton said.

"The police must have taken them."

"I'm not sure," Milton said. "I got there five minutes after they did, and they were already bringing her out. They didn't stay, either. There was no obvious investigation. No one was dusting for prints. No forensics. They even left my bag."

"Bali isn't London," Victoria said. "How shall I say this? Standards are *different* here."

"I get that," Milton said. "I've worked in places like this before, and what happened to her was much too quick to be anything other than a set-up. I'm speculating, but if you asked me to guess, I'd say that someone took the drugs and then called a friend in the police to get Sakura out of the way." He sucked his teeth. "Anyway—it doesn't make much difference either way."

"She's definitely in trouble. The police won't need the drugs to charge her with smuggling. The standard of proof is looser over here."

"How quickly will they process her?"

"She could be charged, found guilty, and in prison by this time tomorrow."

Milton exhaled. "That quickly?"

"They don't mess about, especially with a foreigner convicted of smuggling."

Milton had suspected as much. There was no time to waste.

"I need to get her out."

"I thought you might say that," Victoria said.

"*I* have to," Milton corrected. "Not you. I can't involve you in this."

"I'm kind of involved already—seems like I found a hotel room and a doctor for a woman who's about to get life for running drugs."

"And none of that will ever come out," Milton said.

"Didn't say it would," Victoria said. "But I'm helping anyway. I spoke to a friend of mine while I drove over. He's been a customer in the police station half a dozen times, and he knows the layout."

"A 'customer'?"

"The police don't always see eye to eye with him. Shall we leave it at that?"

Milton remembered what Victoria had said about the work she did for the hotel.

"I'm guessing your friend is..." He forgot the word.

"Laskar Bali," Victoria finished. "That's right. You get nothing done here without their involvement. They're like the mafia. You can rub up against them and lose, or you can go with the flow and accept them for what they are. I've always found them to be helpful, especially when they've been well paid."

"They'll get her out?"

"No," Victoria said. "That would be more than they would be prepared to do. That's on us. But they'll run interference."

Milton nodded. That was better than nothing. "Did they tell you what we'd find inside?"

"There's not much to it. It's a provincial station. Three holding cells in the building at the back, a main office, and that's about it."

"How many policemen?"

"Three, maybe four. There's not enough room for more than that."

Milton made to open the truck door. "I'd better have a look around, then."

Victoria put a hand on his shoulder. "Hold up. I'll come, too."

"No. Stay here. I'll be quicker on my own. And there's no point us both smelling like wet dogs. I'll call you when I've checked it out."

Milton gave her a wink and stepped out into the rain, closing the door behind him.

37

M ilton stepped out of the truck and into the rain. Although the sidewalk—if the narrow muddy strip deserved the name—was on the opposite side of the road, he wanted to keep his back to any passing traffic to avoid his white face lighting up in any oncoming headlights. The next two shacks he approached were both shops of some sort, but closed and shuttered against the storm. Milton couldn't tell, and didn't care, what type of wares they sold; his attention was fixed on the building on the other side of the road. A yellow sign with black lettering was illuminated with a small bulb. *Polisi*. The arrow on the sign pointed through a set of traditional Balinese gates to a squat white single-storey building with a red-tiled roof. Rain hammered off the tiles and poured down onto the ground, almost hiding the small windows at the front of the police station. Milton couldn't see through the windows, but he didn't need to. He wasn't planning on going in through the front.

He stepped over and around the potholes and made his way across to the opposite side of the road, and turned right onto a service road that separated the police station from the neighbouring restaurant. He hurried along, keeping close to the wall that divided the two plots. The restaurant had a handful of patrons inside, so he walked on until he was beyond it. He passed a ramshackle outdoor smoking shack with a couple of locals sitting at plastic tables under a corrugated tin roof, both men staring at their mobile phones as he passed. Milton doubted they'd even registered his presence, let alone looked at him. The heavy drumming of fat raindrops on the tin roof would hide the sound of his footsteps, so he picked up his pace a little.

Victoria had suggested that the cells were at the rear of the building. Milton couldn't see over the wall, but the GPS on his phone placed him just beyond the police station. With the reservation that his position would not be shown with any particular accuracy, he checked behind him and, happy that he was not being watched from the restaurant, he clambered up and over the concrete wall and crouched down behind it.

Milton took a few seconds to examine his surroundings. He was in a small yard dominated by the building he had seen by the road but punctuated with a series of smaller buildings. There was a gate a little way further down the wall that looked as if it would open out into the restaurant's parking lot.

He examined the rear of the police station. The money, such as it was, had obviously been spent on the public-facing elevation, because this side was run-down and basic. The ground was littered with trash and weeds, and several chest-high bushes had taken root. He focused his attention on the rear wall. As he had expected, it was made of block-work coated with a cement render, cracked in places. There was some bowing in the wall and cracks radiated out; there was efflorescence around the cracks. Milton saw that the wall had not been built properly, and that constant water ingress had weakened it. He knew just how to exploit that.

Milton counted three windows, each of them no more than narrow, barred slits. The window on the left had a faint light shimmering through the rain, so he made his way toward it.

He looked up at the window. It was eight feet from the ground. He looked around to see if there was something for him to stand on, but saw nothing. He could retrace his steps and see if there was anything in the yard that he had just left, but he didn't want to waste any more time than necessary. There was a bright flash of lightning above his head, followed a split second later by a crack of thunder. The rain fell even more heavily.

It didn't matter; he wasn't going to get any wetter than he was already. He looked up at the window, bent his knees, and jumped, extending his arms above his head as he did so. He wrapped his fingers around the cold metal bars and heaved himself up, ignoring the burn in his biceps and triceps as he did so.

He pulled himself up so that he could look between the bars and into the cell. It was dark, but, as lightning crackled overhead again, it cast enough of a bright white flash for him to see the figure curled up on the bed that had been cut into the wall.

"Sakura?" he whispered.

There was no response.

"Sakura!"

The curled-up figure stirred.

"John? Is that you?"

He spoke through gritted teeth, trying to ignore the ache in his arms and stomach. "Yes," he said. "It's me."

38

Victoria drummed her fingers on the steering wheel of the truck while she waited for Milton to return. The rain was still teeming down, hammering on the roof and streaming down the windshield. She leaned forward to turn the radio up so she could hear it over the noise of the downpour. Her phone vibrated in her pocket. She took it out and saw that it was Jean-Michel, wondering what time she would be back. She thumbed a quick reply.

Not sure. I'll—

She jumped as the passenger door opened and Milton climbed into the cab.

"Shit," she said. "You gave me a shock."

Milton was soaked, and water dripped from his clothes onto the upholstery.

Victoria finished her text and then turned the radio down. "So? What's going on?"

"She's in a cell at the back, just like you said."

"And now?"

"I just need to get her out."

"Any ideas how we can do that?"

"I told you: this isn't your problem."

"It kind of is." Milton looked as if he was about to rebuke her, but Victoria spoke over him. "I made a couple of calls. You were right—it was Edwin. I fucked up. The reason she's in there is because he sold her out. I just heard—he's put the word out that he has heroin he wants to sell. He offered it to someone I know, and they told me."

Milton nodded. "I'm not surprised."

"So my sending him to help has led to this."

"And there was no way you could've known. I only told you she was sick. I didn't tell you about the drugs. That's all on him."

"Doesn't matter. I recommended him. I should have found someone more trustworthy."

Milton stared through the rivulets of water running down the windshield. Victoria watched his reflection; he was weighing up the pros and cons of asking for help.

"Come on. A helping hand wouldn't be useful?"

"Of course it would."

"So why are we waiting?"

He turned to look at her. "You're sure? We'll have to make quite a mess here."

She nodded.

"All right. Thank you."

"What do you need?"

"Two things. The first is a distraction. Something that'll get the policemen out of the station for a few minutes."

Victoria picked up her phone and started scrolling through her list of contacts to find the one she wanted. She pressed the call button, and, a few seconds later, the man she had just spoken to picked up for a second time. His name was Bagas, and he worked with the Laskar Bali.

Victoria told him what she needed. Bagas owed Victoria a favour and he agreed to help.

Victoria finished the call and turned to see that Milton was watching with one eyebrow cocked.

"What?" Victoria said.

"You've gone native."

"What? The Indonesian? When in Rome…"

"Who was that?"

"A friend with connections. There'll be a distraction in about twenty minutes. I wouldn't expect it to be subtle."

"How much is it costing you? I'll cover it."

"It's not costing me anything."

"Nothing's free."

"Well, no, but they owe me—I'm calling in a favour."

"Okay," Milton replied, but Victoria sensed that they would be coming back to the topic at some point in the future.

"What's the second thing?" she asked him.

"Can I borrow your truck?"

"No."

"Sorry?"

"No, you can't. I saw the way you rode off on that scooter. You're a liability. Where are we going? I'll drive."

"Around the back. Keep the lights off. No point attracting attention to ourselves."

39

They parked in the parking lot of the restaurant, right down at the end next to the gate in the wall. Milton clambered over it again and picked the padlock that secured it. The rain didn't help, nor did the rust that clogged the workings of the lock, but Milton had forced far worse than that before, and it delayed him for only a minute or two.

He had only just hauled the gate open when he heard the sound of automatic gunfire.

Milton hurried back to the truck. "*That's* the distraction?"

Victoria had inched her window down. "I told you they wouldn't be subtle."

"They're shooting up the station?" He shook his head. "Whatever—it'll certainly get their attention. You ready?"

Victoria said that she was, and, as Milton stepped to the side, she rolled the truck through the gate.

∼

KATSURO FLINCHED as he heard the sharp crack of automatic gunfire from close by. He reacted instinctively, ducking down in the car and reaching for his own weapon. He looked left and right as he tried to locate the source of the noise. He peered through the rain and saw two small motorcycles driving slowly past the police station. Each of them bore two young men, and the pillion passengers were both armed with short-barrelled machine guns. The men were focused on the police station. The lead motorcycle turned in a lazy circle as the passenger struggled to change the magazine. Whoever they were, Katsuro saw, they were far from expert. His assessment was confirmed as the other shooter squeezed out a burst in the general direction of the police station. The stubby gun rose in his hands during the burst and, while the first few rounds might have hit their target, the majority of them certainly went high.

He remembered the truck and the two Westerners and joined the dots.

This is a diversion.

He sat up.

They're going to try to get Sakura out.

Katsuro opened the door of the car and eased himself out, staying low. He crept to the side of the road, keeping his head down and working around to the rear of the car. The ripping sound of both shooters firing another long, wild burst was followed by the distinct, individual cracks of more controlled return fire from a police pistol. He looked through the cabin and saw a muzzle flash as someone inside the building squeezed off a round, and then another and another.

He was sure now: this was an attempt to draw the police away from the building so that an attempt could be made to break Sakura out of her cell. Katsuro knew where she was now, but that situation would change if she was allowed to escape. He thought of his father's disapproval and knew that he could not let events unfold without him.

He took a breath, gripped the Glock in a steady hand and then scurried across the road, his head down, and through the gap in the wall that led to the restaurant's parking lot.

40

Sakura shivered on the concrete bunk. It wasn't particularly cold, but then she wasn't wearing anything warm. She got to her feet and paced the small cell, wondering what would happen next. Smith had promised that he would come back for her. He hadn't said when or how, save that it would be soon. She could hear the rain teeming down outside. An occasional flash of light flickered through the window, followed by thunder. Her father had taught her how to calculate how far away a storm was by counting between the flash and the rumble, and now she found herself counting off the seconds.

She thought she could hear something else. Another rumble, this one constant.

A truck or a lorry?

She looked toward the barred window. She heard a scraping noise and then saw Smith's face once again. He didn't have his hands wrapped around the bars like before; he must have been standing on something.

"Sakura."

"I'm here."

"Go over to the corner—over there, as far away from this wall as you can. Wrap your arms over your head and don't look up."

"Why? What's going to happen?"

"Just do it. I'm getting you out, but I'm going to have to make a little mess."

MILTON WATCHED Sakura retreat to the other side of the cell. Victoria had reversed the truck right up to the rear wall, and Milton was standing on the flatbed, more than high enough to look through the window. He leaned down and picked up one end of the thick strap that had, until a few minutes earlier, been keeping the tin roof of the motorcycle shack lashed down. He looped one end of the reinforced material through the bars of the cell window and attached the other end to the tow bar on the rear of the truck. He checked both ends of the strap to make sure they were secure. There was about ten feet of play in it; he would have preferred more, but that was as good as it was going to get. They would have to hope that it was enough.

There were more short, sharp bursts of gunfire from the front of the police station, followed a few seconds later by single shots from pistols. Milton assumed that was the sound of the police returning fire.

Milton jumped down, splashing into the mud. He slapped the side of the truck and then stepped right out of the way.

"Now!"

KATSURO CURSED when he realised what was about to happen. The Hilux had been backed right up tight against the rear wall of the building, and something—a chain, perhaps, or a rope—had been fixed to the bars that covered a cell window. Katsuro swiped rainwater from his eyes as the driver threw the truck into gear and hit the gas. The wheels spun for a second or two on the wet ground before they gained traction, and then the vehicle lurched forward. The rope tightened, jerking the truck almost to a stop. Then it jerked forward again, and, this time, it was accompanied by a crack and then a loud crash.

VICTORIA HIT THE BRAKES. Milton looked back at the building: on the ground, still attached to the strap, were the bars that had previously secured the window. But the truck had not just pulled out the bars; there was a gaping hole where several of the breeze blocks had also been yanked out. Milton had noticed that the building work had been slipshod and suspected that the wall might be fragile. His biggest concern had been that the cell's roof would come down, covering Sakura in debris and injuring her, or worse. Thankfully, that hadn't happened. He hurried toward the hole. Victoria put the truck in reverse and backed it up.

Rapid gunfire came from the front of the police station. A Heckler & Koch MP5, perhaps? The barks of fire sounded too deep to be from a Škorpion or an Uzi. While Milton doubted that the officers in a small police station would have anything more powerful than pistols with which to defend themselves, he was concerned about the amount of ammunition that the submachine guns were chewing through. Victoria's contacts wouldn't be able to keep up the distraction for long.

He stepped through the hole in the wall, waving his hand to swipe away the dust that was drifting down through the air. Sakura was still curled in the corner, her arms wrapped over her head. Milton stepped all the way inside and crossed over to her.

"Sakura? Are you okay?"

She removed her arms from over her head and looked up at him with fear in her eyes.

"What's going on? All that shooting?"

"I'll tell you later," Milton replied, reaching down and helping her to her feet. "We need to go."

41

Milton led Sakura to the hole in the wall and helped her over the pile of concrete that littered the floor. Victoria had opened the passenger door of the truck, and Milton pushed her gently but firmly toward it with a hand in the small of her back.

He bent down and undid the end of the strap that was attached to the tow bar, ensuring that, when they drove off, they would not be dragging the bars after them. That done, he climbed into the back of the truck.

"Go."

Milton sat back as Victoria jammed the truck into gear and floored it. They raced through the open gate and slid hard left as she turned onto the restaurant's parking lot. She spun the wheel to swerve around something that appeared in their path.

"What was that?" Sakura said.

Victoria looked in her wing mirror. "No idea. Can't see anything now. Stray dog."

They raced out of the parking lot and swung hard right, putting the police station behind them. Milton looked back

and saw the flash of another automatic burst and then heard
the whine of motorcycle engines as the *premans*—no doubt
seeing the fleeing truck—took that as their cue to leave. The
bikes were faster than the truck and they quickly caught up
and passed, one on either side. The riders and passengers
were all wearing helmets that obscured their faces, but the
rider on the right raised his hand to Victoria in acknowledgement as he drew alongside, then put it back down on
the handlebars and raced away.

"Hold tight," Victoria said.

The truck lurched from side to side as she guided it
through a seemingly endless succession of backstreets, some
of them only just wide enough for the vehicle to fit. As soon
as they reached what could be called a proper road, Victoria
flicked the headlights back on.

Milton turned to Sakura. "Are you okay?"

"I think so," she replied.

"No injuries? Nothing fell on you?"

"No," she said.

"And the drugs?"

"All out."

"Good."

She looked at him gratefully. "Thank you."

KATSURO GRUNTED as he hit the ground, rolling onto his side
to absorb the hard landing as he leapt out of the way of the
truck. He rolled across the ground, sharp stones digging into
his flanks and the palms of his hands. He came to rest and
lay in the mud, staring at the truck as it raced away from
him. The brake lights flared as the driver slowed before
turning hard right and onto the road.

He got to his feet and checked himself over. He had been lucky; no serious damage seemed to have been done. There were a few minor lacerations on the palms of his hands and down his right arm, but, that apart, he was fine. He had misplaced the Glock, though, and he couldn't leave that behind. Katsuro put his hand into his pocket, pulled out his phone and switched on the flashlight. He knew that he had only a few moments before the police came to investigate what had just happened to the back of their station, and he hurriedly searched the area until he found the pistol.

He shoved it into his waistband and jogged back to the main road. He dropped into the front seat and took out his phone again. He remembered the registration on the truck —B1042PJ—and noted it down. He added what he had discerned of the driver in the brief moments before he had dived clear. She was a Westerner, tanned and with long blonde hair.

That would have to do.

They had Sakura.

He needed to find them.

42

Victoria's truck rumbled into the entrance of the hotel after a twenty-minute journey that had been fraught with the fear that they might be pursued. They hadn't been; Victoria's suggestion that the local station would have only a skeleton staff, and that they would have been distracted by the *premans'* diversion, appeared to have been accurate.

Milton and Sakura crouched down, out of sight of the solitary security guard on duty. It was a precaution, Victoria had said. Better that no one knew they were there. Milton looked up to see Victoria raising a hand in greeting to the guard before the truck made its way into the estate and followed the road to the villas near the beach.

Victoria pulled the truck around to the back of the buildings and turned the engine off. The three of them sat for a moment, listening to the ticking of the engine as it cooled down. There was a flash of lightning over the bay, followed by thunder. The rain had stopped as they had driven away from the police station, and now it seemed as if the storm was being blown away from them.

"Well, that was an interesting evening," Victoria said. She turned to Sakura. "Sorry—we haven't met."

Sakura didn't reply.

"This is Victoria," Milton said to her. "She's a friend."

"I'm Sakura."

Victoria reached back and shook her hand.

They got out of the truck and followed Victoria to the villa that had been reserved for Milton. She stopped at the door, allowing Sakura to go inside so that she and Milton could talk.

"Thanks," Milton said.

"Forget it," she said. "I'd better go. Jean-Michel will be wondering where I am, and I still haven't worked out what I'm going to tell him."

"Perhaps not the truth?"

"I might massage it a little," she said with a smile. "Although we've got up to worse than that before. He probably wouldn't be all that shocked. More annoyed that he was at home while I was out having fun." She half turned, then paused. "Shit—I forgot. You haven't eaten."

"It's okay."

She nodded into the villa. "She might be hungry. The restaurant's closed, but you can get room service. Tell them I sent you—they'll do you something nice." She clapped Milton on the shoulder. "And behave yourself—she's pretty."

Milton was about to protest, but Victoria turned and jogged back to the Toyota. She opened the door and pulled herself inside. The truck rumbled into life and she drove away.

Milton pushed the door open and went into the villa. Sakura was sitting on the bed with her head in her hands.

"Are you okay?" he asked her.

She looked up at him. She looked tired and close to tears. "Not really."

"You've had a day and a half," Milton said. "You need to get some sleep."

She stared at him. "Why would you do this for me?"

"Because you needed a break."

"But you don't know me."

He looked at her earnestly. "You think I was going to forget about you after what you did?"

She frowned, puzzled. "What? What did I do?"

"Upgraded me."

She frowned at him before realising that he was joking. "I'm serious," she scolded him. "Why would you do this?"

Milton sat down on the chair. "Because it was the right thing to do. You needed someone to look out for you today and I was able to help. There's nothing more to it than that."

She bit her lip, as if weighing up what else to say. After a moment, she sighed, scrubbed her nails against her scalp and stood up. "I need a shower. Would that be okay?"

"Of course," Milton replied. He needed one, too, but he could wait. "There are toiletries in the bathroom. I'll hop in when you're done."

Sakura looked at him bleakly, the vigour in her eyes that he remembered from their first meeting all gone. She looked bone-tired.

"What happens next?"

"We get showered and then we get something to eat."

"And then?"

"And then we talk."

PART III

TUESDAY

43

Milton rolled off the sofa and stood, moving as quietly as he could. He checked his watch: it was six in the morning. He crossed the lounge and peeked through the open door into the bedroom. Sakura was still asleep. He wasn't surprised that she was tired. She had been through an ordeal, both physical and mental, and it was going to take her a little while to recover.

Milton pulled on a T-shirt and a pair of shorts and went outside. He closed the door and walked down through the hotel's lush gardens to the beach. He didn't have his running shoes with him, but the prospect of a barefoot run on the sand was a pleasant one. He had always found exercise to be meditative, and he needed some time to himself to work through what might come next.

LIZARDS BASKED in the early heat and a boisterous lorikeet landed in the branches of a palm tree overhead. Milton made his way to the water's edge and looked out over the ocean. It looked as if it was going to be another glorious day. Any sign of the storm that had rolled across the bay the previous evening was long gone, and now the skies were a deep blue, and the sun, rising above the horizon, was a fiery orange.

He turned to the right and walked to the raised promenade that ran parallel to the sand. He popped his earbuds in and scrolled through his music until he found the playlist that he wanted. It was a compilation of seventies and eighties rock, and, when he tapped play, AC/DC's 'Back in Black' began. He broke into an easy stride, matching each step with Phil Rudd's metronomic percussion, and settled into his run.

He relaxed into a loping pace and angled down to the line of the tide, enjoying the slap of his naked feet on the wet sand and the warm water that splashed up his ankles. He let his thoughts return to the previous night. He had called room service while Sakura was in the shower. He had dropped Victoria's name, just as she had suggested, and had ordered a sashimi and seafood platter. The large foil tub, when it was delivered, was loaded with bamboo lobster, flower crab, king prawn, salmon, and yellowfin tuna. The seafood was covered with a generous helping of snapper Thai sauce and cocktail sauce and finished with a sprinkling of soy and fresh wasabi.

Sakura's eyes had widened when Milton peeled back the foil lid. They had sat side by side on the villa's small veranda, watching the twinkling lights of the fishing boats in the darkness of the bay, and eaten as much as they could.

They had talked for an hour. Sakura was determined to return to Tokyo and to Yamato. Milton had asked her what would happen when she got there, particularly without the drugs that she had agreed to deliver for the

Nishimoto-*kai*. Sakura had not been able to answer the question.

As he ran, Milton thought through his options. He could do nothing. Leave Sakura to her own devices and move on. But that would make things worse. She would have no hope of removing herself from the situation in which she had found herself if Milton chose not to help.

The second option—and one to which he had given careful thought—was to find the *premans* whom Edwin had approached about selling the stolen contraband. He could recover the drugs, return them to Sakura, and then she could deliver them to the original buyers. She could return to Tokyo and, perhaps, negotiate the return of her son. But that option was full of problems, the most egregious being that it would make Milton complicit in the distribution of drugs, and he could not endorse that. He would be facilitating pain and misery and, as an addict, that was a line that he would not cross.

The second problem was Victoria's relationship with the *premans*; Milton knew that they wouldn't return the drugs willingly, and that meant that he would have to take them. That might cause problems for her. Finally, helping Sakura to complete the delivery relied upon the assumption that the Nishimoto-*kai* would agree to return her son when she was done. Why would they do that? Sakura would have proven that she was an effective courier; she was beautiful and had a regal bearing about her that was a million miles away from the usual image of a mule. There was value in that, and Milton doubted that the men who controlled her would willingly give her up. He suspected that they would force her to work for them either until she was caught or until, as had so nearly happened this time, something went wrong and she died.

There was a third option, and it was the only one that he really considered viable. He would accompany Sakura to Tokyo and then either mediate for her or persuade the men holding her son that they should reconsider the arrangement.

Milton reached the three-mile point and slowed to a halt. He stood in the warm surf, took a few deep breaths, and then turned and set off back to the villa.

MILTON RETURNED to his starting point and pulled the earbuds from his ears. He took off his T-shirt and used it to mop the sweat from his face. It was already hot, and the mercury promised to climb higher. He dumped the shirt, his phone and the earbuds on the beach and walked out into the surf. He felt the warmth of the water on his calves and then, as he strode deeper, past his knees and then up to his waist and, finally, his neck. He felt the fine sand between his toes and the warmth of the sun on his face.

He had tried not to think too hard about the conclusion to their discussion last night. Sakura had stood up and turned off the small side light next to the bed. She had faced Milton, her hands on the cotton belt that fastened her robe across her midriff. Milton knew that she was about to undo it, and had taken her hands, shaking his head as he did so. Sakura had looked confused and protested that she wanted to thank him. He had smiled at her and said thanks were unnecessary, and certainly not like *that*. She had stood before him for a few moments longer, then removed her hands from his and pulled down the bedsheet. She had been asleep within moments of her head touching the pillow.

Feeling bad about rejecting her, Milton had taken his copy of the Big Book from his bag and sat for a while on the veranda reading it. He had flipped through to the fifth chapter, and, in particular, the discussion of the considerations that an alcoholic should make before starting a new relationship. He had to ask himself one simple question: Was it selfish? He thought back to his relationship with Victoria, a lifetime ago in London, and how perfunctory and egocentric that had been. He applied the same test to anything that might happen with Sakura. She was vulnerable, lonely and afraid. Sleeping with her wouldn't help with any of those problems; it would create new ones.

He had been right to say no.

The warm water caressed his body. The run had been helpful, just as he had expected it would be. It had given him a sense of clarity that had been hidden in a fog of indecision and confusion before.

He knew what he was going to do.

He would offer to go to Tokyo with Sakura. He would find a solution to her problems there.

44

Sakura heard a gentle knocking and opened her eyes. There was a moment of disorientation as she looked around the room and realised that she had no idea where she was. The bewilderment passed, replaced by a sense of dread as the reality of her situation reasserted itself: Takashi's drugs were gone and she had no way of getting them back. Katsuro would have gone to find her at the hotel and discovered that she was not there. It was disaster upon disaster.

She slumped back on the mattress and put her hands to her face.

The knocking returned, a little more insistently. She remembered where she was now—Smith had brought her to a hotel where he had a villa—and she guessed that a maid must be outside.

"Hello?" she called out.

There was no answer.

She swung her legs out of bed and stood. She still felt weak, but the lassitude of yesterday was gone. The room service that Smith had ordered and then hours of sleep had worked wonders.

She went into the living room. The sofa bed had been made, but it was empty. She saw a torn-out page of paper with the hotel insignia left on the table.

Gone for a run. Back soon.

The knocking came again. "Hello? Sakura?"

Sakura went to the door. There was no peephole, so she had no idea who it was. "Hello? Who is it?"

"It's Victoria. John's friend. We met last night."

Sakura opened the door to see the woman who had driven the truck last night standing outside. Sakura had not really had the opportunity to get a proper look at her as they drove away from the police station, but, now that she was right in front of her, Sakura could see that she was pretty. She was older—she guessed around Smith's age—but her skin was smooth and there was a mischievous spark in her blue eyes. She was smiling a little uncertainly, as if reluctant to disturb Sakura.

"I've not woken you, have I?" Victoria said.

"No," Sakura lied.

"Only my husband said he saw John out running, so I thought you'd both be up."

"I woke up a while ago," she said. "Please. Come in."

She stepped back to let the other woman into the villa.

Victoria was carrying a carrier bag with the logo of a local supermarket on it. "I brought you some clothes," she said, holding up the bag. "It looked like we might be about the same size, although I suspect you might be just a *little* bit slimmer than me." She grinned at her self-deprecation, a sincere, broad smile that lit up her face. "I could see you didn't have anything with you."

"That's kind. Thank you."

Victoria waved her gratitude away. "How are you feeling?"

"Better than yesterday."

"You've had a hard few days from the sound of it."

"How much did John tell you?"

"I think I know most of it."

Sakura found, to her surprise, that she wanted Victoria's approval. "The drugs," she said. "It's not what it looks like."

"John told me. They have your son. I understand—I'm sure I'd do the same thing if I had a child."

"I'm grateful for your help," Sakura said.

"I was glad to be able to do a little. I just hope John can help you get the problem fixed. Now—you'd better check those clothes and make sure they're okay."

Sakura took the bag and peered inside it. She saw a pair of briefs and a white bra, both still with the tags attached. "These are new. You didn't have to—"

"Only the underwear," Victoria said.

"I'll pay you back," Sakura said, although she had no idea how she was going to manage that. She had nothing with her apart from last night's clothes. She didn't have her bag or her purse or her phone. She guessed that they were still at the police station.

"Forget it," Victoria said. "My treat." She cast an eye around the room. "John still out running?"

"Yes," she said. "Can I ask you—how'd you know him?"

"We used to work together in London. This is the first time I've seen him in years."

"What did you used to do?"

"He hasn't told you?"

Sakura shook her head.

"It would be better coming from him," Victoria said, noticing her disquiet. "It's nothing to be worried about. We used to work for the government—all very dull—but there are some things that we're not really supposed to discuss with civilians, and I'd rather not make that decision for him. I don't know how much he'd want to say. The good news, though, is that you don't need to be concerned. You got lucky yesterday."

"Did I? It doesn't feel like it."

"Not with... you know, not with the drugs and being arrested, but you were lucky you had him to help. He's a good man and he's very capable."

"I still don't really know why he's doing what he's doing. You, too. You don't know me."

Victoria looked as if she was about to ask something, but then stopped.

"What?" Sakura prompted.

"You and John—are you...?" She let the question hang.

Sakura's face flushed as she remembered what had happened before she had gone to sleep last night: she had made a move and Smith had turned her down. Not many men had ever done that.

"No," she said. "We only just met." She paused. "You said he's a good man?"

Victoria nodded.

"How do you know that?"

Victoria pulled out one of the chairs from the breakfast bar and sat down. Sakura perched on the end of the sofa bed.

"Back when we worked together—when we were both in London—I kind of let things get out of hand. The job I was doing was one that could really get on top of you, and it had been relentless for months. That caused trouble with my first husband and we ended up separating, then getting divorced. I went off the rails a bit. I'll be honest—I was in a mess, and, for a while, it got pretty dark. John helped me."

"How?"

"*I'd* have no trouble telling you what happened, but to do that, I'd have to break a few of the confidences I have with him, and I don't think that's right. He might tell you if you ask, but, as far as I'm concerned, if it weren't for him, I very much doubt I would be here. Certainly not in Bali, married to a lovely man and living a life I would have said was completely impossible ten years ago. Maybe I wouldn't have been here at all. There were moments when it could have gone another way. John made sure it didn't—I'll never forget that, and I'll never be able to pay him back. So when he called and said he needed help?" She shrugged. "I won't say no to him."

Sakura stared at Victoria, unsure how best to respond.

"This is all getting a little deep for a morning chat," Victoria said, getting to her feet. "Have you had breakfast yet?"

"No, not yet."

"Come on, then. Get dressed and come with me. It's time for *sarapan*."

45

S akura took a quick shower and dressed in the clothes that Victoria had brought for her. There was an ankle-length flowing white dress that fitted perfectly and, as she regarded herself in the mirror, Sakura felt better than she had for days.

Smith was in the living room when she emerged. He was shirtless and his skin and shorts were wet. She saw several tattoos on his broad chest and, in the mirror that was fixed to the wall behind him, she saw a tattoo of angel wings that spread all the way across his shoulders and down his back.

"Nice dress," he said to Sakura.

"Thank you," she replied, twirling on her heel so that the thin material danced around her calves. "Have you been swimming?"

"I have. It was gorgeous."

"We're just going for breakfast," Victoria said to Smith. "You can meet Jean-Michel."

"He'll be there?"

"I hope so—he's the chef. Coming?"

"Let me grab a shower," he said. "Give me a few minutes and I'll come and find you."

SAKURA FOLLOWED Victoria as she walked toward the restaurant that was up the slope, a few hundred metres away.

"He didn't used to have those tattoos," Victoria said, chuckling to herself.

Sakura didn't ask how she knew what Smith looked like without his shirt; she had already worked out that there had been something between them in the past.

The hotel was quiet and, apart from a young man in a white uniform who was straightening up the sun loungers, they didn't see anyone else. Victoria waved at the man, calling out something in Indonesian that made him laugh.

"It's a lovely place," Sakura said.

"It is," Victoria agreed.

"How long have you been here?"

"Five years. I can't really imagine working anywhere else now."

They reached the restaurant. It was quiet, with just a handful of couples enjoying their breakfast. Victoria led the way to a table that overlooked an empty infinity pool and indicated that Sakura should sit.

"Coffee?"

"Please."

"Let me go and tell my husband that we're here."

Victoria disappeared into the kitchen while Sakura admired the surroundings. The restaurant was light and airy, with white tiled floors and walls and two dozen tables, each with its own individual reed umbrella to shield the diners from the sunshine. She gazed over the pool to the

Indian Ocean beyond and allowed her thoughts to drift to Tokyo and what Yamato might be doing now. She tried to work out what time it would be there. Japan was an hour ahead of Bali, meaning that Yamato had probably had his breakfast. He liked *okayu* rice porridge or rolled omelettes; she doubted that they would give him either. What would he be doing now? Did they let him play? Did he have toys, or anyone to play with? She didn't know where he was, who was looking after him, whether he was happy or sad, what he had been told when he asked where his mama had gone. She felt her mood slipping and bit her lip to stop herself from crying.

Victoria crossed the restaurant to the table. Sakura wiped her eyes.

"Are you okay?" Victoria asked.

"My son," she mumbled. "I don't know anything—where he is, who he's with... anything. It makes me feel helpless."

She felt Victoria's hand on hers. "You're not alone now."

She looked up and blinked away the tears. Victoria was smiling kindly at her.

"Thank you," Sakura said.

She saw a man in chef's whites emerge from the kitchen. He was carrying a tray in one hand and skilfully negotiated the tables. John appeared at the same time, and the two men reached the table together.

"Excellent timing," Victoria said.

"I'm Jean-Michel," the white-clad man said, extending his free hand. He nodded at Victoria. "Her husband."

Sakura took the man's hand. "I'm Sakura."

Jean-Michel put the tray on the table. It bore a small coffee pot and three short white cups. He turned to Smith. "And you must be John?"

"I am." The two men shook hands.

"I've heard a lot about you," Jean-Michel said.

"All good, I hope?"

"Not at all," Jean-Michel said in a strong French accent. "Victoria says you're *thoroughly* disreputable."

Smith chuckled.

Jean-Michel indicated the pot. "Can I pour you all some coffee?"

"That would be lovely," Sakura said.

Jean-Michel poured as Smith sat down. He was dressed in an airy shirt and loose-fitting slacks and looked much more presentable than he had done earlier. Sakura watched him; she examined his face, the steel in his eyes, the confidence with which he bore himself. He gave the impression of solidity and she decided that she would trust him. In truth, she had little choice, but it felt better to know that she had a capable friend.

"What can I get you for breakfast?" Jean-Michel asked them.

"I don't know," Sakura said.

"I tell you what," he said. "Let me put something together. We've got some fresh fruit, some yoghurt... give me five minutes and I'll be right back."

46

Victoria followed Jean-Michel into the kitchen, saying that she would give him a hand; Milton could see that she wanted to allow him a moment alone with Sakura. He sipped the coffee; it was delicious, bitter yet sweet. He looked across the restaurant as Victoria turned into the kitchen and remembered the years when the only use he'd had for coffee was to chase away the alcohol from the previous night.

"This is lovely," he said, looking at Sakura over the top of his cup. She nodded in reply, looking lost in thought.

Milton wasn't surprised; they had a lot to discuss, but for the time being, he was content to let her enjoy her drink. He looked out over the beach for a few moments, taking in the deserted white sands and gently rolling white-topped breakers before glancing again at Sakura. She looked pensive, thoughtful, but much more like she had done when he had first met her.

"How are you feeling?" he asked her.

"I slept well," she said, "so that helps. I'm still worried, though."

"I'm not surprised."

"I'm *stuck*. I can't do what Takashi wants me to do—I don't know where the drugs are. And if I can't do that…" She paused and bit down on her lip. "And if I can't do that, what happens to my son? What am I going to do?"

"What are *we* going to do," he corrected. "You're not alone. I'd like to help if I can."

She looked down at the table, paused, then looked up. Her eyes were wet. "Why? I don't understand why you'd want to help. This isn't your problem."

"We talked about that," Milton said gently. "I'd like to. And I can. The idea of going against people like that might be frightening to you. It *should* be frightening. But it isn't to me. I've dealt with men and women like that before. I know how to speak to them in a way that will ensure that they listen."

"So, what—this is going to involve violence?"

"I hope not." Milton manufactured a gentle smile to gild that lie. He knew that violence was very likely, and, for the yakuza to take him seriously, he would need to reach back for his dark side.

"Fine," she conceded. "I think you're crazy, but fine. What do we do?"

"I thought about that while I was out running. You really have only one option."

He went through his thinking, explaining why he was discounting the possibility of finding the drugs and then passing them on to the intended recipient.

"But if not that, then what?"

"We go to Tokyo."

Her face crumpled in confusion. "What?"

"We go and get your son back."

She put her hand to her forehead. "Really? Just like that?"

Milton watched her over the lip of his coffee cup. "I'm not pretending it'll be easy. But I'll make them an offer they'll have to consider."

"You know *who* they are, right?" she said. "Takashi is very proud and very traditional. He won't negotiate."

Milton shook his head. "He'll negotiate with me."

"Why?"

"Because I can be persuasive. And I'm not frightened of him."

Her brow crinkled again. "How would we get there? We can't use the airport, can we?"

"No," Milton said. "I don't think that would be a good idea after what happened the last time."

"So?"

"So I'm going to come up with an alternative." He finished his coffee and set the cup down. "Can you give me the rest of the day?"

She leaned back in her chair and exhaled wearily. "Yes, of course. It's not as if I have any other ideas about what to do."

"Stay at the hotel," Milton said. "It'd be best to stay in the villa, but the pool would probably be okay if you need a bit of fresh air. Don't go anywhere else, not even for a walk along the beach. You're safe here—no one except me and Victoria knows where you are. It needs to stay that way."

47

Victoria and Jean-Michel came out of the kitchen. Jean-Michel was carrying a tray that was laden with several bowls, a decanter of juice and three glasses. He laid the tray down on the table and gestured to the coffee. "How is it?"

"Very good," Milton said.

"It's *kopi luwak*," he said. "Traditionally sourced."

Sakura put her cup down. "Traditionally sourced?"

"Made from coffee beans that have been partially digested by a palm civet."

Milton paused, his second cup halfway toward his mouth. "And what's a palm civet?"

"A viverrid," he replied with a broad smile. Milton was none the wiser and let it show. "Kind of like a cat."

"And they harvest the beans from where?"

Jean-Michel's smiled widened. "Their shit," he replied. "They pick them out. It's a local delicacy."

"Crappuccino," Victoria offered with a smile.

Jean-Michel chuckled at his wife. "Would you like another cup?"

Milton couldn't help but smile, too. "I'm good."

Victoria laughed and, after a moment, Sakura did, too. Milton watched as, still chuckling, Jean-Michel placed small bowls in front of him, Victoria and Sakura. Inside each bowl was a handful of rice the colour of aubergine. Jean-Michel picked up a chopping board from the tray and, using a small knife, expertly sliced three bananas into slivers so thin that Milton could almost see through them. He placed the slices on top of the rice before pouring milk over the top of them.

"Coconut milk," he announced, "black rice and banana. Bon appétit."

Milton picked up his spoon and took a mouthful. It was delicious; he had been expecting the milk to be chilled, but it was at ambient temperature and the nutty-tasting rice was slightly *al dente*.

"This is good," Milton said through a mouthful of rice. Sakura nodded in agreement, and a few moments later, all three bowls were empty.

"More coffee?" Jean-Michel asked again, putting the bowls back onto the tray.

Victoria playfully slapped her husband on the arm. "There's a coffee machine in the kitchen if you'd rather something less authentic."

"That would be good," Milton said.

Jean-Michel collected the tray and made his way back to the kitchen.

"What's your plan for today?" Victoria asked.

"I was just talking about that with Sakura. I need to have a think."

"Take as long as you need," she said. "The villa is free until next week. You can have it until then."

"Thank you," Sakura said. She stood. "I'm still feeling a little tired. I might go and lie down if that's okay."

"Call reception if you need anything."

"I will. Thanks again."

They waited as she made her way through the restaurant and out of sight.

"She's a looker," Victoria said.

"If you say so," Milton conceded.

"And?"

Milton smiled and shook his head. "Not a good idea."

"What are you? A monk?"

"No, but something like that is the last thing she needs at the moment."

She held his eye and, for a moment, it was as if they were back in London a decade ago. Milton knew that Victoria had been keen on him from the moment he asked her whether she would like to go for a coffee after her first meeting. He had been attracted to her, too, but believed—at least he told himself—that he was acting with the best intentions in suggesting they share a drink. He had recognised that she was white-knuckling her recovery, holding on for dear life, and he hated the thought that the positive step of attending her first meeting would not be enough to hold back the tide of shame that would carry her straight to the nearest pub. He had been in a similar position, too, and not that long before. He recalled it: the meetings felt alien, progress was imperceptible, and the bottle called. He had wanted to offer her encouragement that things could change if she kept coming back. That a sexual relationship had followed so quickly afterwards was not something of which he was proud, but it didn't mean that he regretted it, either.

The moment passed. Victoria leaned back. "What about you? What are you going to do?"

"I could do with a meeting," he said.

"There's a good one at eleven."

"My head's in a bit of a spin."

"Because of her?"

"Not really. Maybe. I don't know." He exhaled deeply. "Whatever. It usually helps me relax."

"I'll take you," Victoria said. "I haven't been to one for a couple of days."

She looked at Milton as if expecting a sponsor's disapproval.

"I'm not going to tell you off," he said. "I'm hardly one to talk—I haven't been to a meeting for a lot longer than that."

"Be outside the hotel in twenty minutes," she said. "I'll pick you up."

48

Katsuro stood, naked, regarding himself in the full-length mirror in his hotel room. He had taken more damage than he had first thought from his dive out of the way of the truck last night. He was bruised down his right-hand side, all the way from his flank to his knee. The bruising was almost scarlet over the bony prominence of his hip. He took a couple of steps toward the mirror and raised a hand to the scar on his neck, running his fingers over the keloid tissue. Then he stepped back again to look at his full-length reflection.

His powerful torso was covered with tattoos; almost every inch apart from his face and neck and hands had been inked. The tattoos had taken almost ten years to complete. Ten years of painful sessions sitting on a hard floor, with an elderly *irezumi* master repeatedly poking his skin with a sharpened piece of bamboo that had been dipped in ink. Above each breast was a *shisa*, a depiction of a beast that was a cross between dog and lion. The *shisa* on his left breast had its mouth closed to guard the good spirits, and its open-mouthed brother on the opposite breast would protect him from the evil ones. Each beast had taken hours with the *irezumi* master, but both were beautiful, as were the lotus flowers from which they emerged. The old man had described it as beauty emerging from the mud of life, just as the clans had done hundreds of years ago. Katsuro's back was similarly decorated and, when he had the time and money, he was planning on continuing the artwork to his buttocks and legs.

Other than the prostitutes that he visited and other members of the clan who saw him at Sauna Shikiji, hardly anyone had seen them.

But *she* had seen them.

Sakura.

The thought of the moment he had removed his clothes before her for the first time—the memory of her look of befuddlement, which had swiftly changed to horror—angered him afresh. Sakura was *his*. She belonged to *him*. The man who had taken her and was keeping her from him now would pay for his presumption.

FRESHLY WASHED AND DRIED, Katsuro sat on the balcony of his suite with his laptop balanced on his knees. He was staying in the Soori Bali, one of the most expensive hotels on the island. His father was paying for it and Katsuro knew that the old man would not bat an eyelid at the cost. It was some distance from Kuta, and the journey back last night had not been helped by his stopping at a pharmacist to get some dressings for his cuts and scrapes and to stock up on painkillers.

Katsuro sipped his coffee and considered his options. He had no idea where Sakura was, or the location of the drugs.

He had undertaken dozens of jobs for his father since he had started his work for the Nishimoto-*kai*, and, in over a decade of travelling around Japan and outside it, he could not remember anything that had gone this badly wrong. It was, not to put too fine a point on it, a disaster.

And he needed to fix it.

He picked up his phone and tapped out a message before putting the phone back on the glass table at his side. A moment later, it rang.

The male voice sounded cautious. "Yes?"

"I need you to find the owner of a vehicle for me," Katsuro said, closing his eyes and thinking back to the events of the previous day. "Can you do that?"

"No," the voice replied. "But I might know someone who can."

For a price, Katsuro thought. He would end up paying two people for the information, one of them earning a hefty mark-up for very little effort or risk, but that was nothing new. It was, to an extent, how his world worked. The cost of doing business. The man he was talking to was a policeman. Mid-level and nearing retirement with no chance of promotion. Men like him were always amenable to arrangements like the one that Katsuro had proposed.

"It's a white Toyota Hilux, registration B1042PJ."

"How quickly do you need it?"

"I need it now," he said.

"I'll see what I can do," the policeman said. "Do you have an email I can use?"

Katsuro read out a temporary Gmail address.

"I'll be in touch."

~

KATSURO HAD ONLY a few minutes to wait. He heard the ping of an incoming email and opened his Gmail tab. He clicked on the attachment in the email and saw the detail page of an Indonesian driving licence. On the right-hand side of the licence was a fingerprint, but it was the left-hand side that Katsuro was most interested in. Above a printed barcode was a photograph of a woman sitting against a dark blue background. She was good-looking, appeared to be in her mid-forties, and was staring at the camera with a faintly amused expression as if the photographer had caught her unawares. Katsuro reached out his index finger, tracing the name above the photograph.

Victoria Deschamps.

Underneath the woman's name was her address.

The Hilton in Nusa Dua.

Good, Katsuro thought.

She lived nearby.

He would pay her a visit.

49

The meeting was at ten thirty and Victoria pulled up in the parking bay outside Milton's villa in a Jeep at ten. Milton was watching from the window and quietly opened and closed the door so as not to wake Sakura, whom he had found asleep when he returned to the villa after breakfast. Her face had settled into relaxed peacefulness, and he did not want to disturb her. It was evident that she still needed rest.

"All okay?" Victoria said as he climbed aboard.

"All good."

"Sakura?"

"Sleeping."

Victoria nodded, put the Jeep into gear and pulled out. She set off down the narrow, potholed lane that led back to the main road.

"This Good Samaritan thing you're doing?" Victoria said.

"What about it?"

"It's because of AA?"

Milton gave the question a moment's thought. "Going to meetings helped me put things in perspective. You know what I used to do for the Group. I have a lot of guilt. A lot of shame. I can't make amends to all the people I should. The Ninth Step is difficult for me, so I told myself that I'd do it another way. I said that if someone needed me, and I could help, I would. I'll never be able to atone for the things I did, but it's a step in the right direction."

They drove in silence for a moment before reaching the freeway. As Victoria accelerated into the outside lane, manoeuvring her way through a swarm of mopeds, Milton asked her about the meeting they were going to. "Is this one of your regulars?"

"Yes," Victoria replied. "There's not that many English-speaking ones. I can manage in Indonesian, but it's not quite the same."

"You sounded okay when you were talking to the *preman*."

"Far from fluent," she said with an easy smile.

THEY LEFT the Jeep in the parking lot of the Harris Hotel, a modern four-storey hotel and conference centre whose bright white walls stood out among the other, unpainted buildings on Jalan Drupadi. Victoria led Milton down the road, stopping at the Wild-1 café to grab a couple of coffees. The café building was functional, not much more than breeze blocks covered with a thin layer of unpainted concrete. The meeting was being held in a similarly anonymous building, identified by the paper sign outside with the AA logo. Victoria led Milton inside and introduced him to the secretary for the morning's meeting, a smiling elderly man called Frank. The old man welcomed Milton like an old friend and told him and Victoria they should go inside; the meeting was about to start.

Victoria led the way to the front and sat down. Milton had always preferred the back row—far easier there to avoid speaking—but this wasn't his meeting and, if Victoria preferred the front, that was okay with him. The others attending were a disparate group, with a mixture of locals and ex-pat Westerners.

Frank said a few words in Indonesian, and Victoria whispered in Milton's ear, "He's explaining that the meeting is in English, just in case there're any new arrivals who don't know."

Frank switched to English. "We have a guest this morning." He turned to Milton with his hands spread in a welcoming gesture. "Would you introduce yourself?"

"I'm John," he said. "I'm an alcoholic."

The room responded with the usual joint acknowledgement and greeting. The secretary led them through the preliminaries before welcoming the member who was going to share his story. The man introduced himself as Lucas and explained that he was originally from California but that he had come to Bali for the weather and the surfing.

He cleared his throat as he looked for the right place to start his story. "I want to talk about grandiosity. That's the main symptom of my addiction, at least for me. I know a lot of us feel the same way. We have low self-esteem most of the time, but we use grandiosity as a way to hide our vulnerability and low self-worth. That was me, anyway. I managed to get into a place where I hated myself, but I still believed I was better than everyone else. You know what we say in the room: I was lying in the gutter and still looking down on everyone else."

There was a ripple of approval. Milton had always tried

to find the similarities in a share rather than the differences; it was hard, sometimes, but not today. He leaned forward avidly. It was as if Lucas was speaking to him and him alone.

"I was lucky enough to have some amazing friends—people who stuck by me through some awful lows—but, even though they were smart and funny and switched on, I still thought I knew better, all the time. I'd give them advice I was catastrophically unqualified to deliver, and then I'd ignore all of their own help and direction, even though the fact that they weren't raging alcoholics, and I was made, their advice infinitely better than mine. Anyway—long story short, I ended up alienating all of them, and when I finally hit the bottom, I did it on my own. It's different for all of us, but bottom for me was standing on the cliffs at Pecatu and trying to think of a reason why I *shouldn't* jump."

Milton found he was holding his breath, but, even as he focused his attention on the man at the front of the room, he noticed, from the corner of his eye, that Victoria was looking at him.

"I did and said some stupid things when I was drinking," Lucas said, "but coming to meetings and listening to others who looked at the world in the same way—all of them bossed by their own egos and senses of self-worth, even as they hated their own guts—well, that was the moment I knew I'd found my tribe. And, as time passed, I tried to be more humble. I know now that it's not all about me. I know what I think won't always be right—hell, it won't be right *most* of the time. I know now that I need to listen to others. I know not to decide things for others."

Victoria reached across and put a hand on Milton's knee. He looked over at her and saw that she was smiling at him.

"Anyway," Lucas went on, "today is a special day for me. It was one year ago, almost to the hour, that I found myself standing on the edge of the cliff and I realised I had a choice: jump or get sober. I'm so grateful that I got to make the choice. Not everyone is that lucky."

The room broke out into applause. Frank stood, took out a box stamped with the AA logo and took out a small plastic coin. It was a sobriety chip; they were handed out to mark milestones along the path to recovery. This one was blood red to mark the first anniversary.

Frank held up his hands for silence. "Congratulations, Lucas. I just wanted to say that I'm proud of who you've become. I remember you when you first came into this meeting, and the changes that you've made to your life since then are inspirational."

Lucas stood, shook Frank's hand and took the chip. He held it up and, buoyed by the continued whoops and hollers from the others in the room, he took his seat at the front once more.

Frank smiled broadly. "It's always the biggest pleasure to be able to celebrate an anniversary among friends. Do we have anyone else with a milestone today?"

To his surprise, Milton found that he had raised his hand.

"John?"

Victoria was looking at Milton with a mixture of surprise and admiration. Milton found his mouth was dry. He cleared his throat.

"I wasn't going to say anything. I've had a few anniversaries along the way and, save the first month and the first year, I've always kept them to myself. I don't know why—I don't like making a fuss, I suppose. I know—you all probably think that's stupid, and I'd agree with you." He shuffled uncomfortably. "Anyway. I got a lot out of Lucas's share and I thought, seeing as I have an anniversary, too, maybe I ought to share it with you all."

Frank smiled like a father encouraging a nervous child to let go of the edge of the swimming pool. "That sounds to me like the right decision. How long do you have?"

"Eight years," Milton said. "Give or take a day or two."

The room burst into applause for a second time. Frank reached into the box and took out a second medallion. He held it up and encouraged Milton to come forward. He did, uncomfortable at the applause that continued as he made his way to the front and accepted the chip.

"Congratulations," Frank said as Milton sat back down.

Milton shook his head. It was almost as if he had just had an out-of-body experience. He didn't know why he had raised his hand this time when he had kept quiet before; something in Lucas's share had resonated with him, and sitting next to Victoria, as well as seeing the success that she had made of her own recovery, had inspired him. Perhaps he *should* share his milestones and his gratitude. He looked down at the chip in his hand: the AA logo was on the front and the back included a silkscreen printing of a picture that Milton remembered from an old copy of the Big Book that he had been given at the start of his sobriety. It showed two people, Bill W. and Dr. Bob, sitting next to a hospital bed where a third man, Bill D., sat listening to what they were telling him. Their meeting in Akron in 1935 was taken by many to be the first meeting of the Fellowship. The words beneath the picture were reputed to have been Dr. Bob's words to Bill W.: "*If you and I are to stay sober we had better get busy.*"

He closed the chip in his fist and waited for the meeting to come to an end.

50

Victoria led Milton out of the meeting and into the late-morning humidity. The clamour of the street replaced the quiet of the room, and the peacefulness that Milton had felt started to fray at the edges, just as it always did as soon as a meeting concluded.

"You kept that quiet!" she exclaimed. "Eight years. Wow."

"I wasn't going to say anything," he said. "And then... I don't know. It felt like the right thing to do."

"I mean—*eight*. I knew you were up around there some-where, but, my *goodness*, John, that is well done. Very impressive."

"One day at a time," Milton said, using the familiar idiom to deflect her praise. It felt awkward; he still didn't feel that it was earned.

"You feel good for doing it?"

"Maybe," he conceded. "I'm just not very good at it—standing up and getting everyone's attention—but I can't say it doesn't feel good."

He had the coin in his hand and he rubbed his finger

against the stippled edge that decorated the circumference. He pressed it into his palm and closed his fist around it.

"The meeting was good, too, right?" she said. "You know what I always find? I get an answer to a question I might not have known needed answering."

Milton looked over at her. It was a knowing comment; she was talking about Lucas's share.

"What?" he said.

"Making decisions for others? Sound familiar?"

"Sakura? Come on," he protested. "That's completely different."

"Really? I don't think it is."

Milton shook his head. "I'm still not going to take advantage of her."

"Who says you'd be taking advantage? She's a big girl. She can make decisions for herself."

"I realise that."

"And you're being grandiose if you think you need to decide for her."

"Give it a rest," he said curtly.

He knew that she meant well, but, just as had been the case when they knew each other in London, she had a knack for finding his vulnerabilities and then poking and prodding at them until he acknowledged that she was right.

"Sorry," Victoria said. "I'll mind my own business."

Milton was about to apologise for his terseness, but, as he looked over at her, he saw that she was struggling to suppress the smirk that was bending the corners of her mouth upwards. "Piss off," he said, unable to prevent his own grin.

"Eight years sober and a looker who seems to have fallen for you. Not a bad few days."

"Piss. Off."

They walked back to the Jeep.

"What's next?" Victoria said.

"Back to the hotel. I need to talk to Sakura."

"About what?"

"About what happens next. I need to get her to Tokyo. She has some issues there that need sorting out."

"To do with the drugs?"

Milton nodded.

"What about you?"

"I'll go too. She'll have no hope if she goes back alone. It's an old yakuza family—they won't give her a second chance."

"And they won't take kindly to you getting involved in their business."

"No," he said. "They won't. But I think I can make them see the sense in being reasonable."

"You sure about that?"

"I have to try. She's finished otherwise."

They crossed the road, waiting for a gap between two shoals of mopeds.

"How are you going to get there?"

"That's been on my mind. It's not as if we can fly."

"I might be able to help," she said. "Well, not me—Jean-Michel. His brother works in Benoa Harbour. He runs a crew of local stevedores."

"I can't ask you for more. You've done more than enough already."

"Don't be a dick," she said, shoving him on the shoulder. "The last thing I want is you hanging around staring at her with doe-eyes."

"I do not—"

"Yes, you do."

"You said you were going to leave it," Milton protested.

"Sorry," Victoria said. "I will. But I *do* get it. Why you might feel that way about her. She's very cute."

She chuckled as they walked on.

"It might have crossed my mind," Milton admitted.

"*Finally*. Thank you."

They reached the Jeep and paused outside it. "Let's just say—hypothetically—that you might be able to help us."

"I'll speak to Jean-Michel and he can speak to his brother. There're ships in and out of the harbour all the time. One of them must be going to Tokyo, or somewhere nearby."

Milton thought for a moment. While he was unwilling to involve Victoria more directly than she already had been, he knew that the connection could be valuable. Stevedores were the most useful people to know at a harbour; their jobs loading and unloading ships meant that they had easy access to the dock and knew everyone who was worth knowing.

"Okay," Milton said. "Just find out if there's a ship going to Tokyo. Nothing more than that."

Victoria opened the door, swung herself up into the cabin and reached over to open the passenger side. "You got it," she said. "There's something else we need to do, too."

"What's that?"

"I want to introduce you to Eric Blair."

51

Victoria met Milton on the beach. She led him to two loungers that were not overlooked by any other guests. She had a bag with her and, as Milton sat down on the edge of one of the loungers, she unzipped it and took out a handful of documents. She passed them to him.

"I haven't done this for a while," she said. "And I don't have access to the same facilities as before. I'm afraid you're going to have to be Australian. My best contacts are all over there now."

Milton shuffled through the items that she had given to him: there was a passport, a birth certificate, a debit card from Commonwealth Bank, an American Express credit card, a plastic driver's licence and a clutch of membership cards for various clubs and associations.

"So," she said. "Eric Blair was born in Manchester in 1965. He moved to Melbourne with his parents when he was six and he moved back there after finishing his education. Got a decent education, as you'll see from the graduation certificate from high school and the bachelor's degree from

Macquarie University in Sydney. He's unmarried and doesn't have kids. He likes golf and is a member of the Royal Melbourne."

Milton held up the membership card and then a handicap certificate. "He's not very good. He plays off a handicap of twenty-one."

"Do you play?"

"No."

She grinned. "So shut up."

"Job?"

"He works for the Red Cross," she said. "Lots of excuses to travel, and they have awful network security. Eric Blair is a programme management delegate, just finished a posting in Bangladesh and about to move into a role that will have him travelling more widely to make sure that aid budgets are being properly spent. There's a record for you in their HR department, and they'll be paying your wages into the Commonwealth account every month."

"What about the accounts?"

"They have a little money in them, but they won't stand much scrutiny."

"It's okay. I've still got contacts who can flesh that out for me."

"Someone from Group Three?"

"Maybe," Milton said with a smile. He knew that Ziggy Penn would be able to hack into the bank's servers and create months of false transactions for him. He would build a credit history for Eric Blair that would be robust enough to beat all but the most thorough of investigations. Milton would set him to work as soon as he had finished with Victoria.

Victoria shuffled down on the lounger so that she could stretch out her legs. "It's all pretty thorough."

"It certainly is."

"The passport will pass all the usual tests: ultraviolet, machine checks, everything."

Milton looked at the document. It was blue, with the Australian coat of arms on the front cover. Milton thumbed through it and saw the picture that he had emailed to Victoria on the photo page and pages that had been stamped with visas and other evidence of entry to countries all around the world.

"Eric gets around," Victoria said.

Milton closed the passport and put it back with the other documents.

"Do you need anything else?"

Milton dropped the documents into the bag. "No. This is all great. How much do you want for it?"

Predictably, she waved his offer away. "On the house. It was fun. Like I said, I haven't done anything like that for a while. It was good to dust off the cobwebs, prove I still had it in me."

"Thank you."

She smiled. "Forget it." She took her sunglasses from her pocket and put them on. "You going to go and see Sakura?"

Milton zipped up the bag. "I'd better," he said. He got to his feet. "Let me know whether your husband can help."

"I'll call him now," she said.

52

Milton found that the villa was empty when he returned and, for a moment, he wondered whether Sakura had decided that she would try to deal with the mess she was in by herself. That would have been a bad idea, just as it was when she had tried to flee before. He left the villa and made his way down toward the restaurant where, to his relief, he found her on a lounger in front of the pool.

"Feeling better?"

"I slept all morning," she said. "Feel almost normal. Thanks. Where have you been?"

"Victoria and I had some business. It's all done now." Milton sat down on the edge of the lounger next to hers. "There's been some progress. Victoria thinks she might be able to get us onto a boat to Japan."

"Really?"

"Her husband's brother works at the docks. She thinks he might be able to get us onto a ship."

"We wouldn't be noticed?"

"I'd be very surprised if anyone was looking for us at the docks."

She took off her sunglasses. "What do we do when we get there? I need to apologise, right? Figure out a way to say sorry for what's happened."

"That isn't going to work," Milton said. "And, even if it did, what do you think they'll get you to do afterwards? They'll put you back to work."

"But not in Bali," she said. "They wouldn't risk sending me back here."

"Okay, then. Somewhere else. Somewhere you haven't been to before, where you have no experience and no friends. Where—if you get into trouble like this time—you won't have anyone to look out for you. I don't know, Sakura—the status quo doesn't sound like the best idea I've ever heard."

She showed a flush of irritation. "It must be nice to be able to make these pronouncements without having anything on the line," she hissed. "Listen to yourself. I don't know—maybe try to put yourself in my shoes for once. *They have my son.*"

He held her eye, undisturbed by her shortness. "I know they do. And I agree, you have to do something—but you don't need to go back to them and apologise."

"What, then?"

"I told you—you let me handle it."

Sakura sat up on the lounger and crossed her arms over her chest. Milton could see twin spots of heat rising in her cheeks.

"You're not coming," she said, putting as much certainty into her voice as she could.

"Okay," he said.

"'Okay'?"

Milton eyed her. "Not if you don't want me to. But what are you going to do when you get there?"

She hesitated. "I'll see Takashi."

"And what will you say to him?"

"I'll tell him…" She stumbled. "I'll tell him that I want Yamato back."

"And that you won't work for him any longer? And he'll go along with you? Just like that?"

Sakura tried to retort, but bit her lip and looked away. Milton knew that she was no fool. She knew that there was nothing that she could say that she could honestly believe. She knew that he was right.

"I came to Bali to get something from Victoria," Milton said, "and that's all been taken care of now. I don't need to be here anymore. Regardless of whether you want my help or not, I haven't been to Tokyo for a while and I'd like to visit. If you're going that way anyway, then what's wrong with me hitching a ride?"

He saw her resolve weakening, but still she fought it. "I'm grateful for everything that you and Victoria have done, but I can't ask you for more. You've done enough."

"I haven't," he replied. "Not yet."

Sakura frowned in confusion. "I don't understand."

"I still have amends to make."

"What does *that* mean?"

"I'm going to be as honest as I can with you," he said. "You deserve to know—it's only fair."

He leaned forward on his lounger and Sakura sat forward slightly, despite herself, listening.

"I used to work for the British government," he said. "So did Victoria—that's how we know each other."

"She told me, but she wouldn't say what you did."

"I fixed problems. And, while doing that, I did some things that I'm not proud of."

Sakura watched him carefully as he spoke.

"Some of the problems I was asked to fix required violent solutions."

"What? You hurt people?"

He nodded.

"Killed them?"

He nodded again.

"How... how many? One? Two?"

"More."

He looked right at her as he admitted it, and he felt a sense of trepidation, a fearfulness that his honesty might sour the way that she looked at him. He knew himself well enough by now to know that the image he presented to the world—tough, resourceful, capable—was a façade. It was a carapace behind which he hid his vulnerability. He knew that she found him attractive, and found, to his surprise, that he didn't want her to feel differently. But he had to be honest with her. He remembered what Lucas had said during the meeting: he couldn't pretend to be able to make a better decision for her than she could herself. She had to choose.

"I want to be honest with you," he said. "It's not what I've done that you need to be aware of. It's what I can do for you —and for Yamato." He stared at her. "Tell me something? Do you have anyone in Tokyo who can help?"

"Of course I do," Sakura blustered.

"Really? With the yakuza?"

She paused for a moment, then bit her lip. "No."

The silence seemed to last for an age.

He held her eye. "Now you do."

She put a hand to her head and massaged her temples. "Thank you," she said. "Again."

"While we're being honest, there's something else. My name isn't Smith. It's Milton."

"Why would you pretend to be someone else?"

"Because of what I used to do. There are people who would like to know where I am. They don't have my best interests at heart, so I try to stay under the radar. A pseudonym is a good start. The reason I came here was that Victoria is very good at putting together false identities. My old one—Smith—was compromised, so I needed to become someone else. That's what she's been helping me to do."

"So who are you now?"

"My passport will say Eric Blair," he said.

"Right," she said. "Eric."

"I can be John to you, in private—but it'll be Eric if anyone is listening. I've asked Victoria to get one for you, too."

"And what will that say?"

"Jessica Blair," he said.

"*Mrs.* Blair?"

"Provided that's all right with you?"

She smiled.

"Sakura?"

"I'm sure I'll get used to it," she said.

Milton knew that there was nothing to do but wait for Jean-Michel to speak to his brother. He would then have to negotiate with whoever it was who could get them on board a ship bound for Japan. He had no idea how long the process might take, but suspected that they might be waiting a little while. The weather was glorious and, with nothing else to do, it seemed churlish to waste it. He changed into his damp shorts and then returned to the pool area. There were two of them: one was large and mostly shallow, intended for family use; the other, restricted to adults, was suitable for swimming lengths. He dived into the second one, powered under the water before breaking the surface and setting out with strong, confident strokes. He reached the other end, performed a serviceable tumble turn, and set off again in the opposite direction.

He allowed his thoughts to subside, concentrating on the water and the pattern of his stroke. He felt the sun on his back as he crested the surface and felt the burn in his arms and legs, but that was it; after a while, he forgot the number of laps that he had swum, and just swam more.

He turned and saw two people waiting for him at the opposite end of the pool. He swam toward them, gliding through the final few metres and anchoring himself against the side. He looked up, used his hand to shade his eyes against the sun, and saw Victoria and Jean-Michel looking down at him. Victoria had changed into a bikini top and a sarong, but her husband was still dressed in his chef's whites.

"Jean-Michel has good news," Victoria said.

Milton wiped the water from his face. "Go on."

"I spoke to my brother," Jean-Michel said. "There's a ship leaving for Tokyo this evening."

"That was quick."

"You got lucky. The next one isn't until next week."

"Can he get us on it?"

"He can."

Milton planted his hands on the lip of the pool and kicked up through the water, propelling himself out.

"We'd better tell Sakura," he said.

SAKURA WAS STILL STRETCHED out on the lounger, but, while Milton had exercised, she had found a copy of *Vogue* and was flipping through the glossy pages. She looked up as the three of them approached and, seeing their expressions, closed the magazine and dropped it on the floor.

"Is everything okay?"

"Good news," Milton said. "Jean-Michel has found us a ship to Japan."

"When?"

"Tonight," Jean-Michel said. "But there's a wrinkle."

Milton could guess. "Money?"

"I'm afraid so. My brother will need to bribe someone on the ship."

"How much?"

"Not cheap," he said, wincing in anticipation of the figure he was going to have to deliver.

"Go on."

"Twenty thousand dollars."

Milton shrugged. "Okay."

"John…" Sakura protested.

"It's okay," Milton said, raising a hand. "It's fine."

"Twenty thousand *cash*," Jean-Michel added.

"No problem."

Victoria cocked an eyebrow. "You've got twenty grand in cash?"

"I do," he said. "I sold a car before I flew over here. We can use that."

Sakura stood up. "No," she said. "I can't let you do that."

"It's just money. It's not that important to me. I travel light. I don't have expensive tastes. The money is just sitting in my pack, doing nothing. Let me put it to a good cause. This is the safest way for you to get back to Tokyo."

"I'll pay you back," she said. "I'll find the money when we get home."

Milton smiled and said that would be fine. He doubted that Sakura had access to that much money, given that she appeared to have been held in servitude by the Nishimoto-*kai* for months, and, even if she did, he wouldn't have allowed her to give it to him. He had meant what he said: he had never been motivated by money, and, so long as he could afford food and shelter and travel, that was enough. He knew that there was a very good chance that she was going to have to leave Tokyo with her son, and, if he was right about that, she was going to need as much money as possible.

"Are you sure?" Jean-Michel asked.

Milton said that he was.

Jean-Michel nodded. "So I'll tell my brother to set it up."

"What will we need to do?" Sakura asked. "I mean—how do we get on the boat? I'm guessing this isn't legal."

"No," Jean-Michel said. "It's not. But I'll have to ask him. It isn't something I've done before."

"We'll take the bare minimum with us," Milton advised. "A change of clothes and some toiletries. One bag between us if we can. It's not going to be the most comfortable way to travel, but it'll be discreet. And that's what we need—discretion. We want to get back into the country without anyone knowing that we're there."

"And then?"

Milton glanced over at Victoria and then back at Sakura. "We'll figure that out along the way."

54

Sakura heard a soft knocking on the door. She glanced at her watch; it was coming up to nine, and Smith—she caught herself: *Milton*—had said that they would be leaving at ten. He had also said that he had things to do before they left, and had been gone all evening.

"Who is it?" she called out.

"It's Victoria."

Sakura opened the door. Victoria was standing outside with a medium-sized suitcase behind her.

"Come in," she said, stepping aside.

Victoria walked in, leaving the suitcase on the step.

"Are you ready to go?"

"I think so. I still don't know what to expect."

"My brother-in-law will make sure you get on board. You can trust him." She turned and pulled the case in after her.

"I've got some things for you and John in the suitcase. Clothes, toiletries—that sort of thing. Stuff for the journey."

"Thank you." She sighed. "All I seem to be doing is saying thank you."

She waved that off. "Forget it."

Sakura sat down on the sofa. "Can I ask you a question about John?"

Victoria shrugged. "Sure."

"You've known him for a long time?"

"I *knew* him," she said. "That was years ago, though. He wasn't like this then."

"How?"

"It's like I said. I can't say much about—"

"I know what he used to do," Sakura cut in. "He told me. That he's... that he's done bad things. I just want to know what he was like back then."

Victoria gazed into the middle distance, as if calling a memory back. "Intense. He's the kind of man who, if he says he's going to do something, he absolutely will do it. And he was troubled, too. He had this habit where you'd be talking and he'd suddenly glaze over and look right through you."

"Can I ask you something personal?"

Victoria smiled. "Were John and I seeing each other?"

Sakura nodded.

"Is it obvious?"

"It was obvious to me," she said. "It might not be to everyone."

"To Jean-Michel, you mean?" She shook her head and dropped down onto the sofa. "He knows. I told him before I said that John could come out here. It's ancient history. He was different then and I was different then. We both were."

"How long were you together?"

"I wouldn't say we were ever *together*," Victoria said. "It wasn't a relationship—not a serious one, anyway. It was just... you know."

"Sex?"

She nodded. "We were both pretty messed up. Neither of us were happy with our lives, and we relied on other things too much to help us keep going. Sex was just another thing. We were both fucked up, in our own ways, and that was probably what drew us together. Two fuck-ups against the world."

"And alcohol?"

"Why would you say that?"

"Neither of you drink now."

Victoria looked away. "I shouldn't say too much—it's not my place, at least not when it comes to him—but that was a problem I had, yes. I've been sober for six years. It was the best thing I ever did—I wouldn't be as happy as I am now if I hadn't made some pretty serious changes. I left my job, sold everything I owned, and got on a plane. I ended up here, met Jean-Michel, and that's that."

"And how's he changed?"

"John? He seems to have developed a conscience." She chuckled. "He's looking for lost souls who need his help. You might have been lucky to find him. John can be relentless. The people who are after you? They're going to find their lives have become a lot more difficult."

They both heard the sound of footsteps approaching the door of the villa and turned as Jean-Michel opened it and he and Milton came inside.

"Ready?" Jean-Michel said.

"Now?" Sakura replied.

"It's all sorted. We need to get the two of you to the harbour."

55

Katsuro stayed back, out of sight. He followed as Sakura and the *gaijin*, together with Victoria Deschamps and the man he guessed was her husband, made their way through the hotel grounds in the direction of the staff parking lot.

Katsuro had checked into the Hilton earlier and had taken a room on the top floor of the main building that looked down onto the row of villas that faced the beach and the pool. He had known that he would not have been able to locate Sakura by asking for her at the front desk, so he had pulled a chair out onto the balcony and kept watch.

He hadn't had to wait very long. She took one of the spare loungers at the front of the pool and settled down to enjoy the sun and read. The *gaijin* had arrived just after lunch, joined soon after by Deschamps and her husband. The four of them had shared a conversation before Sakura and the Westerner had made their way back to a villa down by the beach.

Katsuro could see the villa from the balcony. He decided the best course of action would be to wait until dark. The grounds were busy, and he did not want to be disturbed while he went about his work. He settled down to watch.

It was evening now. The Westerner had gone out and Katsuro had decided to make his move. He went down to the villa just as Deschamps arrived. He found a hidden spot to observe and saw the *gaijin* and then Deschamps's husband. The door opened again shortly after their arrival, and now the four of them were leaving together.

They reached a white van that bore the hotel's livery, loaded the luggage and got inside.

Where were they going?

Katsuro was frustrated. He knew that now was not the time to make a move, but that if he did not keep them within sight, he would lose his opportunity altogether. He hurried around to the guests' parking lot, got into his rental and drove quickly off the property, waiting on the road outside for the van to appear.

He pulled out and started to follow.

56

Milton watched as the lights of Kuta sped past them through the rear windows of the hotel's delivery van. He and Sakura were in the back, sitting in the cargo space with Milton resting against the rear wheel arch. Sakura was beside him, her body pressed into his. She was nervous; he could feel it in the tautness of her muscles and had seen it in the pinched expression on her face as they had started their journey. The sunset had been stunning tonight—a bright orange tapestry of clouds and reflected light—but it was dark now. Sakura had good reason for nerves; she had no idea what they would find at the dock, or after that. Neither did he.

Victoria was riding up front with her husband. Milton had watched the two of them holding hands. He wondered whether he would ever see her again. It seemed unlikely. He was pleased that she had found happiness, a state of affairs that had seemed beyond her when they had known each other before. It would have been easy to feel jealousy for the settled life that she had been able to stitch together. It seemed idyllic: a charming husband, a job that was undemanding and remunerative, an employer who allowed her to live and work in paradise. Victoria was complicit in the work of the Group, but only in the most tangential way. If she had blood on her hands, she had managed to wash it off. Milton knew that he would not be so lucky.

He would have been much happier if Jean-Michel had let them make their own way to the harbour, but both the Frenchman and his wife were having none of it. Milton didn't know Jean-Michel's brother, and Jean-Michel had explained that trying to arrange a pre-meeting on such short notice had not been possible. Milton didn't like it—being dependent on the actions of others was not something that he would ever be comfortable with—but he knew that he had no choice. He looked out of the tinted windows in the rear doors and saw the lights of the port. Not far now. He felt Sakura's hand sneak into his and entwine their fingers together.

The van pulled to a halt. There was a brief conversation between Jean-Michel and another man in Indonesian, then the sound of relaxed laughter, and the van pulled away again into the main port area. They drove on for a few hundred yards and then the van came to a halt again.

"Nearly there," Milton whispered to Sakura.

She squeezed his hand in response.

Both front doors opened and Milton, hearing a conversation in French, assumed that Jean-Michel's brother had arrived as he had promised. He heard footsteps coming around to the rear of the vehicle and then the sound of the lock being turned. The doors opened. The light of the port washed into the gloomy interior. They were inside the port. The area was industrial, lit with orange sodium lights that flickered and gave the landscape an ethereal quality. Victoria and Jean-Michel were standing next to a third man.

He was stocky and tanned, heavier-set than Jean-Michel but unmistakably his sibling.

"This is Pierre," Jean-Michel said. "My brother."

"*Bonsoir*," Pierre said.

He extended his hand for Milton to shake. His hand was calloused and his strength was obvious.

"I'm John and this is Sakura."

"Good to meet you. Your ship is ready to depart. We need to hurry—it is this way."

Milton reached back into the van to retrieve the suitcase that Victoria and Jean-Michel had filled with supplies for him and Sakura. They walked for five minutes, through large towers of stacked shipping containers. Eventually, they emerged on the dockside. There were a variety of merchant vessels moored by the docks, ranging from small vessels that looked like fishing boats to much larger container ships.

"Which one is ours?" Sakura asked.

Pierre extended his finger and pointed directly in front of them to a large blue-painted ship. It had a red line from bow to stern and the deck was stacked with four storeys of large shipping containers. The hull was painted with letters: CMA CGM.

"What do the letters mean?" Sakura asked.

"The owner," Pierre said. "It is a French company. This is the *Fidelio*. She's a big ship—75,000 tonnes—and very safe. It will be a smooth trip for you."

At the rear of the ship, rising majestically above the superstructure, were the accommodation decks and the bridge. Pierre led the way to the aft gangway that extended from a doorway down to the dock. It appeared that the work to prepare the *Fidelio* for the voyage was done. Apart from a few solitary stevedores, there was no one around.

"You need to get aboard," Pierre said. "She's leaving in fifteen minutes."

Milton wheeled the suitcase to the gangplank where the others were waiting.

"Thank you," he said to Jean-Michel.

The Frenchman put out his hand and Milton shook it.

"Bon voyage," he said.

Victoria stepped up, wrapped her arms around Milton and drew him into a hug. "Be careful," she said.

"I will."

"Look after her," she whispered. "She's a good one."

Milton squeezed her for a moment and then let go. She put her hands on his shoulders to bring him down a little, then kissed him on the cheek.

"And she likes you," she whispered into his ear.

Milton gently withdrew, annoyed with himself to find that he could feel heat in his cheeks. Victoria stepped over to Sakura and embraced her and then stood back and gestured that they should make their way up the gangplank. Milton picked up the suitcase. Pierre put his fingers to his lips and let out a shrill whistle; he raised his hand and, as Milton turned to look, he saw a silhouetted figure waiting for them in the doorway.

Milton picked up the case and stepped out onto the walkway. They climbed the shallow incline and stopped at the top to look back. The van had turned around and was rolling between two stacks of containers. The brake lights flared briefly as Jean-Michel slowed for a turn, and then it disappeared from view. Milton raised his hand to the watching Pierre, and then, with a hand on Sakura's shoulder, he gently impelled her to the top of the ramp and the door to the ship beyond.

57

K atsuro kept his distance as the white-liveried van made its way back toward the hotel. He had followed it to the harbour, but there had been no easy way for him to continue once it had passed through the security gate. It looked as if the driver of the van had bribed the guard to let them in, and that wasn't an option that was available to him, not without running the risk of compromising his anonymity on the island. The last thing he needed was to arouse the attention of the local authorities and, frustrated and angry, he had slotted the car at the side of the road and waited for the van to reappear.

The reason for the trip was obvious: they were arranging for Sakura to leave the country in such a way that her departure would not be noticed. They would get her onto a ship, and that would be that; she would be gone. Katsuro was irked at the turn of events, but not yet ready to give up. Ships were slow. They took a long time to reach their destination. All he needed to know was where she was going and, with that in hand, he would be able to fly ahead of her so that he could be waiting whenever and wherever she reached land.

Victoria Deschamps would know where she was headed. Her husband, too. Katsuro would arrange a meeting with one of them and extract the information that he needed, and then he would act upon it.

This was just a temporary setback, he told himself. Nothing more. He would still find her and bring her back to his father.

The van reached the hotel and rolled slowly into the grounds. Katsuro followed it and waited as it negotiated the security barrier. It drove ahead, turning off the road and heading toward the small parking lot where the hotel kept its vehicles. Katsuro pressed his key card against the reader, gave the guard a cheerful wave as he went by, and parked the car in the guest lot. He got out, reached around to pat the Glock that was pressed up against the small of his back, and arranged the folds of his shirt so that it was hidden.

He walked purposefully to the front of the hotel and looked for a spot where he could see into the second lot. He was ambling in that direction when he saw Deschamps and her husband walking hand in hand toward him. He stepped behind an oversized plant pot that held a large flame tree, and stooped down so that he could pretend to tie his lace. The two of them walked by him, lost in conversation. He could hear what they were saying: the woman was going to go and get a drink, and the man was going to check that the kitchen was closed up for the night. Katsuro gave them thirty seconds and then followed, watching as the woman went right, toward the bar by the pool, and the man went left.

He stopped and considered whom to follow. The woman was heading into a busier part of the hotel. She had definitely been involved with Sakura, but he thought it unlikely that he would be able to get to her without betraying his presence to witnesses. On the other hand, the man was going to the kitchen to check that it was closed down. That sounded as if it might be quieter; perhaps, as it was late, there would be no one else there at all. More importantly, given that he clearly had been involved in getting Sakura to the dock, it was reasonable to expect that he would have the information that Katsuro needed.

He followed him toward the kitchen.

58

The crewman who met Milton and Sakura inside the door led them through the guts of the ship to a staircase and then took them up to the third floor. He explained that the crew accommodation was on the second and third floors, and that the two of them had been assigned the quarters that were reserved for paying guests. The companionway was bland and functional, and the man directed them to the end. Milton was not expecting much, but was pleasantly surprised as the man opened the door and stood back to let them go in.

A short corridor led from the companionway into the cabin, past two doors through which Milton could see a walk-in closet and an en suite bathroom. The cabin was low ceilinged, with cream-painted walls. A large double bed filled the main area of the narrow accommodation, covered with a tightly stretched brown counterpane and decorated with pillows. A large flatscreen television was fixed to the wall, with cheap fine-art prints on either side. Beyond the bed was a seating area, a wooden divider separating it from the rest of the cabin. Thick curtains covered the windows, and a door looked as if it led onto a small balcony.

"Meals are served in the mess," the crewman said. "It's down the other end of the corridor. You got a microwave and a coffee machine in the cupboard. You need anything else?"

"No," Milton said. "We're good."

They heard a deep boom as the ship's horn sounded.

"We're getting underway," the man said. "Probably best to stay in the cabin until we're out of the harbour. If you need anything, my name's Claude. I'll come and see you in the morning and I'll give you the full tour."

"Thank you," Milton said.

Claude—who Milton suspected had benefited the most from the twenty thousand dollars that had bought their passage—gave a little bow of his head, backed out into the corridor and shut the door behind him.

"This is better than I thought," Sakura said.

She was standing within inches of Milton and he could smell the shampoo in her hair.

"We'll be fine," he replied with a wry smile.

She turned to face him, stood on tiptoes and, before he could do anything to stop her, kissed him softly on the lips. Milton paused, letting her lips brush his. He realised that he didn't *want* to stop her. He felt her fingertips pulling at the top button of his shirt. It opened and her hands moved to the next one.

"You don't need to—"

She silenced him with another kiss, harder this time and with more urgency.

She undid the last of the buttons on his shirt and pulled it off. He closed his eyes as she traced her fingers lightly over the scars on his chest. He felt her caress the round dimple from a 9mm round that had nearly ripped through his liver.

She traced the linear scar that had been the gift of a Macedonian thug who had been determined to open him up with a knife. She ran the tips of her fingers across the IX that was inked over his heart.

"What does this mean?"

He opened his eyes and looked down. "It's a reminder of someone I knew."

"How?"

"He was a good man trying to make up for things he regretted. His example is one I try to follow."

"Like now? Like you're doing with me?"

"Yes," he said.

She kissed him again and then reached for his hand, leading him toward the bed.

59

K atsuro followed the man as he turned onto the path that led to the staff area behind the pool. He stayed back as the man opened the door to the kitchen and went inside. Katsuro waited for a minute until he was sure that the area was quiet and then followed. He pulled his pistol, slid his finger through the trigger guard and then gently pushed the door.

It opened.

The room inside was a large kitchen. There was a prep station, a sauté station, a pizza station, and a salad station. The man had grabbed a cloth and was wiping down a large stainless-steel counter.

Katsuro cleared his throat.

"Kitchen's closed," the man said, not looking around.

"I'm not hungry," Katsuro said.

The man looked around and saw the pistol aimed at him.

"Nice and quiet, please."

"Hey," the man said, his eyes fixed on the gun. "That's not necessary. There's no money in here."

"I don't want money."

"So what do you want?"

"Lock the door, please," Katsuro said.

He held the pistol on the man while he reached into his pocket and pulled out the key.

"Quickly," Katsuro said, stepping closer and jabbing the man in the ribs with the pistol.

The man put the key in the lock and turned it.

"Give it to me."

The man dropped the key into Katsuro's hand.

"Now—over there. Sit down."

There was a wooden chair pushed up against the wall and the man lowered himself onto the wicker seat. Katsuro reached into his pocket and took out two cable ties. He tossed them to the man.

"Your right wrist first, please."

The man looked at the ties in his lap and then back up to Katsuro. "What?"

"Secure your right wrist to the arm of the chair—please don't make me ask you again."

The man stared from Katsuro's face to the muzzle of the gun to the tie in his lap and, correctly identifying his situation as far from promising, he did as he was told. He looped the tie around the arm of the chair, fed his wrist through and then used his left hand to draw it closed.

"And now your left hand."

It was more difficult for the man to fashion the loop with one hand fastened to the arm of the chair, but he managed. Katsuro drew nearer, the gun level with the man's head, and tightened both ties all the way to their stops.

"That's better," he said. "Now—I have a question for you. Just one. If you tell me what I want to know, there's no reason for me to hurt you. Do you understand?" The man swallowed, his larynx bobbing up and down, and nodded. "Good. The girl—Sakura. Where is she going?"

"What? Who?"

Katsuro turned his wrist and crashed the butt of the pistol across the man's face.

"Let's try again. Where is Sakura going?"

The man turned his head to the side and spat out a streamer of blood. "Who?"

Katsuro swallowed down his anger. His instinct was to press the muzzle against the man's head and pull the trigger, but, while that might sate his irritation, it would not bring him the information that he needed. He glanced to his left and saw the large industrial stove with six burners. He turned the dial to open the gas and pressed the trigger to light it. A blue flame caught and burned hot. A row of knives were arranged on a magnetic strip and Katsuro took down a paring knife.

He raised the knife so that the man could see it and then very deliberately lowered it into the flame. He held it there as the metal started to heat, aware that the man's attention was fixed on it. The imagination was a powerful thing, and it would do the man no harm to envisage what Katsuro might do with the blade.

The metal changed colour as it oxidised. "Was that your wife?" Katsuro said. "The woman you went to the dock with tonight. Victoria Deschamps."

"Don't mention my wife again."

"Or what, *monsieur?*" He spat the word derisively. "I'll tell you what I'm going to do if you don't tell me what I want to know. I'm going to ask you again, and you really should give some thought to answering me honestly. If I don't think that you've told me the truth, things won't be so good for you or her. First of all, you and I are going to have fun with this

blade. Once we're done, I'll go and find your wife and introduce myself to her. She's a good-looking woman. Not as
good-looking as Sakura, not as young, but you've done well
for yourself. We'd have a good time before..." He paused.
"Well, you know what will happen to you and to her. One of
you is going to tell me what I want to know. Wouldn't it be
better if you told me now, before I need to start thinking
about using"—he held up the knife—"this?"

The man watched the blade and Katsuro knew that he
was going to get what he wanted.

60

V ictoria opened the door of their villa and went through into the kitchen. It had been a long day and she was ready for bed. She opened the fridge to take out the ginger so that she could make tea for her and Jean-Michel, but there was none in the usual place. She remembered: they had used up all of the root last night. It didn't matter; there was always plenty in the kitchen. She would pop over and get some and encourage Jean-Michel to finish up so that he could come back with her.

She locked the door and set off across the hotel grounds, headed for the pool and the staff entrance to the kitchen. She thought of Milton and wondered how he was. It had been a strange experience to see him again after so long. The past couple of days had dredged up memories that she had buried under the silt of time, and some of them had not been pleasant to recall. The low points of her drinking years had come back to her: the empty hopelessness that she had felt when she woke up with no memory of what had proved to be her final night of booze, the desperation and fear as she had waited outside the church hall in Kensington for her first meeting. Milton had guided her through the first few months. The affair had been inevitable, and, although it had been a mistake, she did not regret it. His change in the time between then and now was startling, and she could see why Sakura had fallen for him. Sakura had been fortunate to find him, just as Victoria had been, and, if anyone was able to extricate her from the situation into which she had fallen, it would be him.

Victoria reached the pool and skirted it, going around to the staff entrance of the kitchen. She reached for the door but paused, thinking that she had heard an exclamation from inside. She held her breath and listened harder and, this time, she was sure: two people speaking, one of them in distress.

Jean-Michel.

She checked behind her, confirmed that she was alone, and reached for the compact Glock 19 that was cinched behind her belt, the metal pressed up tight against the small of her back. She held the gun in her right hand while she slowly reached down for the door handle and, as quietly as she could, tried to turn it.

It was locked.

That made no sense. Why would Jean-Michel lock the door? He usually took half an hour to close down the kitchen, and he hadn't been gone that long yet.

Something was very wrong.

She heard another exclamation from inside.

Very wrong.

She reached into her pocket and took out her bunch of keys. They opened all of the main doors, including this one, in the event that she needed to get into a room after hours.

She slipped the key into the lock and turned it, wincing a little at the click as the pins disengaged. She gripped the pistol and turned the handle, very slowly pushing the door open and sliding inside.

61

K atsuro laid the flat of the knife against the man's neck. The metal still glowed blue and the skin sizzled as he pressed it in place. The man screamed, but the dishcloth that Katsuro had stuffed into his mouth muffled the noise. Katsuro wasn't particularly concerned about being discovered; he didn't intend to be here for very much longer. The man would break, but, even if he didn't, there would be other ways for him to find out where Sakura had gone. There would be records of the departures from the dock; he might even be able to access them online. It wasn't so much the destination that Katsuro wanted to extract from his prisoner. He wanted to know about Sakura and, more to the point, the man with whom she was travelling.

He rested the knife on the stainless-steel counter and picked up his pistol again.

"Ready to talk?"

The man's eyes blazed with pain and hate, but he gave a shallow nod. Katsuro pressed the pistol against the man's forehead, right between the eyes, and used his free hand to remove the dishcloth.

"Where did they go?"

"Tokyo," he said, gasping through the pain.

"Better. Thank you. What is the name of the ship?"

"The *Fidelio*."

Katsuro tightened his grip on the trigger. He would ask another question and then that would be that. This man had seen his face, and Katsuro was not in the habit of leaving loose ends.

"The man she is with—who is he?"

"His name is Milton."

"His full name?"

"John Milton."

"And how does she know him?"

"She met him on the plane to Bali. You're here for the drugs she was smuggling?"

Katsuro smiled thinly. "I am."

"One of the packages split. Milton saved her life."

"And what does he do?"

"I don't know. You'd have to ask him that."

"Well, yes," Katsuro said, stepping back. "I intend to."

He took another step, the gun still aimed at the man's head. He increased the pressure on the trigger and relaxed his arm, anticipating the recoil. He was about to shoot when he saw motion to his left, from the doorway. He shuffled two steps to his right, putting the man in the chair between him and whoever it was who had just opened the door.

"Get away from him!"

It was the woman. The wife. Deschamps.

Katsuro kept the gun trained on the man's head. "Don't do anything foolish," he called back.

He knew that he was safe as long as he stayed where he was. Deschamps would not be able to take a shot at him without risking that her husband would be hit. He needed to leave, though, and that was going to require some careful negotiation.

She took a step closer to them and looked at her husband. "Are you all right?"

"Stay back," the man replied.

Katsuro glanced left and right, looking for an alternative exit. "You should listen to your husband."

"Get away from him—*now!*"

"I will," Katsuro said. "I'm going to leave, but I need to know that I can do that without you taking a shot at me."

With the gun unwavering in his right hand, he reached out and collected the knife with his left. He kept behind the man, his eyes on the woman.

"Put the knife down," she said, taking another step toward them. "Hurt him and—"

"Relax. I'm going to cut him loose."

He stepped up next to the chair, pushed the muzzle of the gun against the back of the man's head and reached down with the knife. He slipped the point of the blade inside the plastic tie that secured the man's left arm and sliced through it with a flick of his wrist. He did the same with the tie on the right.

"This is what we're going to do," Katsuro said to Deschamps. "You're going to step away from the door. I'm going to keep your husband between the two of us while I cross the room. You don't do anything and I don't do anything. I get to the door and then I'm gone—as simple as that. No one needs to get shot. Are you okay with that?"

"Fine," she said. "You do anything to him, though, and I'll put one through your heart."

"Of course." He kept his attention on the woman as he

stepped up to the man and held the gun against his back. "Get up, please."

The man did as he was told. Katsuro grabbed the man's left shoulder with his left hand, angled him so that his body would act as a shield, and then guided him to the door. Deschamps stepped away, allowing him a clear path to the exit, her gun aimed with a steady two-handed grip. Katsuro backed up against the door and pushed it open with his heel.

"I'm going to leave now," he said.

"Don't ever come back," Deschamps said.

"I don't intend to. And some advice for you? It would be unwise to follow me."

"Just go."

Katsuro pushed the man away from him and backed through the door. He shut it with his foot, took the key from his pocket and quickly locked it. It wouldn't stop the two of them for long, but it ought to buy him enough time to leave the hotel. He hid the pistol inside his open linen jacket and started for the parking lot. He needed to leave the island. Sakura and John Milton were headed for Tokyo. He needed to get on a flight so that he could arrive before them.

PART IV

WEDNESDAY

62

Milton eased open the sliding door that led from the cabin onto the balcony. He looked back at Sakura tangled up in the bedsheets. She was asleep, her hair loose and strewn across her face, one arm extended across the part of the bed that, until a moment before, he had occupied. He stepped out into the cool half-light of the early morning, dressed in only a pair of shorts. He had his phone in his hand, the screen showing a missed call.

Milton leaned on the railing of the balcony, looking down. The drop to the ocean was four storeys—well over fifty feet—and the sight gave him a momentary judder of vertigo. He leaned back and looked out at the horizon instead. The ship had set sail just over two hours earlier and the lights of Benoa Harbour and the island were distant specks on the horizon. He rested his elbows on the railing and checked his phone. He had seen a notice on the way to their cabin that said the ship had equipment that allowed the crew to use their own phones while they were at sea. Milton had a signal now and, as he scrolled through the notifications, he saw that the missed call was from Victoria. He tapped the screen to call her back and waited for the call to connect.

"Hello?" she said.

"It's me."

"John?"

"Yes. What's wrong?"

"You've got a problem."

He slid the door closed. "Go on."

"We had a visit from someone who was very interested in finding out where Sakura has gone."

She explained what had happened. Jean-Michel had gone to the kitchen and had been surprised there by a man with a gun who had tied him up and threatened him until he had revealed everything that he knew about Milton, Sakura and the plan that he had just helped put into place.

"Is he okay?"

"He got a nasty burn," Victoria said. "The guy heated up a knife on the stove and held it against his neck. We're at the hospital now. He'll have a scar, but, other than that, no damage."

"Shit, Victoria. I'm sorry."

"For what? It's nothing to do with you."

"Of course it is. It wouldn't have happened without me."

"Forget it."

There was a pause and Milton could hear the sound of hospital activity in the background.

He switched the phone from left hand to right. "The guy —do you know who he is?"

"He didn't say anything," she said.

"Description?"

"I got a pretty good look. Asian, very well built, dark hair, dark eyes. Well dressed. Knew how to handle a gun."

"Anything else?"

"Tattoos," she said. "He had one that started up around his ear and ran down his neck. Looked like the tail of a dragon."

That was plenty to be going on with. "What did Jean-Michel tell him?"

"He gave him your name."

"My real one?"

"Yes. He doesn't know the legend."

"What about where we're going? Did he tell him?"

"He did," Victoria said. "I'm sorry."

"Don't be. *I* should be apologising, not you. This is because of Sakura. Please—tell Jean-Michel I feel awful about it and I hope he's okay."

"I will. What are you going to do?"

"I'm not sure. I need to think."

Victoria told him to be careful and ended the call. Milton stared at the display, lost in thought, until it switched itself off. He had hoped to be able to sail all the way to Tokyo without detection, but that seemed unlikely now. He was going to have to improvise a little.

63

Milton went back into the room and sat down on the bed next to Sakura. He put his hand on her shoulder and gently shook her awake.

"What is it?" she mumbled sleepily.

"I need to ask you something," he said.

"Come back to bed."

"Once we've spoken."

She scrunched up her eyes and settled back down against the pillow.

Milton shook her again. "Wake up, Sakura. It's important."

She sighed, but, this time, she opened her eyes and raised herself up on her elbow so that she could look up at him. "Is everything okay?"

"The man who you were supposed to meet in Bali. The man Takashi sends to chaperone you—can you describe him?"

"Why?"

"Please."

She swallowed. "He's shorter than you, but bigger. Muscular. Dark hair and dark eyes. Cruel eyes."

"Tattoos?"

She nodded. "All over his body. It's *irezumi*—it means inserting ink. It's a yakuza tradition."

"Including on his neck?"

She nodded. "A dragon." She reached up and held her finger against the skin just below her ear. "The tail," she added, tracing the finger down her neck to her breast. "It runs from his face to here, above his heart. Why?" She stopped, her mouth falling open as she realised the possible reason for the questions. "Have you seen him?"

"I haven't, but I just heard from Victoria. He threatened Jean-Michel."

"Oh, God," she said. "Is he okay?"

There was no need to give her the details. "He's fine," he said. "A little shaken up, but nothing to be worried about."

She slumped back against the mattress. "I knew it. I knew he'd find me."

"You need to tell me everything about him. What's his name?"

"Katsuro."

"Miyasato's brother?"

She nodded. "He comes to make sure I do what I'm told."

"But he's Takashi's son—why does it have to be him? Surely there's someone less senior?"

"It was Katsuro's idea. He insisted."

"Why? You're not telling me everything."

"He thinks..." She stopped, trying to find the words. "He thinks we're having some sort of relationship. We're not. I mean—nothing you'd say was normal."

"I don't know what that means."

"I..." She stopped again. "After Miyasato died, after Takashi took Yamato and forced me to work for him, it felt like I didn't have anyone. I was on my own. I was scared. And Katsuro is Takashi's son. And so I let him..." She looked down. "I let him think that perhaps I had feelings for him." She looked up at him, anxiety on her face. "I don't. It's not like..."

"Not like us?"

"Don't look at me like that," she said, her eyes sparking.

"I didn't mean it like that," he said. "I'm not saying anything. I'm not judging you."

"I'm glad," she said sarcastically. "You're not qualified to do that, not until you've walked a mile in my shoes."

There was a steeliness in her expression that had not been there before. Milton could say whatever he liked, but he could see that she would need to be persuaded that her admission about Katsuro and her made no difference to him. That would have to wait, though; he needed to understand what they were facing so that he could plan a way to keep her—and himself—safe.

"Tell me about him."

She waited until her temper had died down. "He's crazy... and dangerous. He doesn't think the rules apply to him." She gave a shudder. "There was one time—the second or third time I made the run to Bali—when one of the *premans* we were selling to made a move on me. It was nothing—he put his hand on my leg—but he did it right in front of Katsuro just after he'd introduced me as his girlfriend. I was watching Katsuro's face when he did it. He laughed it off, but there was something in his eyes..." She shuddered again. "The next time I came back, that guy wasn't there. I remembered his name, so I Googled him. He'd been murdered the day after he came on to me. The newspaper said he'd been stabbed more than fifty times and left at the side of the road. I told Katsuro. He told me he did it. Straight up, made no effort to pretend it was anyone else. He said I was his—'You belong to me'; those were his words —and that he'd do the same thing to anyone who didn't respect that. He's a psychopath."

Milton could see that recalling these memories had frightened her, and there was no need to ask for more tonight.

"All right," he said. "Get back to sleep."

"You too?"

Milton nodded. He filled two glasses of water from the bathroom sink and put one on the table next to her and the other next to him. He lowered himself onto the bed and slipped between the sheets. Sakura slid over so that she was next to him. He flicked off the light and put his arm around her. He could feel the tension in her body and, although she lay still, he knew that she was still awake. Milton closed his eyes, even though he knew that he was going to find it difficult to drift away, too. He thought of the yakuza and a tattooed killer, and whether the promises he had made to Sakura had been too ambitious, even for him.

Sakura woke early. The sunlight was streaming in through a gap in the curtains. She was sure that she had closed them the previous evening. Milton must have got up at some point and opened them. She rolled onto her side and looked at him fast asleep next to her. His breathing was deep and sonorous, and for the first time since she had met him at the airport a few short days ago, he looked at peace.

She watched him for a few more moments, her eyes tracing the scars on his chest. What sort of a life had he led to earn them?

"Stop looking at me," Milton murmured, making Sakura jump. He opened his eyes and looked at her with a gentle grin.

"I thought you were asleep," she said.

"I was," Milton said, rolling onto his back and stretching his arms above his head. "And then I got the feeling I was being watched."

Sakura got out of bed and crossed the cabin to the coffee machine.

"Coffee?" she asked, looking back at Milton. She hoped that he had been watching her walk across the room—that was why she hadn't put any clothes on—but he was engrossed by his phone.

"Please," he said, tapping the screen.

"What are you doing?" she asked as she poured some water from a jug into the machine.

"A bit of planning. You might want to get dressed. We need to talk about what we're going to do when we get to Tokyo."

Sakura sighed, trying not to pout. She was hoping for something more than a conversation to start the day, but they had a week on board the freighter, so there was no hurry. As she waited for the coffee machine to warm up, she opened the suitcase that Victoria had prepared for them and picked out some suitable clothes.

THE CABIN WAS QUICKLY FILLED with the aroma of fresh coffee. Sakura, dressed in a simple cream blouse and tight-fitting blue jeans, opened the door to the balcony and carried the cups through. Milton joined her. He was wearing baggy cargo pants and a T-shirt, neither of which fitted him particularly well, but he still managed to look good.

They sat in silence for a few seconds, enjoying the view over the ocean. The water was deep blue, with occasional white-topped waves rippling past, and a few isolated clouds were moving slowly across the sky. Sakura could hear the call of seagulls. They were probably following the boat's wake, hoping for food.

Milton turned to her, a serious expression on his face. "We need to plan today, and, to do that, I need to know everything you can remember about the Nishimoto-*kai*. The names of all the people you know. The places they go. Any weakness or foibles that I might be able to take advantage of. Anything you can think of. The detail might seem small, but it could be something that I can use against them."

"Where do you want me to start?"

"With your husband. How did you meet him? How did he end up working for them? We'll start there and see where it takes us."

It took Sakura almost an hour and three cups of coffee to tell him what she knew. Milton recorded her on an app on his phone, turning it off only during the moments when she couldn't stop the tears.

"My father, Hachirō, is Takashi's brother. The two of them became yakuza at the same time. They were *chimpira* —the lowest of the low—but they got more serious about it as time went by. This was the seventies and eighties, when it meant something to be yakuza, not like now. Takashi became important, but then my father and mother had me, and my father decided that it wasn't something that he wanted to do anymore. He left and set up a little sushi place —he still has it today. He and Takashi stopped talking when he left, and they've never reconciled."

"What about your husband?"

"Takashi had two sons: Katsuro and Miyasato. We all used to play when we were younger, and Miyasato and I started to date. It got serious, but then my father and Takashi fell out and they forbade us from seeing each other. We didn't listen. We'd find ways to be together and, eventually, we decided that we wanted to get married. We did it without telling any of them."

"How did they take it?"

"It was weird—Takashi didn't mind at all. Miyasato and

Katsuro were both *chimpira* then, and I think Takashi took satisfaction from the fact that we got married despite my father saying that we shouldn't. My father was furious. He told me I'd made a mistake. I said I loved Miyasato, but it didn't make any difference. He didn't talk to me for three years. It was only when Yamato was born that he softened. Before then, though, it was Takashi who helped us—he was like a second father to me.

"Miyasato and Katsuro were just like Takashi and my father. Katsuro enjoys being yakuza. He likes the things he's asked to do. He has always been a violent man, and he takes pleasure in causing pain and suffering. Miyasato was more like my father. Gentle and thoughtful. He didn't tell me everything that he was asked to do—I could see that he was unhappy, but he said that he couldn't see any way that he could leave." The look of regret returned to her face. "I should have been more forceful," she said. "I should've *made* him leave, but I didn't. It would have made things different for us. He might still be alive."

"But something changed—something made him want to leave?"

She nodded. "There was a girl—I don't know her name. She was seventeen or eighteen, I'm not sure. There were four of them—Katsuro and three other *chimpira*. They picked her up off the street and took her to a warehouse that Takashi owned. They... they did things to her, over the course of a week, and, after that, they murdered her. Katsuro bragged about it and Miyasato found out. He came home and told me, and that was that—we decided that we had to leave."

"You didn't tell the police?"

She shook her head. "Miyasato said they cremated the girl's body—there was no evidence, just what he'd heard."

"You think it was true?"

Sakura nodded. "Katsuro told me himself. And it's the kind of thing he does. And, even if there was evidence, it wouldn't have mattered. Takashi has connections with the police in Sanya, where he has his place. He would have found out and, when he did, he would have done everything he could to protect his son. And the penalty for speaking to the authorities is severe. Miyasato would have been killed— me too, probably, and the baby."

"And so he quit?"

She shook her head. "Not quite. We'd made up our minds that we would leave, but we had no money. Takashi would have come after us if we'd stayed in Japan, so we decided that we would go to London. I had a friend there who said that we could live with her until we were settled, but we knew that we would need money. That was when Miyasato had the idea about the sword."

65

Milton refilled their mugs with fresh coffee and Sakura continued.

"Takashi is old now, like my father. The yakuza isn't what it once was. The government cracked down, and other organisations have taken its place. Takashi and my father are traditionalists. Old school. They both collect things that remind them of a time when Japan was different. You know—nostalgia. The older they get, the more they look back at a time when they'd say things were better. My father collects porcelain."

"And Takashi collects swords?"

"Yes. I remember him being into them even when I was little. He had a large collection then, and it's bigger now. There's one, in particular, that he was especially fond of. It belonged to a man they say was the last samurai. This man —I forget his name—was the link between what Japan used to be and what it would become. Takashi paid a fortune for the sword. He bought it from a collector for hundreds of thousands of yen. Millions, maybe, I don't know."

"And your husband stole it from him?"

"Yes. He didn't tell me what he was planning to do—I would have stopped him if he had. He knows someone who knows Satoshi Furokawa. He's the leader of the Chinese Dragons."

"Who are?"

"One of the groups who have taken the place of the yakuza. Younger. More violent. No code—that's why men like my father and uncle hate them. Furokawa wanted the sword, too, but Takashi outbid him when it came up for auction."

"So Miyasato offered to get it for him?"

"It was simple. He just took it down from the wall in Takashi's penthouse and walked out with it. There was no security—Miyasato was his son, and, anyway, who would be *stupid* enough to steal from a man like him?" She laughed bitterly. "He sold it to Satoshi and came back with the money. We were ready to leave. I'd cleared out the bank account and we just had to go to pick up Yamato. It was too late. Katsuro was there. He killed our nanny." She paused and composed herself. "They put us all in the back of a car and drove us out of the city. I had to watch while they..." She stopped, the memories coming back all too easily. "While they..."

"It's all right," Milton said. "I don't need to know."

She waved his comment away and swallowed. "I had to watch while Katsuro shot Miyasato. He made him dig a trench in the woods outside Takayama and then shot him and buried him in it." Sakura blinked and the tears started rolling down her face. "It was the last time I saw Yamato, too. They took him away and told me that I had to work for Takashi to make up for what Miyasato had done. Katsuro was given responsibility for me. And you know what happened after that."

Milton leaned over and put his hands on hers. "I'm sorry."

SAKURA FELT DRAINED by the time they were finished. Recounting the events leading up to her husband's death had been difficult. She had tried to stay focused on giving Milton the information he wanted, but, now that she was done, she felt as if she never wanted to talk about it again.

Milton refreshed their coffees.

"What now?" Sakura asked him.

"We've got four days to plan what we're going to do when we get to Tokyo."

"Four? You said it was a week to Tokyo."

"We're not going all the way to Tokyo. Change of plan. The ship stops in Manila before then, and we'll be getting off there. We'll take a plane the rest of the way."

"Why?"

"It's faster, for one. But that's not it. Katsuro knows we're aboard. If I were him, I'd be thinking about arranging a welcome for us in Tokyo, and I'd rather avoid that if we can."

66

Takashi Nishimoto stood in the corner of his office, looking out as the sun set over the skyline of Tokyo. To his left, he could see the Tokyo Tower, its white and orange lattice high above Minato. Its partner, the equally vertiginous Skytree, was farther away, but both towers bullied the smaller skyrises and tower blocks below them. Takashi's building, at twelve storeys high, was tiny in comparison to the buildings in the centre of the city, but here, in this benighted part of Tokyo, it was one of the tallest.

Takashi held his palms against the glass and looked down at the wards of Arawaka and Taitō below. Seventy years earlier, during his childhood, this had been Sanya. It had been an undesirable district full of *doya*, cheap lodgings for day labourers and itinerants. When Takashi had become *oyabun* of the Nishimoto-*kai*, the first building that he had purchased had been the *doya* in which he had been born. His mother, a prostitute who had lived on the poverty line until he and his brother had dragged her with them into prosperity, had not been able to afford anything better.

Takashi and Hachirō had burned it down for the insurance and now a small park stood in its place. The two of them had planted cherry trees in tribute to their *mama-san,* who had always loved them so.

The area around the tower belonged to Takashi. He had been born here, he lived here, and he was sure he would die here. The authorities had tried to wipe Sanya from the map by renaming it, but, to Takashi, this would always be his home no matter what it was called.

He took his hands from the windows and turned to look at the plush living space. He had the entire top two floors of the building and had spared no expense in decorating them in such a way that anyone fortunate enough to be invited to visit could not fail to be impressed by his wealth and taste. He had always been inspired by Louis XIV and the palace of Versailles and had hired an interior designer to recreate that look for him in Tokyo. French classicism with a Japanese twist. The apartment was decked out in gold, with wide mirrors that reflected the grandeur. There were chandeliers, floor-to-ceiling marble, and ceilings painted with scenes from Greek myths. The rooms totalled ten thousand square feet and, although the apartment was worth a fraction of those that could be found in Toranomon or Azabudai, Takashi had no desire to live in those wards. This—this apartment in this building in this part of the city—suited him just fine. He never left the building; everything he needed was here, and, for a man with enemies, like him, it was better to remain in a place that he had made almost impregnable.

The tranquillity of his afternoon was disturbed by the buzzing of his phone on his Mazarin desk. He crossed the room and picked it up. He looked at the display and saw, with a grunt of irritation, that it was his son, Katsuro.

"Tell me you have good news, Katsuro-*chan*," he said, using the diminutive because he knew it would irritate his son.

"I do, *Otōsan*."

"Where are you?"

"Manila."

"Why?"

"The ship they are on is docking in three days. I will deal with them here before the ship reaches Tokyo."

"That's not the good news that I was hoping to hear. What about the packages that you lost?"

"I have been unable to locate them, Father. I believe they have been taken. They are gone."

"That is disappointing."

"Forgive me."

Takashi sat down on the semicircle ivory couch and stretched out his legs. There was a fountain behind the couch, and a portrait of his late father, Akari, was displayed on the seventeenth-century lacquered Kaomi Nagashige coffer that he had purchased last year.

"Father? Are you still there?"

"What about the man she is with? The Westerner?"

"His name is John Milton. I was hoping you might be able to ask our mutual friend for assistance in finding out a little more about him."

"You want me to do your job for you?"

"I ask only because it will save time. I am sure that I—"

"Stop whining, Katsuro. I will see what I can find out."

"Thank you, Father. Again—I am sorry."

"Being sorry doesn't make up for the mistakes that you have made. You have been negligent. Sloppy. You know how much I despise that."

"I do."

"We will discuss what to do when you return."

Without waiting for a reply, he disconnected the call.

Takashi returned to the window and thought about Katsuro's failure and what his own father would have done in the circumstances. He did not need to speculate: he knew. He would have insisted upon *yubitsume*, the removal of a fingertip to signify disgrace. Takashi's father had been a low-level yakuza, and his *otōsan*—Kazuo Nakanishi—had made sure that the edge of the knife he used for discipline was dull so that atonement was as painful as possible. Takashi's father would have insisted that the precedent be followed, but Takashi wasn't a *complete* monster. He would do Katsuro the favour of whetting the blade before he gave it to him.

He looked up at the collection of swords that he had mounted on the wall of the apartment that faced Mount Fuji. He had *tachi* and *tantō* crafted by Masamune, the greatest swordsmith ever to work in Japan. He had a *katana* made by Kamakura that he had bought at auction in California for three hundred thousand dollars. The blades were beautiful, and each bore its own historical relevance. They reminded Takashi of a better time, when Japan had not been sullied by the influence of the West.

His eye drifted right, to the empty mount where he had once displayed the *tantō* that had belonged to Yoshida Shōin. That blade was not as expensive as the Masamunes, nor as impressive as the *katana*, but it was more important than anything else on the wall. Shōin was the fulcrum upon which the lever of history had balanced: before him had been honour and integrity and principle; after him came immorality, disgrace and humiliation. The *tantō* was the embodiment of that change. That Takashi's own son might take the blade from him had been almost more than he could bear. *Yubitsume* had been too good for him; Takashi had ordered fratricide, and Katsuro had carried out his duty to the letter. Perhaps he should have had Katsuro kill Sakura at the same time rather than indulging his thirst for revenge by having her work for him as a mule.

It didn't matter.

Katsuro might be a fool, but he was also a killer. Sakura had contributed to Miyasato's disgrace, and now she would pay the same price as him.

PART V

SATURDAY

67

M ilton stood on the deck, leaning on the railings and watching what was happening on the deck below. It was just after midnight and the ship was off the coast of Coron, one of the small islands that made up the Calamian Group in the Philippines. It had taken the freighter three days to travel to the Calamians from Bali. Milton and Sakura had spent most of that time in their cabin, venturing out only to eat and to exercise. Milton had found that the gangway around the perimeter of the ship was more than long enough to serve as a running route and had managed to run for five miles every day.

"Monsieur Blair."

Milton turned. The crewman who had assisted them— Claude—had joined him at the rail.

"Good evening," Milton said.

"How have you enjoyed the voyage so far?"

"I've enjoyed it very much."

"It is surprisingly comfortable, *non*?"

"It is."

"And your companion?"

There might have been a salacious edge to the comment, but Milton let it pass unremarked. "She's fine, too. Thank you."

"You said you wanted to see me?"

"Yes," he said. "I do. I was hoping you might be able to help."

Claude spread his arms. "Of course. What do you need?"

"We arrive in Manila later today?"

"Around lunchtime," he said. "It depends on the harbourmaster, but it will be around then, give or take. We'll wait at anchor until they're ready for us."

"Would it be possible for us to get to shore ahead of the ship?"

"Why?"

"I don't know how much you've been told, but we're trying to stay off the radar."

"I had gathered as much. Not many people choose to travel this way unless they have a reason for it."

"Exactly," Milton said. "I'm worried that we're being followed, and I'm worried that the people who are following us will have realised that there is a chance we might try to disembark when we dock."

"I see," Claude said. "And you'd like to do it more discreetly?"

"Is that possible?"

"I should think so," Claude said. "The port here is a little tricky to navigate, so they'll send over a pilot when we arrive. I could probably arrange for the two of you to go back with it. It'll cost, though. The crew will have to be paid to look the other way."

"I have another couple of thousand dollars in cash, but that's it."

"That might be enough. I can ask."

"Thank you," Milton said.

68

I t was five o'clock in the morning and Sakura was still a little drowsy from being woken so early.

"Is this really necessary?"

Milton finished packing their suitcase and struggled to close the lid. "Sorry. It is."

She crossed to the curtains that covered the balcony doors and pulled them back. In the distance, she could see the bright lights of Manila sparkling in the darkness. The jagged skyline, punctuated by skyscrapers, was full of flickering lights. She saw the outline of a huge Ferris wheel, each empty pod lit from within.

"But why the rush? The boat doesn't dock until lunch."

"I've arranged an early transfer," Milton said, pressing his palms on the suitcase to force it shut. "We need to get going."

KATSURO HAD TAKEN up position in the terminal building of Manila's North Port. He was next to a large plate-glass window that allowed him an excellent view of the harbour and the darkened sea beyond.

His journey from Bali to Manila had been uneventful. He had flown first class, as was his preference, but the Air Asia seat was average and the service was patchy, at best. He had spent the time watching a film, but had been distracted by thoughts of Sakura and the situation into which she had pitched him. He was angry that she had betrayed him and frustrated that his father would think less of him because of it.

He had consoled himself with the knowledge that he had outsmarted her and the *gaijin*, Milton, who was helping, and had planned appropriate punishments for both. Katsuro would allow her to live—for a little while, at least—but the *gaijin* would not be so fortunate. He had insulted the Nishimoto-*kai* with his impudence and now he would pay the price. Katsuro would collect his debt and would enjoy himself as he did it.

He raised a set of binoculars to his eyes and focused them on the brightly lit freighter, which was sitting at anchor while it waited for a vacant pier. He had spoken to a member of staff and, under the guise of being someone who enjoyed watching big ships, he had confirmed that it was the *Fidelio*. Katsuro adjusted the focus of the binoculars before zooming in on the ship. It was too far away to make out anything at all, but it didn't matter. Sakura would be on board and, when she disembarked, he would follow her.

A bag lay at Katsuro's feet with the essential provisions that he had picked up after his arrival yesterday. He had contacted a merchant with whom he had had dealings before, and had purchased a pistol and ammunition. In the bag, wrapped in an oily cloth, was a SIG Sauer P228. It was the standard-issue sidearm for the Philippine Air Force.

Next to the gun were a couple of boxes of ammunition, and attached to the front of the pistol was a tubular silencer that had cost well over three times what it should have. Expensive, but he might need it.

He looked at his watch. A little after five. The freighter was due to dock at midday. He would find them, follow them, and deal with them. He would be on a plane back to Tokyo with Sakura before the end of the day, and hoped that his actions here would be enough to temper the punishment that he knew his father would mete out for his failures.

69

Sakura followed Milton as he led the way down into the bowels of the boat. They descended several flights of stairs before following a passageway that led them to an open door. The man who had been helping them on the ship was waiting there. The door looked out into darkness, but she could smell the salt and felt the droplets of water that were whipped inside by the wind.

"Be careful," the man called out over the sound of the ship's engines. "You've got a drop to the tender. There's a rope ladder—you'll need to go down backwards."

Milton went first. He left the suitcase with the man, turned around and then climbed down, quickly disappearing beneath the lip of the door. The man picked up the suitcase and lowered it over the side; when he leaned up again, the case was gone.

"Your turn, *mademoiselle*," he said. "Be careful. The ladder will be a little slippery."

Sakura walked up to the door and looked out. There was a rigid inflatable boat alongside, much smaller than the freighter. The tender had been tied up alongside with two hawsers, close enough to the bigger ship that there was almost no gap between them. A rope ladder dropped down six or eight feet to the deck. Milton was standing below, one foot braced on the splashguard and both hands holding the ladder steady for her.

Sakura turned around, held onto the ladder with both hands and started to descend. The wind whipped at her as soon as she was outside the door, and the rope was wet and a little treacherous underfoot, as the man had warned her. She made slow progress, making certain that each foot was secure, carefully going hand over hand until she was close enough for Milton to reach up for her. She felt his strong hands on her hips as he guided her down the last few rungs.

"That was fun," she said.

A middle-aged man in uniform stepped around them, clambered up the ladder and disappeared through the freighter's door. Sakura looked up as the man reappeared, untied the hawsers and tossed them down to Milton. He raised his hand in farewell, then stepped back and closed the door.

Milton collected the suitcase and slid it beneath one of the lightweight aluminium seats. Sakura watched as he reached into his pack and took out a bundle of banknotes. The tender was crewed by two men, and one of them came over and put out his hand. Milton gave him the money, exchanged a few words, and then sat down. Sakura sat next to him.

"You had to pay them?"

He nodded. "Claude arranged it. These guys are local. They'll get us ashore without anyone seeing us."

"Are you worried about that?"

"I think it's a good idea to be careful."

The outboard engine whined as the pilo͠
throttle and the tender sped away from the freiɡ
wrapped her arms around Milton's abdomen ͙͙
tight; her skirt had ridden up almost to the top of her thighs. There wasn't any way of sitting in the boat in a more digni-fied fashion, but neither the pilot nor his colleague seemed to be paying her any attention.

The boat shot across the calm water between the freighter and the shoreline, ripping through the small waves with barely a shudder. Sakura's hair streamed behind her in the wind. They slowed as they entered a small marina with a variety of boats moored up against the dock. The rigid inflatable pulled alongside a small wooden jetty and the second crew member hopped out to tie them up. Sakura unwrapped her arms from Milton's midriff and got to her feet, adjusting her skirt for the sake of her modesty. She wanted to get to a mirror to see what sort of state her hair was in, but that would have to wait. The crewman put out his hand and helped her to cross over to the jetty. Milton handed their luggage over to the crewman, who set it down beside Sakura, then jumped over to the jetty. He turned to thank the two men.

"We all set?" Milton asked.

"No immigration?"

"We're not in that part of the dock," he said. "They told me the way to get through without being stopped. We should be fine."

He picked up the suitcase in one hand and Sakura linked her arm through the crook of his other elbow.

"That's the terminal building just there," Milton said, nodding at the modern building to the north. It looked

ncongruous and was surrounded by large shipping containers. "We'll avoid that and get a taxi somewhere else."

"And then?"

"We've got a plane to catch," he said.

70

The road outside the terminal was quiet. Milton turned away from it and led the way north until they reached a transit shelter with a screen advising that the next bus was not due for another hour. Milton set the suitcase down and looked around. He had ordered a cab and was becoming concerned that it might not arrive when he saw a car in the distance. It had an illuminated sign atop it. Milton stepped out and flagged it down.

The driver wound down his window and leaned out. "Mr. Blair?"

"That's me."

The driver didn't comment upon the incongruity of picking up two passengers outside the port at five thirty in the morning. He popped the trunk and Milton loaded their case inside. He opened the rear door for Sakura and then slid inside next to her.

"You want the airport?" the man said, looking down at his phone.

"Yes, please. Fast as you can. We've got a plane to catch."

～

THE DRIVE to Ninoy Aquino International took less than twenty minutes. They spent most of the journey in silence. Sakura was pensive. Milton guessed that she was thinking about her son and whether the mess that she had found herself in could be fixed. They arrived at the drop-off and Milton paid the driver, collected their case and led the way into the building. He had already purchased tickets on the next flight to Tokyo, but it wasn't boarding for another hour. They passed through security and found a small outlet next to the gate where they could sit down and get breakfast.

Sakura peered at him over the rim of her coffee cup.

"What's up?" he asked her.

"What are we going to do when we get there?"

"Do you have a safe place to stay?"

"My father's house."

"No," Milton said. "That'll be the first place they look. We'd be better in a hotel."

She nodded. "I can book somewhere. The Gracery, maybe?"

"Where's that?"

"Shinjuku. The centre of the city."

"Busy?"

She nodded. "It's big. A thousand rooms or something like that."

"That sounds ideal."

"I'll book it."

Milton gave her his credit card. Sakura took out her phone and opened a browser.

"Does your father know what's been happening?"

"No."

"Nothing at all?"

"We haven't spoken for months. He didn't approve of Miyasato."

"He'd help you, though? If he knew what had happened?"

"I think so," she said. "He's still my dad."

"Does he still have any connections with the yakuza?"

She shook her head. "Not since he and Takashi fell out —they haven't spoken for years."

"But he'll still have contacts?"

"I don't know," she said.

Milton was probing for potential sources of intelligence. If her father was too divorced from his old life to be useful, he would just have to find another way in.

"How would your father react if he found out what Takashi has done to you?"

"What do you think? He'll be furious."

"Good," Milton said. "We're going to need his help."

The crew called the flight, and the passengers started to assemble in front of the gate.

Milton stood. "Come on," he said. "We'd better get moving."

71

Milton looked out of the Perspex oval window and down at the city. Tokyo looked enormous from this height; it *was* enormous. Ten thousand feet below, thirty-eight million people were going about their daily business. Vast sprawls of buildings carved up by networks of roads and railways spread out almost as far as he could see. They were still too high for him to be able to discern the most obvious landmarks, but, as the airplane banked around to the right, he saw the snow-capped slopes of Mount Fuji. Sakura was looking out of the window, too, and Milton could guess what she was thinking: she was home, and had no idea what she might encounter.

Sakura waited for the plane to level out before turning to Milton. "What do we do when we land?"

"You can call your father," he said.

"And say?"

"Can you think of somewhere safe to meet?"

She considered the question for a moment, and quickly came to a conclusion. "Tatsumi Shindo. There are bars and cafés there. My father and I had a tradition on his birthday.

We'd go to a bar—New Motsuyoshi, usually—and I'd buy him a shot of his favourite whisky. Always single malt. It was a tradition, every year, until we fell out over Miyasato."

"Describe the area to me."

"It's just down from Tomioka Hachiman. It kind of feels like it would have fifty years ago. There's a central street with all these little bars on either side of it."

"Busy?"

"It's always packed. Tourists go there, but it's still popular with locals."

"And the bar?"

"It'll be busy."

"That's where we'll suggest, then."

"Why do we need to go somewhere that's busy?"

"We can hide in a crowd. The last thing we need is for them to know we're there—not until we want them to, anyway."

The plane touched down a few moments later and taxied to the gate. Sakura and Milton waited until the other passengers had wrestled their bags from the overhead lockers before Milton took down their case and Milton's battered old leather satchel. Sakura had transferred the clothes that Victoria had given her into a smaller case purchased at Ninoy airport that was small enough to be taken as carry-on.

"Ready?" Milton asked her as they waited at the end of the queue.

She nodded.

"So, immigration," he said. "We're together—okay?"

"You're visiting Tokyo to meet my father for the first time."

"Exactly. All right?"

She nodded again.

Under different circumstances, he thought, the explanation for his arrival in the country might have been something that he could have considered possible. He chased the thought from his mind.

THE IMMIGRATION OFFICIAL looked at their passports, then back up at them, then down at the passports again. He said something in Japanese to Sakura and handed her passport back to her, then looked at Milton.

"Mr. Blair," he said, switching to English, "this is your first time in Tokyo?"

"It is," Milton said.

"Your business?"

"I'm here to meet my wife's father."

"Where does he live?"

"Ota City."

The man glanced between the two of them. If he had any reservations, he signalled that they had been dismissed by stamping the first empty page of the passport. There was no requirement that Milton have a visa to enter the country and, as the man handed the passport back to him, he gave a curt nod and offered a gruff, "Welcome to Japan," and waved them on their way.

Sakura reached into her handbag and pulled out a large pair of sunglasses and a broad-brimmed floppy hat, both purchased at the Manila airport at Milton's insistence. It wasn't much of a disguise, but it would be better than nothing.

He set off toward the exit with Sakura alongside.

"Remind me which hotel you booked?"

"The Hotel Gracery. It's in Shinjuku. There's a statue of Godzilla outside."

"Of course there is," Milton said.

He smiled as he diverted to the nearest ATM. Sakura took out her bank card and drew out enough money to pay for their transport and five nights' accommodation. She asked if they would need longer, and Milton shook his head. He didn't intend to hang around. He would acclimatise himself to the city, try to gain a better understanding of their enemy, and then work on his plan. Three days might be all the time that he would need if things went as he hoped they might.

They found a taxi and Milton asked the driver to take them to the Gracery. The streets were crowded with Tokyoites making their way round the city with the usual combination of orderliness and determination. He again noted with amusement that the sidewalks were organised with regard to the speed of the pedestrians: fast, medium paced and slow.

Sakura reached out and took his hand in hers. "When were you here last?"

"A year or two ago," Milton said.

"I used to love it," she said. "Before—you know."

Milton could imagine how the events of the last few months would have soured the city for her.

"You won't be able to stay," he said. "Once we have Yamato, you'll need to go."

"I know. I'll take him to England."

"That was your plan before, wasn't it?"

She nodded.

"Do you think Takashi knew that?"

"I don't know. Maybe."

"Unless you're *sure* he doesn't, I'd go somewhere else—at least for the first few years. You don't want him coming after you."

"You said that you'd be able to fix things."

"I might be able to," Milton said. "But it might not go the way I want it to, and, if it doesn't, he won't be happy. We'll need to think about where you might go."

"Would you come?"

He stopped. "Sorry?"

"With me and Yamato—would you come with us?"

Milton was caught off guard. He had given the prospect a little idle thought during the voyage from Bali, but hadn't really treated it seriously. The fact that he had entertained it at all was a departure for him; he would usually have dismissed it out of hand. He hadn't considered being with anyone for years and was settled in his itinerant lifestyle. He had no commitments and no ties and, most important of all, there was no one close enough to him who could be harmed thanks to that association. Milton was drawn to danger; that had always been the case. There were people who had run afoul of him over the years, both before and after his time in the Group, who would have liked nothing more than to inflict pain on him. Beyond that, he knew that life with him would be difficult. His moods were unpredictable and his alcoholism often made him impossible to be around. He had made the decision long ago that he would travel alone and, in all the time since he had left London, he had never really met anyone who had given him reason to question that conclusion. There had been women for whom he might have been persuaded to change his mind, but the right moment had never arrived before now.

He reached into his pocket and felt for the chip that he had been given at the meeting. He ran his finger over the stippled edge. Eight years sober. He was a different man now than he had been when he had taken his last drink. Perhaps he could allow himself the possibility of happiness with someone else.

He looked over at Sakura and wondered: might this be different?

"John?"

"I don't know," he said. "Let me think about it."

THEY REACHED Shinjuku and Milton could not help but chuckle as the Gracery came into view. Sakura hadn't been kidding: there *was* a large model of Godzilla next to the hotel. It towered over Toho Cinema in Shinjuku, and, at night, the beast was reputed to move and his eyes were said to flash.

"Only in Tokyo," Milton said, pointing up to it.

They checked in and made their way up to their room on the fifteenth floor. It was pleasant enough, if a little over-priced; Milton was relaxed about that, happy that it offered them anonymity and a base from which he could plot out their next move.

"I'm going to take a shower," he said to Sakura. "You should call your father and tell him that you need to see him."

She looked pained. "Do I have to?"

"You think he won't want to see you?"

She gazed out of the window and out over the city. "I don't know."

"He's your father," Milton said. "Yamato's grandfather. You need to tell him what's happened."

"I know. You're right. It's just because... it's because I'm ashamed. He tried to bring me up a certain way and I repaid him by marrying the one man he told me I couldn't."

"He told you that you couldn't do something and you did it anyway? Isn't that what all daughters do?"

She shrugged.

"He won't ignore you when he knows what's happened. Call him. Tell him you need to see him this evening."

"What about you?"

"I'll take you there and then I'll leave you to it."

"You won't come in and meet him?"

"The two of you need to speak first. I don't want to be a distraction."

"But you will meet him? I'd like you to—and he'll like you, I'm sure of it."

"Afterwards," Milton said. "It'll be better if it's just the two of you to begin with."

73

K atsuro held the binoculars to his eyes and watched as the *Fidelio* was guided through the mouth of the harbour, a tug negotiating it through the passage to a vacant pier. It was much closer now and he could make out the crewmen gathered on deck. He looked for Sakura, but couldn't see her. She would be waiting inside and would disembark via the gangplank. There was no way that she would be able to leave the ship without him seeing her.

His phone buzzed in his pocket. He took it out and saw, with a quick jolt of unease, that it was his father.

He accepted the call. "*Otōsan?*"

"Where are you?"

"Manila."

"Why?"

"I told you, Father. They took a ship—it is just coming into dock now."

"And you think Sakura is on board?"

"I do."

"You are an *idiot*," Takashi spat.

"What?"

"She's not on a ship."

"How do you know that?"

"Because she's *here*."

"No," he said. "That can't be."

"She just called my brother to arrange a meeting."

"In Tokyo?"

"'In Tokyo?'" Takashi repeated, mimicking his confusion. "Yes, you fool, in Tokyo."

Katsuro wanted to swear, but he bit his tongue. "How?"

"I imagine they flew. She told him that they had just left the airport."

Katsuro felt fresh rage: that Sakura had tricked him again and that she had given his father another reason for criticism.

"I see," he said. "I'll be there as soon as I can."

"Why? So you can make another mistake?"

"I am sorry, *Otōsan*," he said. "I accept that this is my responsibility—allow me to fix it."

There was no reply, just buzzes and clicks over the line.

"Father?"

"Fine. One more chance, Katsuro. *One*."

"Thank you, Father. When and where are they meeting?"

"A restaurant in Tatsumi Shindo."

"What time?"

"Four. I will send you the details."

Katsuro looked at his watch. It was midday. It would take an hour to get to the airport, between four and five hours to fly to Tokyo, and then another hour to cross the city. He wouldn't be able to get there in time.

"I'll leave now, but I won't be back until tonight. Send Tsukasa and Wakabayashi and I'll take over after that."

Katsuro tried to apologise again, but the line was dead. He took a moment to breathe, then packed away the binoculars and got up. He looked outside and saw that the *Fidelio* was being tied up. Katsuro gritted his teeth as the ship sounded its horn; the long, honking boom was the punchline to a bad joke at his expense.

74

Sakura had showered and dressed in fresh clothes and, as she stood next to Milton in the elevator, he smelled the scent of the complimentary shampoo that the hotel left in the bathroom. Sakura had confirmed that she would meet her father in Tatsumi Shindo. It was to the east of the hotel and, rather than take a taxi, Milton decided that they would use the metro. They walked to Seibu-Shinjuku Station, bought tickets and descended to the platform, where they caught the first eastbound train on the Shinjuku Line.

Sakura was silent for much of the way.

"You okay?" Milton said at last.

Sakura just nodded. Milton glanced across at her and saw that she had a faraway look on her face. She had reported that her father had been curt when she had called him, and it was obvious that she was nervous about the prospect of seeing him again and, in particular, admitting that she was in a precarious situation and needed his help. Milton wasn't surprised that she was anxious, but he hoped that the filial bonds between the two would be strong enough to withstand their recent disagreements. He had been considering the next move and had concluded that their chances of success would be significantly improved if they had him on their side. He was Takashi's brother, after all; who better to provide intelligence on their adversary than a sibling, especially one who was about to be given a reason to bear a serious grudge? Takashi had killed his daughter's husband, kidnapped his grandson and then enslaved his daughter as a drug mule.

If *that* wasn't enough to win his support, then Milton had no idea what would be.

They arrived at Takadanobaba Station. Milton kept his wits about him as they disembarked, looking for anyone who might have been following them. There was no one who stood out, no one displaying the kind of suspicious behaviour that only the most accomplished street artistes could hide. There was no reason to think that they would have been spotted since they had arrived in the city, but Milton was not interested in letting down his guard. They traversed the station, changed onto the Tozai Line and settled down for the nine stops that would bring them to Monzen-Nakacho and the final walk to their destination.

THEY EMERGED into a district that Sakura referred to as Mon-Naka, explaining that it was a shortening of Monzen-Naka-cho. It was one stop away from the hipsterish Kiyosumi-Shirakawa and was more down-to-earth and less ostentatious than its neighbour. Sakura pointed out the Fukagawa Fudoson Temple and told him that the streets around here remained popular because they refused to be gentrified, still retaining the atmosphere of a bygone, roguish Tokyo. Dusk was falling and strings of bulbs and other illuminations were being lit, the smoke from charcoal grills drifting through the air.

They made their way to a narrow street, perhaps fifty metres long, that was packed with tiny bars. A network of lanes and alleyways split away from the street, with signage that must have been from the seventies and eighties still fixed to the walls. A lattice of cables crisscrossed overhead, and locals and a handful of Western tourists loitered around the bars. Milton was pleased; it was busy, with more than enough people to obscure them or, should events take an unfortunate turn, enough witnesses to dissuade against violence.

They walked by the Tomioka Hachiman Shrine, picking a path between the street vendors who had set up stalls to sell dumplings and bottles of drink and trinkets.

"Which restaurant?"

"New Motsuyoshi," she said. "It's just over there."

Milton saw a small building that was on the corner of the street and an even narrower alleyway. It had yellow-painted wooden facing, a stainless-steel chimney that vented the kitchen, and a helium-filled inflatable that was styled as a lantern bobbing to and fro against its tether. The interior looked too small to take more than a handful of customers, so a number of diners were eating their meals outside. They gathered in small groups in the alleyway, using chopsticks and foil plates.

Milton saw a large machine with a series of labelled buttons, perhaps sixty of them arranged down its front-facing surface, together with slots for coins and notes. "What's that?"

"Where you order your meal. Choose what you want, press the button and pay for it, then take the ticket it gives you to the kitchen. They split it; you keep the stub and then present it when the food is ready."

"And no tables?"

"Standing only. It won't be too busy yet, but if you come back in a couple of hours, there'll be even more people in the street. It doesn't look like much, but the food is excellent."

She was about to say something else when she stopped. She stared at the restaurant and, as Milton turned to follow her gaze, he saw an older man waiting at the entrance.

"My father," she said.

He was a short man, aged perhaps fifty, dressed in a simple pair of loose slacks and a cream shirt. He was looking down at his phone and hadn't seen them yet.

"You'd better go."

She stayed where she was. "It's ridiculous. I'm afraid of him—of my own father."

"You'll be fine."

"What do I tell him?"

"Tell him everything. There's no point in holding anything back. You'll feel better having it off your chest."

She swallowed and gave a nod that bore as much conviction as she could muster. "Okay."

"Call me when you've finished speaking to him."

"Where will you be?"

Milton gestured down the street to another restaurant. "There," he said. "I'll be able to see you."

Sakura nodded and, after a deep breath, made her way to the entrance. Milton watched. Sakura must have called her father's name; he turned and Milton heard him cry out in delight as he wrapped his arms around her. She hugged him back and, as she did so, the man looked out into the street and saw Milton. Their eyes met. Even from that distance, Milton could see that they had clouded with suspicion. And why not? Milton was, after all, a *gaijin*, a foreigner. He was a long way from the more obvious tourist areas of Tokyo, and perhaps it was obvious to the old man that he had delivered Sakura here.

Milton walked on. Two men passed him going in the opposite direction, toward the restaurant. They were both in their twenties and dressed in tracksuits and training shoes. Milton turned back and watched as the men continued by the restaurant; as they did, Milton saw them slow just a little so that they could look inside. Milton readied himself to retrace his steps, but the men continued on their way without stopping.

Milton continued along the street to the restaurant that he had seen earlier. He bought a bottle of strawberry Ramune and found a spot against a street lamp from where he could watch the restaurant.

n hour passed before Milton's phone buzzed. He took it out of his pocket and saw that Sakura had sent him a message.

All good. Come and meet my father.

He dropped the empty plastic bottle in the trash and made his way down the street to the restaurant; there was a queue to get inside now, but Milton ignored the annoyed glares from the waiting diners as he slid to the side, bypassed the ticket machine and located Sakura. She was standing at the back of the room, looking out so that she could see him and, as he stepped between two people eating stew from paper plates, she raised her arm and waved. Her father was standing with his back to Milton, but, as his daughter signalled, he turned to look.

Milton examined him. He was older than he had guessed from before, perhaps in his late sixties to early seventies. Milton saw that his clothes, while spotlessly clean, had been repaired many times. They looked as if they might have been expensive once; Milton saw a man who had once been prosperous, but who had fallen onto harder times. The fact that the clothes were well repaired and clean suggested he still had pride in his appearance.

Milton put a smile on his face as he reached the pair.

"*Chichi*," Sakura said, using the affectionate term for *father*, "this is the man I was telling you about."

The old man looked at him, his eyes narrowed just a little. "You're John?"

"I am," Milton said. "And you must be Sakura's father."

The man bowed a little.

"It's very nice to meet you," Milton said.

Milton suddenly felt awkward under the older man's scrutiny. Too late, he realised he should have asked Sakura more about what the etiquette was when meeting someone. Was he supposed to bow, too? Deciding against it, he reached into his pocket and took out the small orange box that he had purchased from a stall near the restaurant while he had been waiting.

The old man looked quizzically at the box.

"It's a gift," Milton explained.

Sakura smiled at her father. "Open it, *Chichi*."

The old man did as she suggested and removed the lid. The box contained some sort of pureed fish that was—according to the stallholder who had sold it to Milton—quite a delicacy.

Sakura looked at him. "*Kamaboko.*"

"The man who sold it to me said that it's good."

The old man laughed loudly. "It is," he said in accented English. "You make a good first impression." He put out his hand. "My name is Hachirō. It is good to meet you."

76

They settled into the corner of the room and talked. It was obvious that father and daughter had shared a difficult conversation; Sakura's eyes were reddened and her father spoke with a catch in his throat.

"Where did you learn English, Hachirō?" Milton asked, seeking a gentle introduction to another conversation that he knew might prove to be challenging.

"She hasn't told you?"

Milton shrugged. "No. I don't think so."

"I lived in London for three years," he replied with a smile at his daughter. "That's where I met Sakura's mother."

"Were you studying?"

He nodded. "At UCL." His smile faded a little as he continued. "I liked it and I always thought I might settle there, but then my father died and I had to return to help with the family business."

Milton knew enough about what that business entailed not to enquire too closely about it; the details would come when it was necessary.

"My wife—Sakura's mother—came back with me and,

eventually, Sakura arrived." His smile returned, but it was accompanied now with a sadness. "We had many happy years here until she passed. We had a house overlooking Tamahime Park. Do you remember it, Sakura?"

"Of course," she said.

Milton thought about what Hachirō had just told him. Sakura had said nothing about her mother. He hadn't known that she was English, but the mixed heritage—Asian and European—explained her unusual looks.

"Do you want to eat, John? Are you hungry?" Hachirō asked him.

"I'm fine," he said.

"Then I suppose we should talk about my brother."

He changed the subject without preamble, and the warmth that he had shown was immediately replaced by a flinty cold.

"Has Sakura told you what happened?" Milton said.

"She has. Thank you for what you have done for her."

Milton raised his hands. "There's no need to thank me."

"I disagree. Most people would not have done what you did. You have put yourself in danger for the sake of a stranger."

"I was happy to do it. And even happier now that I've got to know her."

"And you do not need to do anything else," he said firmly. "I will take over from here."

Sakura frowned; her father evidently had not fore-warned her that he had made that decision.

Milton cocked an eyebrow. "Are you sure about that?"

"My brother is responsible for what has happened to her. I will speak to him."

"I understand that the two of you aren't on the best of terms."

"Not since I left the family business," he said, relying on the euphemism for a second time.

"And you think he'll listen to you?"

"I will make him listen," he said resolutely. "As I say—thank you for what you have done, but I would prefer it if you left things to me from now on."

Milton paused, looking between father and daughter as he made up his own mind. Hachirō looked steadfast, his arms crossed over his chest and his chin forward, a defensive posture that was impossible to miss; Sakura, on the other hand, looked concerned. Milton could understand why. Her father was old and, given the situation that she had just explained to him—and the stakes involved—she was clearly worried that he was going to do something that would involve him coming to harm. Milton could see that Hachirō was a prideful man, and he knew, from his own experience, what pride often led to.

"I'm sorry," he said. "I can't let you do that."

"I wasn't asking you," the old man said, his eyes growing cold. "I am *telling* you."

"I mean this with respect, but that's not your decision to make. I have a stake in this, too."

"I am Sakura's father—"

"I'm not talking about Sakura," he said, cutting over him. "Your nephew—Katsuro—was sent to chaperone her in Bali."

"I know," Hachirō said darkly. "She told me."

Milton wondered how much the old man had been told, and, after a quick glance at Sakura and registering the infinitesimal shake of her head, assumed that it wasn't nearly the whole story.

"Katsuro made an attempt to find her—to find us—and he followed us to the hotel where we were staying. He attacked a man who helped us. The man is the husband of a friend of mine. I can't let that go uncorrected."

"This is a family matter," the old man said, still unconvinced.

"We're going to have to disagree."

Hachirō clenched his jaw. "You seem determined to put yourself in harm's way. My brother is a dangerous man. We have been estranged for many years, but we are still family. You are not. I can have a conversation with him that you cannot. I can tell him things—home truths—that, if you tried, would have you killed."

"I understand that."

"And it makes no difference to you?"

"Has Sakura told you what I used to do?"

He looked to his daughter. "No."

"Your brother doesn't frighten me. I know what the 'family business' is, and that doesn't frighten me, either. I've dealt with criminals before, and they've always overestimated their own influence and underestimated me. It's usually a mistake they regret."

Takashi Nishimoto took the elevator down from the penthouse to the floor below. It was his private elevator and could only be operated by way of the key card that he carried in his wallet. Its twin, operating in the same shaft, was for public use, although that was limited to the first ten floors only so that security could be maintained. Takashi could access any floor he chose via this elevator, but the only way for anyone else to reach the eleventh and twelfth floors was to take the public elevator to the tenth floor and then, once they had been cleared by security, to climb the stairs.

The elevator chimed and the door opened. The eleventh floor was just as opulent as the twelfth. Even the lobby here had been lavished with expense. There were marble columns, a small fountain and a painted ceiling. A pair of sinuous gilt armchairs—Takashi knew that they were properly described as *fauteuils*—sat on either side of the two elevators.

His private floors were very different from the rest of the building. The state of the decor on the eleventh and twelfth floors was a world away from that of the others. The floors below had walls that were sodden with damp, the moisture forcing the paint to peel away in scabrous patches and encouraging mould to spread. The damp continued into the apartments themselves, and many would have been condemned if it were not for the friendly inspectors from the Bureau of Social Welfare and Public Health that Takashi had on his payroll. Takashi did not care that the building had been allowed to rot. The tenants who lived behind those doors were not in a position to demand that improvements be made. They could leave if they so chose; the demand for accommodation in Tokyo was greater than supply, and it would take his agents five minutes to find new tenants who would be grateful for the roof over their heads.

The eleventh floor had been reserved for Takashi and his immediate family. There were five apartments, each vast and with generous en suite facilities. Takashi's own sleeping quarters were here, together with a room for Katsuro.

One of the other rooms was used by the men who were responsible for his security. The clan was much weakened now, denuded by years of government oppression and Takashi's waning enthusiasm in the face of his advancing years, but he was still rich, and money could buy the loyalty of good men. He had a team of six, and, at any one time, there would be two downstairs at the entrance to the building and two up here. Genzō was on duty up here now. He was in his twenties and was possessed of brawn rather than brain. That suited Takashi. Anyone allowed to ascend this high up the building needed to be presented with a clear idea of what would befall them if they had bad intentions, and Genzō's appearance was an eloquent way of presenting that message.

The building was perfect for Takashi in many ways. It

generated huge profit from the outsized rents that he was
able to charge, and it offered him the security to sleep easily
at night. There had once been disputes between the various
families when lines were crossed and honour infringed, but
no one had ever been foolish enough to attempt to attack
him here. The same was true of the authorities.

Yamato had his room on this floor, too. Takashi nodded
to Genzō, opened the door and went inside.

The nanny came out of the kitchen with a bowl of soup
in her hands.

"Takashi-*sama*," she said as she bowed.

He removed his shoes and smiled a greeting. She was in
her late forties, but looked older.

"Yamato?"

"Sleeping."

He opened the door of the child's bedroom and peered
inside. The boy was fast asleep on a futon, his arm over his
eyes as if he was shielding them from the light.

"How is he?"

"He misses his mother."

Takashi watched the boy for a moment. Did he regret
that his mother had been taken from him? Yes. A child
needed its mother, and all Yamato had were the surrogates
that Takashi provided. But what had happened was not
Takashi's fault. Sakura had made her own decision when
she corrupted Miyasato and conspired to humiliate him.
There were consequences for that; she was reaping them
now, and her son was suffering because of it.

Takashi could have abandoned the boy. He could have
arranged for him to be adopted. In the far north of Japan, on
the island of Hokkaido, was an orphanage run by a man
Takashi had had dealings with in the past. He was venal and
degenerate, but had somehow managed to persuade the

government to pay him to look after unwanted children. Takashi understood that the children were kept in squalid conditions; when they were eighteen and the government stopped their support payments, the orphanage spat them out into the world, where they inevitably drifted into the underclass and became drug addicts or alcoholics, or died— often both.

Takashi had considered that as a possible future for Yamato, but had decided against it. In the end, the boy was his grandson and he did not deserve to have the sins of his parents visited upon him to that extent. And, more, Takashi was concerned about his successor. Miyasato would have been perfect, but his treachery had made that impossible. Katsuro was wholly unsuitable, a conclusion that had been reinforced by this week's misadventures in Bali. Who else was there? Yamato was young enough to be brought up the right way, to be imprinted with a respect for history and the proper ways of doing things. Takashi was old, but he was still fit and healthy; his own parents had lived into their nineties. He had time enough left to mould his grandson so that he might be his successor.

He turned to the nanny. "Does he need anything?"

"No, Nishimoto-*sama*. He has everything he needs."

Takashi glanced at the sleeping child. He would bring the boy up, but that did not mean that he found it easy to love him. He looked like his father, and that reminded Takashi of his betrayal. He knew that would be a challenge that he would have to overcome.

He closed the door and left the apartment without another word. He took the elevator back up to his penthouse, poured himself a drink and took it to the window so that he could look out over the city. The child *had* served an additional purpose in guaranteeing his niece's compliance.

Her obedience had been won until now, but her recent behaviour had suggested that his hold over her was not as firm as it had once been. He would wait for Katsuro to find Sakura and bring her to him, and then perhaps he would show her what it meant to cross the *oyabun* of a yakuza clan. Miyasato had betrayed him; it seemed that his daughter-in-law had been infected by the same foolishness, and it was time for her to pay the price.

78

Sakura excused herself, saying that she needed to visit the bathroom. Hachirō waited for her to pass out of earshot before turning back to Milton with a steely expression.

"Who are you?" he said.

"What did Sakura tell you?"

"That you used to work for the government."

"That's right."

"Doing what?"

"I was a problem solver."

"She says that you are a capable man. What kind of problems did you solve?"

"I can't tell you that."

"And you think that this qualifies you to stand up to my brother? And his son?"

"You're going to have to trust me. I know that they're yakuza. The fact that that doesn't concern me should be all you need to know."

"What about you and Sakura?"

"What about it?"

"What are your intentions?"

It was a curiously old-fashioned turn of phrase. "I want to help her."

"I am not a fool, John. My daughter is an attractive woman. What do you hope to achieve by helping her? You must have an agenda."

Milton shrugged. "I don't. Do I think she's attractive? Yes —I do. Has that influenced my wanting to help her? No—it hasn't. She needed me. I think she still needs me. And I would have helped her regardless of what she looks like."

"And so when this is done? What? You will walk away from her?"

"I don't know," he said, thinking back to what she had asked him.

Hachirō watched him, his eyes still cold. Milton looked down and noticed a tattoo that was just visible above the collar of his shirt. Not enough of it was visible for him to be able to say what it was, but Milton guessed that there were other tattoos across the older man's body. Hachirō noticed that Milton had seen the tattoo and, without speaking, he reached up and undid the top two buttons of his shirt, then opened it just enough for Milton to see a koi carp that leapt from an azure-blue pool to the side of a snake's tail. The serpent was wound around a cherry blossom tree.

"You know what this means?"

"You were yakuza. I know—she told me."

"Takashi is not to be trifled with—and neither am I. Let me ask you a question—your job solving 'problems': did it occasion you to kill?"

"It did."

Hachirō nodded. "I thought so. I have, too. Many years ago, but you should be in no doubt that I will kill again if that is what I need to do to protect my daughter and my grandson. Do you understand?"

Milton held Hachirō's eye and nodded. It was a shot across the bow, and Milton understood why he had seen it necessary to deliver it. He suspected, too, that they were the words of a father who was ashamed that he had abandoned his daughter, and was determined to atone for his absence in her life. Perhaps he blamed himself for what had happened to her. Milton knew all about blame and could see that the old man held himself responsible for the situation in which Sakura had found herself.

"I understand," Milton said.

79

The tiny restaurant became full to capacity and, with more people pressed into the restricted space, it became loud and stuffy. Hachirō suggested that they go for a walk to continue their discussion. Milton would have preferred to stay off the street, but persuaded himself that the chance of them being seen and recognised in a busy district like this was minimal.

They wandered until they reached Fukagawa Park and found a bench that overlooked the Fudōdō temple.

Milton sat down next to Hachirō. "Where can I find Takashi?"

"He owns an apartment block in Sanya. He has the top two floors for himself. He rarely leaves."

"Describe it to me."

"Twelve storeys. He has a private elevator. The public elevator only goes to the tenth floor."

"How do you get to his floors?"

"You get out at the tenth floor and the guards check to see whether you are allowed to go up. If you are, they show you to the stairs. Takashi has bedrooms on the eleventh floor and his living space on the twelfth."

"What are the other floors used for?"

"Accommodation. Unpleasant apartments for people who can't afford anything better."

"How many guards?"

"Enough."

"Armed?"

"Of course."

Milton filed that away. It was useful intelligence, but no substitute for going to reconnoitre the property himself.

"You said you wanted to help," Hachirō said. "What do you have in mind?"

"You know that Miyasato stole from your brother?" Milton said.

"Sakura told me everything," Hachirō said. "The *tantō*."

"Miyasato stole it for someone else."

"Yes. Satoshi Furokawa."

"What do you know about him?"

"I know the group he represents is not to be underestimated. The Dragons are more powerful than the yakuza now. A young man who starts out in Shibuya or Roppongi is not going to be as impressed by tattooed old men like me and Takashi as they would have been twenty years ago. I suppose that's progress, at least of a sort. It's young guys, often with normal, legitimate jobs, but they supplement their income with violence and other criminal activity. I don't know Furokawa, but I hear he used to work in the film industry. He moved into adult films and then, when that became less lucrative, he recruited girls to speak to men on the internet."

"Chat rooms," Sakura said.

"If you say so—lots of money, either way. Furokawa used

it to buy muscle and used that to take control of the organi-
sation. It's not regimented like the yakuza. There's no tradition." He held up his hand and showed Milton that he had
lost half of his pinkie. "They'd think that atoning for
mistakes with a finger was barbaric stupidity—that's one
point upon which we might agree, come to think of it."

"Could you find out where I could find him?"

"They're based in Ikebukuro. I could ask around." He
stopped, then laughed. "Is that your plan? Get the sword
back, give it to Takashi and he gives you Yamato. Is that
right?"

"I think it might be worth considering."

Hachirō shook his head. "It would be a waste of time.
Furokawa won't sell it."

Milton held the older man's eye. "I wasn't planning on
buying it."

"So how are you going to get it?"

"Let me worry about that," Milton said. "Just find out
where he is."

MILTON ASSUMED that Hachirō and Sakura would appreciate
a few moments alone and said that he would wait for her
outside the entrance to the temple. He stood in the street
and watched the pedestrians making their way into and out
of the busy district. It was loud with the buzz of conversation, the calls of stallholders seeking to drum up trade, and
the hum of distant traffic. The streets were lit up now in the
neon glow of the signs that were fixed to the walls and the
bulbs that were strung from one side of the road to the
other.

Milton thought about what they had discussed. He had a

better idea of the situation than he had had before and, with the benefit of that information, he could see the outline of a course of action coming together. He was not quite there yet, but he could trace the framework. The stolen *tantō* was the key, and, with that in mind, he knew that he would need to speak to Takashi. That would begin the slow escalation of risk, but it would not be the end of it. He was going to need to watch his back if he wanted to leave the city in one piece.

He kept an eye on the street and, as he did, he spotted something that gave him pause. One of the men who had passed the restaurant when he had arrived with Sakura was standing at the mouth of an alleyway twenty-five feet away. Milton glanced at him, careful not to warn him that he had been spotted, and then looked away. It didn't take him long to find the other man: he was loitering near the gate that pedestrians used to exit the area around the temple. Neither man was particularly good at surveillance, and certainly not proficient enough to hide from someone with Milton's experience.

He cursed under his breath. He didn't know how, but the Nishimoto-*kai* had found them.

Hachirō said that he was going to get something to eat and invited them both to come with him. Sakura said that she was tired and would prefer to go back to the hotel. Hachirō smiled, kissed his daughter on the cheek, and, with a meaningful look at Milton, said his farewells and set off back into Monzen-Nakacho. Milton took Sakura by the hand and started in the opposite direction.

"If I tell you something," he said, "you have to promise me that you won't show any reaction. No panic, no fear, nothing like that. Is that okay?"

"Yes," she said, although her voice was uncertain.

"We're being followed. There are two men who were waiting for us outside the temple. I saw them earlier."

"Whose? Takashi's?"

"That would be my guess."

"Couldn't be a coincidence?"

"No," Milton said. "I'm afraid not. They've managed to find us."

"How?"

"It wasn't us," Milton said. "I was very careful on the way here and I didn't see anyone."

"So? My father?"

"More likely. Would your uncle have put him under surveillance?"

"How would he know to do that?"

"Katsuro knew we were headed here. He would have reported that."

"I don't know," she said. "My father didn't know that he might be followed. He didn't know anything about this."

"I'm not blaming him," Milton said. "But it's the only explanation I can think of. It doesn't matter. I spotted them easily enough, and that tells me that they're not very good— it should be simple enough to lose them."

"What do we do?"

"We behave perfectly normally," Milton said.

"And then?"

"And then I'll take care of it."

Milton had considered losing them with a quick direction change to which they wouldn't have time to react, and knew that would be an easy enough way to ensure that they were clean before they went back to the hotel. But, the more he thought about it, the more their presence suggested an opportunity.

"You've done this before?" Sakura said.

Milton smiled. "Now and again. Just do what I tell you and we'll be fine. Okay?"

"Yes," she said.

"Good."

MILTON LED the way back to Monzen-Nakacho Station. They bought tickets, passed through the gates and descended to the track. They had to wait a minute for a train and Milton took the time to check that the two men were still with them; they were, standing at the other end of the platform and doing a bad job of pretending not to be observing them.

"They're still there?" Sakura asked.

"They are. That's good. That's what we want."

The train arrived and they got on and sat down. Milton looked down the carriage to make sure that the two men had embarked with them; they had, taking seats next to the second set of doors. Milton looked away again, keen to ensure that they didn't realise that they had been made.

Sakura turned her head to look in their direction.

"Don't look," Milton said. "Pretend they're not there."

The train set off to the east, crossing the Sumida River by way of the Eitai Bridge. They rolled into Kayabachō Station. Milton looked out of the window and saw that the platform was busy with people, too busy for what he had in mind. He looked up at the map of the line that had been fixed to the wall of the carriage.

"How far are we going to go?" Sakura asked him.

"I need a quiet place to get off," he said. "What do you think?"

"This is Tokyo," she said. "It's hard to find somewhere quiet."

"Quieter, then," Milton said.

"Somewhere like Kagurazaka or Waseda?"

Milton looked at the map: her suggestions were six and seven stops away, respectively. The train pulled out again and he watched the stations that they passed through, looking for one that was suitable for what he had in mind. Nihombashi, Otemachi and Takebashi were too busy.

Kudanshita was quieter, but Milton saw a uniformed police officer idling next to the exit. He was beginning to get twitchy as they passed through Iidabashi; the carriage was emptying, and he didn't want the two goons to be spooked by the lack of other passengers whom they could hide behind. Milton gave thought to the option of tackling them on the train between stations, but then they rolled into Waseda and he saw that it was perfect.

"Now," he said, getting up. "Act normal."

He took Sakura's hand and led her down onto the platform. There were glass gates that protected the edge of it and, as they passed through them, Milton glanced left and saw that both tails had disembarked with them. He turned to the exit and started walking, Sakura alongside him. The station was immaculately clean, just like all the others that they had transited through, with the harsh strip lights overhead reflecting off the polished stone floor. It was also empty.

"We're going to take this exit," Milton said as they approached the opening to a passage that was marked with an exit sign. "I want you to keep walking. Go up to the surface and see if you can find a taxi for us."

"What about you?"

"I'll be right behind you."

Milton gripped her hand as they turned off the platform, and then released it and gave her a gentle nudge in the back to encourage her onward. There were stairs leading upwards at the end of the passage, and she reached the bottom step and began to climb. A second passage opened into this one, just before the stairs, and Milton ducked into it and waited, out of sight of anyone approaching from the platform. He had seen CCTV cameras on the platform, but did not see any here; he might have been fortunate. He waited, hearing the sound of approaching footsteps, and then one man saying something in Japanese and another answering.

He held his breath and waited. The two men passed the opening, walking quickly, their attention fixed on the stairs. Milton let them pass and then stepped out and closed the distance to them. They were on the stairs by the time he reached them, and appeared not to have noticed him until he grabbed them both by the collars of their jackets and hauled them backwards. They both lost their footing and tumbled down the steps. Milton followed them down and straddled the closest one, dropping down to a crouch and delivering a stiff downward jab that landed on the point of the man's chin. His eyes rolled up into his head and he went limp, out for the count. His partner was on his back, dazed from his fall but still aware enough of his peril to reach into his jacket for a knife. Milton hopped off the first man and closed the distance to the second with two strides, reaching down and fastening his hand around the man's wrist. Milton had the advantage of being above him; he levered the man's hand back, pushing against the joint until his fingers loosened and he dropped the knife.

The man yelped with pain.

Milton bent at the waist and pressed down with his forearm against the man's throat.

"You speak English?"

The man gasped for breath. "Some."

"You work for Takashi Nishimoto?"

"Yes."

"I want you to deliver a message. Tell him that I want to see him. He's lost something very important to him—a sword. Tell him I have a proposal to get it back. Nod if you understand."

The man did his best to nod. Milton kept the arm bar

over his throat, pressing down a little harder as he reached out with his right hand for the discarded knife.

"I'll come to his building tomorrow at midday," he said. "Nod."

The man did.

"And don't try to follow us," Milton said. "You're not very good at it."

He put the knife in his pocket, removed his arm from the man's throat and stood. The yakuza stayed where he was, on his back, looking up at Milton with a mixture of bewilderment and fear. Milton zipped up his jacket and turned to the stairs, taking them two at a time as he climbed away and left the two of them behind him.

81

Sakura was outside the entrance to the station. She had found a taxi and it was waiting by the side of the road.

"Well done," Milton said. "Let's get going."

He opened the door for her and then joined her in the back. The driver asked where they were going, and Sakura, after checking with Milton, told him to drive them to the Gracery.

"What happened?" she asked him in a quiet voice.

"I spoke to one of them."

"'Spoke'? What does that mean?"

"It was all very friendly. I asked him to deliver a message for me."

"To who?"

"Takashi," he said. "I'm going to go and meet him tomorrow."

Her eyes widened. "Why would you do that?"

"I've been thinking about the best way to get you and Yamato out of this mess in one piece," he said. "It's like I said to your father—if I can get the *tantō*, we'll have something to negotiate with. I'll offer it to him in exchange for your and Yamato's safe passage to somewhere you can start again."

"It's not *just* the *tantō*," she said. "It's the principle. You heard my father—Takashi is traditional. Miyasato dishonoured him—he dishonoured his own father and brought shame onto the family. That's why he's made me do what I've been doing. It's not about the money or the deal with the *premans*. I'm not saying that's insignificant to him, but it doesn't have to be *me* who moves the heroin. He's doing that to make a point. To me, to my father, to anyone else who might think to do what Miyasato did. That's how he is, John. It's what he does."

"I understand that," Milton said. "And the *tantō* isn't all I'm going to offer him."

"What else do you have?"

"It's not what I have," he said. "It's the trouble I could cause."

"You're going to threaten him? That won't go down well."

"I'll imply that working together will be better than working against each other. I understand what you're saying about honour, but he's a businessman, too. I think he'll see the good sense in my proposal."

They sat in silence for a moment as the taxi was slowed by the traffic in Shinjuku.

Sakura looked over at him, her face set with determination. "I'm coming, too."

"No, you're not. That would be a really bad idea. I know this is going to be frustrating and difficult, but you have to trust me. We know they're looking for you—we saw that tonight. Right? It's important that we don't give them the opportunity to get to you before I've been able to discuss what a deal between us and them might look like."

"What does that mean? Stay in the hotel?"

"That's exactly what it means."

"What about my father?"

"They didn't follow us to your father, so I think we have to assume that they're watching him. I'll go to his sushi bar and speak to him again tomorrow."

"Do you think you'll need his help?"

"It won't hurt."

Milton hadn't completely settled on a plan, but he had an idea of how he might secure the *tantō* so that it could be returned to Takashi. He thought that he would be able to manage it himself, but it would be considerably easier with the benefit of a second pair of hands. He just had to work out how much risk that would entail for Sakura's father. He was evidently capable and was very far from an innocent, but he was old and had made the decision to remove himself from situations that might involve questionable ethics. Milton knew that Hachirō would want to help his daughter, but he did not want to take advantage of the old man's parental obligations at the expense of his future well-being. Milton would make an assessment of the risk before deciding.

"John," Sakura said quietly, "I'm afraid."

Milton put his arm around her shoulders. "What of?"

"I'm afraid for you. They might kill you."

"That's not easy to do."

"And then Yamato and my father, then me."

"It won't come to that." Milton squeezed her, drawing her body against his. "There's a way through this. Give me a couple of days and it'll all look very different."

"You promise?"

Milton couldn't do that, but he knew it was what she needed to hear.

"I promise."

82

Takashi stood at the penthouse window, his arms folded, looking out at the view while his fool son explained just how he had made such a mess of what ought to have been a simple enough assignment. He had landed at the airport an hour ago and had hurried across town to see him. He had started to apologise as soon as he had stepped through the door. Takashi had listened without seeking to hide his impatience. He considered himself to be hard, but fair. He had little tolerance for failure, though, and even less for incompetence. Katsuro had failed—that was incontrovertible, since the drugs had not been delivered to the *premans* as contracted—and now he was trying as hard as he could to argue that he had been unfortunate and not simply negligent.

"I don't understand," Takashi said when his son had finished. "This wasn't the first time you have escorted her. What happened?"

"I don't know. She didn't come through the airport as she should have done. The man she was with—the *gaijin*—he took her through a private door before immigration."

"Why would he do something like that?"

"I don't know, Father."

"How did she know him?"

"I don't know. She was alone when she boarded the plane in Istanbul—I checked with her chaperone."

"What *do* you know?"

Katsuro launched into a long and self-serving apologia that took in the woman's arrest and then the Westerner's efforts to break her out of the cell in which she was being held, just—Katsuro said, underlining his bad luck—as he was about to take care of her himself. He explained that he had found out the name of the woman who had been helping the *gaijin*, and that he had interrogated her husband after Sakura had been secreted out of the country by sea.

"And then they leave the ship under your nose. How did they do that?"

"I don't know, Father."

Takashi folded his arms when his son was finally finished. "It sounds to me as if you were always one step behind them. I expect proactivity—you were just following events. I am not surprised it ended so inauspiciously. You have let me down."

"That's unfair, Father."

"Stop whining. You know what they say. Only death will cure a fool."

It wasn't a threat—Takashi had already murdered one son and had no intention of killing a second—but he knew that the criticism would sting, and that Katsuro had always been driven by a quest for Takashi's approval. It was a trait that he had developed as a young boy. He and Miyasato had been competitive, as was so often the case with brothers of a similar age, and Takashi had fostered that competitive spirit by rewarding the one who showed most promise and punishing the other. He wondered whether he had inadvertently contributed to Katsuro's problems.

The intercom on his desk buzzed. Takashi silenced Katsuro with an upheld hand and went over to it. "What?"

"Shinoda and Kodama are here," said Fumio, his second-in-command.

"Perhaps we'll have a little good news," Takashi said to Katsuro. "You might get the chance to redeem yourself." He clicked the intercom. "Send them up."

Takashi had been surprised when told that Sakura had been in contact with Hachirō, telling his brother that she was on her way back to Tokyo and that she wanted to meet. Takashi had sent Shinoda and Kodama to sit outside his brother's house and follow him to the rendezvous. Since Hachirō had no reason to suspect that he was under surveillance, Takashi was expecting them to report where Sakura was staying; when he knew that, he would send Katsuro. It would have been simple enough to hand the assignment to someone else, but he wanted to provide Katsuro with an opportunity to make amends.

He heard a knock on the door and nodded to his guard that he should open it and let the two of them inside. He fixed himself a drink and took it to the leather sofa that was angled to take advantage of the view from the wide picture window. Shinoda and Kodama came inside and, after demonstrating their respect with deep bows, they came closer.

Takashi frowned; both of them had been injured. Shinoda had a deep purple bruise across the side of his face, the contusion spreading from his right eye socket all the way down to his cheekbone. Kodama had a bruise across his nose, and there was evidence of dried blood around a cut that looked to run into his scalp. Takashi closed his eyes, anticipating disappointment when he had hoped for good news.

"What happened?"

"I'm sorry," Kodama said.

"For what?"

"It didn't go as we expected," he said, bowing his head again. "The girl was with someone else."

"Who?"

"A *gaijin*," Shinoda said, taking over.

Katsuro jumped in. "Describe him."

"Six feet tall, dark hair, a beard, blue eyes."

"It could be him, Father," Katsuro said.

Takashi waved for Shinoda to continue.

"We followed the old man to a restaurant. He met his daughter. They spoke for an hour and then the *gaijin* arrived. We couldn't get close enough to hear what they were saying."

"Go on," Takashi said, stifling the flare of anger that he felt at the prospect of Sakura *still* somehow contriving to stay a step ahead.

"We followed her, like you said. They took the metro and got off at Waseda. We stayed with them, but, the *gaijin*..." He paused, evidently embarrassed at the failure that he was going to have to recount. "The *gaijin* jumped us. We came around the corner and he tossed us both down the stairs. Kodama was knocked out and he was too strong for me."

"And?"

"He said that he had a message for you. He is going to come and see you tomorrow. He has a proposal. He said to say that you've lost something very important and that he could help to get it back."

"What have I lost?"

"He said a sword."

Takashi stood and, without even a backward glance at the two men, walked back to his position at the window.

"Boss?" Kodama asked, trepidation in his voice.

"Go," Takashi said. "Get out."

He heard them as they crossed the wide space back to the door and the stairs that would deliver them to the tenth floor and the elevator. He should have insisted upon punishment for shoddy work, but he was distracted by the message that they had delivered. He still had no idea who this *gaijin* was, and why he was helping Sakura. The woman was attractive, but would a stranger really put himself in harm's way just because of that? It didn't make sense. The man, whoever he was, was effective and tenacious.

"Why would they go to Waseda?" Takashi said.

Katsuro didn't answer.

"Do you not think that is unusual?"

Katsuro shrugged. "I don't know."

"Think, Katsuro. There is the university, but it's not the kind of place a tourist would visit. This man—I think he is cunning. He knew that they were being followed, he spotted that pair of idiots, and he deliberately chose a station that would be quiet so that he could accost them."

"Shinoda and Kodama are idiots, though."

"You would know." He ignored his son's pained expression and turned back to the window. "They are, I agree, but they should've been good enough to follow a foreigner without giving themselves away. Whoever this man is, he had the experience to spot them and then the confidence to ambush them. And to send me a message."

"Stupidity, Father, not confidence."

"Perhaps."

Takashi gazed out at the stupendous view of the city, the millions and millions of lights twinkling against the black canvas of the night, and found that he was anticipating the prospect of making the *gaijin's* acquaintance.

PART VI

SUNDAY

83

Milton awoke early, as usual, and dressed without disturbing Sakura. She had been tired upon their return to the Gracery last night, her fatigue amplified by the fright that she had been given upon the revelation that Takashi's men had been following her father. Milton did not speculate as to how they had discovered that they were in Tokyo, but knew it could only really be one of two possibilities: either the Nishimoto-*kai* had put Hachirō's house under surveillance, or they had tapped his phone. Perhaps both. He had to assume that Hachirō would still be under surveillance, and concluded that he would be even more careful when he returned to the hotel after meeting him later that morning. He doubted that Takashi would have enough decent surveillance experts to follow him without him being aware of their presence, but he would conduct a thorough dry-cleaning run to make absolutely sure.

He went to the bureau, found a pad of paper with the hotel's logo and a pen in the drawer, and sat down to compose a message. He addressed it to Sakura and told her

that he was going to see her father and that he might be out
all day. He told her to call him if she needed anything, but
reminded her that she should stay in the hotel. He
wondered if he should just wake her up and tell her himself,
but, as he looked over at her and saw her laid out in calm
repose, he decided that it wasn't necessary. She needed to
sleep. If he was able to bring matters to a conclusion today
as he hoped, she was going to need to be refreshed for what
would come next. There would be a lot of travel before she
and her son were able to start their new life, and she would
need a full tank to manage what that might entail.

He left the note on the pillow next to her head and
quietly made his way across the room and out of the door.

MILTON WENT DOWN to the reception desk.

"Excuse me?" he asked the young woman attending to
guests. "Is there an internet suite here?"

"It's on the first floor, sir," she replied with a smile. "Just
swipe your key card to gain entry."

Milton followed her instructions and found the room
next to the escalators. There was a series of terminals positioned between wooden partitions, as well as a printer. The
room was empty and Milton sat down at the first terminal,
woke the screen and opened a browser. He navigated to
Google and searched for information on Satoshi Furokawa.
It appeared that he was not averse to publicity; there were a
number of articles in the mainstream press, many of them
lauding him as a successful entrepreneur with a series of
profitable businesses in the technology sector. Milton
followed the links from one story to the next, building up a
picture of Furokawa and those with whom he associated. He

printed out the most useful articles and pages, folded the small stack of papers, and slid them into his pocket.

He erased his search history, logged off, got up and left the room. He took out his phone and tapped out the address of Hachirō's sushi bar and then, armed with directions, he left the hotel and headed for the metro.

84

Hachirō Nishimoto's sushi restaurant was fifteen miles to the southwest of the hotel. Milton rode the Yamanote and Ikegami Lines until he reached Gotanda Station. He emerged from the subway into a busy residential neighbourhood. Tall apartment blocks lined both sides of the street, with the ground floors given over to businesses. Milton let his phone guide him to the address he wanted; the restaurant was next to another restaurant advertised as the Siddhartha Palace and beneath a salon offering hairstyling and make-up.

Milton walked by the restaurant and continued along the street, looking ahead for anyone who might be showing an unusual interest in the building. He thought that it was likely that Hachirō would have been followed to work, or that the clan had people watching his premises, but, try as he might, Milton couldn't see anything that might have betrayed someone carrying out surveillance. That didn't mean that he would be careless, but, beyond that, he wasn't overly concerned. He intended to visit Takashi later that day, and then he would make absolutely sure that he was clean before he returned to Sakura.

Milton turned back and approached the restaurant. A laminated menu had been placed on a wooden pedestal, and a decorative wooden sign, complete with characters that Milton did not understand, had been placed on a seat in front of it. A series of paper panels, each bearing Japanese script, had been hung in the window, and the door, when he checked, was open.

He pushed it open, setting off the tinkling of a bell over-head. Purple curtains hung just inside the door, and Milton parted them and stepped inside.

The restaurant was tiny. Four wooden seats with leather tops were positioned before a counter that looked to have been made from a single piece of blackened oak. There was a fridge to the right and a large tank of water to the left. There was a block of knives on the counter, and traditional Japanese art had been hung on the wall. Openings in the wall behind the counter looked to offer access to the kitchen.

"Hello," Milton called out.

Hachirō came out from the kitchen, wiping his hands with a cloth that hung from the belt of his trousers.

"Milton-*san*," he said.

"Call me John, please."

"John."

"This is a nice place."

"Thank you."

"I looked online before I came over. Award-winning?"

Hachirō waved a hand dismissively, although Milton could see that he was pleased that it had been brought up. "It is for my saltwater *uni*," he said. "Most restaurants that serve sea urchin use preservatives to make sure they keep their shape. Mine are natural. My *uni* stays as it is because I store it in saltwater that is the same temperature as the ocean. The taste is the same as if it was just fished out of the water."

Milton sat down on one of the chairs.

Hachirō cocked an eyebrow. "Where is my daughter?"

"At the hotel. I think it's safer for her there."

"On her own?"

"No one knows that she's there."

"Are you sure?"

"I am," Milton said. "But your brother *is* looking for her. We were followed after we left you last night."

"What?"

"I'm afraid your brother has been watching you. He either has someone at your house, or he's bugged it, or he has a way to intercept your phone calls. There were two of them. I was trained to notice unwelcome attention when I worked for the government, and these two were obvious."

"What happened? You're sure they didn't follow you to the hotel?"

"Quite sure. I led them in the wrong direction and then I had a little discussion with them. I gave them a message to deliver to your brother. That's what I want to talk to you about."

Hachirō nodded. "Have you eaten?"

"No."

"Then I will make breakfast and then you can tell me what I need to know. Do you like sushi?"

"Of course," Milton said. He couldn't really say no.

"Good."

Hachirō took a bamboo mat from beneath the counter and spread it out, placing a nori sheet atop it. He moistened his fingers in a bowl of water and took a small ball of sushi rice, layering it over the nori sheet.

"I did a little research this morning," Milton said.

"Into Furokawa?"

"Yes. He's not shy about publicity."

Hachirō took a bowl of pre-prepared ingredients—bell peppers, green onions, cucumber strips and smoked salmon —and arranged them over the sushi rice.

"His generation is louder than mine. The *hangure* crow about the money that they have made. I always found it a little pathetic."

"It's also not very bright," Milton said. "It wasn't hard to follow the breadcrumbs that he's left across the internet."

Hachirō lifted the bamboo mat from the side closest to him and rolled it, pressing down to make sure that the cylinder that he created was firm. He took a knife, moistened the blade, removed the mat and sliced the roll into half a dozen equal pieces. He arranged them on a plain white plate, took little jars of wasabi, soy sauce and ginger, and, together with a pair of chopsticks, he slid the plate across the counter to Milton.

Milton split the chopsticks and, a little clumsily, grasped a piece of the roll and dipped it in the wasabi.

"Just a little," Hachirō advised. "It's hot."

Milton put it in his mouth and immediately raised his eyebrows. Hachirō was not joking; the wasabi paste was potent.

The old man went to the fridge and took out a bottle of sake. He held it up. "I know it's early."

"Not for me," Milton said, feeling sweat prickling on his lip. "I don't drink."

"Some green tea, then."

He dropped tea leaves into a clear pot, added hot water

and, after allowing it to steep, he strained it into a cup. Milton sipped it. The sushi was salty and the tea was bitter; it was a pleasant contrast.

"Thank you," Milton said.

He took out the sheaf of paper that he had printed at the hotel and tapped a finger against the first page. It was a photograph of Satoshi Furokawa with an attractive girl on his arm. He was dressed in a tuxedo and she in a cocktail dress, and, in the background, they could see a red carpet and a banner that advertised the premiere of a Christopher Nolan film.

"What's this?" Hachirō said. He took out a pair of spectacles and put them on so that he could read the caption beneath the photograph. "'Local entrepreneur Satoshi Furokawa and his sister Natsuki Furokawa attend Tokyo premiere.'" He snorted derisively. "'Local entrepreneur.' I've heard it all now."

Milton laid a finger next to the woman's photo. "He's indiscreet, but it was even easier to find details on her. She's younger than him—he's thirty-five, she's twenty-six. She runs a boutique selling furniture to customers with more money than sense. There's a biography on the business's website. Says she's close to her family and particularly to her big brother."

Milton flipped the pages. The next was a printout of a map.

Hachirō looked down at it. "And this?"

"Natsuki is a keen runner. This is from Strava."

"Should I know what that is?"

"It's an app that lets you share your workouts online. It's a terrible idea, especially when you let it auto-post to Facebook. I've looked at her runs from the last two weeks, and they all start and stop at the same place."

Hachirō squinted at the map. "That's Yoyogi Park."

"She starts here, where the red line begins, every morning at a quarter to six, before she goes to work. She runs into the park, does two laps and then returns. I Googled the address where she starts and stops. Yoyogi Uehara. It's residential. That's where she lives."

"Why is this relevant?"

"Someone like Furokawa is not going to be easy to reach. The sword, too—he'll know that your brother will want it back, and he'll have it somewhere safe, maybe in a vault or somewhere that I wouldn't easily be able to get to if I tried to steal it. But I don't need to steal it. Natsuki is his weakness. If I can get to her, I can get to him. He'll deliver it to us."

Hachirō shook his head. "No," he said. "I don't want anything to do with that."

"I'm not proposing that she be hurt," Milton said. "That's not how I work."

"So what *are* you proposing?"

"That I take her and keep her somewhere and tell Furokawa that he can only have her back in exchange for the sword."

"And you need my help to do that."

Milton nodded. "I need a vehicle and a driver to help me get her away, and then I need somewhere where she can be kept while I negotiate with her brother, and someone to keep an eye on her to make sure she doesn't leave until the exchange has happened. I might be able to manage it alone, but it wouldn't be easy. The chances would be higher that she *would* be hurt, too."

Hachirō's skin, tanned and wrinkled like old leather, grew taut as he clenched his jaw. "No," he said. "This is what I used to do. Hurt people. Frighten them. I made a promise to myself twenty years ago that I would never do that again."

"And that was a worthy decision," Milton said. "I promised myself something similar. But she won't be hurt—you have my word on that. She has no stake in this save the fact that she's related to Furokawa. The worst thing that happens to her is she's shaken up a little and then she has an inconvenient few hours. That's it."

"You don't think there's another way?"

"I can't think of anything with a better chance of success."

Hachirō took the empty plate and stacked it in a dish-washer tray.

"We have to do *something*," Milton pressed. "Your brother kidnapped your grandson and punished your daughter for something that his own son did. Neither of those things is right, and I want to help set things straight. The only way I can think of doing that is to offer him the sword."

"So Takashi benefits from his behaviour?"

"He would tell you that a wrong was righted. It doesn't matter either way; you need to see beyond that and get to the goal, to reunite Sakura with Yamato and then keep them both safe. I'm open to other ideas, but I've given it a lot of thought and this is the best I've got. I'm going to do it with or without you, Hachirō. I'd hoped you'd agree to help, but I can't force you. But I have to be honest—if you don't help, there's a decent chance I'll find myself in trouble and, if that happens, you're going to have to figure out how to fix this on your own. I imagine that means persuading your brother to see sense."

"I know what I said yesterday, but I've been thinking about it. It won't work. He and I have no relationship, especially not now. He blames Sakura for leading Miyasato astray. He'd kill me the moment he saw me coming."

Milton spread his arms. "So?"

Hachirō was quiet for a moment and then nodded, his decision made. "What choice do I have? When do you intend to do it?"

Milton looked at his watch. It was ten o'clock. "I'm seeing Takashi at midday," he said. "Assuming I can agree to an exchange with him, I don't think it would serve any of us to wait."

"Tomorrow, then?"

"Yes," Milton said. "First thing."

Hachirō ducked his head in acknowledgement.

"Do you have a pen and paper?" Milton asked him.

The old man reached beneath the counter and brought out the pad that he used for orders and a pencil. Milton tore off the top page and started to write.

"What are you doing?"

"A shopping list," Milton said. "You still have connections?"

"Just a few old men who learned the error of their ways."

"But perhaps one or two who didn't?"

"Perhaps."

"Good. There are some things I'm going to need you to get."

85

Milton concentrated on his surroundings as he walked toward Takashi Nishimoto's tower block. This used to be Sanya, but the district's name had been expunged from official records in the sixties by a government that was embarrassed by the poverty that was cheek by jowl with the prosperity of the rest of the city. Instead, the area had been divided into the districts of Kiyokawa and Zutsumi. This area was the former, and it did not look too different to the other districts that Milton had visited since he had arrived in the city. The buildings looked in good condition, and there was no shortage of supermarkets and neighbourhood stores that offered groceries and other necessities to the men and women who passed in and out of their doors. But, as Milton looked, he saw the subtle signs that suggested that Kiyokawa was not as affluent as the other districts that he had seen. He saw children in patched clothes, parents eking out as much wear from them as possible. Men in cheap plastic flip-flops sat on park benches, sipping alcopops from colourful Chu-Hi cans. There were hotels and hostels and *kichinyado* lodgings with signs in the windows that offered the cheapest rates that Milton had seen since arriving in Tokyo. The buildings might have been substantial and well appointed, a world away from the shanties of other cities that Milton had visited—Rio, Juarez, Manila—but there was the same atmosphere of thwarted ambition and desperation. The people who lived here were not so different.

Milton passed through a park, making his way around two men who were playing *shogi* on a board that they had laid on the ground, and then through a scrum of kids who bustled around him with their hands outstretched, begging for change. He left through a set of iron gates and turned on to the road that led to Takashi's stronghold.

The tower block sat on the north side of a crossroads, a modern-looking structure with twelve storeys. It was slender, with an exterior staircase that ascended to the top. Milton counted seven windows per floor, suggesting three or four apartments on each. There was a trio of men loitering outside, younger than the retired day labourers who shuffled between their hostels and the dive bars where they drank their problems away. Milton was the only Westerner on the street and, as they noticed his approach, they turned to face him and stared at him with threatening eyes.

Milton walked by the three men, ignoring them, and pushed the door to the foyer and went inside. The walls were yellowed with what looked like water stains running down them, and the tiled floor was badly cracked in several areas. The air smelled unpleasant. Fetid. There was a desk on the other side of the room that looked as if it was where the concierge worked, if that was not too grand a title for anyone who worked in a building such as this. Milton saw two elevator doors behind the desk and two more young men, both in their early to mid-twenties, who watched him suspiciously.

Milton approached the desk.

"I'm here to see Takashi Nishimoto," he said.

The man stared at him. The two heavies next to the elevator doors were watching, too. Milton recognised them: it was the pair who had followed them yesterday. They both had bruises that bore evidence of the beating he had administered.

"Do you speak English?"

"I speak it," the man said.

"So tell Takashi that I'm here to see him. My name is John Milton. He's expecting me."

The man took a phone from the desk, turned away from Milton and made a call. Milton waited, using the time to recce the ground floor of the building. There were those two elevators, served by a shaft that ran up the middle of the building. There was a set of stairs opposite those and a door that looked as if it might be a communal bathroom. Three other doors, all arranged around the elevator lobby, looked to contain the first of the building's apartments.

The man behind the desk finished his call and made his way across the lobby to where the two guards were standing. There was a short conversation, and then the man and one of the guards came back to Milton. It was the second of the two thugs from the metro station, the one Milton had told to deliver his message.

"Come," the guard ordered, moving his shirt aside just far enough for Milton to see the knife that he wore in a sheath on his belt.

The man took him to the elevators and told him to wait. Milton looked around; he had been correct in his assumption that the door to his right was a bathroom; a third guard emerged from it, wiping wet hands against the back of his jeans. Milton turned his attention to the elevators. The one on the left looked normal, with the standard button to summon it. The one on the right had a card reader next to the button; Milton guessed that the elevator was restricted to Takashi and his guests, a private way to ascend to his floors at the top of the building.

The elevator to the right pinged, the door opened and a man stepped out. He was in his mid-fifties to early sixties, with weathered skin and jet-black hair.

"Takashi?" Milton asked.

"No. I am Fumio—I work with Takashi. Who are you?"

"My name is John Milton," he said. "I sent a message yesterday—the two men over there thought it would be a good idea to follow me and Takashi's niece. We had a chat and I told them to tell Takashi that I'd be coming over today. Here I am."

"I see. And what do you want?"

"To speak to him."

"He has sent me to talk to you."

"I don't want to talk to you. I want to talk to him."

"I am sorry, Milton-*san*. He is busy."

Fumio turned on his heel and took a couple of steps back toward the elevator.

"He'll appreciate what I have to say," Milton called out. "He lost something recently and I may be able to help him get it back."

Fumio turned back.

"What is it that you think Takashi has lost?"

"I told your boys—a sword. One that used to belong to Yoshida Shōin." He watched as Fumio assessed this information. "But if he's busy, well, I suppose I'll be on my way."

Fumio eyed him suspiciously. "You have it?"

"I'd like to speak to Takashi."

The older man chewed the side of his mouth, thinking.

"It's up to you," Milton said. "If he's not interested, that's fine. Others will be."

Fumio nodded, his mind made up. "Please—come."

Milton did as he was told. The guard searched him quickly and not particularly efficiently. Milton was not carrying a weapon, but noted that it might be possible to sneak something inside if this was the standard of security that Takashi employed.

Milton raised his arms above his head as the man patted down his torso. "No weapons and no wires."

Fumio approached the elevator on the right, took a key card from his pocket and held it against the reader. The unit emitted a chirp of satisfaction, a light turned green and the doors opened. Fumio stood to the side and gestured that Milton should enter. He did, moving to the back of the car and then turning to watch as the guard and then Fumio followed. The older man took a small key from his pocket and inserted it into a keyhole next to the control panel. He turned the key, waited for another light to switch from red to green, and then held down the button for the twelfth floor.

Milton stood with his hands clasped in front of him as the elevator ascended. Fumio and the guard had no idea who he was and, more particularly, of what he was capable. It would have been simple to disarm the guard and then kill them both. The noise would be contained within the elevator car; no one would hear a thing. Milton could arrive at the penthouse to greet Takashi with the knife and then play the game that way. But that wasn't what he had planned. It would be too risky; he didn't know where Yamato was, and the possible repercussions for Sakura, her son and Hachirō were too great.

Milton had another plan. One which, unusually for him, did not involve violence.

He rocked on his heels as the counter above the doors ticked past the floors. When the number twelve lit up, the elevator slowed and then ground to a halt. With a pneumatic sigh, the doors began to open.

86

Takashi turned as the door to the apartment opened, curious to see his visitor. He had heard a lot about the Westerner: the man who had foiled Katsuro in Bali and then Manila *and* bested the two men who had followed him and Sakura after they had met Hachirō. Fumio was astute, too, and he had gone down to assess the man and decide whether he was fit to be brought up to see him. He evidently considered that he was. Fumio stepped out of the elevator, followed by the *gaijin*.

"This is John Milton," Fumio said in English. "He says that he wishes to discuss a matter of some importance with you."

Milton stopped about ten feet away from him and bowed. "Takashi-*sama*. Thank you for agreeing to see me."

Takashi raised his eyebrows. At least the man had some manners. Proper comportment was, he thought, growing rarer and rarer these days. The man was dressed casually in jeans and a white shirt. His face was severe, with an old scar that sliced from his nose to his ear. He had the most intense blue eyes that Takashi had ever seen. Takashi looked carefully at his first lieutenant to see if he could learn anything from the expression on his face, but it was blank.

"Milton-*san*," Takashi said, "welcome." He gestured to the desk in the corner of his vast living room. "Please, sit."

Milton sat down and Takashi took the seat behind the desk. Fumio stayed where he was, a few feet away from them, and the guard stayed by the elevator, close enough to get to Milton if he tried to do anything foolish. Takashi looked at Milton for a moment, appraising him. There was something in the way he held himself, the way that he had sat down in the chair, that gave Takashi reason to be cautious. There was a confidence to his bearing that was at odds with the way that he should have reacted. Takashi was used to inspiring fear. This man didn't look frightened—not at all—and that gave Takashi cause for concern.

He steepled his fingers on the desk. "So—what is this business that you wish to discuss?"

"You lost something recently. A sword. It was stolen from you by your son, Miyasato, and then sold to Satoshi Furokawa."

"And how is this your business?"

"I may be able to help you get it back."

"Do you work for Furokawa?"

"No," Milton said. "I work for myself."

"What is it that you do?"

"I fix problems for people."

"Like Sakura?"

Milton showed no reaction. "That's right," he said. "She needed help—I provided it."

"How could she afford to pay for that?"

"I don't charge. She was a deserving case. You treated her very badly."

"Her husband stole from me," Takashi said. "She is lucky she did not suffer the same fate as him."

"We'll have to agree to disagree about that," Milton said. "She told me what happened, and your brother confirmed it. Your son stole the sword from you to order. Furokawa was his patron. I'm sure you considered how you could retrieve it, but, with respect, you're old and the yakuza have been overtaken by people like Furokawa. The sword was stolen more than six months ago and you haven't tried to get it back. I think you've given it up."

"You make many presumptions."

"Are they wrong?"

Milton paused to allow Takashi to answer, but he chose to hold his tongue.

"I didn't think so. You can't go up against him without risking serious consequences. It's different for me. He has no idea who I am." Milton smiled. "I can take the sword back and there would be no link to you. Even in the unlikely event that I was discovered, how could anyone know I was working on your behalf?"

"Because I owned the *tantō?*"

"He could draw that conclusion, I suppose, but he won't be able to prove it."

"You think it would be easy to take it from him?"

"I'm sure it won't be."

"So why should I believe you when you say that you could?"

"You could ask your son about me," he said. He looked around. "Where *is* Katsuro?"

"My son is a fool. That tells me nothing."

"I suppose not. Look—I'll give you a flavour of what I used to do. I used to work for my government. Solving problems. Unfortunately for me, I seemed to have developed a conscience as I've grown older. Sakura was lucky to find me when she did. I met her, realised what she had been forced to do, and decided that I would help. So we do need to be clear about one thing—I'm not offering to work for you. I'm working for her, and trying to find a way for you to get what you need to leave her and her son alone."

"And this is your solution?"

"It's one of them," Milton said.

"The other?"

"Less pleasant for all involved. I'd rather not have to go down that path. This way is better—you get to walk away with your property returned and your pride intact."

Takashi stared at him. "You are *threatening* me, Milton-*san?*"

"Just stating a fact. Sakura and Yamato are going to be reunited and they're going to live peaceful, happy lives, far away from here. I'm doing you the service of allowing you to choose how that happens."

Takashi paused for a moment, drumming his fingers on the desk as he watched Milton. The man was sitting quietly, just staring at him. There was something about his gaze that was disquieting, but Takashi kept his expression neutral.

He made up his mind. The *gaijin* could pretend to have leverage, could flaunt his confidence, but he had nothing. *Takashi* had the leverage; Yamato was downstairs, under his control. He was concerned about making a hostile move against Furokawa, but the *gaijin* was right; Takashi could deny any involvement. And there was something about the man sitting before him that suggested that it might not be an entirely fanciful hope that he could do what he had said he could do. Takashi's collection would be complete once again if Milton could recover Shōin's *tantō*. That was a prize worth the gamble.

"Fine," Takashi said. "I agree. The *tantō* for the boy."

"And Sakura, too. Her debt is expunged. I have your word that they will never be bothered again?"

"You have my word," Takashi said.

Takashi rose and offered his hand. Milton shook it. The *gaijin*'s grip was firm and unyielding.

"When do you plan to do this?"

"Soon," Milton said.

Takashi tried to remove his hand, but Milton held on.

Fumio took a step toward them; so did the guard.

"I want to see the boy first," Milton said, still grasping Takashi by the hand and staring into his eyes.

"You do not trust me?"

"Of course not. I trust you about as much as you trust me."

Milton let go. Takashi considered the request, concluding that it was not unreasonable. He would have asked for the same assurances had the roles been reversed.

"Fumio," he said, "please take Milton-*san* to see Yamato."

He turned his back on Milton and walked over to the window. Far in the distance, low clouds were obscuring the top of Mount Fuji. He didn't look back until he heard the click of the apartment door closing. He turned and walked into the living room, examining the empty brackets on the wall where the *tantō* had once been displayed. He reached up and ran his finger across the bracket, then looked at the thin film of dust that had stuck to his skin. It would be good to have the blade again; if the *gaijin* could deliver it, perhaps he would meet his demand.

Perhaps.

87

Milton followed Fumio out of the apartment and into the lobby. This time, they took the stairs rather than the elevator. Milton paid attention as they descended; the door that opened onto the floor below was locked. Fumio pressed his key card against a reader until it was recognised and the lock opened.

The eleventh floor was equally opulent. The stairs opened out onto the lobby, with the two elevators directly opposite. The carpets were thick and the walls decorated with marble and classical art that was obviously expensive. Four doors opened out from the lobby, each, Milton assumed, accessing one of the four apartments that had originally been built here; he guessed that they had been remodelled for another purpose, perhaps as bedrooms.

Fumio turned right and approached one of the doors. He rapped his hand on it and, after a moment, Milton heard a woman calling out in Japanese. Fumio replied in kind and, a few seconds later, the door swung open. A small elderly woman stood behind it. Fumio said something to her and Milton watched her eyes flash at him, full of distrust.

"Follow me," Fumio said.

Milton looked around the rooms beyond the door, committing the layout to memory: a bathroom to the left and a small kitchen to the right, a short corridor and then a large bedroom. The bedroom was beautifully appointed. There was a double bed piled high with plush cushions, a bookcase that was filled with books, and several wicker baskets of toys. The framed posters on the wall celebrated Japanese history: there were images of the first shoguns, an armoured samurai posing with a *katana* held above his head, and—in an inclusion that Milton suspected was a concession to the room's young inhabitant—a classic film poster for Ishirō Honda's *Godzilla*. The space was large—perhaps thirty-five square metres—with a series of windows that offered spectacular views of the city outside. A child was sitting next to the baskets of toys. Sakura had shown Milton a picture, and he recognised her son. Yamato was engrossed in a battle between two Transformers.

"There," Fumio said. "The boy."

The child looked up as Fumio spoke, glanced from him to Milton and then, dismissing them both, concentrated on his play once more. Milton took out his phone.

"I need to take a video," he said.

Fumio shrugged that he didn't care. Milton opened the camera app, slid his finger across the screen until he had selected video, and then started to shoot. He focused on the child, crouching down a little so that he could record the boy's face and then, nodding that he was finished, he stood up.

Fumio led the way back through the flat. Milton had not ended the recording and, with the phone clasped in his hand, he made sure that he had a visual record of the layout. Fumio opened the door and took Milton to the restricted elevator. He pressed his card to the reader, pressed the button, and waited for the car to arrive and the door to open. He indicated that Milton should get inside, then unlocked the control panel and pressed the button for the ground floor.

As they descended, Milton turned his thoughts to what he had learned. Takashi wielded power and influence, but he was an old man and not imposing in any physical sense. Fumio was old, too, and neither would pose him any sort of challenge if it came to a confrontation. The guards were younger, but they did not strike him as particularly thorough or effective. He didn't want to have to return in anger but, if that was necessary, he could see a way to get in and collect the boy. He held out hope that things could be remedied peacefully, but he knew there was a good possibility that he would have to call on his demons. That did not concern him and, in that sense, his visit had been profitable; he felt more prepared for the eventuality now than he had before.

88

Sakura jumped to her feet as the door to the hotel suite opened and Milton walked inside. She had been anxiously waiting for him to return all day.

"I told you to keep the sign on the door," Milton said.

"I forgot," she apologised.

"The more people who see you, the more danger you're in. That includes the maid."

"I'm sorry. I had some clothes I wanted to launder—I took the sign off so that they knew I was here when they wanted to return them."

Milton's face softened. "I just want you to be safe," he said. "That's all."

He drew her into a hug and she nuzzled into him, enjoying the firmness of his body and his scent, quickly becoming familiar.

"Where have you been all day?"

He gently pulled away from her. "I saw your father."

"And?"

"He's going to help."

She frowned. "Are you sure it won't be dangerous? He's old, John."

"No," he said. "It won't be dangerous, at least not for him. I wouldn't have asked him if it was."

"And then? You've been gone all day."

"Like I said—I went to see Takashi."

Her stomach dropped at the mention of that name. "Where?"

"At the tower block," he said, then smiled. "I have some good news."

She reached for his arm. "Yamato?"

He nodded. "I saw him."

"Oh my God," she said, feeling her knees weaken.

He guided her back to the bed and encouraged her to sit down.

"How is he? Is he okay?"

"He's fine. They have him in an apartment."

"What was it like?"

"Very nice. It's just below the penthouse."

"How was he?"

"He seemed happy enough."

"What was he doing?"

"Playing."

"Are they feeding him?"

"I'm not an expert, but he looked healthy. Here—you tell me."

Milton took out his phone, selected the video and handed it to Sakura. She pressed play and immediately gasped as she saw Yamato's little face. He was playing with two Transformers, banging one robot into the other. She was buffeted by dizziness and felt her eyes filling with tears.

"See?" he said. "He's fine."

She breathed in and out, trying not to cry. "It's the first time I've seen him properly for weeks."

"You'll see him for real soon."

She scrubbed back on the footage, watching his face as he concentrated on his game. He was biting the corner of his lip, and she remembered how he had always done that, all the way back to when he was a toddler. She blinked back her tears and felt a wave of love that threatened to sweep over her.

"It's okay," Milton said, his hand atop hers. "This is good news. You'll have him back soon."

"What did you say to Takashi?"

"I've made a deal with him. You and Yamato for the sword. I need to get it for him, and then he promised to release Yamato to me and to leave you both alone."

Sakura felt befuddled by emotion: the prospect of seeing her son again was intoxicating, but she realised that it was almost perfectly balanced by her fear for Milton's safety.

"Furokawa is worse than Takashi," she said.

"I know he's dangerous," Milton said. "I spoke to your father about him. Everyone has a weakness, and I know his. He'll give me the sword and no one will be hurt."

"How can you say that?"

"Do you trust me?"

"Yes," she said. "Of course."

He took her hand in his. "So *trust* me." His smile broadened. "It's nearly over. You'll have Yamato back by this time tomorrow and you'll both be safe."

Sakura still felt faint. The thought of being reunited with Yamato would have been enough; she would have run with him, taken him far from Japan. She would gladly have settled for the uncertainty of discovery just to have him with her. But Milton was offering more than that. He was offering freedom.

"Thank you," she said. She turned a little so that she could look into his eyes. She saw steel and determination, but, behind it, she saw a sadness that she could not understand. Perhaps she could persuade him to stay in Tokyo for a little while?

Perhaps she could persuade him to stay for *longer* than a little while?

M iyasato and Sakura had rented a house in Hiroo, and Sakura had kept it after her husband had been killed. Katsuro had been watching the property all day in the hope that he might see some sign of occupation. There had been nothing. It was past ten in the evening now, and the salarymen who commuted into the city had all returned home. The street was quiet and, gradually, the flickers of TVs in downstairs windows were extinguished as the inhabitants turned in for the night. Downstairs lights clicked off and upstairs lights flicked on; another thirty minutes passed and, eventually, those lights were extinguished, too.

Katsuro opened the door of his car and stepped out. He was wearing a pair of thin nitrile gloves, had a pistol in a clip-on holster that he wore on his belt, and carried a small bag with a set of tools inside. He walked along the street to the house, checked that he was not being watched and, satisfied, turned onto the driveway and made his way to the front door. He tried the handle. It was locked. He took a couple of steps away from the door and regarded the narrow alleyway between the house and its neighbour. It was not really wide enough to be called an alleyway, more a gap between the two properties. Katsuro turned his body to one side and slipped into the darkness between the walls.

He took a deep breath, realising that the aperture was narrower than he remembered from when he'd broken in six months ago. He inhaled and felt the walls pushing against him from front and back. He shuffled along the passage, his barrel chest barely fitting, pausing halfway to get his breath. He continued on, grateful when the passageway widened as he reached the rear of the house.

He took a deep breath and climbed over a bare cinder-block wall and into the courtyard. He paused, looking at the windows of the house, keeping his weight on the balls of his feet. If Sakura was inside and had heard him approach, he would have to move quickly. The windows that overlooked the small courtyard were obscured by paper blinds. The one clear window—he remembered that it belonged to the kitchen—showed no light or any other sign that anyone was at home.

The courtyard was small—perhaps ten feet by twelve—and the only decoration was a small table and chairs. There was a child's scooter that had fallen onto its side. The walls to the courtyard were bare cinder blocks, and the only nod Sakura and Miyasato had made to decoration were planters filled with colourful shrubs. The plants had not been cared for recently; they had grown too large for their pots and were being slowly choked by weeds.

Katsuro crossed to the sliding glass doors and examined the locks. He knew that he could just force the lock, but that would betray the fact that he had been here; even though Sakura was likely not home, he preferred that she remain unaware that he was looking for her in the event that she did return. He stooped down next to the lock, put his bag down and opened it. He took out a thin set of lock rakes and used them to ratchet the tumblers in the lock; whoever had installed the doors clearly had not considered anyone trying to enter the house this way and had used a lock that a child could pick. Katsuro removed the pistol from the holster, opened the door and leaned his head inside. He couldn't hear anything. He listened intently, but, apart from the noise of a car passing nearby, it was silent. No television, no radio, no sounds of anyone moving about inside, no breathing that might have suggested that she was upstairs, asleep.

Katsuro slipped his shoes off and arranged them so that the toes were pointing away from the door, then stepped onto the tatami mat inside the house. He walked across the mat to the sliding door that led into the house proper, still listening intently. The room beyond was the kitchen.

He stopped and listened again: still nothing.

He checked the house room by room. The stairs leading to the upper floor of the house creaked as he put his weight on them, but he was increasingly sure that he was alone inside the property. He cleared all three bedrooms. All were empty.

Katsuro returned to the master bedroom and picked up a photograph from the small dresser. Sakura and Miyasato in happier times. He looked at his brother and felt a fresh jolt of disgust at what he had done. Stealing from their father... it was abhorrent. After all the advantages that Miyasato had been accorded... He had been the favourite, hand-picked to take the clan and move it forward. Miyasato could have done it, too; with his brain and Katsuro's muscle, they could have taken the fight to the *hangure* and all the other pretenders and restored the Nishimoto-*kai* to a position of pre-eminence.

And then, what? Miyasato had squandered all that potential for *that woman*. Katsuro, on the other hand, had carried out his father's wishes without compunction. Miyasato was guilty of the most heinous of betrayals and deserved the fate that Takashi had decreed and that Katsuro had arranged.

He didn't miss him. The two of them had never been close, and, as Miyasato had concentrated on his wife, the rift had deepened. They had had no relationship at all at the end; Miyasato was a dog who had deserved to be put out of his misery.

Katsuro was glad that he had been chosen to pull the trigger.

He replaced the photograph, made his way back down the stairs and went into the small study. There was a laptop on the desk and he flipped it open. The machine emitted a bleep and the screen lit up. He sat down and looked at it. The screensaver was a picture of Sakura and Yamato; the two of them were eating ice cream, and the boy had a dollop of it daubed on his nose. Katsuro tapped a key and the screensaver was replaced by the log-in screen. It prompted him for a password.

Katsuro stared at the blinking cursor. He typed YAMATO and hit return. Nothing. He tried MIYASATO. Nothing. He leaned back in the chair and gazed around the room. There was another photograph on the bookcase to his right and a yellow Post-it note had been stuck to the frame. He pushed the wheeled chair across the room so that he could swipe the Post-it. A combination of letters, numbers and symbols had been written across it in red ink. He wheeled back to the desk and, carefully referring to the note, he typed in the characters and hit return for a third time.

The log-in screen disappeared and was replaced by Sakura's email browser.

There were more than sixty unopened emails. Most were marketing spam, but one that had arrived yesterday caught his eye.

The sender was noted as GRACERY and the subject line was YOUR RECEIPT.

Katsuro's tongue flicked out of his mouth and he licked his lips. He opened the email and saw that Sakura had paid for a room at the Gracery Hotel in Shinjuku for the next five nights, reserving it in advance and then paying for it upon check-in. He printed the receipt, collecting the paper from the printer that chugged away inside the cupboard beneath the bookshelf and folding it so that he could slide it into his pocket.

Katsuro knew the Gracery. It was large, and there was no indication on the receipt of the room that had been booked. That didn't matter. Katsuro knew where she was now, and he knew of several ways that he could get the more particular information that he would need so that he could pay her a visit.

90

Milton and Sakura ordered room service from the hotel restaurant. The place was Italian themed and they both chose pizza. Their food arrived and they ate it sitting cross-legged on the floor. Sakura found that she had no appetite. Milton was not similarly afflicted and demolished his.

Sakura pointed at the empty box. "Let me guess. Eat when you can, sleep when you can?"

Milton laughed. He nodded down at her almost untouched meal. "Are you going to eat that?"

Sakura pushed the box toward him.

Milton switched on the TV and found a music channel. An old Fleetwood Mac video was playing. He put the remote down and turned to her.

"What is it? You've barely said two words."

"I'm thinking about what you said."

"About Yamato?"

"You really think he'll be here tomorrow?"

Milton took a slice of her pizza and took a bite. "That's the plan."

"I don't have anything for him. His clothes. His toys. Everything's in my house. I could go back—"

"No," he said, cutting over her. He swivelled so that he could look directly at her and set down the pizza slice. His eyes, frosty blue, were full of conviction. "You can't go home until I say so."

"Five minutes? In and out, that's all. I—"

He took her hands in his and squeezed. "*No.*"

"John," she said, "you're hurting me."

A flicker passed across his face. "I'm sorry." He released her hands. "Please. *Please*, Sakura. They will be watching the house. I promise you—it's the most obvious place they'll look. We can't take the risk."

"But you said he agreed with you. Me and Yamato for the sword."

"I know he did, but I don't trust him. You have to promise me—you have to *swear*—you'll stay here, in the room, until I come back tomorrow."

"I know."

"Say it."

"I will," she said. "I'll stay here until you get back. I promise."

Milton eyed her for a moment, as if deciding whether she was speaking truthfully, before picking up the slice again and taking another bite.

"What will you do afterwards?" she asked him.

"What do you mean?"

"When this is all over?"

"I don't know," he said.

"This could be our last night together."

"Why? You think I'm going to get hurt?"

"I don't know. Furokawa is dangerous."

"I'll be careful."

"You haven't said what you're going to do."

"It's a good plan," he said. "I'm going to be okay."

"You can't say that for sure. And, even if you *are* okay, you still haven't said what you'll do afterwards. You said it yourself—you like to move around. Maybe you've already decided that's what you'll do. Go somewhere else."

She could feel tears pricking at her eyes. He took her hands again and held them more gently this time.

"I don't know," he said, pulling her toward him. "I haven't decided yet. But tomorrow's tomorrow. Why don't we worry about that then?"

"So, you might stay?"

"Perhaps," he said. "At least until I know that you're okay."

"And then?"

"We can think about that."

"But if I'm not safe, you'd stay longer?" She blinked the tears away and smiled up at him. "Maybe I need to find something dangerous. You wouldn't want me to undo all the good that you've done, would you?"

He chuckled and shook his head. "That sounds like blackmail."

She took the slice of pizza from his hand, dropped it back in the box and then lowered herself into his lap so that the two of them were facing one another. She kissed him softly on the lips.

"I'll do whatever I have to do to get my way," she said.

PART VII

MONDAY

91

Milton lay in bed, awake but with his eyes closed against the dawn light that was seeping through the hotel windows. Sakura slept soundly beside him, her breathing deep and regular. It was just before five in the morning and, outside the window, Tokyo was starting to come to life.

They had gone to bed last night, but not to sleep. It had been after midnight before Milton had drifted away and, even then, his sleep had been disturbed by Sakura tossing and turning beside him. He knew how nervous she was about the coming day. It was impossible for her to hide it, but Milton had done his best to reassure her that everything would work out.

He opened his eyes and turned to look at her. He remembered her question: would he stay? His reply at the time had been genuine—he hadn't decided—but he was leaning toward remaining in Tokyo for a little while longer. He told himself that he was only considering that so that he could be sure that Takashi would be true to his word, that

Sakura and Yamato would be safe, but he wasn't fooled. He found, to his surprise, that he did not want to leave and it was all because of her. For the first time in as long as he could remember, the idea of staying in one place—of adopting something approaching a mundane life—was appealing to him. He had always told himself that he did not deserve happiness, and that he was not entitled to put someone else at risk for the sake of his own happiness. That had been his bulwark against self-indulgence, his motive for running from all of the women who had drawn close to him since he had fled London.

He felt now that the bulwark had been weakened.

Milton slipped from the bed, careful not to disturb Sakura, and went into the bathroom. He went through his ablutions as quietly as he could and returned to the living area to collect his clothes from where they had been abandoned the previous evening.

"John?"

It was mumbled, thick with sleep.

"Come back to bed."

He went to her and crouched down so that he could kiss her behind the ear. "I've got things to do."

She smiled sleepily at him, turned over, and fell back into sleep. Milton pulled on his shoes and jacket and reached into his pocket. The sobriety chip was there and he ran his finger around it again, feeling the raised edge, taking a moment to reflect on what he had achieved in the eight years that had passed since he had taken his last drink. Progress. He could admit that to himself now. He was a different man now, changed from the implacable killer of before. He still had his demons and knew that they remained close at hand and ready to slip their leashes if he let them, but he had balance, too. He looked at Sakura.

Maybe, he thought.

Maybe.

92

Hachirō was waiting outside the hotel, as they had arranged. He was sitting in the driver's seat of a battered old delivery van across the road from the entrance. The van was a little the worse for wear, but the rear windows were blacked out and the engine was running. Milton couldn't have cared less about the condition that it was in; he would be satisfied as long as it was reliable and offered a little discretion.

Hachirō reached across the cab to open the door.

"It sticks from the outside," he said.

Milton climbed inside. "Good morning."

"Morning."

They pulled away.

"Did you get it?"

Hachirō nodded at the glove box of the van.

Milton opened it, reached inside and took out an object wrapped in a dirty rag. He unfolded the rag to reveal a Glock 23. It was a little over seven inches long, nice and compact. He turned the gun over in his hand, feeling the weight of it, before popping out the magazine and pulling the slide back. He pressed the rounds out of the magazine and dropped them into his pocket before replacing the magazine.

"Any problems?"

"No."

Milton had asked whether Hachirō would be able to find a weapon. The old man had said that he could, and Milton had not probed for any other information. He suspected that he still maintained contacts with the underworld. The weapon's serial number had been filed off; Milton did not intend to fire it, especially given he had no idea in which crimes it had been used before.

Milton put the gun away.

"What about the masks?"

Hachirō reached down and passed over a plastic carrier bag. There was a half-length *menpō* mask inside. It was of a design that would have been worn by a samurai, intended to protect the face while also intimidating the enemy. This one had a dark russet finish, a bulbous nose and extravagantly arched eyebrows.

"You have one, too?"

Hachirō nodded.

"The cable ties?"

"In the bag."

Milton reached in again and took out a bunch of plastic cable ties, still with the price tag attached.

"Good," Milton said. "How much do I owe you?"

"Nothing," the old man said. "It would be fairer to ask how much I owe you. You still don't have to do this."

Milton didn't answer, and they were both quiet as Hachirō navigated the streets toward Yoyogi Park. It was early, yet the streets of a city as vast as Tokyo were never really quiet.

"It's not far," Hachirō said. "You still think we should do it at the park? Outside?"

"Nothing has changed."

"There might be witnesses."

"I imagine so."

"So we go to her apartment, perhaps?"

"Too hard to get her out without being stopped. Did you buy the van with cash?"

"Yes," Hachirō said.

"And you gave a false name?"

"I did."

"So it won't matter if we're seen. We'll be out of the way before anyone can stop us. What about the restaurant?"

"It is ready."

"It'll be fine," Milton said. "This is the best way."

93

They arrived at the lot on the western edge of Yoyogi Park. Hachirō parked side-on to the open ground, just as Milton instructed. A running track traced the perimeter of the park, and it ran between the trees and the open space that was being used by three old men who were performing impressive feats of callisthenics. Milton would have preferred that they were not there, but he doubted that they would offer a significant threat, and certainly not one that could not be cowed by his waving the pistol in front of them. He hoped it would not come to that, but was prepared to frighten them if that was what it took.

Milton checked his watch. It was just before six.

"Ready?"

Hachirō nodded. "How long until she's here?"

"Should be twenty minutes."

Natsuki Furokawa had followed the same pattern for the last six weeks: she started recording her run at five forty-five, heading west and entering the park; she ran around it twice, passing this spot for the first time at twenty minutes past six, give or take a minute or two either way.

"I'll be here," Hachirō said.

"Kill the engine for now," Milton said. "Don't attract attention."

Hachirō nodded.

Milton got out of the van and walked into the park. He had visited the area the previous afternoon, after he had broached the plan with Hachirō. It was one of the largest open spaces in the city and had housed US troops during the American occupation of the city after the war. It was really two separate parks, split down the middle by a road. It had been busy during Milton's reconnaissance, with fashionistas and hipsters from nearby Harajuku mixing with street performers, singers and dancers. There were far fewer people here now than yesterday: the three old men, a handful of dog walkers, the occasional jogger and cyclist.

Milton felt a moment of uncertainty. There were plenty of things that could go wrong with his plan. He patted the Glock in the inside pocket of his jacket; the pistol felt heavy and cumbersome. He had carried a weapon of some sort for most of his adult life, but this time it felt different. He was going to use it to frighten a young woman who had done nothing wrong and had attracted his attention for the sole reason that she was the sibling of a criminal.

Milton followed the path to the east. It was bounded to the left by a metal fence and, to the right, he saw rose, cherry and plum gardens. He was admiring the view to the striking red bridge that forded one side of a pond to the other when he saw a woman jogging in his direction. She was wearing a white tracksuit top and leggings and was listening to earbuds that led to a phone strapped around her upper arm. Her ponytail bounced left and right as she pounded along the trail.

Right on time.

Milton turned and started back. She was a minute or two away from him. He looked back to the parking lot and saw Hachirō open the back doors of the van, then make his way back into the cab to start the engine; Milton heard it cough and then the steady grumble. He looked around: the three old men had finished their exercises and were walking away to the south. The park was quiet. They had been fortunate.

Milton reached into his pocket and found the grip of the pistol, sliding his fingers around it as he picked up his pace.

94

Natsuki rounded the corner, maintaining a steady pace. She was in the zone: lost in the repetitiveness of her stride, the outside world closed out by whatever it was she was listening to. Milton stood next to a bench at the side of the trail and pretended to stretch, waiting for her to reach him. The park was still quiet, the only potential witness a dog walker still a quarter of a mile away.

The woman approached and, when she was alongside, Milton turned and wrapped his right arm around her waist, immediately arresting her momentum. He looped his left arm around her, too, locking his hands and hoisting her off the ground. She wasn't heavy, and, in her shock, it took her a moment to think that she should struggle. Milton was already halfway to the van by then, and, besides, she was no match for him. He doubted that she was more than a hundred and twenty pounds soaking wet, and, as he squeezed her against his chest so that he could lock her arms against her torso, there was little that she could do to stop him from crossing the distance to the back of the van and shoving her inside.

She hadn't seen his face yet and now he reached down for the *menpō* mask that he had left beneath the van. He put it on and climbed into the back. Natsuki screamed at the sight of him; Milton reached around for the pistol and showed it to her, his finger held up against his lips. The look of terror on her face made Milton feel worse than he already did, but there was nothing else for it.

Hachirō shut the rear doors and hurried around to the cab. The gearbox protested as he forced it into gear, and the suspension groaned as the van pulled away.

Natsuki backed away from Milton, all the way to the divider that separated the back of the van from the cab. Only a little light filtered through the opaque film that darkened the rear windows, but it was enough for him to see the fear on her face.

"Do you speak English?" Milton asked her.

Natsuki nodded in reply before her eyes flicked down to the pistol. Milton lowered it.

"I'm sorry about this," Milton said. "I'm not going to hurt you."

"What do you want?"

"I need to get your brother's attention."

"Who are you?"

"You don't need to know that."

"You are an enemy of my brother?"

Milton wondered about that; he wasn't Satoshi Furokawa's enemy per se, although he suspected that Furokawa might see things a little differently now that he had abducted his little sister.

"No."

"So why are you doing this?"

"He has something I want. Now I have something he wants. I'm going to swap one for the other—you for it." He pointed to the phone on her arm. "Could I have that, please?"

She tore the Velcro fastening apart and handed the armband to Milton, the phone still inside the plastic pouch. Milton took the phone out and powered it down. He didn't know how long it would take for Natsuki's abduction to be reported, but he knew that eventually they would try to use the GPS to locate her. It wouldn't work if the phone was off.

"He'll kill you," she said. "Satoshi—I mean it, he'll kill you. I don't think you realise how much trouble you're in."

"Just sit quietly, please," Milton said. "Do as I say and you have my word that you won't be hurt and this will all be over soon."

He reached into his pocket and pulled out the cable ties.

"No," she said. "Please."

"Hands."

He showed her the pistol again and, suitably cowed, she extended both her arms toward him. Milton made a loop with a tie, fed her wrists through it and then drew it closed.

Milton held onto the wheel arch as the van turned to the right. He looked at Natsuki and hoped that the bond between sister and brother was enough for Furokawa to give up the blade that he had recently spent so much to acquire. Milton's research suggested that the relationship between them was strong, but he was going to have to test it. It was the unknown element of the plan, the weakest link; if Furokawa refused to trade Natsuki for the *tantō*, or if he called his bluff, then Milton's scheme would collapse and he would be left with a kidnapped woman, no sword and a disappointed Takashi Nishimoto. He had no idea what that would portend for Yamato, but he doubted it would be good.

95

It took them half an hour to reach their destination. Hachirō slowed the van and then reversed it. The vehicle bumped over the surface of the road and drew to a stop; Hachirō opened the driver's side door and hurried around to the back. He opened the doors, keeping out of Natsuki's sight but just within Milton's view. Milton looked out and saw that they were in a narrow alleyway, with industrial dumpsters at the closed end and buildings that reached up several storeys, blocking most of the light so that all that was left was weak and grey. Hachirō's face wasn't covered; Milton pointed and the older man acknowledged his forgetfulness, going back to the front of the van and returning with an *Oni* mask, a red-faced and angry demon with long, curved fangs.

Milton made sure that his own mask was still in place and turned back to Natsuki. "We're getting out now," he said. "I'll help you."

He took the woman by the arm and guided her to the van's door. Hachirō took her other arm and she slid her legs over the edge. Milton and Hachirō, one on each side, guided her around the van to a door that Hachirō had opened for them. It was dark inside, lit by a single naked bulb. It was the storeroom for the restaurant; Milton saw bags of rice and trays of fresh produce, including a tank of water that held the *uni* of which the old man was so volubly proud. The storeroom was not large, perhaps ten metres square, but it would serve for the time Natsuki would be kept here. Milton did not intend it to be for long.

They guided her to a wooden chair and helped her to sit.

"I'm sorry about this," Milton said. "I'm going to have to tie you to the chair."

"I won't try to run," the woman protested. "You don't need to do that."

"It won't be for long. I'm sorry."

Milton separated four ties from the bunch. He took a knife and sliced through the tie that he had used to secure her in the van, then used the new ones to attach her ankles and wrists to the legs and arms of the chair. She sat quietly while he worked and didn't struggle; Milton felt a fresh blast of regret for worsening her morning still further, but he didn't know her and was not prepared to take the chance that she might try to escape. He was going to have to leave her with Hachirō and, although he had no doubt that Sakura's father was capable, he was also old and Natsuki was fit and strong. Just one more reason not to take chances.

Milton finished and tested the ties; they were good. "I want you to listen to me very carefully," he said to her. "You're not near anyone who would be able to hear you if you called out, so I'm prepared to leave you like this. But that's only if you're quiet. If you make a nuisance, we *will* use a gag. Do you understand?"

The indignity of her situation had turned her fear into anger. "He'll kill you. You're dead men. Both of you."

Milton added a little steel to his voice. "Last chance. Will you be quiet, or do I tape your mouth shut?"

She stewed for a moment, tension written in the stiffness of her posture. "I'll be quiet."

"Good. Now—I'm going to blindfold you."

Hachirō handed him an empty hessian rice sack and Milton pulled it over the woman's head. He nodded to the older man and pushed his mask back so that it was resting against the crown of his head. He took Natsuki's phone from the armband and powered it up. It had a fingerprint reader and, before she could protest, he isolated her index finger with his left hand and pressed the phone against it. The screen woke. Milton opened the settings and used her finger again to disable the autolock. He knew that he wouldn't be able to translate the messages that had been sent to Natsuki, so he gave the phone to Hachirō, who scrolled through them until he had located one from her brother. Milton transferred the number into his own phone and then powered hers down again.

He double-checked that the ties were secure and went to stand with Hachirō in the alleyway. Hachirō removed his mask so that they could speak freely.

"So, what next?" he asked.

"I need to call Furokawa."

96

M ilton took out his phone and entered Satoshi Furokawa's number.

The call was answered by a man speaking Japanese.

"Hello, Satoshi," Milton said.

Milton had watched interviews with him on YouTube and knew that he spoke excellent English.

"Who is this?"

"You can call me Eric."

"How did you get this number?"

"It was on your sister's phone. Please listen carefully, Satoshi. I have Natsuki with me. She was running in Yoyogi Park this morning, the same as she always does. I don't have any interest in hurting her. You can have her back, but we need to agree to the terms before I let her go."

"Who are you?"

"I told you—you can call me Eric."

"Do you know who I am?"

"I do."

"And still you would do something like this? Do you know how stupid that is?"

"Calling me stupid's not nice, Satoshi. Let's keep this as polite as we can—I'd much rather we can come to an arrangement that suits us both. As I said, I don't want anything bad to happen to your sister."

"I don't believe you. You don't have her."

Milton knew that Satoshi would likely pursue that line, and was prepared for it. He looked down at the phone and selected the button that would change from an audio to a video call. He lowered his mask, tapped the screen and waited for Satoshi to accept the call. He did, and a moment later, Milton was looking at his face. It was familiar from the videos that he had studied, but Milton's call had given him reason for ire, and it was obvious from the clenched jaw, the intensity in his eyes and the deep furrows across his brow.

Milton took the phone back into the storeroom and held it so that Natsuki was framed.

"Here she is," Milton said.

"Show me her face."

"Satoshi?" Natsuki tried to stand, forgetting that she was restrained. "Satoshi? Is that you?"

Milton reached forward with his left hand and removed the sack from the woman's head. He kept the phone where it was, allowing Furokawa to see his sister.

Natsuki spoke in rapid Japanese, panicked and garbled, but Milton took the phone away before Satoshi could reply. He went back into the alley and nodded to Hachirō that he should go and replace the sack over her head.

Milton killed the video, switching back to audio only. "Happy?"

"What do you want?"

"We both have something that the other wants. I have your sister. And you have Yoshida Shōin's *tantō*."

"This is Nishimoto's doing? Seriously? You work for that old bastard?"

Milton didn't deny it; a little confusion as to his motivation might prove helpful. "You'd be a hypocrite to complain. You stole the sword from him."

The line was quiet for a moment as Satoshi digested the information. Milton knew that it was a lot for him to take in: his sister abducted and now offered in exchange for the sword that he had gone to such lengths to acquire.

"My sister for the *tantō?* Yes?"

"That's right."

"When?"

"I don't want to inconvenience Natsuki for any longer than I have to."

"Today, then? This afternoon?"

"That works for me."

"All right. Where and when?"

97

K atsuro made his way around the block that included the Gracery Hotel. He was careful, very aware that to compromise his suspicion that Sakura was inside the building at this juncture would be an infuriating mistake. His father was rightfully upset with his performance, Katsuro knew, and he would only be able to rectify the damage done by punishing his sister-in-law for her disloyalty and disobedience.

He just had to find her first.

Sanban-dori Street was adjacent to the entrance to the hotel. He found a seat in a small restaurant, took out his phone and Googled for information on the hotel. The Wikipedia page suggested that it had nearly a thousand rooms that were spread over thirty floors. Katsuro tapped his fingers against the edge of the table. He needed to know Sakura's room number, and knew that there was no point in asking at the reception desk; the hotel would treat guest information as confidential and would not willingly provide it to a third party. He couldn't very well force them to tell him, and he didn't have the expertise to access their servers from outside the building.

He navigated back to Google and found a list of florists in the area. The Kabukien Flower Shop was five minutes away and its website advertised that it delivered to local businesses. Katsuro dialled the number for the store and waited to be connected. He kept an eye on the comings and goings through the entrance to the hotel as he ordered a bouquet of flowers to be delivered to Sakura Nishimoto, a guest staying at the Hotel Gracery, room number unknown. He paid for the flowers with a dummy credit card, thanked the woman at the store and ended the call.

He attracted the attention of the waitress, ordered a matcha parfait and tipped the woman generously when she returned with his food. The ice cream was served with sweet red adzuki beans, preserved chestnuts and chewy warabi mochi. Katsuro—who had always had a sweet tooth—took the long-handled spoon and slotted a scoop of the ice cream into his mouth. He had an hour or two to wait here while the flowers were being prepared, and knew that he wouldn't have any problems with the waitress moving him along thanks to his generous tip.

He scooped out another mouthful and sucked the spoon clean as he watched the activity at the end of the street.

98

M ilton walked from Hachirō's restaurant to Gotanda Station and went down to the Yamanote Line, waiting for a train to take him north. The carriage was quiet and he found a spot at the back where he could sit without being disturbed. There, he ran through his plan again, probing and prodding it to ensure that he had considered all of its possible weaknesses. He had needed a place to meet Satoshi, and his knowledge of Tokyo was not strong enough for him to come up with a suitable location. He had asked Hachirō and realised that he had been fortunate with the date. The Sannō Matsuri was one of the three most important festivals in Tokyo, taking place over the course of a week with frequent parades and events centred around the Hie Shrine. It was underway now, and the main parade was scheduled for this afternoon.

His plan was not, Milton knew, either particularly elegant or clever, but it was the best he could do at such short notice. There were issues with it: there was the collection of the blade from Satoshi and the release of his sister, both of which could go wrong; he knew that there was a very good chance that Satoshi would have men and women waiting to follow him after the meet, and he was going to have to rid himself of them. Finally, and assuming that the exchange was successful and that he was able to go black—confirming that he was not being tailed—he would then need to negotiate a second exchange: swapping the *tantō* for Yamato and Sakura's safety, all the while aware that there was a good chance that Satoshi would be looking for him.

Lots of weaknesses. Lots of vulnerabilities. But no other choice.

Milton would have to do the best that he could.

99

The florist had said that the flowers would be delivered in the early afternoon and, wanting to make sure that he was in place in plenty of time, Katsuro made his way inside the hotel at half past eleven and went up to the desk.

"Can I help you?" the receptionist asked.

"A room, please."

The woman looked at her screen and shook her head. "I'm sorry. We're almost completely full."

"*Almost* full? What do you have?"

"I'm afraid all we have left is a deluxe twin room with a view of Godzilla. It's expensive—nine thousand yen a night."

"I'll take it," he said.

The woman smiled, evidently recalculating her impression of Katsuro's worth. "How many nights would you like, sir?"

"Two, please."

The woman smiled again and busied herself with making the reservation. She took his details, asked whether he would like breakfast included, charged his dummy credit card and, once she was finished, printed a key card for him.

"You're up on the tenth floor," she said. "The elevators are just over there."

"Thank you," he said.

He wandered in the direction of the elevator lobby, but, once he was out of sight, he diverted and took a seat on a leather banquette where he could watch the activity in the reception area. There was a small coffee table next to the seat, and he took a copy of the morning's *Asahi Shimbun* and busied himself with the front page while keeping an eye on the men and women who made their way inside.

———

100

Milton walked from Tameike-sannō Station and passed through the first of the red *torii* gates that led to the shrine. The area was as busy as Hachirō had predicted, with a large crowd of people jostling to pass through the gates so that they could make their way into the streets around the shrine. Milton saw musicians playing from floats and others carrying *mikoshi shrines*. Many of those taking part in the festival wore traditional dress: kimonos with colourful *obi* sashes, *yukata* robes and *zori* sandals; there were also a number of men wearing just *fundoshi* loincloths. Many of the revellers in the crowd sported costumes that included masks. Milton saw some in *noh* masks, others with traditional fox or devil masks, and others still in contemporary *kigurumi* masks. He took his own mask from his bag and put it on, arranging the elastic band so that it sat comfortably behind his ears.

He checked his watch. It was nearly ten minutes to one and he was supposed to meet Satoshi on the hour. Milton was relieved that Furokawa had agreed to make the exchange so quickly; it meant that there would be a limit to the amount of time that he had to hold Natsuki, and, more practically, it would make it difficult for Satoshi to put anything into place that might complicate matters.

Hachirō had proposed the steps of the *haiden*, the main hall of worship, for the meet and, as he approached, Milton could see that the location would work well. There was a flight of stone steps that led up to an impressive building with a gabled roof and stone lions guarding the entrance. Milton walked along a parade of stallholders, waiting for the crowd to open enough for him to approach the steps to the temple. He climbed up and turned back so that he could survey the area. He saw Satoshi almost at once. He was making his way through the crowd, surrounded by a retinue of younger men who must have comprised his security. The men at the front barged through the crowd, clearing a path so that Satoshi's progress could be more serene. Milton stepped to the side, putting himself in their way.

The man in the front—big and mean, with a buzz cut and heavy rings on his fingers—reached up to move Milton aside. Milton intercepted his hand, isolating his index finger and bending it back before the man could do anything to stop him. He gave a curiously feminine yelp of pain, his knees buckling as Milton used the pain from the stressed joints to move him out of the phalanx that protected Satoshi.

"Hello," he said. "I'm Eric."

The other men stepped up, but Satoshi stood them down with a flick of his hand.

"The mask," he said. "Take it off."

"No," Milton said, releasing the big man's finger.

"I don't blame you," Satoshi said. "You are right to be frightened."

"I'm not frightened. This is me being practical. I don't

want to have to deal with these boys in the event you find out who I am. It'll be better for them."

Satoshi looked older than he had done in the photographs that Milton had seen. He was dressed in a smart dark suit with well-shined shoes. He was carrying a bag, medium sized and made of leather, and he held it up so that Milton could see it.

"I have something for you," Satoshi said. "Where is my sister?"

"You'll have her in a moment. Open the bag, please."

Satoshi unzipped the bag and held it open. Milton glanced inside the bag and saw the *tantō*. He knew that there was a possibility that Satoshi would try to fob him off with an imitation, or something less exclusive, so he reached inside and turned the handle so that he could see the inscription written on the core. He had read the story about the sword's discovery in America and had seen close-up photographs of it. The inscription matched.

"Happy?" Satoshi said.

"Yes. Thank you."

"So where is she?" Satoshi said, looking around.

Milton pulled out his phone and called Hachirō.

"Okay," he said when the call was answered. "We're good."

Milton disconnected the call and stared at Satoshi.

"In a few moments," he said, "your phone will ring. It will be Natsuki, and she will tell you that she is safe and well. When that happens, I'll leave and you'll never see me again."

"Are you sure about that?"

"I'm sure."

"I disagree. I think I *will* see you."

"I told you—I'm not frightened. I took your sister once.

Don't make me think you're coming after me or maybe I'll take her again. I looked after her very well this time. Next time? I don't know."

Milton heard the ringing of a phone. Satoshi reached into his pocket, pulled out his cell and looked at the screen. Milton saw his relief, quickly mastered, before he answered the call and spoke in rapid Japanese. He kept his eye on Milton before finally nodding his head. Milton took that as his signal to leave. He descended the steps down into the crowd. The men who had accompanied Satoshi did not seek to impede him, nor did they give pursuit. Milton had doubted that they would; if he was to be followed—and he was certain now that he *would* be followed—he knew that the tails would be waiting out of sight. He would detect them only by concentrated vigilance, looking for repeats: a person seen more than once, a coat that he recognised, perhaps even the same pair of shoes that he had noticed from before. He would shake them off before making his way back to the hotel.

He called Hachirō. "It's me."

"Did you get it?"

Milton glanced down at the leather bag. "I did. Where's the girl?"

"I took her to Hachiōji," he said. "Near the Imperial Museum. I let her out there."

"She didn't see your face?"

"I wore the mask."

"Good."

Milton passed through the red gates and started back toward the station. He looked behind him, but it was too busy for him to be able to spot any obvious tails. He would shake them on the subway.

"What now?" Hachirō said.

"I'm going to go back to Sakura, and then I'll arrange to deliver the sword to your brother."

"You won't be able to trust him," Hachirō warned.

"I know," Milton said.

He could have added that he didn't trust anyone, and that he hadn't for years, but there was no need. He told the old man that he would be in touch if he needed more help and then ended the call. The station was ahead. He tightened his grip on the bag and joined the queue of pedestrians waiting to descend to the tracks, his eyes open, watching for followers, but distracted—if only a little—by the prospect of delivering the good news to Sakura.

101

The clock in the lobby showed two o'clock as a delivery driver made his way through the revolving doors with a huge bouquet of purple *kosumosu* and orange *kinmokusei* cradled in his arms. Katsuro watched over the top of the newspaper as the driver, wearing a polo shirt branded with the florist's logo, carried the bouquet to the concierge's station. Katsuro turned the page and watched as the concierge discussed the delivery, eventually accepting the flowers and sending the driver on his way.

He waited as the concierge signalled to a bellhop, an older man dressed in the uniform of the hotel, who collected the flowers and made for the elevator lobby. Katsuro folded the newspaper under his arm and followed.

The bellhop summoned the elevator and, once it had arrived, held it open for Katsuro. He pressed the button for the fourteenth floor.

"What floor for you, sir?"

"I'm on the fourteenth, too," Katsuro said, standing back and unfolding the newspaper so he could pretend to read the back page.

The elevator ascended, collecting an additional passenger on the second floor and then depositing him on the ninth. The doors closed and they ascended once more, stopping for the third time as they reached their destination.

The doors opened and the bellhop indicated that Katsuro should go first. He did, pausing in the lobby to untie and then refasten his shoelace. Corridors led away to the left and right. The bellhop bid him a good afternoon and made his way left, following the sign for rooms 1402 to 1430. Katsuro followed. The corridor then took a sharp right-hand turn, and Katsuro paused until the bellhop had turned at the junction and disappeared from sight. He picked up his pace a little, slowing again as he heard a brisk knock against one of the doors around the corner.

"Who is it?"

Katsuro recognised Sakura's voice.

"I have a delivery for you, madam," the bellhop said. "Flowers."

Katsuro heard the sound of a door opening.

"Thank you," Sakura said.

"Would you like me to bring them inside?"

"Please," she said.

Katsuro turned the corner, just in time to see the bellhop step through the open doorway to room 1428. The door, on a pneumatic hinge, was slowly closing. Katsuro picked up his pace along the corridor and reached it before it could close.

He stopped it with his foot.

102

The bellhop set the flowers down on the bureau. They were lovely, a dozen heads of *kosumosu* and *kinmokusei* wrapped in cellophane and arranged with their stems inside a tied pouch of water. Sakura guessed that they were from Milton, and was thinking about the best place to put them when she noticed the door, which was on a pneumatic hinge, had stopped before it could close.

It was pushed open.

A second man stepped inside.

Katsuro.

The bellhop noticed the terror on her face and started to turn back to see what had caused it. Katsuro was holding a silenced pistol and, as the bellhop realised the danger he was in—too late—Katsuro raised it, aimed and fired. The bellhop was close, no more than three metres away, and Sakura knew that Katsuro was an accurate shot. The bullet struck the man in his chest, just below his throat. He stumbled back, blood already running from the wound, before

Katsuro closed in on him and fired a second shot into his head.

The bellhop fell to the floor at the same time as the pneumatic hinge closed the door.

Sakura grabbed a paperweight from the bureau and raised it, ready to dash it against the side of Katsuro's head. He put his free hand against her sternum and shoved her so hard that she fell backward, her tailbone striking the carpeted floor with a jolt that shuddered all the way up her spine.

He leaned down and grabbed her by the wrist, then yanked her back to her feet, his nails digging into her skin.

"Katsuro, *please*. Don't—"

He let go of her wrist and, before she could raise her arms to defend herself, he cracked the butt of the pistol against the side of her head. The shock was numbing. She stumbled and fell again, her ears ringing. She thought she was going to black out.

Katsuro grabbed her and hauled her up for a second time.

"Please," she said again. "*Please.*"

He raised his hand again and backhanded her, moving so fast that she had no time to dodge it. She tried to push Katsuro away from her, but had no leverage. He pushed again, and she felt the glass of the large windows against her back.

"I'm sorry," she said. "The bag split—I nearly died. I texted you. You didn't come."

She looked for something else that she might be able to use as a weapon, but there was nothing.

Katsuro raised his hand again, but more slowly. He brought it to the side of Sakura's face and used his fingertips to stroke the tender skin on her cheek.

"Do you know how much trouble you've caused me?" he said. He smoothed away a tear from her cheek and then put the pistol down on the bureau.

"I'm sorry."

His hand slid down to her jawline and, with a sharp movement, he clamped his fingers around her neck. His right hand joined his left and he pushed hard, sliding her up the window by a couple of inches. She groped for his forearms and clung to them, trying to pull herself up to relieve the pressure on her neck. Her feet flailed, searching for purchase, something to relieve the pressure, but they found nothing and banged hopelessly against the glass.

She struggled to speak. "Can't... breathe."

"You think *this* is how you see Yamato again?"

Her lungs emptied. "Please."

Katsuro pushed harder, sliding her further up the window until his arms were locked. Her muscles ached as she tried to lever herself up against his forearms, trying to keep her weight off her neck. The effort was significant and she was tiring fast.

"Give me a reason why I shouldn't kill you."

She tried to speak, to beg for her life, but nothing came.

Katsuro adjusted his grip, digging his fingers into the soft tissue on either side of her neck. Sakura's peripheral vision bent and wobbled, and then the edges started to go grey, throbbing with her pulse, expanding and flooding her field of vision as the periphery got darker and darker and darker. She could taste blood in her mouth and felt a pain at the tip of her tongue; she must have bitten down on it. All she could see now was a narrowing circle of light in the centre of her vision. She closed her eyes tightly, trying to conjure an image of Yamato before the circle closed.

She saw him, just quickly—his smile, the spark of life

that jumped in his eyes—and then the circle started to winnow away and the black was almost complete.

Katsuro released her. She fell to the floor and gasped for breath. The darkness receded, fading to grey and then white. The sudden rush of blood throbbed in her head.

"Just *saying* sorry is not going to be good enough," Katsuro said. "You're going to have to *show* me how sorry you are. You're going to have to persuade me that I can still trust you. That's how you get Yamato. Not by consorting with a *gaijin*."

"I'll show you," she rasped. "I promise. Whatever you want. What do I need to do?"

"Get your things," he said, waving his hand at the bag by the bed. "We'll spend a little time together and think about that."

103

Milton walked to the hotel, looking up with wry amusement at Godzilla. He was in an optimistic mood. The first part of his plan had promised to be the most difficult, with the most moving parts to manage, yet he had pulled it off without significant issue. He was too jaded by experience to allow himself to believe that the conclusion would be as easy, but perhaps Sakura's emancipation was not too distant a prospect after all.

He nodded to the bellboy who held open the door for him, and made his way across the foyer to the elevator. He pressed the button to summon it and waited as it descended. He stepped in, pressed the button for the fourteenth floor, and looked at himself in the mirror as the doors closed. He looked tired, but he knew that the effort he had expended over the last few days had been worth it.

The elevator arrived and Milton walked to the room. He put his hand in his pocket for his key card, held it to the reader, waited for the click and the green light, then pushed the door open.

He stopped.

The room had been disturbed, with a chair kicked over and the items from the bureau scattered over the carpet.

Sakura was on the other side of the room. She was on her knees.

There was a man in front of her.

He turned at the sound of the door.

Milton recognised him.

Katsuro.

Milton saw a pistol with a suppressor on the bureau.

Katsuro swivelled, grabbed it and took aim.

Sakura sprang at the man, her shoulder colliding with his arm at the moment he pulled the trigger. The pistol fired, but the shot went high, cracking into the ceiling above Milton's head.

Katsuro pushed Sakura away and then backhanded her with the pistol. She dropped to the floor and lay still.

Milton sprang forward, raised the bag and flung it, sending it across the room in a flat arc. It slammed into Katsuro as he was about to aim for a second time. Milton ran, head down, closing the distance between them. He lowered his shoulder, but Katsuro had turned and was braced for the impact. The two men crashed together, Milton grabbing for Katsuro's gun hand and forcing it up into the air. The pistol fired again, the shot blasting into the ceiling. Milton isolated Katsuro's fingers and twisted them back until the gun fell to the floor. Milton kicked it with the toe of his boot, sending it spinning across the room.

Katsuro butted Milton to free his hand, then wrapped his arms beneath Milton's torso and twisted, using Milton's momentum against him as he flung him against the window. The glass was reinforced and Milton bounced off it, straight into a right-hand punch that Katsuro seemed to have conjured from nowhere; there was almost no preparation, no drawing back of his fist, just a lightning-fast blow that cracked against the point of Milton's chin. He fell back against the window again, Katsuro following up and fastening both hands around Milton's throat. Katsuro lifted Milton up, apparently without effort, and held him against the window as he tightened his grip around his throat. Milton felt the strength in Katsuro's hands, tried to jam down with his forearms in an attempt to break the hold, but his opponent's arms were like iron rods, hard and unyielding. He drew back his right hand and punched Katsuro in the face, but the blow had no effect. Katsuro tightened his grip and, unable to break free, Milton drove the point of his knee into Katsuro's groin. His grip weakened and Milton kneed him again, and then again; Katsuro grunted, spun on his heel and flung Milton across the room.

Milton crashed into the desk, which collapsed beneath his weight. Katsuro followed and Milton kicked out at him. The Japanese caught his ankle and yanked hard, pulling him from the table and onto the floor. Milton scrambled up, but again Katsuro was onto him, both hands knotted into his shirt as he heaved him up and threw him against the wall. Milton saw Katsuro's gun on the floor and grabbed it, bringing the extended barrel around, but not fast enough. Katsuro slapped the weapon out of his hand; it spun through the open balcony door and fell out of view. Katsuro grabbed Milton again, dragging him up and spinning, throwing him against the wall for a second time. The impact was harder; Katsuro's momentum had increased, and the wall had already been weakened. Milton crashed through it, landing on his back amid a pile of fractured plasterboard.

Katsuro stomped through the hole in the wall, his broad

shoulders opening it wider; more plaster fell to the carpet. Milton braced as Katsuro came at him once again.

104

The room next door was identical to the one that they had just been inside, apart from the fifty-something businessman in bed with a much younger woman. It was dark, the blinds drawn and the room lit by a flickering candle on the bureau. Clothes had been strewn across the floor and there was a bottle of rum and two glasses.

Milton scrambled to his hands and knees, but was too slow to evade Katsuro as he grabbed the back of Milton's shirt with one hand and his belt with the other, lifting him off the floor and driving him, like a battering ram, into the opposite wall. Milton fired his elbow backwards, the bone deflecting off Katsuro's rock-hard abdominals, and then, as the Japanese locked both hands around Milton's head and squeezed, his fingers reaching for his eyes, Milton butted him and then pushed with his feet. Both men crashed through a half-open door and into the small bathroom. The back of Katsuro's head cracked against the wall, but the impact didn't even daze him. There was a smaller vanity mirror on a reticulated arm that was fixed to the wall;

Milton yanked it from its mount and smashed it into Katsuro's face. The bigger man jerked away just enough that it struck only a glancing blow. He hit Milton with a left to the ribs and then a right to the side of the head, then fixed him in a headlock and leaned back and suplexed him, the momentum turning Milton upside down and sending him through the thin partition wall and back into the bedroom.

The man and woman were still in bed, frozen by the spectacle. Milton scrambled up, reached for one of the rum glasses, and flung it at Katsuro. He swiped it away with one meaty paw, the alcohol splashing over him, and closed in. Katsuro swung lefts and rights, big punches that would have fractured bone had they landed, but Milton was just fast enough to duck and swerve out of the way. He retaliated with his own strikes, hooking right and left into the bigger man's ribs, but the blows had no effect, and Katsuro, as if angered by Milton's resilience, picked up his foot and kicked out with it, his boot landing square in Milton's sternum and impelling him back onto the bed. He fell back onto the legs of the pair and rolled off again, landing on his shoulders and corkscrewing to get his legs back underneath him.

The candle that lit the room was inside a glass bowl. Milton scrambled over the woman and reached for it, jamming it at Katsuro's alcohol-sodden clothes. The room went dark before the candle lit the alcohol that had doused the fabric, bluish flame quickly sweeping across it. Katsuro ignored it for a moment, rounding the bed and drilling down with a right that flattened Milton against the carpet. He stomped down at him; Milton caught his boot and swept his standing leg, and the bigger man collapsed on top of him. Milton felt the burn of the flame on his skin and wriggled clear, hopping out of range as Katsuro's wild downward swipe missed him and demolished the table instead.

Milton was starting to feel dazed, knew that he was badly outmatched, yet could not bring himself to retreat. Sakura was in the room next door, and he couldn't leave her. Katsuro stood, worked off the burning jacket and flung it behind him. Milton looked for something to use as a weapon, saw the bottle of rum that the pair had been drinking from, and grabbed it by the neck. He smashed it against the table, the alcohol splashing over his trousers, and held the shattered remains out in front of him. Katsuro came on and Milton swung the bottle, a swipe from right to left and then another from left to right; the bigger man evaded each with surprising dexterity. Milton stabbed out with it and Katsuro blocked, the daggered edges cutting furrows along his forearm. He ignored the bloody tracks, slapping the bottle out of Milton's grip and then shoving him with both hands. Milton stumbled back, losing his balance and falling through the curtains and out of the open door onto the balcony.

Milton was on his back, the sky spread out above him, fluffy clouds scudding along on a gentle breeze. The balcony was narrow, no more than a metre deep, and there was nowhere for Milton to go. Katsuro filled the doorway, his broad shoulders brushing either side of the opening, blocking any chance Milton might have to escape. Milton leapt to his feet and punched him, his fists bouncing against Katsuro's chest and into his ribs, doing no obvious damage and having no effect. Katsuro seized him with both hands, pinning Milton's arms to his sides, and then butted him in the face.

The day spun.

Katsuro butted him again and started to lift. Milton's back was against the rail, a fulcrum against which he could start to feel himself turning. His right foot came off the floor and then his left. He jammed his leg between Katsuro's, locking his ankle behind the bigger man's knee, trying to anchor himself. It would take only a few more inches, an extra degree or two, and Milton would be over the edge.

There was nowhere to go.

The end of the road.

He knew it, and so did Katsuro. There was no gloating, no words whatsoever, but his face, impassive until now, cracked into an ugly grin. He clutched Milton's throat with his left hand and drilled him in the gut with his right, each fresh strike loosening his ankle, releasing the anchor that held him in place. Milton tried to butt him, but the left hand held him out of range. Katsuro squeezed, his fingers closing around Milton's throat, constricting his windpipe and arteries.

Milton felt his leg go limp, his foot sliding out from behind Katsuro's knee.

Katsuro grinned more widely, started to push harder, then stopped. The grin flashed into a frown of pain and then anger. Katsuro held Milton in place with his left hand, reached around with his right hand and clawed for something on his back. He turned sideways to Milton for a moment, and Milton saw a corkscrew sticking out of his shoulder. Sakura was standing in the balcony doorway, her hand held up, empty now. Katsuro twisted his hips and backhanded Sakura across the face, hard. Her head cracked around and she fell out of sight, hidden behind Katsuro's considerable bulk.

It was a distraction, and that was all that Milton needed. He took his chance. Katsuro was holding him so that he could not advance, but he was not preventing him from sliding over the balcony. He held onto the rail with his right hand and kicked up, flipping over the side so that his legs windmilled through a full circle, the rail acting as a pivot. He locked in his grip, knowing he had seconds and no more, remembering the layout of the balconies and knowing that there was another just below.

He took a breath and then let go.

105

M ilton fell, his legs cycling for a second until his left hand slapped against the rail of the balcony below, followed by his right. The sudden deceleration felt like it might tear the balls of his upper arm bones from their sockets, and the blaze of pain loosened his right hand enough that he fumbled the rail. He dropped again and grabbed at the rail of the next balcony, holding firm this time. He dangled for a long second from just his left hand, but then he found a spot between the glass balustrade and the floor of the balcony to jam the toes of his right foot. He grabbed the rail again with both hands and vaulted up and over it.

The balcony door was unlocked, and Milton slid it open and walked inside. The room was empty, with no personal possessions or suitcases that might have suggested that the guest or guests were absent.

Milton assessed his body: the pain down his ribs from where he had been pummelled, the blood running from his nose and the cut in his scalp, the ringing in his ears that might presage a concussion. Katsuro had delivered a comprehensive beating; Milton was not confident that he could take him in a straight-up fight, let alone in the state that he found himself now.

But Sakura was still up there with him.

He had to try.

Katsuro watched as the *gaijin* dropped from the balcony rail and fell out of sight. They were fourteen storeys up; there was no way he would be able to survive a fall like that. He would have gone to the balcony to look down and check, but he had the corkscrew stuck in his shoulder, Sakura was mumbling something on the floor, and the man and the woman in the bed were both screaming. Katsuro reached around until his fingers touched the wooden handle, and then he yanked the corkscrew out of his flesh and tossed it to the floor. He hauled Sakura to her feet and dragged her through the hole in the wall, back into her and Milton's room. He collected the bag that the *gaijin* had thrown at his gun hand. He unzipped it and saw with astonishment that it contained the *tantō* that had been stolen from his father. It was a surprise, but a welcome one; he would be able to tell the old man that he had found Sakura *and* recovered the blade. He looked for his pistol, but it wasn't on the balcony. There was a gap between the glass barrier and the floor, and the only thing that he could think was that it had slipped through and fallen to the ground below.

Sakura was still dazed. "Get up," Katsuro said.

She mumbled Yamato's name. He picked up a glass of water and dashed it in her face.

"We're leaving," he said. He zipped up the bag and slung it over his shoulder. "You say anything or do anything and

I'll go straight to Yamato. I'll throw him out of the window, just like the *gaijin*. Understand?"

She blinked the water out of her eyes and nodded.

"Good."

He took her hand, hauled her out of the room and turned left. A guest had just stepped out of one of the elevators, and Katsuro picked up their pace enough to get to the door before it could close. It slid open and he ushered Sakura inside. He saw that her throat was marked from where he had choked her out, and bruises were forming on her face from where he had struck her.

He decided against trying to take her through the lobby and hit the button for the second floor.

The elevator came to a halt and the doors opened.

"Move," he said, dragging her with him.

Katsuro led the way along the second-floor corridor until he reached a green-lit sign for the fire exit. He kicked the bar to open it, shouldering his way through and starting down the stairs. The fire exit opened onto an alleyway at the side of the hotel and Katsuro led the way calmly along it. At the end, he could see the usual throng of people who had gathered to watch the statue of Godzilla as its eyes shone and its mouth opened and closed. He took her hand and dragged her into the crowd.

106

Milton opened the minibar in search of something he could use as a weapon and found a corkscrew, much like the one that Sakura had used against Katsuro. He hurried across the room and, very carefully, pushed down on the handle of the door. The corkscrew had a wooden handle and he held that tight in his palm, the screw itself poking from between his fingers. He opened the door, slowly at first, listening for anything that might suggest that someone was outside. He heard nothing, opened the door all the way and then looked out, left and right. The corridor was empty. There was a cleaning trolley parked in the corridor. He grabbed a towel and used it to wipe the blood from his face. The white cotton came away streaked with red; Milton knew he had been battered, and could only guess at how bad he looked. He would have to clean himself up.

He tried to orient himself and saw a sign for an emergency staircase fifteen feet to his left. He ran to it, opened the door and ascended the stairs two at a time. He started from the twelfth floor, reached the thirteenth and kept climbing until he reached the fourteenth floor. He opened the door cautiously and looked out into the corridor. The couple from the room next to theirs were outside. They saw Milton heading in their direction and backed away, turning and running before he could reach them.

Milton knew that he didn't have long before the alarm was raised. He ran to his and Sakura's room, took out his key card, held it to the reader and opened the door. The room was empty. He looked for the bag with the *tantō* and saw that it had been taken. He looked through the hole in the wall and saw that that room was empty, too.

No Katsuro.

No Sakura.

He had her.

Milton went back into their room. Katsuro had the *tantō*, and, with it, the last piece of leverage that Milton might have been able to wield. He collected his travelling bag from the wardrobe and left the room. He took the emergency stairs and hurried down to the basement. The stairs opened onto a short corridor, uncarpeted and with unfinished walls. There were doors leading off it on either side and, at the other end of the corridor, another door with a round glass window. Milton could see a kitchen filled with men in white tunics.

He found a staff bathroom and locked himself inside. He pulled the cord to switch on the light and examined himself in the mirror in greater detail. He had been bloodied and beaten. He ran the taps until the basin was full of cold water, and then dunked his face in it. He rubbed the water over his skin, then scrubbed his scalp. When he pulled back and looked down, he saw that the water had been dyed with the red of his blood. He took a towel and dried himself, then checked that his clothes would pass muster. Save for a couple of patches of sticky blood—not his, he thought—he was presentable enough.

He opened the door and went through into the kitchen, picking a route between the stainless-steel counters, the industrial ovens and a large hob, ignoring the startled looks from the staff and the occasional protest in Japanese. He arrived at the other end of the room and a door that, when he opened it, led to a sloping service alley that led up to street level.

Milton walked up it, checked left and right for signs of Katsuro or the police, and then melted into the early afternoon crowd.

107

K atsuro led the way, Sakura's hand tight in his, almost dragging her along behind him. He wanted to be alone with her and he knew just the place. They called the streets around Seibu Shinjuku Station the "Sleepless City," on account of the number of love hotels and hostess bars that were established there. Katsuro ignored the Nigerian touts who tried to lure the unwary to visit their businesses, although, to be fair, he was insulated from the most fervent attention by the way that he looked. There were yakuza here, too, men from families that had been more resilient than the Nishimoto-*kai*. Katsuro looked at them jealously and tried to ignore his resentment that his father's lack of ambition had seen them wither away while other clans—and *hangure* newcomers—had been allowed to flourish. Katsuro knew all the stories about his father and uncle from the seventies and eighties, the tales of their successes that had become almost legendary in the retelling. They became less credible, though, when he looked at what his father was reputed to have been and compared that to what he had become. Katsuro knew that there was a place for his family in the Tokyo underworld, and that all that it lacked was an ambitious leader who was willing to take a risk. That was not his father, not anymore; nor had it been his brother.

Perhaps it could be him.

They arrived at the building that his father owned and he nodded to the manager, ignoring the man's alarmed look, as he led the way into the private rooms at the rear.

"Nishimoto-*san*," the man said. "You're bleeding."

"I'm fine."

"But your face…"

"It's nothing."

"And your *shoulder*. What happened?"

"I just need to clean up. Get us a room."

"Room six is free. Second floor. Can I get you a drink?"

"Champagne."

"I have a nice bottle. I will bring it for you."

Katsuro led Sakura up the stairs and around the building until they reached the room that the manager had indicated was empty. It was a simple space: a bed with a television fixed to the wall and a small en suite bathroom. Its purpose was simple, and, because of that, comfort was not a prerequisite. He opened the door to the bathroom to check that there was no way that Sakura would be able to escape and saw, to his satisfaction, that the window was no more than a sliver.

"Clean yourself up," he said to her. "You look awful. I'll shower after you."

She didn't protest and went inside. He heard the sound of running water and dropped down on the bed, wincing at the wound in his shoulder. He ran through what he would do with Sakura once he had finished with her this evening. She was a beautiful woman, and there was a pleasure to be derived from being with the woman who had chosen his brother as her husband. His early interactions with her had been driven by his own resentments, but that had changed. He had begun to hope that their relationship might evolve into something more. He knew that she tolerated his demands in return for her safety and the safety of her son, but he had hoped that—in time—she might see beyond that. Katsuro was not naive enough to think that she might love him, but perhaps she would one day accede to him without the same fear in her eyes. He could see now that they had not reached that point yet. She still resented him.

He would just have to try harder. She would see sense in the end.

There was a knocking on the door. Katsuro opened it and saw that the manager had brought him the bottle of champagne with two flutes. He took the bottle and dismissed the man.

Katsuro removed the foil from the bottle and held it with his left hand so that the seam where the two parts of the bottle joined was facing up. He opened the bag and took out the *tantō* and, with a quick downward stroke, brought the blade down against the annulus of the bottle, breaking it and ejecting the cork across the room. He stood the glasses on the bedside table and started to pour.

108

Milton wandered, telling himself that he was making sure that he was not being followed but, really, just walking with no idea where he should go. He knew that he would have to tell Hachirō what had happened, but he didn't know how to start. Everything that could have gone wrong *had* gone wrong: he had lost the sword *and* Sakura. And it was his fault. He knew that. His fault and no one else's. He had been careful with their arrival into the city, and had been as sure as he could have been that they had not been detected, but he had overlooked *something,* and the consequences could not have been worse. Katsuro had found them. Milton had erred and now Sakura was going to pay the price. He didn't know what he was going to say to her father.

How presumptuous he had been. Milton had long since accepted that he could not have the life that others had, knew that the comfort of a normal existence was not something that was available to him. He was an alcoholic, and there was an axiom in the Fellowship that alcoholics didn't have relationships; they took hostages. The nomadic life that he had chosen was not one that could be shared. But his actions here hadn't been just presumptuousness. They had been based in selfishness, too. What was he thinking? That he was going to play happy families with Sakura and be a father to her son?

He realised now, with blinding clarity and scalding shame, that that was *exactly* what he had thought. There had been other women through the years who had had feelings for him, and he had denied them all.

Ellie Flowers.

Matilda Douglas.

Sharron Warriner.

Each time, he had considered how his life might change and, however much that might have been attractive, he had decided against it. Death trailed in his wake. It always had, ever since he had joined the army, and more so as his career took him to the SAS and then the Group. It still trailed him now. This one moment of foolishness, of thinking that he could be the same as everyone else, would lead to Sakura's death.

Milton stopped at a walkway, merging into the throng that waited obediently in lines three deep for the lights to tell them they could cross the road. He allowed the tide to carry him along, over the road and then left. On each side, smaller streets branched off like tributaries. He saw one street—he caught the name, Maneki-Dori Street, on a sign—and turned onto it. It was quieter than the main drag and, as he walked deeper and deeper, he turned again and then again until he wasn't sure where he was. He had found his way into a grid of pedestrianised streets, narrow and busy with locals and tourists. A thicket of signs had been fixed to the walls on either side, and doubled-sided chalkboards were propped open next to the walls. The signs were in

Japanese and English, and some mentioned Golden Gai. Milton remembered reading about the area on his previous visit: this particular network of streets was jammed with bars, many of them little more than a counter and a few stools. They were often barely six feet wide, and there were steep staircases that led to even smaller bars above.

Milton knew he shouldn't be here. Every meeting he had ever been to, every share he had ever heard, all of them had included the same refrain: *One drink is too many and a thousand is never enough.* Milton remembered that and all of the other warnings and ignored them all. He picked a bar at random—the sign above the door said Nessun Dorma—and paid the seven-hundred-yen cover charge for one of the six stools at the bar.

Milton reached into his pocket and took out his eight-year chip. He put it on the bar and looked down at it, turning it with his finger. He flipped it and looked at the scene that was printed on the back: Bill W. and Dr. Bob, the founders of the Fellowship, trying to persuade Bill D. that he didn't have to drink.

"What do you want?"

Milton looked up. The bartender was staring at him. "Sorry?"

"What do you want to drink? You can't just sit there."

Milton looked at the bottles stacked in shelves that had been crammed into narrow alcoves in the wall.

"Whisky," he said. "Give me a double."

109

K atsuro called a cab and had the driver take them to Sanya. The streets around the building had their usual atmosphere—a low-level throb of enmity and possible threat—but Katsuro knew that no one would be foolish enough to approach him. He was an imposing man, and, although it carried less fear than it had in its heyday, the Nishimoto name still had weight. He walked by the *hiyatoi rodosha*—the labourers—who were drinking cheap sake from the bottle, taking in their malevolent stares and returning one of his own. It felt good to have Sakura by his side. He liked the way they looked at her, and then the way they looked at him. He knew that they were jealous.

He reached the tower, stepped into the lobby and nodded to Kodama and Shinoda, the members of his father's security detail who were on duty. He went to the elevator, pressed his key card against the reader, and ushered Sakura inside. He had the *gaijin's* bag over his shoulder and was looking forward to his father's reaction when he delivered the *tantō* to him. What had happened in

Bali would be forgotten. Takashi had been depressed for weeks at the loss of the sword, and Katsuro would be able to make up for his errors by returning it to him.

THE ELEVATOR REACHED the twelfth floor and the door slid open. He stepped straight out into his father's apartment. The old man was sitting at the large dining table with a set of *karuta* cards laid out before him. Fumio was nearby.

"*Otōsan*," he said, bowing his head.

Takashi looked up and removed the wire-framed glasses that he used for close work. He saw Katsuro and looked behind him to where Sakura was standing.

He cocked an eyebrow in surprise. "What is she doing here?"

"I found her. She was staying in Shinjuku with the *gaijin*."

"He did that to your face?"

Katsuro had seen his cuts and bruises in the mirror at the hotel. "He did. He had this."

He took the bag the *gaijin* had left in Sakura's room and placed it on the table.

"What is it?"

"Open it, *Otōsan*."

Takashi looked at his son dubiously, then reached for the zip and drew it back. He looked inside.

"Take it out. You will be pleased."

Takashi reached into the bag and withdrew the *tantō*. He held it up in his right hand and used the left to remove the scabbard. The light caught against the dark metal of the blade.

"The *gaijin* arrived while I was attending to Sakura,"

Katsuro explained. "He had it with him. It's the *tantō* that Miyasato stole, isn't it?"

Takashi held the blade out, moving it left and right with subtle flicks of his wrist. "Where is the *gaijin* now?"

"Dead."

"How?"

"He fell from the fourteenth floor."

"Are you *sure?*"

"I threw him over the balcony myself. I am sure."

Takashi flicked his wrist and slid the sword back into the scabbard. He laid it on the table.

Katsuro frowned. "You don't seem pleased."

Takashi waited a moment before he spoke. "The *gaijin* contacted me and proposed an exchange—the sword for Sakura and Yamato. Taking matters into your own hands might have complicated things."

"No one told me about that," Katsuro protested. "How was I to know?"

"Did you not think to contact me when you discovered where she was?"

"I didn't want to concern you until it was done."

"No, Katsuro. That's not it at all. You wanted to impress me."

Katsuro clenched his fists in irritation, both at his father's disdain and for chastising him in front of Sakura, who stood silently behind him.

Takashi stood and took the sword across the room to the wall where his collection was displayed. The empty brackets were at head height, with the other weapons arranged around them. Katsuro had no interest in the *tantō*, nor what it represented, save that it was valuable. When his father died, he would sell it and the rest of the collection to assemble a fund with which to reinvigorate the Nishimoto-

kai. Takashi placed the blade back onto its mounts, nudging it a fraction to the left so that it was perfectly symmetrical.

He spoke without turning back. "Is there anything else, Katsuro-*chan*?"

Katsuro felt a flash of irritation and couldn't hold his tongue. "A thank-you, perhaps?"

Takashi turned and stared at him coldly. "Really?"

"I thought you would be pleased."

"Why? Because you have made up for your own mistakes?"

"But the *tantō*? I—"

"I am pleased that it has been returned, but you should have spoken to me before deciding on a course of action. You don't *think*, Katsuro-*chan*. You never have. You are impetuous. Impulsive. I am pleased that you have been able to return the blade, but neither of us should be under the misapprehension that you were not lucky to find it, nor that you didn't think about what might have happened if you had made yet another mistake. That is the difference between Miyasato and you. Your brother would have considered the consequences and then acted. You act first and then, when things go wrong—as they did this week—you cause more chaos and confusion trying to fix them."

"And Miyasato is dead." Katsuro couldn't keep the note of gloating out of his voice.

"Something I regret every day."

Katsuro bit down on his lip so hard that he drew blood. He looked down at the floor.

"Is there anything else?" Takashi asked him.

"No, *Otōsan*." He turned to Sakura. "Come."

"No," Takashi said. "Wait. I will speak to her."

110

Milton stared at the glass of whisky. It sat on the bar in front of him. He held the sobriety chip in his right hand, flipping the coin between his fingers like a gambler preparing to make a bet.

He had been in the bar for two hours and been wrestling with his conscience. He wanted to drink. He wanted oblivion, to drink himself to blackout, where he would be able to forget about Sakura and Yamato and everything else. He knew that it was false, that his demons would wait until he was drunk and then they would come out to play. They would hover at the edges of his consciousness, just as they always did, and wait for their opportunity, for the moment when he would not be able to restrain them. Milton wouldn't care. Why should he? He would be out of his mind by then, and consequences were for tomorrow. He knew that letting them in might mean violence, but he was past worrying about that. He might end up in a cell. Or beaten up. He might end up dead.

He didn't care.

And yet, despite that, he had not yet raised the glass to his lips.

The bartender was looking at him.

He glanced up at him. "What?"

"You okay?"

"Fine, thanks."

"It's just that you've had that for a couple of hours now."

"Is that a problem?"

"My boss won't be happy."

"I paid the fee to sit down. If your boss has a problem, tell him to come and have it out with me."

The bartender stayed where he was. He looked down at the chip that Milton was flipping between his fingers. "I don't want to intrude—"

"So don't."

"—but I know what that is."

"Do you?" Milton laid the chip down and rested his finger atop it, self-consciously covering the scene on the back. "I'll tell you what it is. It's something that weak men use to give themselves a pat on the back and tell themselves that they're doing well. It's a waste of time."

"Don't know if I agree with that."

"Don't really give a shit what you think."

"I'm in the Fellowship."

"Seriously?" Milton scoffed. "You work in a bar."

"I needed a job. This was all I could get."

"Okay. Whatever."

The bartender was in his early thirties, had a hipsterish beard and was dressed in monochrome colours. He scratched his neck, revealing a sleeve of tattoos, but did not look as if he was going to take the hint and leave Milton alone. Milton stared at him, but, for once, it didn't have the effect that he expected.

The bartender put out a hand. "I'm Daitaro, by the way."

Milton ignored it. "I'm not really interested in a conversation."

Daitaro held his eye. "I've been going for a month. Thirty-two days, actually. They say you should do a meeting a day for the first thirty, right? That's what I've done. It's really helped."

"Good for you."

Daitaro pointed down at the coin on the bar. "I got my thirty-day chip yesterday, but I don't recognise that one."

"You don't take a hint, do you?"

The barman was still undeterred by Milton's attitude. "How long have you got?"

"Eight years."

Daitaro nodded his head appreciatively. "Amazing."

"I thought so," Milton said. "But it turns out I was just postponing the inevitable."

"How's that?"

"What is this—an intervention?"

"It's good to share. That's what they say."

"That's what they say," Milton repeated with a weary sigh. "Fine. I drink to forget."

"Forget what?"

"What else is there? The things I've done. I had the idea that if I followed the Steps, tried to make up for everything, then I'd be able to live with myself. With my memories. But it's not true. I don't want to be the one to break it to you, friend, but the stuff they sell us—it's a crock of shit."

"And yet you've been sober for eight years. What's changed?"

Milton drew back his lips, feeling his teeth against them. "There was someone I knew who needed my help. She was in a mess—a *real* mess—and I said I'd come here to help her clear it all up."

"Grandiosity, then? Thinking we know better. That we can always fix things. We're told to look out for that, aren't we?"

"They tell us a lot of things."

"But you thought you were the one who could fix it all for her?"

"She didn't have anyone else. But then... but then I tried to get it straightened out and there was a mistake along the way and it was probably my fault, and now..." He paused just in time to stop from telling a complete stranger what had happened. "And now things are worse than they were before. And the funny thing is, it's not the first time that's happened. I've tried to help others before. Thought I was getting better at it. Turns out I'm not—I'm getting worse. That's always been how I've tried to make amends. And now, once I've got it through my thick head that it doesn't work, I'm finding it hard to think of a reason why I shouldn't drink."

"Can I tell you my story?" Daitaro rested his elbows on the bar; it was obvious that he was going to give Milton the benefit of whatever was on his mind no matter what Milton said, so he just shrugged his indifference. "Look." He reached into his pocket and took out his wallet. He flipped it open and laid it out on the bar between them, then tapped his finger against a photograph in a clear plastic panel. "That's my boy."

Milton couldn't help himself. He looked down and saw a child, no more than six or seven, dressed in a white karate *do-gi*, the suit bound by a green belt. The boy was in a fighting pose, his arms raised, and was smiling at the person behind the camera.

"His name's Kenji. He's six. Big into karate. His mother died last year. Diagnosed in January, dead by March. Breast cancer. I tell myself that was the time I started drinking, but, in truth, I'd been drinking for years. I couldn't go out now that I was alone with Kenji, so I started drinking at home. There was this one time, a couple of months ago, when I got him to bed and he fell asleep earlier than usual. I was always drinking in the evenings, but I'd had a difficult call with the insurers dealing with Yui's life policy and I thought I'd do it properly. You know—go to town on it. I worked out afterwards that I'd had almost two bottles of sake."

Milton looked up. "Afterwards? What happened?"

A flicker of pain passed across the bartender's face. "I used to smoke, too. Spliffs. I lit one and left it in an ashtray on the side of the sofa. I fell asleep with it there and it must have fallen down. When I woke up, the room was on fire. I managed to get Kenji out, thank God, but we lost everything. The house. All our stuff. He had a teddy that my wife made for him when she was sick—gone."

Milton looked down at the photograph of the child. Yamato was younger, he thought, but not by much. Kenji might have lost his mother, but he still had his dad. Yamato was not so fortunate. His father was dead and his mother soon would be, one way or another. Milton doubted whether there would be any reason for Takashi to keep Yamato without the controlling influence that the child could exert over Sakura. The best Yamato could hope for was to reach adulthood with his wits about him and then try to escape the wreckage of his upbringing. But Milton knew that the child would need incredibly good fortune to make it even that far.

Daitaro sighed. "We all have a rock bottom, right? When things can't get worse. That's mine. It took something as bad as that to realise that I had no control over my drinking and what the consequences would be if I didn't do something about it. My boy could've been dead. Or orphaned. I went to my first meeting the next day and I've been every day since. And here we are. One day at a time, right? I feel better now —like I have a plan. I feel like maybe I've got a chance. Look —I don't know you, and I know you're probably not interested in what I have to say, but it feels like I have to say it anyway. I doubt the reasons you stopped drinking have changed. We get challenges to our sobriety all the time. I wanted a drink last week and it took a meeting for me to see why that was a bad idea. Maybe instead of sitting here in a bar with a whisky—maybe you should find a meeting, too. There's one in Shinjuku later tonight. I could tell you where it is?"

Daitaro looked at Milton expectantly. Milton looked down at the glass and the brown liquid inside and exhaled. He ran his finger across the sobriety chip. He thought of Sakura and Yamato and knew that they needed him, and that he would be no use to anyone if he allowed himself to take a drink. He flipped the wallet with the picture of the boy closed and slid it back across the counter. He reached into his pocket for his bankroll and peeled off enough notes to pay for the untouched whisky.

"Pour it away."

"What about the meeting?"

"Maybe tomorrow. We'll see."

111

Takashi looked at Sakura. His niece had her head down, looking at the floor by her feet. He found his thoughts jumping to his brother. Thinking of Hachirō caused the same flicker of anger that it always did, and he took a moment to compose himself before he addressed her.

"Look at me."

She raised her head. She had been weeping, her eyes red.

"I gave you a chance. I offered you an opportunity to make up for what you did. Work for me and perhaps you could see your son again. And yet, despite my generosity, despite my *kindness*, you treat me like this?"

"It wasn't my fault, Takashi-*san*," she protested. "The bag split inside me. I nearly died."

"Did you come to me?" Katsuro butted in, evidently concerned that his version of events not be challenged.

"I told you where to find me," she said.

"And you weren't there when I arrived."

"The police—"

"And then you come here with a *gaijin*," Katsuro cut over her.

"I wanted to see Yamato," she said. "Milton told me he would help."

"You disobeyed my father—"

"Be *quiet*, Katsuro," Takashi snapped. He glared at his son until he looked away, then turned his attention back to Sakura. "I had already promised that you would see the boy again. You knew what you had to do."

"I know," she said. "I am sorry. I should have stayed in Bali. But I was desperate. I let him persuade me that he could fix my problems. I was wrong. Please, Takashi-*san*."

Takashi turned away from them both. "It doesn't matter now. Your apology is worthless. It is the same with your excuses. You led my eldest son to disgrace. Despite that, I offered you a chance. You have rejected it and given me reason for disappointment in my youngest son."

"*Otōsan*," Katsuro whined.

"Quiet, Katsuro. Not another word."

Sakura dropped to her knees. "Please, Takashi-*san*. I am sorry. Truly. I didn't know what else to do, but I've never wanted to offend you."

"It is as I said—too late. Your words mean nothing. You cannot be trusted. I have listened to others who have suggested that I show clemency toward you, and look how you have rewarded me. You bewitched Miyasato. You bewitched the *gaijin*. You have bewitched Katsuro."

Katsuro frowned. "*Otōsan*, I—"

"Shut *up*. I have heard enough from you to last a hundred years."

Katsuro chewed the inside of his lip, his fists clenched.

Takashi turned back to Sakura. "Do you know what I wanted to do after what you did to Miyasato? I thought about having Katsuro kill you. That was my first instinct, but then I decided that was not punishment enough for your crime. You cost me my son. Death would be too good for you. Instead, I decided to remind you, every day, of the shame of what you did. I spoke with an old friend—Yoshio Wakasa. Do you remember that, Fumio?"

"I do," his *wakagashira* said, concern on his face at the direction the conversation was taking.

"Wakasa-*san* is an old friend. I used to work with him, years ago. He used to run *baishun* snack bars in Kyoto. You know what they are?" The fear on Sakura's face was replaced by horror. A *baishun* snack bar was a brothel by any other name, and she knew it. "Wakasa-*san* had a dozen then, but now that he is older, he keeps just two or three. He is always looking for new girls, and we agreed on a price."

Fumio looked agitated. "A word, *Oyabun?*"

Takashi waved his request away. "Do you know what happens in a *baishun* snack bar to a woman like you, Sakura, a *hāfu*? The men will see your Western blood and they will take pleasure in breaking you. You will be used, over and over and over, many times a day, until you are so used up that there is nothing left. And then, once you are of no use?" He shrugged. "You would be abandoned, likely an addict, with no one and nothing. Fumio persuaded me against it before, didn't you?"

Fumio nodded unhappily.

"He reminded me that you are my brother's daughter and that a fate like that would be too cruel, even given your crime. It was Katsuro's suggestion that you work with him and the *premans*. He persuaded me that it would be unpleasant for you and valuable for us. He was right in that last regard, but wrong in the first—it was not unpleasant enough."

"Please," Sakura said. "Takashi-*san*, I want to work for you. I know I have a debt to pay. Let me pay it."

"No," he said. "Your debt to me will be extinguished. Wakasa-*san* made me an offer for you before, and I believe he will honour it. The debt will be paid, but you will belong to him from now on." He gestured to Katsuro. "Take her downstairs. There is an empty room next to Yamato's. Lock her in, but do not let her see him. He will be on the other side of the wall, and that is the closest that she will ever be to him again. She leaves for Kyoto in the morning."

112

Milton rode the metro to Gotanda Station. He had been tempted to go straight to Takashi's tower block, but reason had intervened as the train had rumbled into the platform, and he had decided against it. He needed a plan. He knew that Yamato was there. And Sakura? She was probably there, too. Milton did not care whether he himself lived or died, but he wanted to ensure that, whatever happened to him, he maximised the chances of getting them both out alive. And, if he was going down, he would do his best to take Takashi and Katsuro with him.

All of that meant that he needed to prepare. He needed a plan and he needed a weapon.

Milton emerged from the station and followed the same route as before, eventually reaching Hachirō's restaurant. He pushed the door open. It was just after eleven and the place was as quiet as Milton had expected, with just a single couple sitting at the counter, settling up their bill. Hachirō saw Milton, frowned, and then—perhaps realising that the expression on his face did not portend good news—he hurried the customers out and flipped over the sign on the door. He closed it and turned the key in the lock.

"What is it?" he said.

"I'm sorry," Milton said. He tried to go on, but found that his mouth was dry.

The blood drained from Hachirō's face. "Tell me."

113

Fumio stayed at the edge of the room as Katsuro led Sakura to the elevator. Takashi went to his swords and took down Yoshida Shōin's *tantō*. He held it in his right hand, marvelling at the perfect balance, the craftsmanship that was necessary to create something as perfect as this.

"What is it, Fumio? You don't agree?"

"I'm sorry, Takashi, but no—I don't."

"Why? No—let me guess. My brother."

"I understand your anger for what she has done."

"Do you?"

"Of course, Takashi. I share it."

"I doubt that," he muttered.

"But you know what will happen to her in a place like that. Wakasa is an animal. She will be defiled."

"It is no more than she deserves. What she was doing with Katsuro and the *premans?* I didn't hear you disapproving then."

"I *did* disapprove. You know that I have never agreed

with the drugs. The *ninkyodo* is clear—dealing drugs is not our way."

"And yet you've been happy to take the money that it makes."

"And perhaps I was wrong to do that. I reconciled myself to Sakura's role as a mule because of your promise—that, once she had completed the task, she and the boy would be free. *This*, though? She has made mistakes, but the blame lies with the *gaijin* and, with respect, *Oyabun*, with Katsuro. The punishment for her behaviour is too harsh. She is your niece. Hachirō's daughter."

Takashi snorted. "I haven't spoken to Hachirō for twenty years. You think I owe him anything? I don't. Not a *thing*. He never approved of Miyasato. You remember what he was like —when they told us they wanted to marry? He always looked down at my boys, both of them, from when they were children. You know him. You know what he is like. His attitude, always looking down at me, always disapproving."

"I agree, Takashi. He is. But this? Condemning his daughter to a life with Wakasa? It is too much."

"Perhaps it is time he should know what it is like to lose a child."

"There are other ways to show him that. I beg you, *Oyabun*. Be merciful."

Takashi looked at his old friend and, for the first time, wondered if their long association had much longer to run. Takashi was traditional, but he was practical, too. Fumio was right about the *ninkyodo*, but Takashi had concluded that the code was increasingly irrelevant. It forbade the selling of drugs, theft, robbery and anything that might be considered shameful; but how could a yakuza who observed the *ninkyodo* hope to compete with rivals who did not, with men like Satoshi Furukawa who had no honour? Takashi had survived this long because he was a pragmatist. He had been able to balance honour and ethics with the ability to compete and make money; without the latter, there would be no yakuza, and then there would be no honour at all. If Fumio could not see that, then perhaps it was time that he retired to the villa in Shizuoka of which he had always spoken so fondly.

"No, Fumio. I will not kill her. This is her fate. It is what she deserves."

"And the boy?"

"I will bring him up as my own. We both know that Katsuro does not have it in him to succeed me. This week has removed all doubt of that. I am fit and well. If I can live another fifteen years, another twenty, then that should be enough to mould him into the man that Miyasato would have been."

"And his mother? What will Yamato say when he finds out what happened to her?"

"He will know by then what she was and what she did. He won't care."

"This is your decision, *Oyabun?*"

"It is."

Fumio nodded. "Then I will see that it is done."

He bowed, dipping at the hip, but, when he straightened back up, Takashi noticed that he would not look him in the eye. He knew then, for sure, that Fumio's time had come. The villa, perhaps. But he was his first lieutenant—his *wakagashira*—and had been in the business for decades. There was nothing that he didn't know. Perhaps, Takashi mused, it would be safer to bring his service to an end with a little more finality. Katsuro had never liked Fumio. The order to end him would be one that he would be happy to follow. Katsuro was, at least, good for that.

Fumio bowed again. "Good night, Takashi."

Takashi waited for Fumio to leave in the elevator. He replaced the *tantō* on its mount and went to his study. He had a large monitor on his antique desk, and, as he woke the screen with a tap on the mouse, the feed from the four cameras in the lobby at the foot of the building was displayed. He wasn't looking for anything in particular, but there was something about what had happened that evening that had him on edge. Shinoda and Kodama were on duty, both men sitting behind the reception desk, neither showing any real diligence. They were lazy and not particularly effective. He remembered that Milton had schooled them both when they were supposed to be following Sakura after she had met her father; he recalled what Katsuro had said about the *gaijin* and hoped that he had been right in reporting his demise.

Takashi opened his humidor for a cigar and was about to take it out of its plastic wrapper when he saw movement on the screen. He looked at the time—just after eleven—and, although it was not so late that activity in the lobby would be unusual, there was something about the way that the figure was moving—head down, furtive—that caught his eye. Takashi watched as the figure moved across the fields of view of the four cameras: a shot from behind by the camera in the elevator lobby, then from the right as the man moved into the main area, then from the left as he passed the desk. The final camera was mounted above the door, and the figure made the mistake of glancing up at it as he passed through the door.

Takashi rested the cigar on the lid of the humidor and picked up his phone.

"*Otōsan?*" Katsuro said. "What is it?"

"Come back upstairs. We have a problem."

PART VIII

TUESDAY

114

M ilton woke up in the storeroom. He looked at his watch and saw that two hours had passed since he and Hachirō had finished their conversation. Milton had told the old man that he would grab a little sleep to refresh himself in readiness for what he intended to do. He looked around the room, the space where they had kept Natsuki Furokawa while Milton negotiated with Satoshi. That seemed like a long time ago now, everything that he had hoped to achieve—the retrieval of the stolen sword and its exchange for Sakura and Yamato's safety—no more than a bad joke, a rejoinder to his foolish temerity. Things were worse now than they had been then.

He heard the sound of footsteps in the main body of the restaurant. He went to the door and opened it slowly, pulling it back an inch so that he could look through the crack. A couple of low lights had been lit, and Milton could see Hachirō sitting at one of the tables, his head bowed. Hachirō didn't respond as Milton made his way into the room. The older man brought a hand to his head and then turned. His face was pinched, with no colour in his cheeks. His eyes were red-rimmed and burned with cold fire.

"There's a jug of water on the table over there," the old man said. "Help yourself to anything from the kitchen."

Milton lowered himself onto one of the stools at the counter. The older man stood, put on a dark coat and reached under the counter for a shotgun that Milton had not seen before.

"Where are you going with that?"

"To see my brother."

"No," Milton said. "You can't."

"Why not?"

"Because he'll kill you."

Hachirō took a box of shells and poured a handful into his pocket. "Then that is what will happen."

The old man started toward the door.

Milton got up and stepped across his path. "Wait."

"Please," Hachirō said. "Get out of my way."

"I know where they're keeping Yamato. I've seen him— I've been in the same room. It's probably where they'll have Sakura, too. Let me do it. I know you probably think I won't be any help, but this is what I used to do. I can get them out."

Hachirō considered Milton's suggestion. Milton knew that he was no fool, and that he must have realised that he wouldn't last five minutes if he tried to take on his brother alone. Milton was worried that Hachirō's notion of honour might override his good sense, that he would rather die in glory than accept help, but the old man was more pragmatic than Milton had given him credit for. His need to see his family rescued and justice delivered was greater than any desire to seek vengeance for himself.

He shook his head, but, before he could speak, there was a knocking at the door.

Milton stood. "Are you expecting anyone?"

"No," he said.

"Give me the gun."

Hachirō did as he was asked. Milton took the shotgun and stepped back so that he was at the side of the room, in a position where he would be able to cover anyone coming inside without being seen until it was too late.

The knocking was repeated with more urgency.

Milton nodded.

Hachirō went to the door, turned the key in the lock and pushed down on the handle. Milton raised the shotgun and slipped his finger around both triggers. Hachirō saw who was standing outside, scowled, and stepped back to allow the visitor to enter. It was a man, dressed in black, with a hood that covered his face.

Milton stepped away from the wall so that the man could see him and the shotgun.

"It's all right," Hachirō said. "I know him."

The man removed his hood and turned to face Milton. It was the man from the tower block: Takashi Nishimoto's lieutenant.

"This is Fumio," Hachirō said.

"I know," Milton said. "We've already met. What do you want?"

"I'm here about Sakura and the boy," he said. "I want to help."

115

Milton stepped forward, holding the shotgun level with his finger on the triggers.

"Turn around," he said. "Nice and easy."

"I'm not here to cause trouble," Fumio said.

"No?"

"I have something Hachirō needs to hear. You, too, if you care about Sakura."

"Put your hands on the table."

Fumio did as he was told. "I've known Hachirō for many years," he said. "We haven't always seen eye to eye."

Hachirō snorted. "You could say that."

Milton frisked him.

"I'm not armed. I am an old man. I am not a threat."

"You'll understand if I want to confirm that for myself."

"Of course."

Milton glanced up at Hachirō. "How do you know him?"

"We grew up together in Sanya. Him, Takashi and me. But I haven't seen him for twenty years."

"Not since you left," Fumio said.

Milton finished frisking Fumio. "Sit down."

"We don't agree on many things," Fumio said as he lowered himself onto one of the stools. "But I have always respected you."

Hachirō grunted disdainfully. "What do you want, Fumio?"

"Katsuro brought Sakura to Takashi this evening."

"And?"

"Your brother is angry. He blames her for what happened to Miyasato. He always did. You know what she was doing in Bali?"

"I do now," Hachirō said, looking at Milton.

"That wasn't his first choice for her punishment. He wanted to sell her to Yoshio Wakasa. I persuaded him against that then, but I won't be able to this time."

Hachirō stiffened.

"Who?" Milton asked.

"He is a pimp," Fumio said. "He has brothels in Kyoto. Takashi has ordered me to contact Wakasa."

Hachirō stood; Milton held a hand out, cautioning him to stay where he was. "Where is Sakura now?"

"On the eleventh floor. Next to Yamato's room. You've been there—I took you."

Milton eyed him with suspicion. "Why are you telling us this?"

"Because I do not agree with what Takashi is doing. The yakuza *ninkyodo* forbids it, yet he does it anyway. I have been thinking about my role in all of this for some time. I knew what Sakura was doing with Katsuro. The drugs—I knew about that. I argued against it, but Takashi did not listen to me. The function of a *wakagashira* is to advise the *oyabun*. He doesn't care for my opinion any longer. What is the point of a *wakagashira* who does not command the respect of the boss? My usefulness to him is at an end."

Hachirō glowered. "You are here because you are afraid for yourself?"

"No. I am here because I do not want to see your daughter sent to Kyoto and there is nothing that I can do to stop it myself. I thought you should know."

Milton rested the shotgun on the counter and stepped behind it to sit opposite Fumio.

"Takashi is at the tower?"

"He never leaves."

"And Katsuro?"

"The same."

"I'm going to go and get Sakura and Yamato," he said. "I have some questions about the best way to do that. If you want to help, I'll need you to answer them."

Fumio nodded. "What do you want to know?"

116

F umio stayed for thirty minutes, answered all of Milton's questions, and agreed with the plan that he proposed. There were no thanks once the conversation had concluded; Milton could see that Hachirō was at the edge of fury, and that there was nothing that Fumio could do or say that could have rehabilitated him from his involvement in what had happened to Sakura. Fumio left with the promise that he would help Milton as much as he could. Hachirō let him go without a word.

"Do you trust him?" Milton said once the door was locked once more.

"About this? Yes. He was always very traditional. The *ninkyodo* is important to him. What Takashi is proposing..." He paused, his mouth twisting as if he had tasted something unpleasant. "It will go against everything that he considers to be honourable."

Milton looked at his watch. It was half past midnight. "We need to get to work," he said. "We have a lot to do and not very long to do it."

Milton assessed his own physical condition. He was

bruised and sore from the beating that Katsuro had delivered. His ribs were sore and his shoulder was still tender
after he had arrested his fall from the balcony. He would
have liked to wait and recover a little, but Sakura and
Yamato did not have the luxury of time. It was tonight or not
at all, especially for her.

"What do you need?" Hachirō asked.

"Your shotgun."

"What about the Glock?"

"I want something a little more imposing, but I'm going
to need to modify it. It's a little long to get into the building
without it being seen. Do you have a saw?"

"I have a toolkit in the storeroom. There's a saw there.
What else?"

"Sugar."

"I have plenty."

"What about instant cold packs?"

"Yes, in the freezer."

"What about a salt substitute? Potassium chloride."

"Yes," he said. "I think so."

"Could you get them for me? And a metal tray and
aluminium foil."

Hachirō busied himself assembling the ingredients that
Milton had requested while Milton started to work on the
shotgun. Hachirō kept a plastic box of tools for general
maintenance and Milton took out a hacksaw and attended
to the barrels. He worked the blade back and forth, cutting
through the metal so that first one barrel and then the other
was cut right back. Milton lined up the saw against the butt-
stock and sliced that in half, too, reducing it so that it was
little more than a crude pistol grip.

Hachirō returned with the items that Milton had asked
for: an instant cold pack, a plastic tub that was labelled 'Salt

Lite,' a bag of sugar. Milton needed potassium nitrate for what he had in mind, and set to work producing it. The cold pack contained two pouches: one filled with water and the other with ammonium nitrate. He sliced open the pouch with the nitrate and dissolved it in a jug of water. He strained the solution through a coffee filter, added the salt substitute and then heated the solution until the potassium chloride had dissolved.

"What are you doing?"

"Making a distraction," Milton said.

He put the glass jug with the solution into the freezer so that it cooled, and then waited for the potassium nitrate to crystallise. While he was waiting, he held up the sawn-off and asked whether Hachirō had a bag that would be big enough to take it.

Hachirō opened a cupboard and pulled out a padded courier bag emblazoned with the logo of the restaurant. "I used to employ a local boy to deliver meals in the neighbourhood."

Milton unzipped the bag and laid the shotgun inside. He opened the box of shells and stuffed them in his pockets, an even amount to both left and right.

The bag gave him an idea. "Did your delivery driver have a helmet?"

Hachirō went back to the cupboard and took out a crash helmet.

Milton held it up. "Perfect."

117

F umio returned to the tower block and took the elevator to the tenth floor, where he had an apartment at the front of the building. It was a million miles away from the opulence of the quarters on the floors above, but Fumio had never minded that. He was not interested in ostentation. He liked money and had salted away a small fortune over the years, but showing it off had always struck him as both gaudy and unwise, given that it might attract the attention of the authorities or others who might try to take advantage of his advancing years in an attempt to relieve him of it.

He went over what he had done as the elevator ascended the shaft. He had not expected Hachirō to greet him warmly; they had been estranged for years, and the recent treatment of his daughter, even though it had been at the instigation of Takashi, would inevitably also be attributed to him. Fumio had wondered whether he would be given the opportunity to pass on his information, but Hachirō had had little choice once he knew what Fumio was there to say. The *gaijin* had asked a series of questions and had struck Fumio as measured and confident. He looked as if Katsuro had given him a significant beating, but the cuts and bruises were evidently not enough to persuade him against further intervention. Neither he nor Hachirō had trusted Fumio enough to tell him what they were planning, but that didn't matter. Milton was going to make an attempt to infiltrate the building and recover Sakura and her son; Fumio hoped that he had given him the information he needed to increase the odds of success.

The elevator arrived. Fumio took out his key, unlocked the door and went inside, slipping off his shoes. He had a small sitting room and bedroom with *tatami* mats on the floors. The sitting room had a short-legged *kotatsu* table with a futon pinched between the tabletop and the frame. He had a futon to sleep on in the bedroom and a bookcase for his books. It was simple, almost ascetic, and it suited him well. He took off his coat, hung it on the back of the door and went through into the tiny kitchen.

Katsuro was standing next to the hob. The burner had been lit, the blue flame lighting up the gloom.

"What are you doing here?" Fumio said.

"Where have you been?"

"For a walk."

"It's late for a walk, isn't it?"

"It helps me to think."

"What do you need to think about?"

"I don't agree with what your father has decided to do. I wanted to think about how I might be able to change his mind."

"I don't believe you. Where did you go?"

"Get out. I'm tired and I want to go to bed."

Katsuro smiled and shook his head. "My father asked me to come and speak to you. He won't believe that, either." He took a knife from the block and held it so that the metal could be heated by the flame. "Shall we start again? Where did you go tonight?"

118

Sakura knew there was no point in trying to sleep. Of course, she was terrified of what tomorrow might bring for her, but that wasn't the reason for her agitation. It was what Takashi had said before Katsuro had led her down here: this apartment was next to the one in which her son was being held. She went to the wall now and laid her palm against it, then leaned in closer so that she could listen for any sound that might leak from that room to this. She could hear nothing. It was late, two in the morning, and Yamato would be asleep. The thought of him so close to her and yet so far away was maddening.

Katsuro had laughed at her as he had delivered her here.

She walked across the apartment to the front door and tried the handle, afraid that it would be locked but also afraid that it would be open. It was locked. The door did not appear to be particularly strong, but she doubted that she would be able to force it, and certainly not without attracting the attention of Katsuro or anyone else who might be on the floor. She went to the large window in the sitting room; it opened at the top, but not enough for her to climb out. Even if that had been possible, she was eleven floors up. There would be no escape that way.

She looked down and wondered about Milton. She had seen what Katsuro had done to him. He had beaten him and then forced him over the balcony. She had watched him fall. They had been even higher at the hotel than she was here, and she knew that there was no possibility that he might have survived. He was dead, and her father had no idea where she was and what was about to happen to her.

She left the window and lowered herself back onto the futon. She closed her eyes, even as she knew that sleep would be impossible; her only option was to wait out the hours until the morning and then pray that she might have the opportunity to speak to Takashi again. She tried to think about what she would say to change his mind.

119

Hachirō rolled up to the junction over which Takashi Nishimoto's tower presided. He brought the van to a stop and killed the engine. It was four in the morning and the two of them had been busy. Milton looked out of the dusty windshield at the building. There were lights in some of the windows, but just one on the two top floors.

Milton gazed up at the building. "You think he'll be inside?"

"He never leaves. You heard what Fumio said—he hasn't stepped foot outside for months."

"You're sure you're okay to wait?"

"I will be here."

"I don't know how long I'll need."

"I'm not going anywhere."

Milton nodded his acknowledgement and reached for the door handle. Hachirō put out a hand and grasped him on the shoulder.

"Thank you," he said. "I don't blame you for what

happened. It wasn't your fault. You didn't have to help her, and you did. You don't have to do this, either, and you are."

"I do. I'm not leaving her up there. Or Yamato, either."

Hachirō released his shoulder. Milton took the bag and opened the door.

"You have a message for your brother? Anything you'd like me to say?"

"Tell him to go to hell."

Milton pushed the door open and stepped down. "I'll see you when I'm done."

MILTON PUT the motorcycle helmet onto his head and lowered the visor. He hoisted the delivery bag with the sawn-off and slung it across his shoulder. He didn't look much like a delivery driver, but he wasn't planning on getting to the top floor through subterfuge; he just needed a little leeway when he arrived, and he hoped that his appearance might be enough.

He made his way across the road and approached the entrance to the building. There were two men sitting on the kerb outside the doors, drinking from bottles of spirits and speaking in slurred Japanese. One of them pointed at Milton and the other looked, then called out; Milton took a diversion to avoid them and then turned into the lobby.

He opened the door and quickly reconnoitred the interior. It was much as it had been before, but, thanks to the late hour, there were fewer people. There were no occupants passing into or out of the building. The concierge at the desk was absent, but there were two guards standing by it and, as he approached, Milton recognised them from the metro station: the inept tails he had identified and disabled.

They had suffered a run of bad luck; their unfortunate streak was going to continue.

Milton had observed the security from his previous visit, and had noticed that the guards had not concerned themselves with anyone unless they tried to use the restricted elevator. That made sense; the building must have accommodated several hundred Tokyoites, and it would be impractical to check identification for all of them and their guests. The man nearest the desk called out to Milton; Milton responded with "*Haitatsu*," the word that Hachirō had suggested would be understood to mean delivery. He held up the bag to underline his point, and the guard waved him toward the elevator with a grunt of assent.

Milton turned into the elevator lobby and, when he was out of sight of the desk, pushed open the door to the restroom. He took off the helmet and dropped it on the floor, then unzipped the courier bag and took out the solid clay-like substance that he had made in the restaurant. He had taken the potassium nitrate crystals and added sugar and then heated the mixture in one of Hachirō's skillets. He had poured the resultant sludge into a boat that he had made from aluminium foil and left it in the delivery bag to cool. He prodded it now; it looked ready, with the doughy consistency that he wanted. He peeled the foil away, dropped the mixture into the basin and lit it with his lighter. It took only a moment before it caught light. Smoke gushed out of the basin, quickly thickening until visibility in the room was reduced by the haze and then almost completely eliminated. Milton retrieved the helmet, opened the door to the bathroom and let the smoke escape. He yelled out the second Japanese word that Hachirō had taught him.

"*Kaji!*"

Fire.

Milton placed himself behind the door and waited for the guards to arrive. It took just a few seconds; the first man came inside, saw the smoke and froze. Milton swung the helmet into the man's head. It was a hefty blow and the man fell, limp, to the dirty floor.

The door opened again. This guard, too, stood stock-still. Milton grabbed him from behind, forced him down and rammed him head-first into the far wall. The guard fell, face down, and Milton dropped astride him, grabbing a handful of hair and then driving his head against the tiles until he stopped struggling.

There was blood on the helmet. Milton wiped it off with a paper towel, put it back on and, with his finger around the trigger of the shotgun that was still hidden inside the courier bag, he backed through the door and returned to the lobby. Smoke was pouring out of the bathroom and filling the lobby area. Milton walked briskly to the now abandoned front desk and the switch for the fire alarm that he had noticed on his previous visit.

He smashed the glass, pressed the button and heard the wail of the alarm.

Takashi woke up to the sound of the alarm. He lay in bed for a moment, staring up at the ceiling and waiting for it to be disengaged. One of the disadvantages of living in a tower block was that there were moments like this; on the other hand, he employed men to staff the lobby twenty-four hours a day, and one of the tasks for which they were responsible was the quick investigation and, usually, identification of false alarms. Shinoda and Kodama were on duty tonight. They would fix it.

The alarm did not stop.

Takashi got out of bed, slipped his feet into his slippers and took his robe from the hook on the back of the door. There was a private flight of stairs that led from his suite to the living space on the top floor, and he climbed them and then looked out of the windows for any sign of smoke. He had a view out of all four sides of the building and, if it was on fire, he was confident that he would be able to see the evidence.

There was no smoke. There was nothing.

Takashi went through into the study. He heard the door to the apartment unlock and open.

"*Otōsan?*"

It was Katsuro.

"In here," Takashi called.

Katsuro was breathless.

"The elevator isn't working," he said. "I had to take the stairs."

"It's the fire alarm. The systems are linked—they'll be locked until the board is reset." Takashi could see that his son was agitated. "What is it?"

"You were right. We have a problem. I just finished with Fumio."

"Where did he go?"

"To see Uncle Hachirō."

Takashi sighed. "Why?"

"To tell him about Sakura."

Takashi slumped down into his chair.

Katsuro winced a little. "The *gaijin* was there, too, Father."

"You said he was dead."

"It appears that I was mistaken."

Takashi made a fist and cracked it against the table.

"Father, I'm sorry—"

"Stop apologising, Katsuro! If you did your job properly, you wouldn't need to."

Katsuro looked as if he was ready to say sorry again, but Takashi stilled his tongue with a flash of anger. "What did Fumio tell him?"

"He said they asked about your security. Fumio told the *gaijin* that Sakura was to be sent to Kyoto. He thinks he'll try to get her before then."

The alarm blared on. Takashi wondered: could it be

Milton? He woke the screen and scanned the feeds from the four cameras in the lobby. Each feed took up a quarter of the screen, and he searched each quadrant for Shinoda and Kodama. Neither of them was visible. He moved the cursor to the bottom of the screen and dragged the time bar backwards so that he could review what had happened leading to the sounding of the alarm. He jumped back ten minutes. Shinoda and Kodama appeared in shot, joined shortly thereafter by a fast-food delivery rider in a motorcycle helmet. The rider had a quick exchange with Shinoda and then walked out of shot. Takashi glanced at the next feed, showing the doors to the elevators. The rider appeared in shot briefly, then disappeared. He didn't use the elevators or the stairs. The restroom was there, though, just underneath the camera.

Takashi scrolled forward in thirty-second chunks until he noticed Kodama turning in the direction of the restroom and then making his way across to it. Takashi saw smoke drifting up to the camera that was fixed above the restroom door.

Katsuro watched over his shoulder. "The fire started in there? The *bathroom?*"

Takashi watched, with a growing sense of panic, as Shinoda followed Kodama across the lobby to investigate. He, too, went into the restroom.

Neither man came out.

Takashi tapped the mouse to jump forward for another minute and saw the rider emerge into shot once again. The man crossed back to the desk, went around it and activated the alarm on the wall. He still had not removed his helmet.

He tapped the icon to return to a live view.

Tsukasa and Genzō were in shot now. They must have gone down to investigate.

Genzō was behind the desk, fiddling with the alarm control board.

Takashi took out his phone and called him.

"Yes, *Oyabun?*"

"There was a fast-food delivery rider. I watched on the camera. He set the fire and activated the alarm. Look in the restroom."

Takashi watched as Genzō left the desk and started toward the elevators. He crossed the lobby to the restroom door and disappeared out of shot, but came back out and reported almost immediately.

"*Oyabun*, they've both been—"

Genzō didn't get the chance to finish the sentence. Takashi watched as the delivery rider stepped out from behind a pillar and closed quickly on where Genzō was standing. He had taken off his helmet and swung it against the side of the guard's head. Takashi saw the impact on the screen and heard the crunch on the open line, then heard the clatter of the phone as it fell to the floor. Genzō toppled sideways, his head bouncing off the floor. He spasmed once, then lay still. The man who had struck him knelt down and frisked him, moving from pocket to pocket with brisk efficiency. He took a square of plastic—Genzō's key card—and then turned and looked straight up into the lens of the camera.

It *was* the *gaijin*.

Takashi watched as he went to the elevators. He held a key card to the reader, but the car did not arrive. He opened the door to the emergency stairs and disappeared from view.

"I'll get Tsukasa and Wakabayashi," Katsuro said.

Takashi made a fist and slammed it against the table.

I must be cursed, he thought. *My first son betrayed me and my second is a fool.*

121

Milton had not anticipated that the elevators would be connected to the fire alarm; he chided himself for his sloppiness. He should have realised that was likely. His plan had been to take the communal elevator to the tenth floor and then climb to the eleventh and then the twelfth floors by way of the stairs, but that was out of the question now. He ascended on foot, taking the stairs two at a time, maintaining a steady pace. Each floor was scaled by two flights, one turning back on the other by way of half-landings. Milton was sweating by the time he reached the fifth floor and, as he arrived at the eighth, his thighs were complaining.

The fire alarm was still ringing out and the fact that it had not been silenced seemed to have served as the signal for the inhabitants of the building to evacuate. They spilled onto the stairs and started down: mothers and fathers with children clutched to their breasts, elderly couples clinging onto the handrail as they made their descent, single men and women sharing worried glances. Milton had the strap of the delivery bag over his shoulder, his right hand inside the open zip. He bumped through the men and women and children, careful that his finger was rested along the shotgun's receiver and not against the trigger, where a jostle might lead to an involuntary discharge.

The stream of people thinned out by the time Milton reached the ninth floor, and then, as he reached the tenth, there were none. Milton was pleased. There was a good chance that things were going to get messy. No people meant no witnesses and no chance that an innocent bystander might get hit by an unlucky ricochet or a shotgun blast through a wall.

Milton reached the eleventh floor and stopped to catch his breath. The door ahead was more significant and sealed by a hefty electronic lock. He took out the key card that he had confiscated from the guard in the lobby and held it against the reader. He was rewarded with an electronic buzz and then the sound of the lock disengaging.

Milton took the shotgun out of the bag, pushed the door open and, with the gun raised, carefully stepped through the opening.

Fumio had told him that Sakura and Yamato were on this floor. Milton paused, weighing up whether he should take them now and go, or whether he should attend to Takashi first. He knew the *oyabun* was trapped at the top of the tower, and that Milton might never get another chance to get to him. If Takashi was allowed to live, he would redouble his security.

But if he didn't get to Sakura and Yamato now...

He had no choice.

122

Takashi grabbed the empty leather briefcase that he kept next to his desk. He crossed the room to the safe that was hidden in the floor, beneath the Agra Jail rug that had cost him nearly a hundred thousand dollars. He yanked the rug away and spun the combination dial, lining up the wheels and their notches, and then slid the bolt and pulled the door up. He reached inside and started to withdraw the bundles of banknotes that he kept there for emergencies such as this. He lined the briefcase with a first course and then added a second on top. He lowered the lid and pressed down the clasps to secure it.

He went to the monitor and looked at the feeds from the security cameras on the ground floor. A steady stream of people, most of them still in their nightclothes, were emerging from the stairs next to the elevators. They hurried outside and milled around the building, no doubt wondering why there was no sign of the fire that had triggered the alarm. He could now see the red and blue lights of a fire engine. The precinct was at Shiori Park, just five minutes away, and the alarm reported to it directly.

It felt as if events had careened out of his control. He had very deliberately built himself a redoubt at the top of the building. It should have made him safe, yet this man—the *gaijin*, Milton—had trapped him. He was a prisoner in a gilded prison, waiting for the arrival of the executioner.

He went through into the main living space. Katsuro was speaking on his phone. He saw his father and ended the call.

"Tsukasa is downstairs. He's resetting the elevators. They should be online again in a minute. He'll come up when they are, and then we can ride straight down to the ground floor and go outside. It's going to be fine, *Otōsan*. I won't let anything happen to you."

123

Fumio had explained that Sakura was being held in the apartment to the immediate left of the elevator shaft. Milton approached it and took out the key that the old man had given him. He inserted it into the keyhole, turned it—hearing the click as the lock disengaged —and then carefully pushed down on the handle. He readied himself, his right index finger laid across both shotgun triggers, and stepped inside.

Fumio had not been sure whether Sakura would be alone, and Milton went inside one slow step at a time. It was dark, with all the lights off and the curtains drawn. He assumed that the layout was the same as the apartment in which Yamato was being held, and proceeded along the corridor to the bedrooms. He heard the creak of a floor-board to his left and saw a flash of motion just in time to avoid the standard lamp that was swung—very awkwardly —at his body. The momentum of the lamp drew Sakura out of the doorway in which she had been hiding. Milton lowered the shotgun and put up a hand.

"It's me," he said.

"John?"

She stumbled at him, wrapped her arms around his neck and held on tight. He put one arm around her, but kept his attention on the apartment. Then, after a moment, he gently disengaged her.

"I thought you were dead."

"Not yet," he said.

"How did you—"

"Later. I'll tell you later. We need to move quickly. Is there anyone else in here?"

"I don't think so."

"You're sure?"

"Yes. I'm sure." She reached for him again. "You came to get me."

"One of Takashi's men came to see your father. He told us what Takashi was planning for you."

She stiffened against him. "Kyoto. He said I was going tomorrow."

He gently removed her arms from around his neck for the second time. "Not anymore."

"We need to get Yamato."

"We're doing that now. Stay behind me."

Milton turned around and led the way out of the apartment and back into the lobby. He tried the door handle to the adjacent apartment; it was open. He stepped inside. The lights were on and, as he turned into the living space, he saw the elderly woman that he remembered from before. She had just come out of one of the rooms to the side, and now she looked down at the shotgun, then up at Milton. She looked terrified, just as she should.

"English?" Milton asked her.

She swallowed and didn't respond.

Sakura stepped around Milton and spoke to the woman

in Japanese. Milton heard Yamato's name and saw her gesture down at the shotgun; to underline, presumably, why truthfulness would be the best policy. The woman nodded her understanding and indicated that Milton and Sakura should follow her. Milton was aware that there was a chance she might be trying to trick them, and that Takashi might have stashed a guard in the apartment, but, as they passed through the corridor to the bedroom, it appeared that his suspicion was unwarranted. He looked into each of the rooms as they passed and saw nothing.

The woman stopped at the door to the boy's bedroom. There was a key in the lock. Milton indicated that she should open it and stood back, covering her with the shot-gun. She turned the key, pulled the handle down and pushed the door. It swung open. Milton waved her inside and, as she did, he reached around the door and found the light switch. He pressed it, waited for the bulb to flicker on, and then surveyed the room. There was a bed and a desk and a box of toys. Yamato was in bed, sitting up, a duvet pulled up to his neck.

"*Yamato-tan!*"

Sakura stepped around him and rushed across the room, sweeping her son up in her arms. Milton moved to the side of the room, where he could cover both the old woman and the open doorway, and gave Sakura and Yamato a moment. He did not want to dawdle, but he knew that Sakura had not seen him for months and a few seconds would make no difference.

"Stay," Milton said to the woman.

"No," she said, finding her English. "The fire."

As if on cue, the alarm stopped.

"No fire," Milton said. He nodded to the wardrobe on the other side of the bed. "Get in there, please."

She frowned her disapproval, but her compliance was easily won with a quick wave of the shotgun. She opened the door and stepped inside, bowing down so that she fit beneath the metal rail from which a small collection of the boy's clothes had been hung. Milton removed the rail, swept the clothes onto the floor, and then closed the door. He slid the rail through the handles, fashioning a makeshift bar.

Yamato was looking wide-eyed at him and what he had done to the woman who, Milton assumed, had been his nanny while he had been held here.

Milton looked back at Sakura and Yamato. "Is he okay?"

"He seems fine," she said, an obvious relief in her smile.

"We need to leave," Milton said. "Stay behind me again."

He led the way out of the apartment and paused at the door to the stairs, straining his ears for sounds of movement or anything that might suggest that they were not alone on the floor. He heard nothing save the wail of a different siren from the foot of the building: a fire engine, he suspected.

He turned to Sakura. "Your father is on the street outside in a white van. Go down the stairs. Don't stop—go straight outside. The lobby will be busy—there will be firemen and people who live here—and Takashi won't be able to do anything to stop you. Don't wait for anything or anyone. Just head outside, get to your father and go."

"What about you?"

Milton opened the door and looked up at the stairs that led to the twelfth floor and Takashi's penthouse.

"Don't worry about me," he said.

"I'm not leaving you here on your own."

"You have Yamato to think about. I'll be fine. I'll see you later. Now—*go*."

He started to climb before she could protest.

124

Takashi emptied the small document safe in the study, removing the bonds that he had purchased over the course of the years, another hundred million yen that he was not prepared to leave behind. He put the bonds into his briefcase and wondered what he should do. Milton was just one man; surely it wouldn't be beyond Katsuro and the others to take care of him? Nevertheless, he was clearly resourceful—he had demonstrated that by retrieving the *tantō* from Furokawa—and it seemed prudent to relocate until he was out of the way. Takashi was irritated with himself for his weakness—if this was twenty years ago, he would have taken down one of his swords and gone after the *gaijin* himself—but he was older now, and with age came greater caution.

He opened the desk drawer and fumbled for the Type 94 Nambu pistol that his father had used in the war. He had a small box of 8x22mm cartridges and he thumbed eight of them into the magazine. Takashi shoved the pistol into his dressing gown pocket, collected the briefcase and went through into the living space.

Katsuro was pushing the button for the elevator.

"It's still not working?"

Katsuro shook his head.

"What are they *doing* down there?"

"It won't be long," Katsuro said. "Are you armed?"

Takashi pulled out the pistol and held it up.

"That's it?"

"I have the guards. I have you. I shouldn't need anything else. Where is *your* weapon?"

"I lost it at the hotel. The *gaijin*..."

Takashi sighed in resignation. Katsuro frowned angrily, then put the unspoken criticism aside and looked around the room. His eyes settled on Takashi's collection of swords. He went over to them. "Can I use one of these?"

Takashi was tempted to tell him that they were too precious, but this was an emergency. And, after all, he reminded himself, they were weapons of war. They were meant to be used.

Katsuro reached for the *tantō* that he had retrieved.

"No," Takashi said. "Not that. Too small." He pointed. "The Kamakura."

The *katana* was a curved, single-edged blade with a circular guard and a long grip. The blade was eighty centimetres long from the guard to the tip. The sword was seven hundred years old and had cost a small fortune to acquire. Katsuro took it down and held it in both hands.

His phone buzzed again. He switched the katana to his right hand, answered the call, shared a brief conversation, and then put the phone back into his pocket.

"That was Tsukasa. The elevators are fixed. He's coming up."

"At last. I'll go down with him. You'll need to go and get Yamato."

"You want to take him?"

"Yes, Katsuro, I do. We'll go to the villa."

Takashi owned a property in Hakone, near Mount Fuji. It was near to the hot springs, and every year for the last twenty, Takashi had visited it for a week to enjoy *hanami* season; the explosion of cherry blossoms that transformed the mountain. It was not as easily defensible as the tower block, but there was no reason to suspect that Milton knew of its existence.

He heard the sound of the lock disengaging.

"Katsuro," Takashi warned.

The door opened and the *gaijin* stepped inside. He was toting a sawn-off shotgun. He aimed it into the room. Katsuro stepped in front of his father; Takashi reached for his pistol.

The *gaijin* shook his head. "Don't do that."

To their right, the elevator pinged as the car began to rise through the shaft. The digits in the display flicked from 1 to 2 and then 3.

The *gaijin* nodded in the direction of the elevator doors. "I think that's going to be a little late."

Takashi started to edge to the right. Katsuro was still covering him, although the *katana*—as impressive as it was —now looked less of an option when compared to the shot-gun. Katsuro saw that, too, and Takashi watched as his son bent down, laid the sword flat on the carpet and then stood again.

The elevator continued to rise: 6, 7, 8, 9.

Katsuro flexed his shoulders, his slab-like muscles bulging. He lowered his arms and settled into a ready stance. "You want to try again?"

10, 11, 12.

The *gaijin* stared at him. "Not really."

Milton pulled one of the triggers. The sawn-off boomed, a 12-gauge shell firing and the heavy load of lead shot blasting out and peppering Katsuro in the chest. He slid down the wall, leaving a swash of blood across the magnolia paint.

The elevator door opened. The *gaijin* swivelled and Tsukasa stepped out just as Takashi stumbled inside. The shotgun boomed again. Takashi was facing into the elevator car and couldn't see what happened, but heard a grunt of pain and felt a warm spray over the side of his face. He ignored it, pressing the button for the ground floor.

He heard a click—the sound of a shotgun being broken apart—and kept hammering the button, knowing it wouldn't make any difference but unable to stop. He turned his head, almost too frightened to look, and saw Tsukasa's body spread out next to Katsuro's. The *gaijin* was walking toward him, pressing two new shells into the shotgun and, as the elevator doors started to draw together, he closed the breech, aimed and fired.

125

The elevator doors were almost closed when Milton fired both barrels. Birdshot fired out, a spread that peppered the wooden panelling, some of it spraying into the car. He heard the sound of it chiming against the metal of the elevator's wall, but wasn't able to see whether he had been able to strike Takashi. The car started to descend: Milton watched as the numbers fell from 12 through 11 and 10 and 9, recording the car's progress down to the ground floor. Takashi was hit or he wasn't; Milton couldn't be sure, and, if he had managed to escape, there was little that he could do now.

He needed to move fast.

The two men he had shot were still alive, but neither looked as if that was a state of affairs that would persist for long. The man who had come out of the elevator had landed face up on the floor. His gut had been torn open by the bird-shot, and, as Milton watched, the man gave out a long final exhalation. His eyes rolled back and he lay still.

Milton saw a bag on the floor near to where Takashi had been standing. He opened it and saw bundles of banknotes and what looked like financial instruments. He zipped it closed and tossed it across the room to the door.

He moved over to Katsuro. His face was twisted into a mask of pain, and his shallow breathing brought a crunching sound. Milton recognised it: among all the other damage the birdshot had done, Katsuro's lungs had been punctured.

"Can't breathe?" Milton asked him.

Katsuro nodded, his eyes wide with fear.

Milton frisked Katsuro's body, found his phone and pocketed it.

"Please," he gasped. "Help."

The long sword that Katsuro had set down was by his feet. Milton collected it, marvelling at the perfect balance, the sensation that it could be moved quickly and easily. He pressed the tip of the blade against Katsuro's breast and pushed down. The metal slipped through the fabric of his shirt and pierced his skin. Milton maintained the pressure until he felt the blade come up against the solidity of the floorboard beneath Katsuro's scapula.

"That's for Sakura."

Katsuro gasped and blood bubbled out of the corner of his mouth and ran straight down his cheek and onto the floor. His eyes bulged, but then twitched as he looked at something behind Milton's shoulder. Milton saw a spark—bitter amusement amid his pain—and when he turned, he saw Sakura standing in the open door. Yamato was behind her, his head poking around her legs.

Shit.

He had *told* them to go downstairs.

Katsuro coughed once, spluttering blood, and, when Milton turned back, he watched the life drain from his eyes.

"Out," Milton told Sakura. "Wait outside."

Milton went to the wall where the swords were displayed and, on a whim, took down the *tantō* that had caused so much trouble. He unzipped the bag with the money, dropped the blade inside, and then closed it again. He picked up the shotgun, found two fresh shells from his pocket and opened the break action. He slotted a fresh shell into each barrel and closed the breach until he heard it click.

He opened the door to the stairs. Sakura and Yamato were waiting there.

"I told you to go down," Milton said to Sakura.

"I was frightened for you."

Milton knelt down next to Yamato. "Try to forget what you saw."

The boy looked close to tears. "Where is *Jiji?*"

"He means Takashi," Sakura said.

"I'm not sure," Milton said, "but I'm going to find him. We need to go. Right now."

Milton could hear the sound of footsteps ascending from below him. Gesturing for Sakura and Yamato to stay back, he took a glance over the bannister: a fireman wearing a silver helmet was climbing up to the eleventh floor. Milton wasn't surprised; the fire department would want to check the floors one by one to confirm that there was no reason for the alarm before they let the occupants back inside again. Milton hid the shotgun behind his leg as the fireman reached the landing. He was wearing full turnout gear: helmet, face mask, a small cylinder of compressed air on his back, a heavy jacket and three-quarter-length rubber boots.

The man saw them and called out something in Japanese; Milton didn't understand it, but the urgent downward jab of his hand that accompanied it suggested that he wanted them to leave.

Milton stepped to the side so that the fireman could pass.

"Wait a minute," Milton said.

The fireman turned back and Milton jabbed the shortened butt of the shotgun against his chin. The blow was hard and unexpected and enough to knock him out. Milton caught him before he could topple down the stairs, and carefully lowered him so that he was leaning against the wall.

Yamato looked fearful. "It's all right," Milton said, unsure whether the boy would understand him. "He'll be okay. I just need to borrow his things."

Milton moved quickly, removing the man's helmet and disconnecting his face mask from the hose that fed oxygen from the tank. He put the helmet on his head and fitted the mask around his face, removed the thick jacket and pulled that on, too. There was a waste disposal chute on the landing above and he hurried up to it, opened the metal door and tossed the shotgun in. He listened to it clang and clatter as it dropped down through the guts of the building.

He returned to Yamato, reached down and hoisted him up, clutching his little body against his chest.

"Let's get you both out of here."

THE LOBBY WAS full of people. The fire department had cleared the building and were allowing the residents to make their way back to their apartments. It was loud: tired children screamed, older residents chattered about the false alarm, radios squelched as the men and women who crewed the fire engines outside reported back from their checks of the building. Milton pushed the door open and made his way out, Yamato clinging onto his neck and Sakura right behind him.

The doors to the private elevator were open and two paramedics were tending to someone inside. Milton risked a glance and saw Takashi. The old man was sitting up, his back resting against the mirrored wall at the back of the car. The glass of the mirror had been broken in several places, creating little points of impact with spiderwebbed cracks that radiated out from them. The medics had removed his dressing gown and Milton saw that the buckshot had peppered his shoulder and arm. Blood ran from each point, and the medics busily prepared dressings to help staunch the flow. Takashi was conscious, and his head turned to follow Milton, Yamato and Sakura as they went past. The boy saw him and reached out an arm; Milton picked up his pace. Takashi looked away. He knew that there was nothing that he could do.

A fireman was just outside the main door and Milton acknowledged him with an upraised hand as he and his charges stepped outside. He could see Hachirō's van a few metres up the road; he had moved it a little to allow the fire engine to park. Milton stepped onto the road and walked away from the building, the red and blue lights of the engine still pulsing against the walls of the buildings that reached overhead.

EPILOGUE

T akashi took a cup of coffee out onto the terrace of his villa near the hot springs at Hakone. It was a little before eight in the morning and the warmth in the air suggested that it was going to be a pleasant day. The property was worth more than triple what he had paid for it, but he had no interest in selling. He didn't need the money, and coming out here made for an enjoyable change from his Tokyo apartment. The villa had a large *onsen*, or hot spring, with natural mineral water that he believed made a difference to the aches and pains of old age. It had generous grounds, too, with cherry trees, hinoki pine, and wild camellias. Lake Ashinoko was the boundary at the southern edge of the grounds, the mirror-flat waters reflecting the snow-capped majesty of Mount Fuji.

Takashi gently lowered himself into his padded chair. He had been fortunate to have escaped the *gaijin* after he had assaulted the tower in Tokyo. He had been shielded from the worst of the shotgun blast by the closing elevator doors, but there had still been enough of a gap for him to have been peppered across the left-hand side of his body. Wakabayashi had intervened before the paramedics could take him to a public hospital, taking him instead to a private physician upon whose discretion Takashi knew that he could depend. Most of the lead shot was close to the surface of his skin, and the doctor had spent a painful hour removing it with a pair of tweezers. Shinoda and Kodama had joined them and, once Takashi had been patched up and the doctor paid, the three guards had driven him out of the city.

He had spoken with his bought-off contacts in the Tokyo Prefectural Police and they had confirmed to him what he had already suspected: Fumio, Tsukasa and Katsuro were all dead. Fumio had been found in his apartment, a single gunshot wound in the centre of his forehead. Tsukasa and Katsuro were found near to the elevator on the twelfth floor, both suffering significant injury from close-range shotgun blasts.

Takashi felt no sadness for the death of his son. It had been different with Miyasato—he had mourned him for weeks—but Katsuro was a dull-witted imbecile and Takashi had already concluded that he was a lost cause. But, while there might not have been much in the way of sadness, there certainly *was* anger. Takashi was very interested in finding John Milton. He had instructed his police contacts that the *gaijin* was to be located and had promised to reward the man or woman who delivered him.

Takashi sipped his coffee and gazed out at the pink blossoms that transformed the flanks of the great mountain to the south. He had been here for two weeks and planned to stay for another few days before returning to the city. This was not such a bad place to relax while the security at the tower block was reviewed. There was a pagoda between the villa and the lake, and it looked as if it were floating amid a sea of blossoms.

Takashi was enjoying the vista when he became aware of someone approaching him from behind.

He turned, expecting to see one of the guards, but, instead, he saw his brother.

"*Hachirō*?"

He was dressed in a simple leather jacket, black denim and a pair of black sneakers. He had a woollen hat on his head and was carrying a small pistol in his right hand.

"What are you doing here?"

Takashi tried to maintain his composure as he flicked his eyes left and right, looking for the men who were supposed to protect him.

"They're not coming," Hachirō said.

He raised the pistol.

"That's not necessary," Takashi said. "We might not always agree, but we're brothers. My wife is dead. Both my boys are dead. I don't have anyone else."

"'*Brothers*'?" Hachirō exclaimed. "It's too late for that. I should have done this years ago. It would have prevented a lot of heartbreak."

He drew closer, levelled the pistol and aimed it at Takashi's forehead.

"Please, *Oniisan*," Takashi begged him, using the affectionate honorific that he hadn't spoken since they had been teenagers, running around the benighted streets of Sanya, before the yakuza and everything that flowed from it.

"Do you think I could ever forget what you did to my daughter? What you were going to do?"

"Did you think about what *she* did to *me*?"

Hachirō shook his head and drew closer. "It's always been about you, hasn't it? You'll never change."

He fired.

SAKURA WATCHED as Yamato played with the toys that Milton had brought back after his Tokyo trip three days earlier. Yamato had told him that his favourite toys were Transformers, and Milton had returned with toy robots with names like Ironhide, Barricade and Bonecrusher. They didn't mean much to Sakura, but Yamato had been beside himself with happiness as Milton took them out of the bag bearing the famous logo of the Yamashiroya toy store.

Yamato had played with them ever since. He beamed with happiness now as he staged a battle between the Autobots and Decepticons; watching him filled her heart with a pure and simple joy that she had thought she would never feel again.

The last two weeks had been everything that she could have hoped for. Her father had located a small house in Odawara, a hundred miles to the southwest of Tokyo, and Milton had found the money to pay the rent for the first two months. They needed to be away from the city, he argued, at least until he was satisfied that Takashi was no longer a threat to them. She had no idea how Milton would be able to be sure about that, but she was happy to trust him.

Her attention was on Yamato and making sure that he felt happy and loved. Mother and son might not have been together for months, but it had made no difference to the strength of their relationship. The boy asked about Takashi and, less often, about Uncle Katsuro, but those questions became less and less frequent as the days wore on. Her father visited regularly, and she had been delighted to see his relationship with Yamato bud and then blossom.

Hachirō was gruff and circumspect most of the time, but that hadn't stopped him from lying on the floor next to the boy and joining in his battles.

She had been happy, too, that Milton had agreed to stay with them. He had been honest with her; he had not promised that the arrangement would be permanent, and had explained his continued presence by a concern for her safety. He could say that if he liked, but Sakura hoped that there was more to it than that. She certainly felt safe, and nothing had happened since they had arrived that gave her any indication that they were in danger from Takashi, but if that was the excuse he needed in order to justify his continued presence in her life—and in her bed—then she was not about to question it. She had long since decided that she would like to spend more time with him and see if their relationship was strong enough to last the course, but she knew that it was not her decision alone. She knew that he had doubts that he would have to satisfy before he was able to make a decision, and told herself that he was worth her patience.

"Mommy?" Yamato said.

"Yes?"

"Can I open it now?"

She frowned. "Open what?"

"The box."

"What box, Yamato-*chan?*"

The child got up and led the way into his small room. There was a box under the bed that Sakura had not seen before, and he pulled it out.

"Where did that come from?"

"Uncle John left it for me."

"When?"

"When I went to bed. He said that I could open it at breakfast. We've had breakfast, so can I open it?"

She nodded, an uncomfortable emptiness in her stomach as she realised what the box might portend. Yamato tore away the tape that secured the lid and opened the box. There were two new Transformers inside.

"Wow," Yamato exclaimed, clapping his hands together in spontaneous wonder. "Look, Mommy. Optimus Prime and Megatron."

The boy held up the toys, but Sakura's attention was focused on what else was inside.

Money.

A lot of money.

She took out a bundle of banknotes and saw that it was composed of ten-thousand-yen notes. She riffled the edge of the bundle; there must have been a hundred notes there, maybe a million yen in total. She put the bundle down and took out the others, stacking them up until she had a pile that was five wide and five tall. She was dazed by it, and it took her a moment to work out that there must have been nearly twenty-five million yen. She and Miyasato had looked at how far their savings would stretch in the United Kingdom, and she knew that the money in the box would be enough to buy them a nice little house.

But Sakura didn't dwell on that.

Milton wouldn't have left the money here—like this, without telling her—unless he had made the decision that it was time for him to go.

She wondered whether she would see him again.

Hᴀᴄʜɪʀō ᴄʟᴇᴀɴᴇᴅ the pistol with a handkerchief and carefully placed it in his brother's hand. He took one final look at him; he looked decades older without the spark of life, his skin as thin as parchment and blood running into his sightless eyes.

Hachirō had meant what he had said: he should have done this sooner.

He had not approved of Sakura's union with Miyasato, but perhaps he had allowed his hatred of what his brother had become to pollute his opinion of his son-in-law. Perhaps, if he had been more hospitable, Sakura and Miyasato might not have taken so foolish a decision as to steal from Takashi.

He didn't blame himself for what had happened, but he knew that the regret would nag at him until he, too, had died.

He retraced his steps through the villa. He could hear the sound of banging from the basement. Milton had shepherded the three guards down there and locked them in. They must have heard the sound of the gunshot and now they were panicking that they might be next. Hachirō had no intention of harming them. They had made bad choices in aligning themselves with the Nishimoto-*kai*, but he knew from his own bitter experience that those choices would catch up with them eventually. It was not his place to punish them.

He stepped outside and looked for Milton. The Englishman had offered to take care of Takashi, but Hachirō had insisted that his brother was his responsibility, and Milton had not protested. He had said that he would take the guards out of the equation and then wait for him outside the villa, but, as Hachirō looked left and right, he couldn't see him.

He walked along the gravel drive to the gate where they had left the car, but Milton was not there, either.

He took out his phone to call him when it buzzed with an incoming call.

"Milton-*san*?"

"Is it done?"

"It is."

There was no response and, for a moment, Hachirō thought that Milton had ended the call.

"Where are you?"

"I said that I'd make sure you were able to do what you wanted to do, and I have. It's time for me to go."

"What about Sakura?"

There was a pause before he spoke. "She deserves stability. She needs it—so does Yamato. And that's not me."

Hachirō thought he heard regret in his voice. "Don't you think that's her decision to make?"

"I know myself too well. Please tell her..." He paused again and sighed. "Please tell her that she should be happy."

"I will."

"And promise me that you'll look after them both."

"Of course."

"Thank you, Hachirō. I've left something in the car for you—it's your choice what to do with it."

"What is it?"

The line was dead.

Hachirō opened the door of the car and saw that something *had* been left on the front seat. It was long and thin and wrapped in a cloth. He picked it up and unwrapped it; the metal object within sparkled brightly in the morning sun.

It was Yoshida Shōin's *tantō*.

He let the cloth fall away and held the blade in his right

fist, feeling the perfect balance and the economy of movement as he swiped it left and right. Takashi had lusted after the blade for years. Satoshi Furukawa had, too, and Miyasato had been corrupted by it.

Hachirō knew that the blade was valuable, but he wanted no part of it.

He turned away from the car and looked out at the still water of Lake Ashinoko. The road dropped away in a steep slope, with the placid water lapping against the rock below. Hachirō drew his arm back and then flung the *tantō* away, as hard as he could. The blade spun end over end, sparking in the light, before the tip sliced into the water and the blade sank quickly from view.

Hachirō felt blank, neither happy nor sad. He looked at the water for a moment and then went around to get into the car. He had a forty-minute drive to Odawara, and he wanted to be there in time to take his daughter and grandson to lunch.

MILTON WATCHED as the car reversed back into the road, turned around and drove away. The road looked to have been cut from the rock, and the terrain on either side of it was steeply sloped. The terrain above it was thick with vegetation, and Milton had not had to look far for a spot where he would be able to keep an eye on Hachirō while also being hidden from him.

He had watched as the old man had tossed the blade into the water. Milton didn't blame him. It was the cause of his daughter's misfortune, and it would have been a constant reminder of her travails every time they laid eyes upon it. They could have sold it, of course, and Milton had wondered whether that would be the decision Hachirō took, but, on the other hand, it was obvious that family meant more to him than money.

Milton wondered what they would do with the money that he had left in the house. He hoped that they would be pragmatic about that, at least. Sakura and Yamato would need funds, especially if she still intended to take the boy out of the country. That was her decision to make, but he hoped he had given her a little more flexibility in her options.

He picked up his bag and slung it over his shoulder. He had kept a little money for himself; enough to book a flight and go anywhere the mood took him. His new legend, Eric Blair, offered him a freedom that he hadn't enjoyed for months, and he was keen to test it out. First, though, he wanted to find somewhere quiet and peaceful where he could relax and find balance again.

He reached into his pocket and ran his finger around the stippled edge of the token that he had received with Victoria in Bali.

Eight years.

He had been close to throwing it all away, and now he saw that his hard-won abstinence—one day at a time—was worth fighting to keep.

He descended the slope, picking his way carefully between the rocks, and reached the road. He would walk back to Hakone and see about taking a train back to Tokyo. After that, he would find a map and lay his finger on it. Wherever it landed would be where he would go.

Milton started to walk.

John Milton will return in
Never Let Me Down Again
- **Spring 2021** -

Search your favourite store now to pre-order and take advantage of the launch price.

GET EXCLUSIVE JOHN MILTON MATERIAL

Building a relationship with my readers is the very best thing about writing. Join my VIP Reader Club for information on new books and deals plus all this free Milton content:

1. A free copy of Milton's adventure in North Korea - 1000 Yards.

2. A free copy of Milton's battle with the Mafia and an assassin called Tarantula.

You can get your content **for free**, by signing up at my website.

Just visit www.markjdawson.com.

ALSO BY MARK DAWSON

IN THE JOHN MILTON SERIES

The Cleaner

Sharon Warriner is a single mother in the East End of
London, fearful that she's lost her young son to a life in the
gangs. After John Milton saves her life, he promises to help.
But the gang, and the charismatic rapper who leads it, is not
about to cooperate with him.

Saint Death

John Milton has been off the grid for six months. He
surfaces in Ciudad Juárez, Mexico, and immediately finds
himself drawn into a vicious battle with the narco-gangs
that control the borderlands.

The Driver

When a girl he drives to a party goes missing, John Milton is
worried. Especially when two dead bodies are discovered
and the police start treating him as their prime suspect.

Ghosts

John Milton is blackmailed into finding his predecessor as Number One. But she's a ghost, too, and just as dangerous as him. He finds himself in deep trouble, playing the Russians against the British in a desperate attempt to save the life of his oldest friend.

The Sword of God

On the run from his own demons, John Milton treks through the Michigan wilderness into the town of Truth. He's not looking for trouble, but trouble's looking for him. He finds himself up against a small-town cop who has no idea with whom he is dealing, and no idea how dangerous he is.

Salvation Row

Milton finds himself in New Orleans, returning a favour that saved his life during Katrina. When a lethal adversary from his past takes an interest in his business, there's going to be hell to pay.

Headhunters

Milton barely escaped from Avi Bachman with his life. But when the Mossad's most dangerous renegade agent breaks out of a maximum security prison, their second fight will be to the finish.

The Ninth Step

Milton's attempted good deed becomes a quest to unveil corruption at the highest levels of government and murder at the dark heart of the criminal underworld. Milton is pulled back into the game, and that's going to have serious consequences for everyone who crosses his path.

The Jungle

John Milton is no stranger to the world's seedy underbelly. But when the former British Secret Service agent comes up against a ruthless human trafficking ring, he'll have to fight harder than ever to conquer the evil in his path.

Blackout

A message from Milton's past leads him to Manila and a confrontation with an adversary he thought he would never meet again. Milton finds himself accused of murder and imprisoned inside a brutal Filipino jail - can he escape, uncover the truth and gain vengeance for his friend?

The Alamo

A young boy witnesses a murder in a New York subway restroom. Milton finds him, and protects him from corrupt cops and the ruthless boss of a local gang.

Redeemer

Milton is in Brazil, helping out an old friend with a close protection business. When a young girl is kidnapped, he finds himself battling a local crime lord to get her back.

Sleepers

A sleepy English town. A murdered Russian spy. Milton and Michael Pope find themselves chasing the assassins to Moscow.

Twelve Days

Milton checks back in with Elijah Warriner, but finds himself caught up in a fight to save him from a jealous - and dangerous - former friend.

Bright Lights

All Milton wants to do is take his classic GTO on a coast-to-coast road trip. But he can't ignore the woman on the side of the road in need of help. The decision to get involved leads to a tussle with a murderous cartel that he thought he had put behind him.

The Man Who Never Was

John Milton is used to operating in the shadows, weaving his way through dangerous places behind a fake identity. Now, to avenge the death of a close friend, he must wear his mask of deception once more.

Killa City

John Milton has a nose for trouble. He can smell it a mile away. And when he witnesses a suspicious altercation between a young man and two thugs in a car auction parking lot, he can't resist getting involved.

IN THE BEATRIX ROSE SERIES

In Cold Blood

Beatrix Rose was the most dangerous assassin in an off-the-books government kill squad until her former boss betrayed her. A decade later, she emerges from the Hong Kong underworld with payback on her mind. They gunned down her husband and kidnapped her daughter, and now the debt needs to be repaid. It's a blood feud she didn't start but she is going to finish.

Blood Moon Rising

There were six names on Beatrix's Death List and now there are four. She's going to account for the others, one by one, even if it kills her. She has returned from Somalia with another target in her sights. Bryan Duffy is in Iraq, surrounded by mercenaries, with no easy way to get to him and no easy way to get out. And Beatrix has other issues that need to be addressed. Will Duffy prove to be one kill too far?

Blood and Roses

Beatrix Rose has worked her way through her Kill List. Four are dead, just two are left. But now her foes know she has them in her sights and the hunter has become the hunted.

The Dragon and the Ghost

Beatrix Rose flees to Hong Kong after the murder of her husband and the kidnapping of her child. She needs money. The local triads have it. What could possibly go wrong?

Tempest

Two people adrift in a foreign land, Beatrix Rose and Danny Nakamura need all the help they can get. A storm is coming. Can they help each other survive it and find their children before time runs out for both of them?

Phoenix

She does Britain's dirty work, but this time she needs help. Beatrix Rose, meet John Milton...

IN THE ISABELLA ROSE SERIES

The Angel

Isabella Rose is recruited by British intelligence after a terrorist attack on Westminster.

The Asset

Isabella Rose, the Angel, is used to surprises, but being abducted is an unwelcome novelty. She's relying on Michael Pope, the head of the top-secret Group Fifteen, to get her back.

The Agent

Isabella Rose is on the run, hunted by the very people she had been hired to work for. Trained killer Isabella and former handler Michael Pope are forced into hiding in India and, when a mysterious informer passes them clues on the whereabouts of Pope's family, the prey see an opportunity to become the predators.

The Assassin

Ciudad Juárez, Mexico, is the most dangerous city in the world. And when a mission to break the local cartel's grip goes wrong, Isabella Rose, the Angel, finds herself on the wrong side of prison bars. Fearing the worst, Isabella plays her only remaining card...

ABOUT MARK DAWSON

Mark Dawson is the author of the breakout John Milton, Beatrix and Isabella Rose and Soho Noir series.

For more information:
www.markjdawson.com
mark@markjdawson.com

Printed in Great Britain
by Amazon

19885849R00302